Capital markets will be affected as least as much a
European Community's drive for greater economic int<
capital controls on 1 July 1990 has far-reaching conseque
cross-border investment, and plans for economic and mo<
fundamental upheavals at the heart of the financial system.   ...king and
monetary and fiscal policy. This volume reports the proceedings of a conference
on European financial integration held in Rome in January 1990, which was
organized by the Centre for Economic Policy Research and the Istituto Mobiliare
Italiano.

In this volume, leading international experts examine the implications of
integration for the structure and regulation of capital markets, the changing
relationships between the corporate and banking sectors throughout the Community, the distortionary effects of differing taxation policies among member states
and possible means of overcoming them, and alternative routes to European
monetary union.

European financial integration

Centre for Economic Policy Research

The Centre for Economic Policy Research is a network of over 140 Research Fellows, based primarily in European universities. The Centre coordinates its Fellows' research activities, and communicates their results to the public and private sectors. CEPR is an entrepreneur, developing research initiatives with the producers, consumers and sponsors of research. Established in 1983, CEPR is already a European economics research organization, with uniquely wide-ranging scope and activities.

CEPR is a registered educational charity. Grants from the Leverhulme Trust, the Esmée Fairbairn Charitable Trust, the Baring Foundation, the Bank of England and Citibank provide institutional finance. The ESRC supports the Centre's dissemination programme and, with the Nuffield Foundation, its programme of research workshops. None of these organizations gives prior review to the Centre's publications nor necessarily endorses the views expressed therein.

The Centre is pluralist and non-partisan, bringing economic research to bear on the analysis of medium- and long-run policy questions. CEPR research may include views on policy, but the Executive Committee of the Centre does not give prior review to its publications and the Centre takes no institutional policy positions. The opinions expressed in this volume are those of the authors and not those of the Centre for Economic Policy Research.

Istituto Mobiliare Italiano

Istituto Mobiliare Italiano (IMI) ranks among the pre-eminent financial groups in Italy, and in some respects, within the top class of European institutions. IMI was constituted in 1931 in order to effect large-scale financial restructuring and recapitalization by making equity investments and long-term loans. From this historical background comes the name Istituto Mobiliare Italiano, where 'mobiliare' means 'concerning securities'.

Following World War II, IMI played a pivotal role in the rebuilding and evolution of the nation's industrial structure, in part as a result of being entrusted with the channelling of funds granted by the Import–Export Bank of the United States under the Marshall Plan.

After the post-war reconstruction, IMI concentrated its activities on the tasks of financing large industrial projects, supporting Italian exports, promoting the development of small and medium-sized companies, and assisting the economic development of Southern Italy.

During the 1980s the IMI Group reorganized its activities and corporate structure. The Group took steps to diversify and coordinate the array of its financial services and re-shape its holdings.

IMI operates through its head office in Rome and ten regional offices in the main Italian cities. It acts as the sole manager of a large government concessionary lending programme, the Fund for Applied Research and Development. It provides commercial banking through Banca Manusardi's head office in Milan and seven branches located in the country's prime urban centres. Its subsidiary SIGE, with headquarters in Milan, provides the entire spectrum of investment and merchant banking services. FIDEURAM's nationwide sales force of personal financial consultants provides the Group's principal direct link with retail savers, and an additional point of contact with small and medium-sized firms. IMI also operates, through subsidiaries, in leasing, factoring, ship-building credit, real estate development and advisory services.

In the international arena the IMI Group provides market-making, brokerage, fund management, corporate finance and investment banking services through the subsidiaries of IMI International which currently operate in London, New York, Frankfurt, Luxembourg and Zurich.

Chairman
Luigi Arcuti

Deputy Chairman
Mario Ercolani

Director General
Rainer Stefano Masera

Deputy Director General
Cesare Barbieri
Luciano Martino
Vittorio Serafino

Secretary General
Enrico Fioravanti

European financial integration

Edited by

ALBERTO GIOVANNINI

and

COLIN MAYER

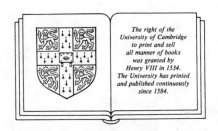

The right of the
University of Cambridge
to print and sell
all manner of books
was granted by
Henry VIII in 1534.
The University has printed
and published continuously
since 1584.

CAMBRIDGE UNIVERSITY PRESS

Cambridge

New York   Port Chester   Melbourne   Sydney

Published by the Press Syndicate of the University of Cambridge
The Pitt Building, Trumpington Street, Cambridge CB2 1RP
40 West 20th Street, New York, NY 10011–4211, USA
10 Stamford Road, Oakleigh, Victoria 3166, Australia

© Cambridge University Press 1991

First published 1991
First paperback edition 1992

Printed in Great Britain at the University Press, Cambridge

British Library cataloguing in publication data

European financial integration.
   1. European Community countries. Economic intergration
   I. Giovannini, Alberto   II. Mayer, C. P. (Colin P.)
   337.142

Library of Congress cataloguing in publication data

European financial integration / edited by Alberto Giovannini and
  Colin Mayer.
    p. cm.
  Proceedings of a conference sponsored by the Centre for Economic Policy
  Research and the Istituto mobiliare italiano, and held in Rome
  Jan. 22–23, 1990.
  Includes index.
  ISBN 0 –521–40244–1
  1. Monetary policy – European Economic Community contries – Congresses.
  2. Finance – European Economic Community countries – Congresses.
  3. European Monetary System (Organization) – Congresses.
  I. Giovannini, Alberto. II. Mayer, C. P. (Colin P.)
  III. Centre for Economic Policy Research (Great Britain)
  IV. Istituto mobiliare italiano.
  HG930.5.E86845 1991
  332.4'5 – dc20   90–45312 CIP

ISBN 0 521 40244 1   hardback
ISBN 0 521 42890 4   paperback

CE

Contents

ix

Figures

Tables

Preface

This volume contains the proceedings of a conference on 'European Financial Integration', which was organized by the Centre for Economic Policy Research (CEPR) and the Istituto Mobiliare Italiano (IMI). It was held in Rome at IMI's head office on 22/23 January 1990. The conference is part of a wide-ranging initiative by CEPR to bring high-quality, policy-relevant academic research to bear on questions raised by the completion of the European internal market and by economic and monetary union. This conference was the first event associated with CEPR's new research programme on Fiscal and Monetary Integration in Europe, supported by the Stimulation Programme for Economic Science (SPES) of the European Commission. The Centre's initiative included a companion conference on 'The Impact of 1992 on European Trade and Industry' held at Urbino, Italy , in March 1990, the proceedings of which will be published in early 1991. Cambridge University Press has also published two special issues of the journal *Economic Policy* on the subject of 1992, in October 1989 and April 1990.

Throughout the organization of the Rome conference we received invaluable advice and support from CEPR (in particular from Richard Portes, Ann Shearlock and Stephen Yeo) and from IMI (in particular from Giorgio Questa, Emilio Barone and Stefania Ferretti): we are grateful to all of them for the help that they have provided. We are also grateful for the additional financing provided by the Ford and Alfred P Sloan Foundations.

In producing this volume we have been fortunate in being guided by Paul Compton, Sarah Wellburn and David Guthrie of CEPR, Professor John Black of Exeter University, and Patrick McCartan of Cambridge University Press. Without their constant efforts and prodding this volume would not have appeared so swiftly and flawlessly.

Alberto Giovannini and Colin Mayer   *June 1990*

Conference participants

Franklin Allen *Wharton School, University of Pennsylvania*
Julian Alworth *Bank for International Settlements*
Yakov Amihud *New York University*
John Arrowsmith *Bank of England*
Emilio Barone *Istituto Mobiliare Italiano*
Susanna Barsella *Commissione Nazionale per la Società e la Borsa*
Margaret Bray *London School of Economics and CEPR*
Giovanni Carosio *Banca d'Italia*
Richard Caves *Harvard University*
Paolo Clarotti *Commission of the European Communities*
Vittorio Conti *Banca Commerciale Italiana, Milano*
Anthony Courakis *Brasenose College, Oxford*
Jean Dermine *Institut Européen d'Administration des Affaires*
Rudiger Dornbusch *MIT and CEPR*
John Flemming *Bank of England*
Günter Franke *Universität Konstanz*
Julian Franks *London Business School*
Francesco Giavazzi *Università degli Studi di Bologna and CEPR*
Alberto Giovannini *Columbia University and CEPR*
Roger Gordon *University of Michigan*
Ronny Hamaui *Banca Commerciale Italiana, Milano*
Martin Hellwig *Univerität Basel and CEPR*
James Hines Jr *Princeton University*
Glenn Hubbard *Columbia Univerity*
Richard Levich *New York University*
Giovanni Majnoni *Banca d'Italia*
Rainer S. Masera *Istituto Mobiliare Italiano*
Colin Mayer *City University Business School and CEPR*
Haim Mendelson *Stanford University*
Michael Moore *Central Bank of Ireland*

Damien Neven *Institut Européen d'Administration des Affaires and CEPR*
Marco Pagano *Università di Napoli and CEPR*
Henri Pages *Banque de France*
Francesco Papadia *Banca d'Italia*
Pierluigi Parcu *Commissione Nazionale per la Società e la Borsa*
Franco Passacantando *Banca d'Italia*
Richard Portes *CEPR and Birkbeck College, London*
Giorgio Questa *Istituto Mobiliare Italiano*
Assaf Razin *University of Tel-Aviv*
Mario Sarcinelli *Ministero del Tesoro*
Luigi Spaventa *Università di Roma 'La Sapienza' and CEPR*
Niels Thygesen *Kobenhavn Universitet*
Alfio Torrisi *Istituto per la Riconstruzione Industriale*
John Vickers *Nuffield College, Oxford*
Xavier Vives *Universidad Autónoma de Barcelona and CEPR*
Philippe Weil *Harvard University*
Michael Woodford *University of Chicago*
Charles Wyplosz *Institut Européen d'Administration des Affaires and CEPR*
Stephen Yeo *CEPR*

Organizers
Alberto Giovannini *Columbia University and CEPR*
Colin Mayer *City University Business School and CEPR*

Foreword

RAINER S. MASERA and RICHARD PORTES

Capital markets will be affected at least as much as goods markets by the European Community's drive for greater economic integration. Indeed, we may say that financial integration in the EC is the key step towards the creation of the Single Market. The removal of the legal and administrative obstacles to free capital movements and the integration of financial markets raise major issues concerning the alleged trade-off between efficiency and stability and the competitiveness of different financial regulatory systems. The implications and effects go far wider than the EC, not just to the 'European Economic Space' but even more broadly to relations between Europe, the United States and Japan. The conference on 'European Financial Integration' organized by CEPR and IMI focused on these problems, which are specific to financial intermediation and have important implications for economic policy.

The reshaping of financial institutions should, first of all, not permit firms and individuals to take advantage of opportunities to circumvent taxation (see Giovannini and Hines). Otherwise competition between institutions and markets may not favour the fittest but rather those with tax advantages. Competitive fiscal deregulation should not be the major driving force of the single financial market. The international coordination of fiscal policies is also important to internalize the 'fiscal externalities' that occur whenever domestic and foreign government debts are traded on international markets, and thereby become close substitutes. In such circumstances, an increase in interest rates in one country results in an increase in the debt burden for all countries. Some fiscal coordination will be necessary to proceed towards monetary union, although its nature and scope will be determined in difficult negotiations (Buiter-Kletzer).

Financial integration will also affect the structure of the financial and banking sectors. In the face of today's high degree of market segmentation and limited contestability in the banking sector (Vives), banks will

xix

probably react to competition by trying to defend their position through mergers, acquisitions and cross-participation agreements. Competitive conditions differ across member countries, and there is asymmetric information between investors and financial institutions. Thus various degrees of competition will coexist initially, and the benefits of integration will be unevenly distributed. These market failures will direct attention to financial regulation issues. Forms of regulation and market institutions should differ between countries and between classes of investment services (Mayer-Neven, Amihud-Mendelson).

Mistakes made in the past should be avoided. Financial regulation must be shaped in the light of economic principles, not following examples like that of the United States, where monetary union was accompanied by geographical restrictions on interstate banking and by the separation of securities and banking businesses, principles that are now being progressively relaxed. The relative weakness and fragility of financial institutions in what remains the largest and most important economy in the world is a profound lesson for Europe.

The globalization of financial markets has removed barriers between banking and credit, investment services and securities operations, collective investment, insurance and foreign exchange operations, within national markets and across borders. Securitization and financial innovation link the various markets in forms hitherto unknown. In these circumstances, it is essential to seek an optimal banking organization. There are lively controversies over the merits of different institutional mechanisms of providing external finance to firms (Hellwig) and over comparisons between the universal bank and the so-called 'multifunctional' group. These two systems of organization for financial intermediaries appear to meet different objectives. The universal bank is a model which has proved its viability. The group may be more suited to the joint production of financial services that are not closely related, such as banking and insurance, but the group's organizational problems pose major challenges.

Financial integration requires monetary coordination. The instability of the exchange-rate regime could have perverse effects on the degree of substitutability of financial assets, thus impeding financial integration; and conversely currency substitution will affect exchange-rate stability (Woodford).

So far, the EMS has been a useful tool to keep inflation under control in an environment made easier by the long-term improvement in the terms of trade of industrial countries. That process is now running out of steam (Dornbusch). The main problem of monetary union is not what the final arrangements will be, but rather how to cope with the transition through economic convergence and efficient regulatory implementation.

The relevance of the issues discussed during the Conference for the activities of international financial institutions like IMI and for research purposes is evidenced by the contents of the papers and by the lively debates of the panel discussion. We hope that this excellent volume will encourage further research and help policy-makers on these key issues for the future of European integration.

1 Introduction

ALBERTO GIOVANNINI and
COLIN MAYER

1 Financial market integration

In contrast to goods trade, liberalization of assets trade has not been centre stage in the postwar international arena. Attitudes towards capital account transactions have been influenced by a belief that controls permit countries some independence in setting their macroeconomic policies. Thus, for example, a country could gain full membership of the International Monetary Fund (IMF) by making its currency convertible for current account transactions while at the same time not being required to liberalize capital account transactions. As a result, there were limitations on portfolio and direct investment flows and barriers to the establishment of foreign financial institutions.

Integration of capital markets in Europe has taken a significant leap forward with the Single Act and the endorsement by the Council of Ministers (in Madrid in May 1989) of economic and monetary union (the Delors Report). These call for removal of virtually all barriers to free trade in financial services and the acceptance of rights of establishment of one member country's financial institutions in any other.

There are several factors that have prompted this change. The first is that capital market integration is a natural extension of the economic integration that was set in motion by the Treaty of Rome. This in part had its origins in the belief that economic integration and political harmony went hand in hand and that conflict between states, which has been so much a feature of European history, could at last be eradicated.

The second is that capital market liberalization is a necessary condition for improvements in efficiency in goods and factor markets. Capital market restrictions distort product market behaviour. Interest rate ceilings artificially depress savings and raise investment; credit controls interfere with domestic sectoral allocations; capital controls impede efficient allocation of resources internationally; and limitations on the free transfer of ownership undermine productive efficiency.

1

The third is that financial services are an important industry in their own right. Elimination of barriers to entry is as relevant to financial services as it is to any other industry.

There is one important respect in which capital market liberalization differs from that elsewhere. As capital markets become more integrated, national monetary policies, financial policies and tax policies become less effective. This is exacerbated by free movement of banks between member states. By agreeing to elimination of barriers to the free flow of capital and financial institutions, governments of the European Community have set in motion a process that has wider implications for monetary control and macroeconomic policy.

An analysis of European financial integration therefore has to address both microeconomic issues concerned with the operation of markets and macroeconomic consequences for monetary and fiscal policy. The authors in this book examine the effects of integration on money, financial markets and taxation from both a positive and a normative perspective. On the positive side, the articles consider the evolution of financial intermediation, securities markets, monetary management and taxation after financial liberalization. On the normative side, they consider the role and interactions of national governments in the new economic environment.

2   Theories of government competition

The Single European Market is an unusual economic concept. It resembles a federation in having integrated national markets. It differs in not having a central government with wide-ranging powers. For example, it differs from a United States of Europe in not having a US Federal bureaucracy. This raises the question of whether the system is viable, let alone desirable.

There are two schools of thought on this which lead to quite different conclusions: the 'Leviathan' and 'optimal taxation' theories of government.

2.1   'Leviathan' governments

The Leviathan school views governments as agents with objectives that are distinct from those of the citizens that they represent. For example, they attempt to maximize the resources under their control by establishing as large a tax base as possible. Regulation in general and capital controls in particular are an essential pillar of the attainment of this objective. By imposing capital controls, governments can limit the portfolio choice of private agents and restrict the operations of financial institutions. They can impose interest-rate ceilings, burdensome capital or reserve requirements and inflation taxes. They can direct resources to their own use, reduce costs of servicing budget deficits below market interest rates and earn revenue from inflation taxes.

The effect of liberalization on this description of the operation of governments has been discussed by Hayek (1976). He focuses on the consequences of eliminating a monopoly in issuance of money. This exposes governments to foreign competition: they have to provide a currency that is at least as good as the best foreign alternative, both in terms of stability of purchasing power and efficiency of payments systems, or face loss of market share in demand for their own currency.

These ideas underlie recent proposals from the UK Treasury on competing currencies. The UK proposal advocates greater freedom of circulation of currencies across national borders and therefore a greater degree of substitutability of national currencies in the demand for money. The papers by Woodford and Weil in this volume examine the theoretical underpinnings of the Treasury proposal. The authors consider whether the traditional problems of monetary equilibria are likely to be worsened by an increase in currency substitutability.

Woodford proves a number of important propositions regarding the characteristics of monetary equilibria in a two-country, two-currency world; these were previously available only in closed economy models. He explores the effects of changing currency substitution and concludes that increased substitution 'does not improve' and in most cases worsens the nature and stability of equilibria.

Weil follows Woodford's methodology but adapts it in one important respect: he introduces money into the utility function. His results are consistent with Woodford's in finding that increased currency substitution in an integrated multi-currency economy may have perverse effects in, for example, increasing risks of hyper-inflation. Furthermore, increased substitutability does not guarantee that the currency of the most virtuous central bank dominates others.

Hayek's analysis of competition between currencies can be extended to other areas of government, in particular regulation and taxation. In the former case, international competition forces governments to remove regulations that put domestic financial intermediaries at a competitive disadvantage in international markets. As a result, regulations converge to the minimum levels necessary to ensure viability of financial markets.

Amihud and Mendelson discuss this in relation to equity markets. Europe currently possesses a large number of fragmented stock markets. Many of these are too small for trades to be efficiently executed and there are substantial advantages in terms of liquidity from integration. But Amihud and Mendelson argue that immediacy and liquidity can be achieved without formal integration. What is required is a set of rules relating to the order in which transactions are executed to provide traders with incentives to supply liquidity. The advantage of not integrating markets is that competition in the execution and settling of transactions can emerge. This avoids the imposition of common systems designed to meet the requirements of the least efficient exchange and allows transactions to gravitate naturally to the most efficient.

Banks are another example. The determination of capital and reserve requirements has in the past been a combination of prudential supervision, monetary policy and tax considerations. Preservation of monetary systems and the use of reserve requirements as a tax base have frequently justified the imposition of onerous capital requirements. But now, as Vives notes, governments are faced with an additional threat to their domestic banking systems from overseas competition. As a consequence, regulatory requirements have to be moderated.

The influence of financial integration on taxation is still more evident. As the international mobility of capital increases, the ability of governments to use capital as a tax base diminishes. Capital income taxes have to be lowered if capital outflows to lower tax regimes are to be avoided. Giovannini and Hines record that there is already a tendency for European corporate tax rates to converge on lower rates.

In summary, according to the Leviathan view, deregulation increases public welfare by constraining the operation of governments. It limits the resources that governments can expropriate and thus indirectly restores control of governments to their citizens.

2.2   'Optimal tax' theories of government

A contending theory of governments is that they are agents of citizens and implement solutions of social optimization problems. Regulation and taxation are chosen by governments to maximize the welfare of their citizens. Far from benefiting citizens, competition between national authorities may create distortions that lead to too little taxation and regulation of mobile factors. In other words, there are externalities between national authorities resulting from a failure of nation states to take account of the effects of their fiscal and regulatory decisions on others. Likewise, in the presence of fixed exchange rates, governments fail to take account of the effect of their monetary policies on inflation elsewhere.

The optimal taxation theory of government suggests that coordination of monetary, taxation and regulatory policies is rquired. It is a solution to the problem created by international externalities. The Leviathan school regards such coordination as collusion between governments to exploit their subjects.

There are four questions raised by the optimal tax theory: (i) is government intervention justified at all, (ii) if so, are there cross-border externalities that justify coordination between national authorities, (iii) what form should coordination take and (iv) who should administer it. Many of the papers in this volume address one or more of these questions. They are relevant to taxation, monetary and fiscal policy, and regulation. We discuss each in turn.

Taxation

Giovannini and Hines describe the problems of the current system of capital income taxation in Europe, and point out that the roots of these problems are in part to be found in the dismal state of public finances during the interwar years. The system of capital income taxation that emerged in Europe was *territorial* in nature, that is one where income is taxed at the source rather than in the country of residence of its final recipients. As noted above, this leads to competition between tax authorities and potential undertaxation of capital income.

Giovannini and Hines examine whether there is a tax system that preserves sovereignty of national authorities in setting tax rates and at the same time minimizes tax arbitrage distortions. They argue that these objectives are met by residence systems of taxation that tax capital income at different rates in countries in which it is earned but tax residents of a particular country at the same rate irrespective of the country in which the income has been earned. This system allows countries to set different tax rates, but requires collaboration in exchange of information and revenues between national authorities. Giovannini and Hines offer an example of such a scheme, by describing in detail a plan of reform of corporate taxation in Europe based on the application of a common notional rate, and a system of rebates at the individual shareholder level.

Monetary and fiscal policy

The UK Treasury proposal on competition between currencies was made in response to the Delors report on monetary union. The Delors report advocates rules to ensure full central bank independence, as well as ceilings on national budget deficits. Buiter and Kletzer criticize these proposals. They provide examples of where national authorities can circumvent restrictions on budget deficits by foreign exchange interventions, open market operations or advances of credit to commercial banks. Buiter and Kletzer's conclusion is that confrontation between monetary and fiscal authorities cannot be avoided by institutional design. While they advocate some degree of fiscal coordination for both distributional and efficiency reasons, they argue for a flexible system that balances requirements for simple and transparent policy rules with different requirements of nations and regions across the Community.

Dornbusch discusses the transition to monetary union. He dismisses as 'naive' the view that membership of the European Monetary System (EMS) automatically reduces inflation. Dornbusch records that inflation problems have worsened in some countries, for example in West Germany. Dornbusch believes that a fundamental weakness of existing transition proposals is that they prevent monetary policy from being used to balance control of inflation and real variables, such as real wages, competitiveness and real interest rates. At the same time, private agents do not change their behaviour and fiscal authorities are ill-equipped to deal effectively with the macroeconomic consequences of real-wage and interest-rate shocks.

Instead, Dornbusch offers two proposals. The first is to discard exchange-rate margins altogether, thereby strengthening credibility of exchange-rate targets by conveying impressions of sound monetary policy. The second is to introduce a transition period during which countries with troubled public finances can correct their fiscal imbalances and demonstrate sustainability of government finances.

Regulation

Financial regulation is most commonly associated with banks. As Hellwig argues, one of the difficulties that arises in this area is that there is no generally accepted theory of why banks exist. This is particularly acute in relation to corporate finance. Traditional economies of scale arguments for the existence of banks do not stand up to close scrutiny. There are two sets of theories that have recently been proposed that provide a more fundamental justification for the existence of banks. The first is information theories that emphasize the role of banks in monitoring companies. Monitoring of banks is avoided by portfolio diversification which allows banks to issue fixed liabilities. The second is theories of commitment in which banks offer financial contracts that are unavailable in competitive markets. They do this in response to limitations on companies' subsequent borrowing opportunities that ensure them of adequate returns on their initial investments. Commitment models provide a justification for the traditional maturity transformation function of banks.

Vives notes that the combination of fixed liabilities and maturity transformation makes banks vulnerable to runs and banking systems prone to
contagion. These externalities justify bank regulation. Vives argues that
in the past regulation has acted as a focal point for collusion amongst
banks. With the integration of financial markets, Vives believes that
attention will shift from collusion to competition. Still, he suggests that
there remain sufficient imperfections in banking markets for only limited
competition to emerge.

One way in which Vives argues that competition will be restrained is
through mergers. Banks may prefer merger to competition which, if it
leads to bankruptcies, can undermine the stability of a financial system.
The theme of mergers is developed by Caves. Caves suggests that there are
two theories of mergers relevant to international acquisitions that have
quite different implications. The first is a traditional economies of scale
motive for merger: firms merge to benefit from unexploited opportunities.

The second, which is the focus of Caves' paper, is a strategic theory.
Economic disturbances occur that alter the opportunities available to
oligopolistic firms. Disturbances provoke rent-seeking mergers that
benefit one firm in an industry at the expense of another. The latter
responds by engaging in a defensive merger. Disturbances thereby give
rise to mimicking mergers across an industry.

Caves' thesis is an elegant explanation for the well-known bunching of
mergers in waves. While Caves' empirical analysis does not support the
strategic model, the fact that structural conditions in some industries may
provide scope for strategic mergers poses threats to the efficient organization of business activities. As Caves concludes, 'it is not easy to identify
these costs of rent-seeking, let alone write rules to limit them. But the
possibility of important resource misallocations from this source should
certainly be kept on the policy agenda.'

While the case for the regulation of banks receives wide support there is
no equivalent theory of the regulation of other financial institutions such
as insurance companies, investment managers and brokers. Mayer and
Neven argue that for at least one group of non-bank financial institutions,
investment managers, the literature on the regulation of the professions is
more relevant than that on banks. Mayer and Neven describe a framework for analysing both the design and implementation of regulation of
financial services. They suggest that the appropriate design of regulation
varies significantly across financial institutions. In particular, for most
financial services, less reliance should be placed on use of capital requirements than in banks. Furthermore, in some parts of financial services,
where risks of investor losses can be limited, self- rather than statutory
regulation may be adequate. This permits a greater degree of flexibility in
the implementation of regulation.

In banking, competition between national authorities risks competitive deregulation and the under-regulation of banks. In response, coordination of bank regulation has been advocated by, for example, the Cook Committee. Mayer and Neven argue that coordination may not be justified throughout the financial sector. Where there are few interactions between financial institutions then systemic risks are absent and international coordination is not warranted.

To summarize, in contrast to the Leviathan view, optimal tax points to a requirement to coordinate government policies in several areas: monetary and fiscal policy, capital income taxation and regulation of banks. Elsewhere, for example the regulation of non-banks and equity markets, international competition between national authorities may be desirable.

For the most part, coordination rather than competition has emerged as a requirement for the financial sector. This raises the question of whether the limited central administration of the Comunity will be adequate for the task. In most respects, the speed with which the path to integration has proceeded to date has been encouraging. In other respects, disagreements over monetary union, taxation of capital income and regulation of non-banks emphasize the weaknesses of the current system. At the end of the day, the success of the process will rely on a judicious mixture of enlightened government and firm leadership.

REFERENCE

Hayek, F.A. (1976) *Denationalization of Money*, London: The Institute of Economic Affairs.

2 Banking competition and European integration

XAVIER VIVES

1 Introduction

European integration poses a challenge to the study of competition in banking and financial markets. The Price Waterhouse (PW) study for the European Commission on the 'costs of non-Europe' in financial markets concluded that important welfare gains could be attained by the increase in competition which would accompany financial integration. This study has been much debated and criticized on the grounds that it overestimates the gains to be obtained by assuming that integration will lead to a competitive market.

The crucial issue seems to be the impact of the process under way on the *degree of competition* in banking, and more particularly in retail banking, where the effects are likely to be the largest. Many other questions revolve around this issue:

Will deregulation induce excessive competition?
How will the benefits of integration be distributed?
What specific predictions on conduct and market structure, trade and
    direct investment can be made?
How will the stability of the financial system be affected?
Are the regulations to be implemented consistent?

In the present paper I try to draw some lessons from recent research in finance, banking and industrial organization on how competition will be affected by the integration process. This is not an easy task since at a theoretical level financial intermediation is still not well understood, and competition among financial intermediaries even less so.[1]

Any attempt to understand the way financial institutions compete must start by examining the role of financial intermediaries, the potential for market failure and the need for regulation. It is argued that financial intermediaries have two distinct roles: the provision of liquidity insurance

9

and risk-sharing opportunities to agents, and the minimization of trans-action (incentive) costs associated with monitoring and signalling in a context of asymmetric information. The liquidity insurance role of banks turns out to be central since it leaves them subject to runs, which may be costly in welfare terms. The real and financial crisis of the 1930s is a case in point.

Under asymmetric information, the possibility of runs, and the existence of economies of scale in monitoring and screening, substantiate the need for regulation to correct market failures. Nevertheless regulation has induced problems of its own; regulatory capture inducing monopoly rents, distortion of investment incentives, inefficient provision of services and moral hazard problems in the form of too high risk taking. These side effects of regulation are crucial in understanding competition in banking.

The recent history of European banking has been characterized by a lack of vigorous competition: regulatory capture and concerted action have been more the norm than the exception. Our central thesis contends that *the main effect of integration will be to change the focus from collusion and regulatory capture to competition.* '1992' will make regulatory capture more difficult by introducing a harmonized system of regulation. '1992', being a *state of mind*, will move the focal point away from the restrictive practices of the past. Collusive activity needs a focal point to coordinate action. The weight of the history of the industry, with its restrictive practices linked to a heavy regulated environment, is being erased by the '1992' idea.

Competition among banks in Europe will increase as a result of integra-tion, but will not result in the perfectly competitive market for financial services envisaged in the PW report. Competition will increase, but will still be imperfect because of the presence of important economic barriers to entry. Banking, and particularly retail banking, does not seem to fit the model of 'contestable' markets. In a contestable market potential com-petition disciplines established firms since they are vulnerable to hit and run entry. Branch proliferation, the creation of networks (like ATM systems), the presence of switching costs for consumers, and reputation effects can serve as effective barriers to entry. In fact, although freedom of capital movement exists already in quite a few European countries and almost all legal obstacles to the establishment of banking subsidiaries have already been removed (with the temporary exception of Spain), trade in banking services is limited and tends to be of the intra-industry type (in which a country both imports and exports financial services) and the market shares of foreign banks vary substantially in different Euro-pean countries. This suggests that there are either hidden restrictions or important barriers to entry.

In summary, competition will be imperfect due to the presence of important economic barriers to entry, yielding an upper bound for the integration benefits lower than the competitive benchmark. This means that the impact of integration will be of a significant magnitude but will not attain levels associated with competitive or 'contestable' outcomes.

Further predictions follow from our analysis:

> *Banks will react to the increase in competition by trying to reduce their rivalry via mergers, acquisitions and cross-participation agreements.* Nonetheless, this will happen in an essentially non-cooperative framework where collusion will be much more difficult to sustain.

> *The increase in competition will be unevenly distributed. Different degrees of competition will coexist in a segmented market and integration will have a differential impact according to classes of bank customers.*

2   Financial intermediation, regulation and side effects

2.1   Financial intermediation and market failure

We take as the starting point for our analysis the consideration that *financial intermediaries emerge as a response to the imperfections and incompleteness of financial markets.* Indeed, in a complete market system à la Arrow-Debreu, financial institutions are unnecessary and irrelevant. The principal source of market failure in our context comes from asymmetric information: moral hazard and adverse selection problems prevent financial markets from being complete. A classical example is provided by Akerlof's lemons problem in the credit market (Akerlof, 1970). A widely accepted thesis asserts that financial institutions reduce market imperfections and improve the allocation of resources.

The *main functions* of financial intermediaries (banks) can be summarized as follows:

(a)   facilitating transactions: the transfer of wealth and payment mechanism;
(b)   portfolio management;
(c)   the transformation of illiquid assets into liquid liabilities, providing liquidity insurance and risk-sharing opportunities to agents;
(d)   the minimization of (incentive) transaction costs by the monitoring of loans and signalling.

If banks were to realize only the first two functions (a) and (b) there would not be any need to regulate a competitive banking sector since, as argued by Fama (1980), the portfolio management decisions of banks (b) would be subject to the Modigliani-Miller theorem on the irrelevance of pure financing decisions. This would be true even if banks were to have a comparative advantage in providing these services in a competitive market.

The sources of *market failure* come from the (c) and (d) functions of banks. In particular, *the risk-sharing deposit contract leaves banks vulnerable to panic runs*.

The optimal deposit contract between the banks and risk-averse depositors, who face private liquidity risks, involves a fixed payment for early withdrawals. There is a good equilibrium which realizes optimal risk sharing, but there is also a bad equilibrium in which all depositors panic and withdraw their funds and the bank collapses. This may happen to an otherwise sound bank (Diamond and Dybvig, 1983).[2] A bank run is costly in terms of real resources since the production process is interrupted and assets are prematurely liquidated. Further, there is the danger of a systemic failure due to contagious bank runs, creating a strong negative externality for the real sector of the economy. According to Friedman and Schwartz (1965) the major causes of the recession in the 1930s were the bank runs and mismanagement of the crisis by the Federal Reserve which contracted the money supply.

Banks are also subject to *failure* because of insolvency. In general, there is no perfect diversification of the risk to banks' assets since their investment projects are large and the monitoring technology they use is limited. Therefore there is potential risk to bank depositors and banks will be subject to *fundamental or information-based bank runs*.

In a panic run depositors withdraw because they fear that others will withdraw first.[3] In a fundamental run depositors realize that the value of assets in the bank is low and that withdrawing is a dominant strategy. Fundamental runs may be based on information about the returns of the bank (Jacklin and Bhattacharya, 1988) or about the behaviour of other depositors (Postlewaite and Vives, 1987).[4]

The role of banks in minimizing transaction costs in an asymmetric information context (monitoring loans and evaluating projects, and signalling the quality of an investment portfolio, based on cost advantages like economies of scale in monitoring and diversification possibilities)[5] does not presuppose that the market solution with unregulated active financial intermediation is optimal. Competition among financial intermediaries may introduce additional complications: intermediation may not emerge even when banks have an advantage in monitoring loans, and intermediation may not be welfare improving because of excess competition among fund seekers (banks and entrepreneurs) which increases the incentive costs associated with bankruptcy.[6]

In summary, we have highlighted *asymmetric information* as a major source of *market failure*. Nevertheless other classical sources are present: the standard deposit contract leaves banks subject to runs creating a negative *externality*, and the economies of diversification may lead to *increasing returns* with associated market power problems.

2.2   Regulation

The response to the potential market failures has been regulation, with the aim of improving efficiency and protecting small investors and depositors. The regulation has tried both to provide stability to the system and to avoid the important negative consequences of panics. In addition, the money creation role of banks has given a monetary policy dimension to regulation, using, for example, reserve requirements as an instrument of monetary policy?[7]

Two basic *types of regulation* have been proposed and used to give stability to financial systems: structure and conduct regulation. Examples of the first are functional separation of institutions (like the separation between commercial and investment banks of the Glass-Steagall act in the US), entry requirements (like minimum capital requirements), deposit insurance and the existence of a lender of last resort. Examples of the second are information disclosure rules, and pricing rules or rate regulation.

The regulatory response to the US banking crisis of the 1930s was the establishment of a *deposit insurance* system (the FDIC). These systems have been quite successful in stabilizing the financial and banking markets. Runs have been very limited since the Second World War. In Europe deposit insurance systems have been created more recently, typically in the late 1970s. Their coverage differs across countries and may involve full or partial insurance usually for deposits up to a certain size.[8] The most striking feature of deposit insurance in Europe is that it remains largely unknown to the public. This is probably because it is common knowledge in Europe that banks in trouble will be bailed out by the government and that it is taxpayers, and not depositors who will foot the bill. This, obviously, leaves unexplained the introduction of the insurance systems.

2.3   Side effects of regulation

Some of these regulations are better founded than others in terms of efficiency analysis. But, in any case, what is important to understand is that the *second best principle* applies to regulation: it is very difficult to be sure of improving welfare through intervention when the first best cannot be attained, as is usually the case. In other words, regulation has its side effects, among them the potential introduction of new inefficiencies. This implies that a careful cost-benefit analysis must be performed before any new regulation is implemented.

Present regulatory theory does not give clear cut recommendations owing to the complexity of the welfare analysis, as we have seen in the bank runs case. For example, runs could be eliminated by a simple structural regulation requiring banks to invest the proceeds of deposits in risk-free liquid government securities. The reason why this may not be such a good idea is that the cost of intermediation would probably go up because of the substantially higher yields of longer-term investments (the liquidity transformation role of banks). Similarly, information disclosure requirements may make banks more vulnerable to information-based runs. Even the rationales for such well-established practices as reserve requirements and the discount window are not completely obvious.[9]

Deposit insurance and the existence of a lender of last resort prevent the occurrence of bank runs but induce a *moral hazard problem*; banks may have an incentive to assume too much risk through risky investments, or to compete by raising deposit rates high, thus forcing central bank intervention. This problem is compounded by the reduced incentives that depositors have to monitor the solvency of the bank under a deposit insurance system. As a consequence, sometimes only partial deposit insurance is offered, or central bank intervention is made discretionary. Nevertheless, particularly for large institutions, whose failure can have a domino effect, an important credibility problem for policy remains. Interest rate regulation and prudential measures, like capital and liquidity requirements and restrictions on asset concentration, have been implemented to reduce the moral hazard problem. Similarly, schemes to make the banking community bear the bail-out cost of insolvency have been proposed. Then bankers would act as a club with appropriate incentives to monitor its members.

The deregulation process started in the 1970s, principally via the money market fund revolution whereby high deposit rates were offered, coupled with deposit insurance and the guarantee of the lender of the last resort. These induced *excessive risk taking* and an increase in the number of failures, the most conspicuous example being the thrift crisis in the US.

It is clear that some of these regulations, for example rate regulation, induce further *distortions*. *Rate regulation* suppresses price competition and induces financial institutions to compete on a non-price basis, through quality or services, and to cross-subsidize products. Although rate regulation could serve as a prudential measure, substituting for equity creating a rent for the bank, it is dominated by a stricter capital ratio requirement.[10]

These distortions can be examined in the context of the classical *Klein-Monti model*[11] of banking competition where the banking firm is a price taker in the bond or interbank market and competes in both the deposit and loan markets with some market power. The model was originally built for a monpolistic bank but the approach has been readily extended to Cournot competition. If the costs of the bank are separable (between deposits and loans), and if the loan and deposit demand functions are independent, then a standard *separation result* emerges for pricing in the deposit and loan markets. The bank equates the marginal revenue from loans and the marginal cost from deposits to the competitive bond rate. The introduction of a services variable that affects positively the demand for deposits and for which the bank can set a price (a zero price means a complete subsidy for the services) allows the examination of the effects of deposit rate regulation. With a regulated rate, a bank will invest in services to equate the marginal cost of investment to the financial margin: the bond/interbank rate (discounted by the percentage of free reserves) minus the regulated deposit rate. This will generally imply that services will be subsidized. A lower deposit rate (or a higher margin) implies that the bank has a greater incentive to invest in services. Deregulation and price competition that imply a lower margin will induce the provision of a lower level of services. It is worth noting that the *subsidization of services* only arises when the bank has some monopoly power.[12]

Interest rates, the pricing of services and entry requirements all pose more fundamental problems of regulation: the possibility of '*regulatory capture*' in favour of the regulated financial institutions.

Until recently, rate regulation has been very popular in Europe. According to a recent OECD survey (Bingham, 1985), market rates were paid on demand and savings deposits only in Italy, Switzerland and the UK. Other countries were subject to regulation or cartel-type agreements that distorted rates. National authorities and regulators have allowed financial institutions in some countries to coordinate their market actions, or to collude, in the belief that this would benefit the stability of the system and that it would make it easier to control the banking sector.[13] Different forms of 'concerted pricing' exist in Belgium, France, the Netherlands and Switzerland.[14] Baltensperger and Dermine (1987) give evidence of the effect of rate controls in raising profitability and margins. Banking has tended to have a higher rate of return on equity than the industrial sector. All of this is consistent with the capture theory of regulation.

Another side effect of protecting the banking system against runs may be the *unwanted protection of inefficient and/or badly managed or fraudulent banks.* It is well known that a very high percentage of bank failures are due to mismanagement and fraud.

In summary, the main side effects of regulation are to induce moral hazard and the possibility of regulatory capture. In any case, conduct type regulation, with its associated principal-agent relationship in a world of asymmetric information, generates information rents.[15]

3   Deregulation and integration

3.1   European banking

Until recently different forms of concerted pricing and collusive agreements in Europe maintained prices for financial services above competitive levels. This is consistent with the evidence gathered so far, the Price Waterhouse (PW) study and the available data on margins.[16] Regulated prices have induced competition on services and cross-subsidization. There is evidence also that higher margin countries have denser branch and ATM networks.[17] The PW study also uncovered large price differences among countries. Although these differences can be attributed to differences in costs,[18] reserve requirements or bundling (in which case the price of a standard bundle may still be the same across countries), the possibility remains that competition differs in degree from one country to another. Market structure could be characterized as a *system of national oligopolies.* Concentration does not appear to have a positive relationship with profits. This should not be surprising given the possibility of regulatory capture. Further, there is evidence of rent sharing with labour.[19]

3.2   Towards a single market

The programme for the integration of the financial sector calls for *freedom of capital movement* and *freedom of establishment* as essential tools, but several European countries still maintain controls on capital movements (Germany, UK, France and the Benelux countries have liberalized capital flows already). Trade in banking services in Europe is limited, tends to be of the intraindustry type (where a country both imports and exports) and seems to be mostly with the rest of the world.[20] Legal obstacles to the establishment of banking subsidiaries have been virtually removed (with the temporary exception of Spain) and there are still restrictions to the acquisition of domestic institutions by foreign banks (need of approval by supervisory authority and other restrictions in some countries like Spain, France and Italy). Nevertheless, the market shares of foreign banks vary substantially in different European countries, suggesting either hidden restrictions or economic barriers to entry.

In order to facilitate market access, the European Commission has established the *single banking license* and the *home country and mutual recognition principles* in its Second Banking Directive. Authorization for a financial institution to operate in one European country would be enough for it to supply or establish financial services elsewhere. The EC second directive calls for home country control on solvency and large exposures, and for a minimum harmonization across countries on several other issues: setting a floor on equity levels, putting limitations on risk concentration, setting standards on investor protection and other accounting and ownership measures. With respect to monetary policy issues (reserve coefficients, for example) and deposit insurance, the *national or host country principle* is called for. Thus, for instance, a foreign bank should join the deposit insurance scheme of the host country.

3.3   The benefits of integration and competition

The PW study predicts that substantial benefits will arise from the integration of financial markets. The study simulates the impact on consumer surplus of the decrease in prices of financial services to the lowest levels found in the EC. The basic idea is to assume that a competitive financial and banking market will prevail following integration. Producers that do not set competitive prices will not survive since business will flow to the lowest priced firms. This accords with the classical competitive view of international trade (although the bundling problem may indicate an overestimation of the attainable price decreases). The study also contemplates existing imperfect competition features, economies of scale, differentiation and associated non-competitive pricing, but seems to assume that integration will be so powerful as to induce perfect competition, exhausting the potential economies of scale. This is certainly too extreme to be taken literally. Probably it would be more appropriate to interpret the post-integration situation, according to PW, as a 'contestable' market, where, even in the presence of economies of scale or product differentiation, potential competition disciplines established firms and enforces a competitive outcome.

The PW study has been much debated. We now offer a qualitative assessment of the effects of integration on competition.

4   From collusion and regulatory capture to imperfect competition

Our first and central thesis contends that the main effect of integration will be to change the focal point of the strategies of banks from collusion and regulatory capture to competition. Nevertheless, competition will be imperfect owing to the presence of important economic barriers to entry, yielding an upper bound for the integration benefits lower than the competitive benchmark.

This means that, although the integration of financial markets will produce, already, substantial benefits, these will be less than those which would follow from a fully competitive structure.[21]

In order to substantiate our claim we will explain why the potential for collusion looms large, how '1992' can change things and the limits to competition in banking.

4.1   Collusion, focal points and '1992'

The theory of dynamic games has illuminated the factors that tend to hinder or foster collusion among firms. The basic idea is that the fear of future retaliation may deter cheating in a collusive agreement. In this respect low discount rates, a small number of firms, symmetry of firms in the market and the possibility of rapid detection of a deviator have been shown to facilitate collusion. Two other factors, multimarket contact and building a reputation for cooperation, may apply with force in the banking environment. *Multimarket contact*, typical in banking, facilitates collusion since a non-cooperative attitude in one market can be punished in others, and the fear of spoiling one market may deter deviations in all markets.[22] In a situation with incomplete information, where firms do not know the relevant information that influences the behaviour of their rivals, there are incentives to build a *reputation for friendly and cooperative behaviour*. In this respect the *history* of the industry, an intangible, plays a crucial role, yielding '*focal points*' and 'usual practices' to firms so as to coordinate their actions and avoid price wars. On the other hand, in a multimarket competition context, market power may be protected by building a reputation for toughness and effectively threatening to fight entrants.[23]

It is well known that tacit collusion, i.e. collusion without legally binding agreements, may be difficult to sustain when the above mentioned factors are weak. Nevertheless, in the banking industry in Europe the collusive factors have been reinforced by regulations that have made life easy for banks.[24] In particular, interest rate regulation and 'concerted pricing' may have provided effective devices to enforce collusion, be it because of regulatory capture or because of improved coordination. In any case the institutional and regulatory framework in many countries seems to have fostered a cooperative attitude and consolidated a tradition of understanding among banks.

A history of cooperation needs a turning point if a competitive attitude is to be developed. It is our contention that 1992 will provide this.

Once regulation is harmonized and kept to its prudential role, the possibilities of regulatory capture diminish dramatically. At the same time, the incentives to deviate from a collusive agreement increase since there is no longer an official sanction to individual banks' decisions. The deregulation and integration process will move the focus towards non-cooperative behaviour, thus destroying the anchor to which restrictive practices are bound.

The case of high yield accounts in Spain serves to illustrate our thesis. Since 1987 there has been total freedom of interest rates, nevertheless only foreign banks and some secondary trademarks of the large national banks, all with a limited network, have openly offered high-return accounts. There seemed to be a tacit agreement between the large banks not to engage in a costly rate war over deposits, trying to prolong the low regulated deposit rates of the past. The strategy also tried to discriminate between informed and uninformed customers. This situation was upset by a large, and efficient, bank that finally decided to launch a very aggressive campaign to attract deposits by offering a new account with high returns and offering to pay for part of the switching cost of consumers (change of all automatic payments through the account). The bank seems to have increased its deposits substantially, thus triggering a generalization of the new high-yield accounts.[25]

4.2   The limits to competition

Non-cooperative behaviour is not to be confused with competitive behaviour. The lack of concerted action and a deregulated market does not mean that a competitive outcome will emerge if there are economic barriers to entry.

A market with no barriers to entry and exit is termed *contestable*.[26] In a contestable market, entry and exit are costless and potential competition disciplines the behaviour of incumbents, even if there is a monopoly. This is so since this type of market is vulnerable to hit-and-run entry. If a firm were to charge a price so as to make a positive profit an entrant could come in, undercut the established firm, get his business, and exit before he could react. The price charged by the incumbent would not be sustainable. Sustainable configurations have very desirable properties: firms make zero profits, if more than one firm is active prices equal marginal costs, the industry configuration is cost-minimizing and there is no cross-subsidization of one set of products by others.[27]

Two conditions are needed for contestability: there must be no sunk costs and there must be some price rigidity, the quantity adjustment of entrants and the switch of consumers to the new offer being faster than the reaction of incumbents.

Are these conditions, abstracting from regulation and collusion, satisfied in banking?

Bain identified several sources of barriers to entry: economies of scale, product differentiation advantages and absolute cost advantages. A barrier to entry is an incumbency advantage: a cost or demand asymmetry which favours the incumbent and allows a supernormal return (or rent).

Barriers to entry are present at different levels of the banking business. Leaving aside legal ones, for example entry and capital requirements, there are many economic barriers and sources of market power. These include investment in physical capital, branches, computer equipment, ATM systems and intangible capital, building up a clientele and a reputation for solvency. These factors may give a bank an absolute cost or a product differentiation advantage.

It is well understood from *location models* that an extensive branch network may crowd space and prove to be an important barrier to entry yielding the bank local monopoly power in the retail market. An incumbent (or a cartel of incumbents) has an incentive to deter entry through *branch proliferation.*[28] This is so since a monopoly incumbent has more incentive to open new branches than an entrant. The monopoly, if successful, will keep its monopoly position, while the maximum payoff for the entrant are the profits associated with a duopoly.[29] Furthermore, the branch and ATM system also involves a *network externality.* For the consumer the size of the network is an important consideration and therefore an individual consumer must anticipate the total number of consumers who will join the bank. This poses a coordination problem which may have multiple equilibria, not necessarily optimal from the social point of view. The bank then has an incentive to enlarge its customer base to elicit growth expectations in the consumers, facing at the same time the problem of whether or not to make its ATM system compatible with those of competitors. In general a smaller or weaker bank will have a greater incentive than larger ones to make their ATM systems compatible. With an integrated network all banks gain since consumers prefer it, but a smaller bank obtains a larger benefit by free riding on the network of the larger competitor. A larger bank will tend to prefer an incompatible system. Nevertheless this will induce an increased aggressiveness on price to capture a larger customer base (with penetration pricing, for example) and may not be worthwhile.[30] In any case denying access to a well-established network poses an important barrier to a potential entrant.

Switching costs are another important source of market power.[31] Consumers face a substitution cost of moving from one bank to another. This cost may be associated with the physical change of accounts, regular bill payments, lack of information, or even bounded rationality. Switching costs are not the same for all customers. It is reasonable to assume that they are decreasing with wealth. This would rationalize the idea that rich people have more alternatives. Banks know it and are able to segment the market by discriminating on price. This way, for example, high return accounts may require large minimum balances, and sometimes they are not even publicized and are kept for 'informed' people. Someone asking for this type of account reveals himself as an informed customer.[32] Switching costs may yield collusive outcomes once firms have established a customer base which remains captive. Nevertheless they also induce intense competition for customers to enlarge the base. Banks may have an incentive to offer an advantageous introductory pricing scheme, such as a high deposit rate, to attract new customers and then, once customers are locked in, to reduce it. In fact, introductory pricing has been used by banks with special accounts for young people and in the launching of high yield money market accounts. If this type of behaviour is anticipated by consumers they will refrain now from accepting these offers out of fear of being 'exploited' later. The result is that switching costs make demand less elastic both now and in the future and, with no change in the tastes of consumers, increase the profits of banks.

Last but not least, *reputation effects* in banking may prove to be crucial barriers to entry. As we have seen confidence in a bank and in the banking system is a delicate matter. The 'quality' of a bank is very much related to the perception of customers about its solvency and probability of failure (think of Swiss banks!). The solvency of the bank will depend obviously on the wisdom of its investments and good management, but also on its customer base. A large base gives stability, because of switching costs, and allows a high level of diversification. A problem is that the quality of the bank is related to the expectations of depositors. With imperfect deposit insurance an interest rate offer may mean different things depending on the evaluation of the solvency of the bank.

By identifying the 'reputation' of a bank with its perceived probability of failure, we can introduce the concept of *vertical differentiation* in banking competition: if all banks were to offer the same rates, and there were no other differential elements, depositors would prefer the safer ones. It is not difficult to imagine a situation where low risk (high quality) banks enjoy larger margins, profits and market shares, thus attracting highly risk-averse customers. Furthermore, vertical differentiation may give banking a *natural oligopoly* structure (regardless of entry costs).[33] If the diversity of the consumers is low (in terms of risk-aversion), or the initial advantage of safer banks is large, the market may not sustain riskier banks (even if entry costs are small).[34]

The natural oligopoly structure may be reinforced by a *snowball effect*. Suppose for example that two banks are already established in a large market and that bank A is larger and better diversified than bank B. A new market is opened and consumers form (rational) expectations about the different probabilities of failure of the two banks. Bank A will capture a larger market share than bank B, snowballing its initial advantage.

Deposit insurance and the presence of a lender of last resort tend to provide stability to the system, but nevertheless some residual uncertainty remains. This seems particularly true in Europe where deposit insurance systems are ignored and intervention rules are not at all transparent. Reputations for solvency and good management take time to build but, once established, they stabilize a clientele. For example, in some European countries savings banks have had, and still have, a premium for being safe. The premium translates into lower deposit rates paid to customers.

In summary, the increase in competition brought about by integration will be limited. Freedom of establishment will be confronted by economic barriers to entry. We have seen how, despite the fact that practically no legal barriers remain in place, investment and entry abroad have not surged to the extent that may have been expected.[35] With regulated rates banks have an incentive to overinvest in services, mainly through an overextended branch system. This overextended network can yield effective protection against entry. One effect of the past rate regulation is thus to create an important barrier to entry once deregulation takes place! Freedom of capital movements will be limited, from the point of view of depositors, by switching costs. The prevailing system of national oligopolies does not seem destined to disappear.

5   Segmentation and the benefits of integration

Our second thesis asserts that *the banking market will remain segmented, with different degrees of competition, and that the benefits of integration will be unevenly distributed.*

As large corporate banking is already an international business with strong competition, integration will not have a large impact on this area of financial services. Retail banking for wealthy consumers and corporate banking for medium-sized firms, on the other hand will see a substantial increase in competition. Mass retail banking will see a much more moderate increase in competition, mainly because of the high switching costs faced by consumers and the presence of barriers to entry. Low-income depositors will probably suffer since the increase in competition will tend to diminish the extent of subsidy to the operation of their accounts.

Segmentation may be either structural or induced by strategic reasons.

Banking is a multiproduct industry segmented *structurally*, both from the demand and the supply sides. Retail banking and the corporate international banking are very different lines of business both because the customers are very different and because delivering the products calls for different skills and resources. This is one of the reasons why it is so difficult to find convincing evidence of *economies of scale and scope* in banking. Global economies of scale in banking are similar to the classical problem of the returns of aggregate production functions. Econometric studies yield (global) economies of scale that are exhausted at low levels of output and there is evidence that average cost dispersion is higher in the same size class of banks than across different sizes, indicating that the issue of scale economies cannot be crucial.[36] The theoretical arguments for the existence of banks seem to point at the greater relevance of *economies of scope*. Nevertheless there is no conclusive evidence of their importance.[37]

As we have seen in our discussion on price discrimination and switching costs, the segmentation of customers is very important from the *strategic* viewpoint. For example, a bank can invest in a large network of branches in order to have a large and stable (risk-averse) clientele, with little opportunity to take their custom elsewhere, and gain a reputation for solvency. This will allow the bank to be soft in pricing, a *fat cat* and enjoy a large margin. Otherwise a bank may decide to have a small network, price aggressively and cater to less risk-averse and better informed clients. The bank will be then a *puppy dog* by committing to be small.[38]

It is worth emphasizing here that some aspects of the barriers to entry we have mentioned, strictly speaking, apply only to retail banking based on a branch network. Some banking services for corporate customers, and for wealthy individual customers, may have some *contestability properties* due to the low switching costs and the alternatives offered by disintermediation. This points also to the consideration of the value of branches as instruments of competition that lower switching costs, given technological developments and deregulation. These banking services are good candidates to be supplied by specialized firms unless there are economies of scope with other services provided by banks. Nevertheless, competition in several markets gives a bank the possibility of using the leverage of a monopoly position in one line of business to monopolize another line of business by *bundling* or tied sales. This way banking institutions may foreclose the entry of non-banks in some threatened segments.[39] The important conclusion is that the segmentation of the banking market implies that different degrees of competition can coexist.

Furthermore, multimarket competition may yield incentives for firms to exit or not to enter a market. This paradoxical outcome, which limits the effects of the integration of markets, comes about because of strategic behaviour. In a context of segmented markets, a firm may exit from a profitable market in order to gain a strategic advantage in another market that more than compensates for the loss in profits in the first market.[40] Similarly, the prospect of integrated markets may induce a firm not to enter a market so as to avoid a more aggressive price response from a rival, since integrated markets imply uniform pricing. Suppose that firm A is in markets 1 and 2 and firm B operates only in 1. The latter may not want to enter market 2 since with the status quo the pricing of firm A is softer because the firm has a monopoly in market 2 and has to charge the same price in both markets.[41]

6   Mergers and the intensity of competition

Our third thesis is that *mergers, acquisitions and cross-participation agreements will tend to soften competition*.

Deregulation and integration will make inefficient some structures already in place. Rate regulation has induced overbranching and a certain tendency to agglomerate at the centre of the market.[42] This is easily explained in terms of location theory, since when rates are fixed firms have an incentive to locate 'where demand is' and to compete in terms of quality (geographical proximity) with more branches. When rates are free this location pattern makes price competition very harsh. Firms have incentives then to *relax price competition* by differentiating themselves, for example by locating further apart. This process is costly and a possible way to relax competition is to buy the rival. In this case concentration in local markets would increase (as has happened with deregulation in the US).

A potential alternative to buying up competitors is to try to drive the rival bank out of business. Nevertheless, when depositors have residual uncertainty about the solvency of banks and the banking system, predatory strategies may backfire. A bank trying to get rid of a rival, perhaps forcing him into bankruptcy, may provoke a confidence crisis without appropriate lender of last resort facilities. Thus, on the contrary, a sound bank may have incentives to help another bank in trouble precisely to avoid a confidence crisis that will hurt everyone. Failure to do so may signal to depositors that the supposedly sound bank may have problems also.[43] These considerations indicate that it may be better to merge with a rival than to attempt to attack him. Merger has the advantages of not entailing the risk of a confidence crisis and of obtaining, at least potentially, increased market power. Nevertheless a certain level of pre-merger predation (but not enough to trigger a crisis) may be optimal, since then the buyer may obtain a more favourable price.[44] On balance, it seems that the costs of predation in banking are much higher than in other industries: *merger thus looks a better alternative than predation.*[45]

In another vein, the overextension of the branch network in some countries may mean that the only entry possibility is by acquisition of an already existing bank. Such opportunities may arise since increased competitive pressures may force inefficient or badly managed banks into insolvency. In this case public and private incentives coincide in the desirability of a rescue *merger* to preserve both the stability of the financial system and the intangible capital of the bank (such as its non-verifiable information about customers and loans).

In general one response to increased competition may be to merge with rivals, both because collusion is easier to sustain with fewer firms and because margins in non-cooperative competition tend to be lower. Another reason to merge is the realization of economies of scale and/or scope. Although we have seen there is no hard evidence in favour of either of these it must be emphasized that measurement and aggregation problems may obscure some potential economies in very specific areas.

The effort to soften competition and to penetrate foreign markets, gaining access to an established network, may promote *cross-participation agreements*. In this situation an individual bank puts some weight on the profits of its allied banks and cooperative behaviour is induced. In any case, the establishment of a European market for corporate control should improve the efficiency of banking and the quality of management.

7   A final remark: the consistency of proposed regulations

We have talked about the strategic incentives of financial institutions in the face of the deregulation and integration process. What about the strategic incentives of national regulators, given the EC directives on integration?

The EC directives on integration have set the ground for a contest among national regulators. Nonetheless, this contest will not necessarily yield an efficient outcome.

The application of the home country principle to solvency and to the approval of banking services, coupled with the application of the host country principle for deposit insurance schemes, gives incentives for national authorities to be very liberal in setting standards to provide national banks with a competitive edge abroad. If disaster happens, foreign taxpayers will foot the bill. At the same time an increase in deposit insurance in one country may make it more attractive to depositors but also too risky for foreign banks. We conclude therefore that, despite the fact that the directives call for minimum standards (harmonization), the system does not give the appropriate incentives to national authorities to internalize costs.

Similarly, monetary policy instruments like reserve coefficients will tend to be set at the lowest possible levels,[46] since any country that does not do this will put its banks at a disadvantage.

NOTES

Carmen Matutes, Colin Mayer, and the participants at the CEPR/Istituto Mobiliario Italiano Conference on European Financial Integration, Rome, January 1990, provided helpful comments.

1 Useful surveys of the banking firm are Baltensperger (1980) and Santomero (1984). An excellent introduction to strategic competition is Tirole (1988).
2 Three conditions are necessary to make panics possible (in the absence of any regulation): (1) Banks must satisfy a sequential service constraint (that is, withdrawals tenders must be served sequentially till the bank runs out of assets). This creates incentives to run and get the money before other people. (2) Investments of the bank can not be totally illiquid.Otherwise by withdrawing early it is not possible to gain anything. (3) Depositors must have a high enough degree of risk-aversion. Otherwise the optimal risk-sharing contract involves a face value lower than the liquidation of the bank assets.
3 There is a problem in the theoretical foundation of panic runs. If depositors have rational expectations they will anticipate the run and will not deposit in the bank. Runs would never be observed in equilibrium. A possible way out is to select the good or bad (run) equilibrium according to a sunspot; then agents would deposit in the bank provided the probability of the good outcome was high enough. Another possibility to obtain the emergence of runs in equilibrium, which does not rely on sunspots, is to consider 'fundamental' or information-based runs.
4 The welfare analysis of information-based runs is complicated. They can be seen to be welfare decreasing when the long-term investment of the bank is irrevocable and depositors are not very risk-averse. If the long-term investment is liquid, however, they are beneficial since all early demands can be met, and the project is liquidated when there is bad news about returns. If depositors have a high degree of (relative) risk-aversion then the reception of bad news does not induce depositors to run since consumers would like to invest more in the uncertain future (Jacklin and Bhattacharya, 1988).
5 See Diamond (1984) and Leland and Pyle (1977).
6 See Yanelle (1989).
7 It has been argued recently that reserve requirements may be an ineffective tool to control the money supply. As Baltensperger and Dermine (1987) argue there is no clear cut case for regulation based on macroeconomic/monetary policy considerations.

8 See Baltensperger and Dermine (1989).
9 The rationale for reserve requirements and the discount window is discussed in Bhattacharya and Gale (1986). Private liquidity shocks of banks (with private information about their portfolio) induces the need for interbank lending to insure depositors. The optimal mechanism involves banks borrowing and lending at a subsidized rate (discount window) and there to be underinvestment in reserves (with respect to the full information situation).
10 See Baltensperger and Dermine (1987).
11 Klein (1971) and Monti (1972).
12 See Faig (1987).
13 Before 1981 the European Commission viewed interbank rate agreements made under the auspices of national authorities falling in the domain of monetary policy instruments and therefore not subject to the competition articles of the Rome Treaty. This position has been revised recently. See Dassesse and Isaacs (1985).
14 In Spain, and until very recently, the heads of the large banks would meet once a week for lunch to 'conduct business'.
15 The classical analysis of this issue is Baron and Myerson (1982).
16 See Baltensperger and Dermine (1989).
17 See Neven (1989).
18 Maybe because of differences in factor prices, scale and scope economics, or just plain inefficiency. The different mix of retail versus wholesale and corporate banking in different countries could play a role also.
19 See Steinherr and Gilibert (1988).
20 See Neven (1989).
21 We are assuming therefore, and this is an empirical judgement, that moving from collusion to imperfect competition will improve welfare.
22 See Bernheim and Whinston (1986).
23 See Kreps and Wilson (1982) and Milgrom and Roberts (1982).
24 Evidence of market power in the US market is not conclusive. Positive evidence of the association between concentration and profitability is given in Rhoades (1977) but Smirlock (1985) argues that it can not be attributed to market power.
25 See Caminal et al. (1990) and Vives (1990) for an overview of banking competition in Spain.
26 See Baumol, Panzar and Willig (1982).
27 That is, the revenues of any set of products exceed their incremental cost.
28 See Schmalensee (1978) and Bonano (1987).
29 Nevertheless, if exit costs are low and there is product substitution, proliferation may not be credible. An established multiproduct (multiplant) firm may have more incentive to exit a location where it faces competition than a single product (location) competitor. The former will reduce price competition by exiting (Judd, 1985).
30 See Katz and Shapiro (1986a, b) and Farrell and Saloner (1985).
31 See Klemperer (1987a, b). See also Caminal and Matutes (1989) for an analysis of endogenous switching costs.
32 For example, in Spain it has been a usual practice of large financial institutions not to publicize high yield accounts and not to offer them to customers unless they are demanded.
33 It is worth remarking that the condition for the emergence of a natural

oligopoly seems to be satisfied in banking: the burden of the increase in quality (increase in the customer base) falls basically on fixed costs (investment in the branch network, ATM systems and promotion). See Gabszewicz and Thisse (1979) and Shaked and Sutton (1983) for an analysis of vertical differentiation.

34 See Matutes and Vives (1990).

35 In Spain, the only country where there are still restrictions to entry, foreign banks have not even exhausted the limited possibilities they have. This is an indication of the existence of important economic barriers.

36 See Gilligan et al. (1984), Shaffer and David (1986) and Humphrey (1985 and 1987).

37 Some positive evidence is provided by Gilligan et al. (1984) although some studies even report slight diseconomies of scope (Berger et al., 1987).

38 It has been shown that smaller firms have an incentive to price aggressively to build a clientele while larger firms would tend to 'exploit' their customer base. See Farrell and Shapiro (1988). The animal terminology for strategies is taken from Fudenberg and Tirole (1984).

39 See Whinston (1987).

40 This may happen, for example, with decreasing returns to scale and Cournot competition (Bulow et al. (1985)).

41 See Mutates and Regibeau (1989).

42 On theoretical grounds this tendency has been shown to obtain in some location models with a uniform distribution of consumers.

43 See Aghion et al. (1988).

44 See Yamey (1972) and Saloner (1987).

45 It could be argued also that lender of last resort schemes may render predation ineffective, protecting institutions against failure.

46 Reserve coefficients are better seen as a tax. (See Romer, 1985.) In some countries with high reserve requirements, like Italy and Spain, harmonization may pose an important problem for the financing of the public deficit.

REFERENCES

Aghion, P., P. Bolton and M. Dewatripont (1988) 'Interbank lending, bank runs and competition', mimeo.

Akerlof, G. (1970) 'The market for "lemons": qualitative uncertainty and the market mechanism', *Quarterly Journal of Economics* **84**, 488–500.

Baltensperger, E. (1980) 'Alternative approaches to the theory of the banking firm', *Journal of Monetary Economics* **6**, 1–37.

Baltensperger, E. and J. Dermine (1987) 'Banking deregulation in Europe', *Economic Policy* **2**, (4), 63–109.

 (1989) 'European banking, prudential and regulatory issues', forthcoming in J. Dermine (ed.), *European Banking in the 1990s*, Basil Blackwell.

Baron, D. and R. Myerson (1982) 'Regulating a monopolist with unknown costs', *Econometrica* **50**, 911–30.

Baumol, W., J. Panzar and R. Willig (1982) *Contestable markets and the theory of industry structure*, New York: Harcourt Brace Jovanovich.

Berger, A., G. Hanweck and D. Humphrey (1987) 'Competitive viability in banking: a restructuration and reassessment', *Journal of Money, Credit and Banking* **14**, 435–56.

Bernheim, D. and M. Whinston (1986) 'Multimarket contact and collusive behavior', mimeo, Department of Economics, Harvard University.

Bhattacharya, S. and D. Gale (1986) 'Preference shocks, liquidity and central bank policy', mimeo, University of Pennsylvania.

Bingham, T. (1985) *Banking and monetary policy*, Paris: OECD.

Bonano, G. (1987) 'Location, Choice, Product Proliferation and Entry Deterrence', *Review of Economic Studies* **54**, 37–46.

Bulow, J., J. Geanakoplos and P. Klemperer (1985) 'Multimarket oligopoly: strategic substitutes and complements', *Journal of Political Economy* **93**, 488–511.

Caminal, R. and C. Matutes (1989) 'On precommitment and competition: endogenous switching costs in a duopoly model', mimeo.

Caminal, R., J. Gual and X. Vives (1990) 'Competition in Spanish Banking', in J. Dermine (ed.), *European Banking in the 1990s*, Basil Blackwell.

Dassesse, M. and S. Isaacs (1985) *EEC banking law*, London: Lloyds of London Press.

Diamond, D. (1984) 'Financial intermediation and delegated monitoring', *Review of Economic Studies* **51**, 393–414.

Diamond, D. and P. Dybvig (1983) 'Bank runs, deposit insurance, and liquidity', *Journal of Political Economy* **91**, 401–19.

Faig, M. (1987) 'Implications of banking market structure for monetary policy: a survey', IMF Working Paper.

Fama, E. (1980) 'Banking in the theory of finance', *Journal of Monetary Economics* **6**, 39–57.

Farrell, J. and G. Saloner (1985) 'Standardization, compatibility and innovation', *Rand Journal of Economics* **16**, 70–83.

Farrell, J. and C. Shapiro (1988) 'Dynamic competition with lock-in', *Rand Journal of Economics*.

Fudenberg, D. and J. Tirole (1984) 'The fat cat effect, the puppy dog ploy and the lean and hungry look', *American Economic Review, Papers and Proceedings* **74**, 361–8.

Friedman, M. and A. Schwartz (1965) *A monetary history of the United States, 1867–1960*, Princeton, NJ.: Princeton University Press.

Gabszewicz, J. and J.F. Thisse (1979) 'Price competition, quality, and income disparities', *Journal of Economic Theory* **20**, 340–59.

Gilligan, T., M. Smirlock and W. Marshall (1984). 'Scale and scope economies in the multi-product banking firm', *Journal of Monetary Economics* **13**, 319–405.

Humphrey, D. (1985) 'Costs and scale economies in bank intermediation' in R.C. Aspinwall and R.A. Eisenbeis (eds.), *Handbook for Bank Strategy*, Wiley.

(1987) 'Cost dispersion and the measurement of economies in banking', *Federal Reserve Bank of Richmond Review*, May–June.

Jacklin, C.J. and S. Bhattacharya (1988) 'Distinguishing panics and information-based bank runs: welfare and policy implications', *Journal of Political Economy* **96**, 568–92.

Judd, K. (1985) 'Credible spatial preemption', *Rand Journal of Economics* **16**, 153–66.

Katz, M. and C. Shapiro (1986a) 'Technology adoption in the presence of network externalities', *Journal of Political Economy* **94**, 822–41.

(1986b) 'Product compatibility choice in a market with technological progress', *Oxford Economic Papers* **38**, 146–65.

Klein, M.A. (1971) 'A theory of the banking firm', *Journal of Money, Credit and Banking* **3**, 205–18.

Klemperer, P. (1987a) 'Markets with consumer switching costs', *Quarterly Journal of Economics* **102**, 375–94.

(1987b) 'The competitiveness of markets with switching costs', *Rand Journal of Economics* **18**, 138–50.

Kreps, D. and R. Wilson (1982) 'Reputation and imperfect information', *Journal of Economic Theory* **27**, 253–79.

Leland, H. and D. Pyle (1977) 'Information asymmetries, financial structure and financial intermediation', *Journal of Finance* **32**, 371–87.

Matutes, C. and P. Regibeau (1989) 'Standardization across markets and entry', *Journal of Industrial Economics* **37**, 359–72.

Matutes, C. and X. Vives (1990) 'Failure risk differentiation and competition', mimeo, Universitat Autònoma de Barcelona.

Milgrom, P. and J. Roberts (1982). 'Predation, reputation and entry deterrence', *Journal of Economic Theory* **27**, 280–312.

Monti, M. (1972) 'Deposit, credit and interest rate determination under alternative bank objective functions', in K. Shell and G. Szego (eds.), *Mathematical methods in investment and finance*, North-Holland.

Neven, D. (1989) 'Lessons from Industrial Organization to retail banking in Europe', in J. Dermine (ed.), *European Banking in the 1990s*, Basil Blackwell.

Postlewaite, A. and X. Vives (1987) 'Bank runs as an equilibrium phenomenon', *Journal of Political Economy* **95**, 485–91.

Rhoades, D. (1977) 'Structure-Performance Studies in Banking: A Summary and Evaluation', SES No. 92, Federal Reserve Board.

Romer, D. (1985) 'Financial intermediation, reserve requirements and inside money: A general equilibrium analysis', *Journal of Monetary Economics* **16**, 175–94.

Saloner, G. (1987) 'Predation, merger and incomplete information', *Rand Journal of Economics* **18**, 165–86.

Santomero, A. (1984) 'Modelling the banking firm', *Journal of Money, Credit and Banking* **16**, 577–602.

Schmalensee, R. (1978) 'A Model of Advertising and Product Quality', *Journal of Political Economy* **86**, 485–503.

Shaffer, S. and E. David (1986) 'Economies of superscale and interstate expansion', Federal Reserve of New York, Working Paper 8612.

Shaked, A. and J. Sutton (1983) 'Natural Oligopolies', *Econometrica* **51**, 1469–84.

Smirlock, M. (1985) 'Evidence of the (Non) Relationship between Concentration and Profitability in Banking', *Journal of Money, Credit and Banking* **17**, 69–83.

Steinherr, A. and P. Gilibert (1988) 'The impact of freeing trade in financial services and capital movements on the European banking industry', Research Report No. 1, Center for European Policy Studies.

Tirole, J. (1988) *The theory of industrial organization*, Cambridge, MA.: MIT Press.

Vives, X. (1990) 'Deregulation and competition in Spanish banking', *European Economic Review*, forthcoming.

Whinston, M. (1987) 'Tying, Foreclosure, and Exclusion', mimeo, Harvard University.

Yamey, B. (19720 'Predatory price cutting: notes and comments', *Journal of Law and Economics* **15**, 129–42.

Yanelle, M.O. (1989) 'Two sided competition and endogenous intermediation', mimeo, University of Basel.

Discussion

JEAN DERMINE

The analysis by Xavier Vives covers a large set of issues ranging from competition among banking firms to competition among regulators. These comments will focus on two issues: *Contestability in banking markets* and *structural adjustments*.

To introduce the discussion, it is useful to position the paper, both in terms of its empirical validity and its use of economic theory. The banking activities under discussion are commercial retail banking activities: deposit taking and lending on retail and small- and medium-size company markets. This focus is quite legitimate given the theoretical development which, rooted in information asymmetry, apply best to 'small' clients; casual empirical studies assign most of the gains expected from European Banking integration to the retail market. As regards theory, the author argues quite rightly that a theory of banking competition is almost non-existent and that the widely used 1970s Klein–Monti model concerns one banking firm. However, it will be argued that the separation theorem obtained in this model is very likely to hold in more complex models, with important implications in assessing the degree of contestability of banking markets. Finally, the author argues convincingly that an analysis of banking competition should address the very specific nature of banking services, i.e. asymmetric information in monitoring loans and in the provision of liquidity insurance.

1   Contestability in banking markets

In view of many bank mergers realized in several European countries, one is forced to wonder about the effective gains to be expected from European integraton. Baumol, Panzar and Willig (1982) have argued that competition does not require a large number of firms if markets are contesable, that is if barriers to entry are low. The view expressed by Vives is that banking markets are not very contestable. Analysis of barriers to entry from the supply and demand sides shows that the degree of contestability is likely to be higher in the retail market.

Barriers to entry on the *supply side* include real economies of scale and scope, financial economies of scale and the initial equity requirement. On the *demand side*, barriers to entry include a demand for joint services (one-stop shopping) and advertising.

2   Barriers to entry on the supply side

The empirical evidence on *real economies of scale and scope*, based on the US retail market, is non-conclusive. Some have argued that these results may not hold in the future as, increasingly, retail deposit, the payment system and credit cards will require an automated technology and an Electronic Fund Transfer System involving very large fixed costs. However, the use of costly technology does not prevent the entry of small firms if they have access to the network, as is the case for Carte Bleue, Visa, Mister Cash or the Eurocheck system. As long as regulations allow entry at a fair price, it would seem that size is not a barrier to entry.

Financial economies of scale stem from the diversification of a loan portfolio and the number of depositors. A large deposit base reduces the uncertainty (variance) of deposit withdrawals and the need for costly liquid reserves. Diversification is particularly important in banking because stable earnings reduce the risk of a bank run. It is doubtful whether financial economies of scale exist on the deposit and consumer loan markets because one does not need a large number of clients to capture most of the reduction in risks. The argument is more valid for small and medium-size company loans concentrated in one region. The correlation of returns is probably high and national or international diversification would help to reduce the variance of return on a loan portfolio.

The European Commission requires a *minimal equity requirement* of ECU 5 millions to set up a bank. It is my view that this requirement should be abandoned and that tests of 'fit and properness' are better indicators of quality than a minimum level of equity. However, the initial equity requirement is unlikely to be a significant barrier to entry, especially as the European Commission will apply a lower requirement (ECU 1 million) to specialized institutions.

To illustrate further the relatively low level of barriers to entry on the supply side, consider the case of money market funds and consumer lending.

In several European countries, especially those with a large supply of risk-free government bonds, it is fairly easy to create quasi-perfect substitutes for bank deposits, i.e. money market funds. The case of France is illustrative in this respect. Deregulated in 1981, money market funds represent 25% of savings and term deposits, with funds ranging in size from FF 100 millions to FF 53 billions. On the consumer loan markets, finance companies are quite active, funding themselves on the interbank market. It appears that a process of certification on ratings enables these specialized firms to assess directly the interbank capital markets. These two examples are illustrative of the Klein-Monti separation results. Banks can provide independent deposits and loan services. With the advance of 'liability management' (meaning access to certified interbank capital markets), separation seems to hold, easing entry into banking markets. Moreover, access to deposit insurance would ease the reputation problem.

Martin Hellwig has argued that entry in the corporate loan market would be more difficult because of the time needed to build up credit risk expertise. This point is valid although the purchase of expertise from other banks could facilitate entry.

In summary, an analysis of barriers to entry from the supply side indicates that they are relatively low in the deposit and consumer loan markets. They could be more significant for the corporate markets because of the need for diversification and the initial investment in credit risk expertise.

3   Barriers to entry from the demand side

The *costs of switching* to another bank, caused by difficult access to information, could reduce the extent of competition in the mass retail market. This barrier to entry could be reinforced further by massive advertising which would need to be financed by a large deposit base. The benefits from *one-stop shopping* – the so-called marketing economies of scope could deter entry in some markets. The demand-type barriers to entry are likely to concern small transactions on accounts for which the benefits expected from a switch are small. Their relative importance remains to be documented. Overall, the analysis of barriers to entry from the demand and supply side predicts great contestability, especially in the deposits and consumer loan markets.

The last comments concern the issue of *over capacity* in banking markets and the necessary structural adjustments. This issue is of particular importance as there is casual evidence of below-cost pricing in the securities, retail and corporate loan markets. The number of financial institutions must be reduced in an orderly manner. Vives argues convincingly that mergers are likely to prevail in banking markets, because of the fear that price wars and predatory pricing could hurt solvency reputation, and possibly lead to bank runs. The wave of bank mergers currently observed in several European countries seem to confirm this prediction.

3 Banking, financial intermediation and corporate finance

MARTIN HELLWIG

1   Introduction

What is the role of banks and other intermediaries in the provision of finance to industry? More generally, how do financial institutions affect the allocation of funds for investment and the evolution of production possibilities in an economy?

Until very recently, questions of this type received little attention from economic theory. Theoretical work on finance tended to rely rather heavily on the Walrasian paradigm of 'perfect', i.e. anonymous, frictionless markets. Within this paradigm, there is no room for a comparative analysis of different institutions because one specific set of institutions, namely the Walrasian market system, is *a priori* taken as given. Reliance on the Walrasian paradigm with its given set of frictionless markets involves an implicit presumption that comparative institutional analysis can be neglected – say because as a first approximation all potentially interesting institutions achieve roughly the same outcome as a Walrasian market system.

In contrast, the role of institutions in the provision of finance to industry is of great interest to economic historians and development economists. Historians observe that financial systems differ significantly across countries and across periods, so the question arises how these differences between financial systems affected the functioning of the different economies. In certain countries such as Germany, large banks seem to have played a prominent role in the industrial expansion of the late nineteenth century. In other countries such as Britain, banks do not seem to have played such a role. Did the prominence of the large banks in Germany make a positive contribution to economic growth? Does the difference between financial systems explain some of the difference between Germany and British growth rates in the late nineteenth century?[1]

The historical literature presents a challenge to economic theory. Here as elsewhere, we need a theoretical framework to move from the observation of the simplest correlations to an assessment of the underlying mechanisms. To evaluate the effects of the large German banks on growth in the late nineteenth century, one has to travel rather far into the world of counterfactuals. Not only does one have to sort out the respeective roles of the supply of funds by the financial system and the demand for funds by industry (Tilly, 1966, p. 138; Landes, 1969, pp. 352ff), but in addition one has to consider what alternatives to bank finance there might have been, i.e. one has to assess the actual system in comparison to some counterfactual alternatives. Explicitly or implicitly, the specification of counterfactual alternatives involves a theoretical assessment of how different institutions work. The question then is what theoretical framework do we have for making such assessments?

These issues are not just of historical interest. Some of the distinctions between bank-oriented and market-oriented systems are still relevant today. Japan in the post-war period provides at least as striking an example of bank prominence in industrial finance as Germany in the late nineteenth century. The historians' discussion of Germany and Britain in the late nineteenth century can be recast in terms of Japan and the United States in the post-war period. Does the difference in financial systems explain any part of the difference between Japanese and US growth rates since the Second World War?

As pointed out above, the Walrasian paradigm of 'perfect' markets is not appropriate for addressing such questions. To be sure, the early work on financial intermediation by Gurley and Shaw (1960) Brainard and Tobin (1961) or Tobin (1969), does fit financial intermediaries into a Walrasian framework. In this literature, however, it is not clear what relation there is between the Walrasian formalism and the rather non-Walrasian informal accounts of why intermediation matters. In the Walrasian formalism, all agents – consumers, producers and intermediaries – appear as anonymous participants in the different markets; transactions costs, indivisibilities and the organization of markets by intermediaries are left outside the formalism. In consequence, the analysis provides some partial-equilibrium insights about the effects of tax and regulatory changes on financial intermediation, but it allows no explicit general equilibrium or welfare comparison of different financial systems.

The challenge to economic theory has recently been taken up again in a thought-provoking paper by Mayer (1988). Like some of the economic historians, but drawing on recent data for the period 1970–85, Mayer suggests that there are systematic differences in performance between financial systems in which banks play a prominent role and financial systems in which banks are not so prominent. He proposes to explain these differences in performance by differences in mechanisms that reduce or eliminate moral hazard in the relation between entrepreneurs and financiers. Specifically, he suggests that the more bank-oriented systems of Germany and Japan involve more commitment of the firm and the bank to a long-term relation, which allows them to enjoy the benefits of long-term contracting to reduce moral hazard.

The importance of moral hazard for finance had previously been stressed by Jensen and Meckling (1976). They had suggested that financial contracts and financial institutions are most usefully explained as efficient mechanisms for dealing with moral hazard. Mayer follows this research program, but he modifies it in an important respect. Whereas Jensen and Meckling had looked at optimal contracts for dealing with one-time moral hazard problems, Mayer is concerned about *repeated moral hazard problems in ongoing long-term relations*. The focus of the analysis is thus shifted from short-term incentive effects to problems of *commitment, contract incompleteness* and *sequential rationality* in long-term relations. According to Mayer, the nature of long-term relations determines the availability of long-term finance to firms; moreover it is this availability of long-term finance, that makes the difference between different financial systems.

Mayer does not actually work out his ideas in the context of a fully specified model, so perhaps his paper should be read as an agenda for research rather than the final theory. In the following survey, I will try to assess where we are in this research. Specifically, I want to consider the following issues:

> Where are we in our understanding of the internal logic of long-term bank-firm relations? More generally, in what sense is ability to support long-term relations the clue to assessing financial institutions?
>
> What does the consideration of long-term financial relations add to our understanding of financial institutions? Where do we go beyond the insights contained in the work of economic historians or the static analysis of Jensen and Meckling (1976) and Diamond (1984)? More generally, where are we in the search for a theoretical framework that enables us to assess the role of banks and other intermediaries in the provison of finance to industry?
>
> How does our theoretical analysis relate to the stylized facts presented by the economic historians as well as by Mayer and others? What clues do we have that theory is in fact telling us the right story?

The focus of my discussion will be on *financial institutions rather than financial instruments*. In contrast to the standard textbook on corporate finance, I am not so much concerned with the types of securities that firms issue or with the return patterns on such securities. I am rather concerned with the institutional environment in which securities are issued and finance is obtained. To be sure, we sometimes associate banks with fixed-interest debt and organized markets with equity. However, such an association of different institutions with different financial instruments does not go to the heart of the matter. In certain countries where stock markets are organized and dominated by banks, a stock issue will be just as dependent on the firm's bank as a bank loan. Recent developments in Japan provide us with an example where organized *bond* markets serve to emancipate firms from the dominance of their 'main banks' (Hoshi *et al.*, 1989b). Thus I see the distinction between bank finance and market finance as largely independent of the distinction between debt finance and equity finance. My concern here is to assess the economic significance of the distinction between the different institutional environments for corporate finance.

2   Inside finance, outside finance and bank finance: theoretical presumptions in historical assessments

It will be convenient to begin the analysis with the debate among historians about the role of banks in the process of industrialization. This debate has focussed on the work of Gerschenkron (1962), which interprets bank prominence in industrial finance as a consequence of economic backwardness. According to Gerschenkron, countries like Germany or Italy in the late nineteenth century suffered from a scarcity of capital as well as entrepreneurship, so bank finance and bank initiative had to step in as a substitute. In this interpretation, capital is regarded as scarce because (i) at this late stage, a hundred years after the beginning of the industrial revolution, the adoption of up-to-date technology required large capital outlays, and (ii) the failure to participate in the earlier stages of industrialization meant a lack of accumulated funds that could be used to finance these outlays. In contrast, Britain started industrialization at a time when required capital outlays were small. When subsequently the required long-term capital increased, accumulated funds from the earlier stages were available so that recourse to bank finance on the German pattern was unnecessary.

In passing, I note that Gerschenkron's assessment of the data has not remained undisputed. In contrast to Gerschenkron, Neuburger and Stokes (1974) suggest that, in the German case, the observed prominence of bank finance for heavy industry with large capital requirements may be a consequence of biassed bank preferences rather than the requirements of industrialization with up-to-date technologies. Indeed, they suggest that the bias in bank behaviour may have induced inefficiencies that retarded growth. Tilly and Fremdling (1976) and Tilly (1986) dispute the finding of inefficiency, but confirm the existence of a specific preference among banks for firms and industries with large-scale capital requirements, among them of course the heavy industries.

This is not the place to pursue these empirical questions. Instead, I want to analyse the theoretical structure of Gerschenkron's argument. This will provide a useful starting point for the subsequent assessment of where we are in our theoretical analysis of financial intermediation and corporate finance.

Consider first the notion of 'capital scarcity'. We must distinguish between capital scarcity at the level of the individual firm and capital scarcity at the level of the economy as a whole. Gerschenkron's argument about the role of banks in German industrial development involves the notion of *capital scarcity at the level of the individual firm*: at the level of the firm, retained earnings were insufficient to finance desired investments. To be sure, differences in interest rates and international capital flows suggest that at the aggregate level, too, capital was relatively more scarce in Germany than Britain. However, the argument about the specific role of bank finance in a situation of 'backwardness' turns on the notion of capital scarcity at the firm level. At the aggregate level, capital was available and only needed to be mobilized to finance large-scale investment. Such mobilization of outside finance in a situation where inside finance is insufficient is precisely the function of banks in Gerschenkron's argument.[2]

At this point, Gerschenkron's argument raises two questions.

(i)   Why should an insufficiency of inside finance be seen as characteristic for a situation of 'economic backwardness'?

(ii) Why should the large-scale provision of outside finance to industry require the intervention of banks or of the government?

The first question really concerns the role of inside finance in an industrially advanced country. It is clear that, in the second half of the nineteenth century, certain advanced technologies required large-scale investments. It is also clear that firms in the more 'backward' countries had not had the time to accumulate the funds required for such investments. However, it is not so clear why firms in the industrially more advanced country should have retained earnings to such an extent that further industrialization could be financed without much recourse to outside finance. To be sure, this was the pattern observed in Britain. But can one generalize from the British experience?

In this context, I note a curious contrast between Gerschenkron's analysis and Mayer's assessment of essentially the same empirical phenomenon in different data. In Mayer's (1988) assessment of cross-country differences in financing patterns in the period 1970–85, the ability of the bank-oriented systems of Japan and Germany to provide outside finance to industry is regarded as a major advantage of these systems over the market-oriented systems of the US and the UK, in which industrial investment is limited by the firms' ability to self-finance. Where Gerschenkron interprets industry reliance on banks for outside finance as a sign of 'economic backwardness', Mayer interprets the relative insignificance of outside finance in the US and the UK as a structural weakness of the market-oriented financial systems in these countries.

From the perspective of the Modigliani-Miller theorem, it is not clear that either assessment is warranted – at least without additional arguments. In a Modigliani-Miller world, the ratio of outside finance to inside finance is irrelevant. For consider two firms with identical investment paths and identical paths of earnings before interest, and suppose that one firm is levered whereas the other firm is wholly equity-financed. The firm that is equity-financed is free to choose between distributions and retentions so as to have a high level of self-finance. The levered firm must have distributions at least equal to its interest obligations, so it has less scope for self-finance. In this case, outside finance just compensates for the fact that the levered firm has to pay interest. But there is no difference in real investment paths. Any attempt to attach substantive significance to the ratio of outside finance to inside finance must therefore be based on additional arguments that move us out of a Modigliani-Miller world.

In Gerschenkron's analysis, the additional argument comes from the implicit hypothesis that firms have a strict preference for inside finance over the different types of outside finance. Under this hypothesis, self-finance is the 'normal' source of funds in an advanced economy, and 'backwardness' is on stage where the 'normal' situation of almost exclusive reliance on inside finance has not yet been reached. Empirically, this interpretation receives some support from the observation that the larger companies in pre-First World War Germany did try to move towards self-finance as soon as they possibly could, and that the banks' ascendancy was reduced apace. (Similar developments are reported by Hoshi et al., 1989a, b and by Fischer, 1990 for present-day Japan and Germany.)

From a theoretical point of view, the question is why a high degree of self-finance should be regarded as 'normal'. What are the mechanisms that make inside finance so much more desirable to firms than outside finance? Moreover what are the consequences of self-finance for the economy as a whole? Is it clear that a heavy reliance on inside finance is socially desirable? In the last part of this paper, I shall try to give at least a preliminary account of where we are on these questions.

I now turn to the role of banks in Gerschenkron's analysis. In his interpretation, the involvement of banks or the government is needed to provide outside finance to industry on any large scale. Outside finance from the anonymous, organized markets of our theoretical models is not seen as an alternative.

Bank finance here is not necessarily just loan finance. During certain periods, especially prior to 1873, German companies obtained substantial amounts of equity finance. However, the shares would be held by banks or by clients or banks acting on the banks' advice, so in many respects, banks were as much involved in equity finance as in loan finance. While share markets were organized, they were certainly not anonymous and free for all as the theoretical models would have it.

The question is to what extent bank involvement in equity and loan finance was actually necessary. The mere observation of bank prominence does not imply that there could not have been a substitute. Perhaps the banks were no more than institutionalized Walrasian auctioneers, without significance for the real allocation – and if they had not done the job, somebody else would have done it! While I do not actually believe that this was the case, we need an additional argument to show why bank finance was important. The Gerschenkron argument means that bank finance could do something that anonymous, organized markets could not have done. So we need to discuss what exactly the comparative advantage of bank finance is. This is the subject of the following sections.

To conclude this section – and before I turn to an explicit comparison of bank finance and market finance – I want to point to another puzzle. If we do find an important comparative advantage of bank finance over direct finance through anonymous markets, why do anonymous, organized markets seem to play such a significant role in the UK and the US? Does the comparative efficiency of bank finance and market finance vary from country to country? Or could it be the case that the efficiency of capital markets in the UK and the US serves investors who want to reshuffle their portfolios, but is of little relevance to firms that want to raise outside finance? Mayer's observations on the contribution of UK and US stock markets to industry funding suggest that the latter might indeed be the case. So do observations about the well-known underpricing phenomenon for initial public offerings, which is just as prominent in the US as it is in Germany or Switzerland (see, e.g. Ibbotson *et al.*, 1988). There is an empirical issue here that needs to be settled before we can usefully proceed with any theoretical assessment. However, it is of some interest to note that, on the question of bank finance versus market finance, Ger-schenkron's analysis implicitly parallels Mayer's more recent questioning of the role of anonymous, organized markets for the funding of industry.

3   What do intermediaries do? Risk diversification versus agency cost reduction

Before considering the advantages of intermediated finance over direct finance through anonymous, organized markets, it is useful to observe that, in principle, intermediated finance has one disadvantage: the chain of transactions between the firm and the final investor is longer, and *ceteris paribus*, an increase in the length of the chain of transactions may be taken to entail an increase in transactions costs. Any proposition that intermediated finance is more advantageous than direct finance must therefore be based on a view that the presumed gains from intermediation are more than enough to compensate for the increased transactions costs.

The literature gives two quite distinct accounts of the role of intermedi-ation. In the early analysis of Gurley and Shaw (1960), financial interme-diaries are there to transform the primary securities issued by firms into the indirect financial securities desired by final investors. Firms issue shares and bonds, final investors desire demand deposits or life insurance policies, and the missing link is provided by intermediaries that issue demand deposits or life insurance policies and that hold shares and bonds. Intermediation is seen as a kind of transportation: just as the transporter takes oranges in Spain and transforms them into oranges in Germany, so the intermediary takes bonds issued by firms and transforms them into demand deposits or savings deposits held by consumers. As mentioned in the introduction, this vision of financial intermediation as a kind of transportation activity is then analysed in a Walrasian model of 'perfect' markets, to which in principle everybody has access on an equal footing.

Why are intermediaries actually needed in the Gurley-Shaw analysis? Why don't firms issue demand deposits or life insurance policies, and why don't final investors hold shares and bonds? *Prima facie*, the answer seems to be that direct finance doesn't permit enough diversification of risks. A small industrial company that finances itself by issuing demand deposits to a thousand consumers may find that the risks of withdrawal are too large. However, the argument does not explain why IBM should not finance itself by issuing demand deposits or life insurance policies. Nor does it explain why the small industrial company should not finance itself by issuing very small demand deposits to a million consumers. Similarly, it may be true that the consumer who holds a life insurance policy issued by IBM is subject to too much firm-specific risk. But then he could diversify this risk if he held a portfolio of life insurance policies issued by a whole set of different companies.

On the side of firms as of consumers, these objections assume that assets are perfectly divisible and that transactions technologies do not involve any scale economies. At a deeper level, we may therefore say that, in the analysis of Gurley and Shaw, financial intermediation is useful because indivisibilities and non-convexities in transactions technologies restrict the amount of diversification and risk sharing that is feasible under direct finance. In the absence of indivisibilities and non-convexities in transactions technologies, a complete system of Arrow-Debreu markets would achieve an efficient risk allocation anyway (see, e.g. Malinvaud, 1972), and there would be no need for intermediation à la Gurley and Shaw. From this perspective, the function of intermediation in the framework of Gurley and Shaw may be seen as overcoming the frictions from transactions costs so as to bring the economy closer to the efficient-markets world of our theory.

Where does this view of financial intermediation leave us with respect to the Gerschenkron thesis? One empirical implication of the Gurley-Shaw analysis is that, as the economy grows and additional independent risks are added, there should be more scope for financial intermediation to exploit the additional benefits of diversification and risk sharing. From this perspective, economic development should be accompanied by a process of *financial deepening*, i.e. financial intermediation should become more important as the economy advances.

I find it hard to reconcile this proposition with Gerschenkron's interpretation of bank prominence in industry finance as a sign of economic backwardness. The problem is a theoretical one. Empirically, both the Gerschenkron and the Gurley-Shaw propositions about the role of intermediaries at different stages of development may be valid, but then they must be referring to different things, i.e. we cannot use the Gurley-Shaw analysis to account for the role of bank finance in the Gerschenkron argument.

The distinction made here is relevant for any assessment of current developments in international financial markets. The innovations that we have seen in recent years and that have generated so much excitement are perhaps an instance of the type of financial deepening that the Gurley-Shaw analysis predicts. Indeed most political evaluations of this process have – explicitly or implicitly – proceeded on the basis of the Gurley-Shaw approach. The innovations are seen as improving the overall efficiency of the markets and bringing them closer to the Arrow-Debreu ideal. However, to the extent that something else is going on in relations between industry and the financial sector, it would be desirable to take account of that as well and to consider more explicitly the effects of financial-market innovations on industry finance.

The second approach to financial intermediation that we find in the literature views intermediaries as institutions that reduce or eliminate problems of moral hazard or asymmetric information in relation between firms and financiers. Financiers typically have less information about firms than entrepreneurs or managers. Moreover, they are subject to various types of moral hazard: moral hazard concerning managerial effort, moral hazard concering the riskiness of the firms' strategies and moral hazard concerning reported return realizations *ex post*. These problems of moral hazard and asymmetric information cause difficulties for the provision of finance to industry (Jensen and Meckling, 1976). Intermediaries are taken to reduce these difficulties by engaging in monitoring and control activities.

Diamond (1984) presents an explicit example in which intermediation successfully reduces the agency costs of outside finance under moral hazard. In his analysis, the feasibility of financial intermediation rests on two key propositions:

(i)   Monitoring and control of a firm involve natural scale economies: a single intermediary can monitor and control the firm at least as effectively as ten thousand shareholders – but much more cheaply.

(ii) If the intermediary has a well-diversified portfolio of firms that he finances, then relations between himself and his own financiers – the final investors – are not much affected by moral hazard and asymmetric information because his own return is approximately riskless, so for him, fixed-interest debt finance is feasible and does not involve any moral hazard.

On the basis of these two propositions, Diamond shows that under certain circumstances incentive-efficient allocations in a system with intermediation actually dominate incentive-efficient allocations without intermediation.

Unfortunately, we know very little about the functioning of intermediation under conditions of imperfect information. Yanelle's game-theoretic analysis of Diamond's example (1989a, b) shows that at this point we do not know what system would actually implement an incentive-efficient allocation with intermediation. Both the scale economies in intermediation and the non-Walrasian character of simultaneous Bertrand competition on deposit as well as on loan markets destroy the usual presumption that competition entails efficiency. At this point, it is not clear whether these results are a pathological consequence of the extreme features of Bertrand competition or whether they point to a deeper difficulty with competition among intermediaries in a non-Walrasian setting. What is clear is that we do not have a good understanding of the strategic interaction between intermediaries under imperfect information. (This may be a problem for the theoretical purist rather than the practitioner who would not expect to observe unfettered competition in banking anyway.)

In spite of this lacuna in our understanding, it seems safe to say that the imperfect-information approach captures an important aspect of the role of intermediation for corporate finance. Diamond's notion of financial intermediation as delegated monitoring (or delegated control) does seem to be closely related to Gerschenkron's account of bank involvement in firms at the early stage of industrial development. As emphasized by Mayer, bank initiative and bank participation in entrepreneurial planning may be a way to obtain enough information and control to reduce the moral and informational hazards of finance to a tolerable level. We may therefore look at the imperfect-information approach to financial intermediation as the theoretical basis for Gerschenkron's view that banks and bank involvement with firms were needed to provide outside finance during the early stages of industrialization in Germany when capital was 'scarce and diffuse' and 'the distrust of industrial activities . . . considerable'. In Diamond's terminology, Gerschenkron's presumption must have been that the sum of the monitoring costs of the banks and direct agency costs of bank deposits was less than the agency costs of direct finance, perhaps even that the agency costs of direct finance were so high that this was never a genuine alternative at all.

The difference between the Gurley-Shaw and the Jensen-Meckling-Diamond approaches to financial intermediation is seen rather clearly if we consider the recent trend towards a securitization of loans. From the perspective of the Gurley-Shaw approach, securitization is an instance of financial deepening allowing improved risk sharing: the risks associated with a given loan do not remain with the initial bank, but are divided up and shared among many security holders. From the perspective of the Jensen-Meckling-Diamond approach, the question would be how securitization affects incentives: if the initial bank expects to resell the debt securities to other institutions, how careful will it be in its initial assessment of creditworthiness? Also, how will securitization affect the security holders' willingness to take action when difficulties arise? From this perspective, some of the enthusiasm for securitization should perhaps be tempered by a rather more careful consideration of liabilities and incentives under the different regimes.

4   Financial intermediation as delegated monitoring

I now consider the imperfect-information approach to financial intermediation in more detail. What do intermediaries actually do to reduce information and incentive problems? Why are there scale economies in these activities? How does intermediation affect the firms' investment behaviour?

The literature contains two distinct answers to these questions. According to Diamond (1984, 1989), financial intermediaries reduce information and incentive problems by *monitoring* the firms that they finance. According to Mayer (1988), financial intermediation provides a mechanism of *commitment to a long-term relationship*. I shall consider both approaches in turn.

'Monitoring' ought to be understood in a broad sense as any form of collecting information about a firm, its investment prospects and its behaviour. The information that is collected is useful because it serves to sort out 'bad' projects and/or to punish 'bad' behaviour. The literature contains the following examples:

> Monitoring of the firm's return realizations makes it possible to conclude contracts in which the financiers' claims depend on the firm's returns (Diamond, 1984; Gale and Hellwig, 1985).
> Monitoring of the firm's characteristics, i.e. a creditworthiness test, makes it possible to avoid bad loans (Broecker, 1990).
> Monitoring of the firm's behaviour during the loan application stage makes it possible to avoid loans to firms following too risky an investment strategy (Diamond, 1989).

In all these examples, the role of monitoring is straightforward. The main distinction is between monitoring that takes place before a contract is agreed to and monitoring in the execution of a contract. The former serves to reduce the proportion of bad loans, the latter serves to improve performance under the given contract.

Monitoring that takes place before a contract is written may give rise to some interesting problem of competition on the market for contracts. If the different intermediaries can observe the outcomes of the other intermediaries' monitoring activities, there may be a *free-rider problem* in that each intermediary may want to rely on the other intermediaries' monitoring without doing any monitoring of its own. Alternatively, if the different intermediaries cannot observe the outcomes of the other intermediaries' monitoring activities, there may be a *winner's curse problem* in that each intermediary must fear that his clients were just the ones that his competitors rejected as bad credit risks. Broecker (1990) shows that the winner's curse problem causes difficulties for competition among monitoring banks, suggesting that perhaps there might been an element of natural monopoly in such a market. These difficulties are not present when monitoring only takes place *after* a contract has been concluded.

In work currently in progress at the University of Basel, von Thadden (1990) studies an example of monitoring within a contractual relation that is particularly interesting because it substantiates Mayer's (1988) suggestion that financial intermediation may lengthen the investment horizon of firms. He considers a model with two investment periods. There are two types of firms, 'good' and 'bad'. Firms can choose between two investment strategies, short-term and long-term. Both strategies require identical amounts of funds in both investment periods. However, the long-term strategy has a relatively low expected payoff in the first investment period and a relatively high expected payoff in the second investment period. Model parameters are specified in such a way that 'bad' firms should not receive funds in either period. However, *ex ante* there is no way for financiers to distinguish 'bad' firms and 'good' firms. After the first investment period, a partial distinction may be possible because there are two sources of information: costless observation of first-period returns and costly monitoring. In the absence of monitoring, banks interpret low first-period return realizations as an indication of poor quality and discontinue financing. Anticipation of such behaviour induces firms to opt for the short-term investment strategy even though the long-term strategy may eventually be more profitable.[3]

In contrast, monitoring may provide the financier with an additional source of information about firm quality, so he can provide the 'good' firm with some assurance that the second period will be funded even if first-period returns are unfavourable. The 'good' firm is thus induced to pay less attention to the problem of second-period finance and more attention to the overall profitability of the two investment strategies. If indeed the overall profitability of the long-term strategy is higher, then monitoring may have a positive return because the prospect of monitoring and of a better decision on second-period finance induces firms to choose the better investment strategy in the first period.

The preceding considerations explain the gains from monitoring as well as the link between monitoring and the investment horizon in von Thadden's model. They do not yet explain the link between monitoring and financial intermediation. Nor do they take account of the costs of monitoring and intermediation. On these points, von Thadden simply follows Diamond (1984), namely he assumes:

> Monitoring involves scale economies, i.e. it is more efficient to have just one financier monitor the firm than many.
>
> In the absence of intermediation, no one financier has enough funds

to finance a single firm, i.e. intermediation is required to exploit the scale economies in monitoring.

The gains from monitoring exceed the – technically given – costs.

The agency costs of finance for an intermediary can be arbitrarily small, say because the intermediary finances many firms and – through the law of large numbers – has an approximately riskless return from these firms which makes fixed-interest debt finance feasible.

With these assumptions, *any* model of monitoring can be turned into a model of financial intermediation as delegated monitoring, at least if one neglects Yanelle's observation that the relative efficiency of intermediation under the given incentive and information constraints may not be sufficient to ensure the emergence of intermediation in an equilibrium of a given game-theoretic model of competitive financial markets. By this procedure, the analysis of financial intermediation is very much simplified because attention is almost exclusively focussed on the monitoring role of financial intermediation. (Note that Diamond, 1989, doesn't even address the refinancing of the intermediaries any more.)

However, there is a certain danger in relying too mechanically on Diamond's procedure for turning models of monitoring into models of financial intermediation as delegated monitoring. By neglecting the refinancing side of intermediation, we may be losing sight of some important phenomena. In a model like von Thadden's for instance, one might use refinancing considerations to explain not only why some banking systems do contribute to long-term investment, but also why others do not. Clearly, the use of monitoring to provide assurance of long-term funding presumes that the financier himself has some assurance that when the time comes he will have the funds available. In this context, it is of interest to note that Germany private banks in the late nineteenth century apparently could be more assured than their English counterparts that short-term liquidity would not be a problem. According to Tilly (1986, 1989), they enjoyed two advantages:

> They served a carefully selected group of clients whose payment needs they closely monitored so that they became rather predictable. They could rely on the discount facility of the Reichsbank to provide for their short-term liquidity needs (albeit at a price). In this respect, the Reichsbank had much more flexibility than the Bank of England, which was tightly constrained under the Bank Charter Act of 1844.

Tilly suggests that these institutional differences were actually responsible for the difference in the commitment horizons of banks in the two countries.

In the same context, one must question the relevance of Diamond's (1984) notion that intermediaries can finance themselves with hardly any agency costs because diversification makes their own portfolios almost riskless.[4] The portfolios held by German banks in the late nineteenth century seem to have been quite risky. According to Tilly (1986), these banks used their information advantages and their freedom from liquidity worries to engage in investment strategies that involved high risks as well as high returns. Indeed quite a few of the banks went under, so the risks did affect the banks' depositors as well. Given this observation, the analysis of banking and financial intermediation must go beyond Diamond and study again the relation between banks and their depositors under conditions that involve a non-negligible probability of bank failure.

Another possible objection to the notion of financial intermediation as delegated monitoring is rather less well founded. Upon reading Gerschenkron's or Mayer's accounts of the involvement of German and Japanese banks in company planning and decision-making, one may feel that these activities reflect more than just 'monitoring'. The word 'monitoring' seems ill-suited for describing the banks' influence on firm behaviour. Thus, when Gerschenkron emphasizes the role played by banks in the cartelization of German industry in the late nineteenth century, one doesn't exactly think of this activity as 'monitoring'.

However, we should not be deceived by the rhetoric of the word 'monitoring'. The real question is how 'monitoring' fits into the overall relationship between the intermediary and the firm. 'Monitoring' as a form of collecting information about the firm is useful only because the information that is collected has consequences for behaviour and resource allocation within the relationship. The notion of financial intermediation as delegated monitoring must encompass such uses of information as well as the act of collecting the information.

At this point, it is useful to recall that many incentive problems are due to information problems. Certain aspects of relevant behaviour are not commonly observable, hence they cannot effectively be made the subject of a binding agreement, but have to be influenced directly, through appropriate incentives. If all relevant aspects of behaviour could be commonly observed, or inferred from other variables that are commonly observed, then moral hazard would not be much of a problem. In this case, contractual agreements about behaviour – effort choices, risk choices, etc. – could be enforced because contract violations would be detected and could be punished.

Thus from the perspective of incentive theory, 'monitoring' is not so much a sorting device as an instrument for improving performance under an incentive contract. Perfect monitoring of all relevant behaviour will eliminate the moral-hazard problems altogether and permit the attainment of a first-best solution. Imperfect monitoring, e.g. monitoring that is subject to error, will not eliminate the moral-hazard problems, but at least it will reduce them. From the theory of optimal incentive contracts, we know that even noisy monitoring will improve performance under an optimal incentive contract (see, e.g. Grossman and Hart, 1983). Upon combining this result with the procedure of Diamond that was outlined above we obtain a new version of financial intermediation as delegated monitoring, one that emphasizes the incentive effects rather than the sorting effects of monitoring.

Monitoring as an element in an incentive-contract relation is not all that far from the accounts of Gerschenkron and Mayer. Consider Gerschenkron's observation that banks played a key role in the cartelization of German industry. Any cartel is subject to the moral-hazard problem that the individual firm has an incentive to undercut and to serve more than its allotted share of the market. Banks that are involved with several firms in the same industry have an incentive to restrain such behaviour in order to increase the aggregate gross return they can earn from the industry. Along the lines suggested above, monitoring of individual firms by banks may then be a device to reduce or even eliminate the moral-hazard problems that otherwise prevent cartelization.[5]

Indeed, on the basis of the arguments of Yanelle (1989b), one might argue that in the absence of any countervailing effects such an involvement of banks in industry cartelization is to be expected. As cartelization increases the gross returns flowing from industry to its financiers, it will also improve the position of the enforcing banks in the competition for funds. In the absence of countervailing effects, the process of competition for funds should thus give rise to a banking industry which is concentrated or coordinated enough to impose cartel behaviour on its industrial clients, using the returns to attract deposits.[6]

One aspect of the historical accounts is missing from the monitoring models, but should be easy to accommodate. Whereas the monitoring models stress the banks' collection of information *about* firms, historically, the provision of information and advice *to* firms has also been an important part of the bank-firm relationship. Today this aspect may be even more important: if Deutsche Bank is involved with the acquisition program of Daimler-Benz, the relationship probably has more to do with Daimler-Benz's demand for information about other firms and industries than with the moral hazard problems in the relation between Daimler-Benz and its financiers. However, there should be an interdependence between the provision of information to firms and the collection of information about firms that is stressed in the monitoring models. One activity supports the other, so there should be economies of scope. More generally, the intermediary that is involved with many industries at once will enjoy economies of scope in the provision of information to its clients. The question then is how the interdependence between information provision to firms and information collection about firms affects the functioning of financial intermediation as delegated monitoring.

5   Financial intermediation as a mechanism of commitment

I now consider the notion that financial intermediation may provide a *mechanism of commitment* in a long-term relationship. So far, I have implicitly assumed that entrepreneurs and financiers can enter into binding contracts that specify all future actions and outcomes subject only to the incentive-compatibility constraints that are imposed by the information structure. If such complete contracts can be written and enforced, then commitment is not a problem.

For several reasons though, the assumption of complete and binding contracts is problematic.

> It may be too difficult to write a complete contract that specifies actions and outcomes for all periods and all relevant contingencies. Many aspects of the relationship may therefore be left implicit – and hence unenforceable in the courts (Grossman and Hart, 1986).
> Even where contracts do contain explicit provisions, the courts may be unable or unwilling to enforce them. They may lack the information required for enforcement, or they may find that contractual provisions conflict with legal rules that take precedence, e.g. anti-usury laws.
> An *ex ante* (second-best) efficient contract may prescribe *ex post* inefficient outcomes for certain contingencies, so *ex post* all parties to the contract may find it preferable to rescind the initial provision and replace the inefficient contract outcome by another outcome that is efficient. Thus an incentive contract with monitoring that requires punishment of 'bad' behaviour will not be 'renegotiation-proof' if the punishment imposes costs on the financier who carries it out as well as on the entrepreneur who suffers it (Bolton, 1990; Gale and Hellwig, 1989).

The relevance of these considerations can be gathered from Mayer's (1988) example of the firm in financial distress that needs a fresh infusion of funds. As in other cases where outside finance is needed, the funds may be available if the financiers can expect to receive a fair portion of the returns whereas they may not be available if the financiers expect to receive only a small portion of the returns. However, the returns to a successful rescue operation – like the returns to a successful new venture – accrue not just during the next few periods but during the entire subsequent life of the enterprise. The question then is to what extent the firm can commit itself to making the financier share in the later returns as well as the earlier returns to the rescue operation.

If the firm and its financiers can write a complete, binding long-term contract, there should be no problem. However, such a contract may not be feasible, say because it is too difficult to specifiy and enforce provisions that concern the sharing of returns that accrue five years hence with today's financiers. If indeed commitment through long-term contracting is infeasible, then, according to Mayer (1988), financial intermediation with a close relationship between the bank and the firm may provide an alternative mechanism of commitment.

Specifically, Mayer suggests that Japanese banks are more willing to engage in corporate rescues than financiers elsewhere because the bank-firm relation in Japan involves a mutual long-term commitment. Some rather striking quantitative evidence on this point is provided by Hoshi *et al.* (1989c). For a sample of Japanese firms, they find that the cost of financial distress is significantly less for firms that have close relations to a 'main bank' than for firms that do not. Specifically, firms that have close banking ties 'appear to invest more and perform better' than firms that do not have such ties.

From a theoretical point of view, the question is why intermediation can serve as a mechanism of commitment. What are the forces at work? In what sense does Mayer's idea carry us beyond the notion of financial intermediation as delegated monitoring?

A preliminary answer to these questions is given by Fischer (1990). Following Mayer, Fischer observes that the main threat to a long-term commitment is due to competition from other financiers at an interim period when it is already clear that the rescue operation (the new venture) was successful, but the returns have not yet been fully reaped. Even if at this interim stage the firm stays with the previous financier, such competition may force the previous financier to improve his terms to a point where he just covers the opportunity cost of additional funds, but no longer receives a compensation for the risks that he took initially and that happened to have come out well. The question is why a 'main bank' relation of the Japanese type should restrain this interim competition.

To answer this question, Fischer considers a model with two types of firms ('good' and 'bad') in two periods. Each firm has one project per period. Financiers that finance a firm in the first period subsequently have better information about the firm's type. This information advantage mitigates the competition from outside financiers in the second period. The outcome of competition among financiers in the second period depends on the distribution of information about the firm's type:

> If no financier has superior information, (Bertrand) competition among the financiers drives their expected profits from the second projects to zero, i.e. all surplus from that project stays with the firm. If exactly one financier has superior information about the firm's type, this financier retains the contract for the second project; indeed he is able to approrpriate some of the surplus on that project beause – as in Broecker's (1990) analysis of competition with prior monitoring – the other financiers are afraid of a 'winner's curse' and bid less aggressively than they would under homogeneous information.
> If two or more firms have superior information about the firm's type, competition among them drives their expected profits from the second project to zero; as in the first case, all surplus from the second project stays with the firm.

Ex ante, before the first project is undertaken, neither the firm nor the potential financiers know the firm's type. From the financiers' perspective, the loss they make on the 'bad' type has to be compensated by the gain they make on the 'good' type. Such compensation may require them to appropriate some of the returns on the 'good' type's second project as well as the return on his first project. If this is the case, one should expect to see a pattern of finance whereby the first project is financed by exactly *one* financier who thereby gains an information advantage, so subsequently he can appropriate additional returns in spite of the potential competition from outside financiers.

Thus for certain parameter constellations, the equilibria of Fischer's model exhibit some of the key features of the 'main bank' relation in Mayer's account:

> In equilibrium, the firm has exactly one financier.
> As the relation between the firm and the financier develops, the financier obtains an information advantage over outside financiers.
> The one financier's information advantage commits the firm to the relation by reducing the strength of competition from outside financiers.
> The commitment of the firm to the financier supports the financier's initial willingness to supply funds to the firm, support a rescue operation or provide startup capital.

Fischer does not actually analyse intermediation. He merely shows that, if financiers have sufficient funds, then exclusive financing by one financier may emerge in an equilibrium because exclusivity serves as a commitment device. However, his model of exclusivity and commitment can be turned into a model of intermediation by the same procedure that was used to turn models of monitoring into models of intermediation. Namely, if there are many small investors, the gains from exclusivity in the financing of a firm cannot be reaped unless there is an intermediary that collects funds and then acts as the unique financier of the firm. As for the monitoring models, the question is simply whether the gains from exclusivity exceed the costs of intermediation.

There are thus similarities as well as differences between the notion of financial intermediation as a commitment device and the notion of financial intermediation as delegated monitoring. Both approaches find that exclusive financing of the firm by one financier is advantageous; yet, if outside capital is diffuse, exclusive financing is only possible through intermediation. However, the two approaches differ in the reasons they give for the advantages of exclusivity. In the monitoring models, exclusivity is a way of exploiting technical scale economies: monitoring by two financiers is more expensive, but no more effective than monitoring by one financier. In Fischer's commitment model, exclusivity is a way of reducing possible conflicts between financiers: at the interim stage, competition between financiers would destroy the 'good' firm's commitment to turn over second-period excess returns in order to pay for the initial finance.

The problem of possible conflict between financiers is an important one that shapes financial relations quite extensively. The problem is particularly relevant just before and in bankruptcy when financiers are most concerned about their shares in the remaining assets of the firm. The creditor who fears an impending bankruptcy will try to withdraw his loan at face value before bankruptcy is declared. At the very least he will try to have some assets singled out as collateral for his loan. Either measure is likely to deepen the firm's difficulties, to precipitate the event of bankruptcy, and to make a reorganization and continuation of the firm more difficult. There is thus a presumption that distributional conflicts between financiers are an important factor in premature liquidations of firms that might more profitably be reorganized.[7] Such inefficiencies too should be avoided if the firm's financing was altogether in the hands of one financier.

At this point, we encounter a rather serious difficulty, which actually concerns both the Diamond and the Mayer-Fischer approaches to financial intermediation. According to both approaches, any one firm should receive financing from just one financier. How then do we explain the observation that firms typically have more than one source of outside finance?

A superficial answer to this question might point to the assumption of risk-neutrality on all sides that is common to all models. Once firms reach a certain size, presumably risk-averse intermediaries have a diversification incentive to share the risks of the firms they finance. While this point is undoubtedly important, it does not entirely answer the question.

In particular, it does not explain why even small debtors have both bank loans and various forms of trade credit. This is the more remarkable since trade creditors do not usually have a comparative advantage in assessing creditworthiness and moreover, in the event of bankruptcy, the rivalry between trade creditors and banks seems to be particularly costly. For the case of secured loans of different types, Weskamp (1989) suggests that having different creditors with different collaterals may be advantageous because the different creditors have different comparative advantages in disposing of assets in the event of bankruptcy. However, even this analysis leaves unexplained the rather substantial amounts of unsecured forms of credit provided by sometimes very heterogeneous sets of trade partners. In other words, if we accept some version of financial intermediation as delegated monitoring or financial intermediation as a commitment device, why do we observe so much additional finance that does not avail itself of the benefits of intermediation?

From a theoretical perspective, it seems that we need a more systematic account of the relation between exclusivity and commitment. The discussion so far has only considered the problem of committing the firm to a long-term relation with its financier(s). We also have to consider the reverse problem of committing the financier(s) to the terms of a long-term agreement with the firm. With respect to this reverse commitment problem, *exclusivity may actually be disadvantageous.*

I give two examples to illustrate the point. First consider the problem of commitment to an *ex ante* efficient contract that prescribes *ex post* inefficient outcomes for certain contingencies. For example, such a contract might prescribe bankruptcy and inefficient liquidation after certain outcomes in order to provide incentives for the firm's management to choose strategies under which these outcomes are unlikely. If there is just one financier, this contract is not renegotiation-proof because, once the given contingencies arise, both parties have an incentive to rescind the initial contract and to carry the firm on. In contrast, a renegotiation is not so easy when there are many financiers. In this case, the distributional conflict between financiers may preclude the attainment of an *ex post* efficient outcome (continuation of the firm) and thereby enhance the credibility of the *ex ante* efficient threat of *ex post* inefficient liquidation in some contingencies. From an *ex ante* point of view, the very inefficiencies that arise from conflicts between financiers may actually be desirable because they weaken renegotiation-proofness constraints and strengthen the financiers' commitment to the initial contract.

Empirically, the argument is illustrated by the contrast between the international debt crises of the 1930s and the 1980s. In the 1930s, most country debts took the form of widely held, publicly traded bonds. When the debtors got into difficulties, renegotiations with the multitudes of creditors were all but impossible, so the bonds just went into default. In contrast, in the 1980s, most country debts took the form of loans from a few hundred banks. Coordination of the creditors and the renegotiations of the debtors with the consortium of creditors were feasible, so the loans did not officially go into default, but were merely rescheduled. From an *ex post* point of view, such rescheduling may be desirable, but from an *ex ante* point of view the prospect of being able to avoid default through rescheduling may have rather adverse incentive effects (Hellwig, 1977).

A second example concerns directly the Mayer-Fischer notion that exclusivity reduces the strenth of interim competition from other financiers and serves to commit the firm to its 'main bank' that has put up the initial finance. Ordinarily we think of competition as a mechanism of protection, so any weakening of competition from outside financiers should expose the firm to the possibility of an abuse of power by the 'main bank'. In the absence of effective competition from other financiers, why shouldn't the 'main bank' raise the interest it demands, say because of 'unforeseen' refinancing difficulties?

To see the impact of these considerations, go back to von Thadden's analysis of intermediation, monitoring and long-term investment. In von Thadden's model, the 'good' firm is willing to choose the long-term project because it has some assurance that interim finance will be available if monitoring enables the financier to distinguish it from a 'bad' firm. Suppose now that the financier's commitment to provide interim finance is not legally binding, say because the courts cannot verify the outcome of his monitoring. In this case, he can threaten to withhold the required interim finance unless his share of the overall returns is increased. In the absence of competition from other financiers, this threat will be effective, and the entrepreneur will have to give in. If he foresees this at the time when he chooses his investment horizon, he may prefer to choose a sequence of short-term projects after all, where he is less exposed to such abuse of power by the financier.[8]

In contrast, if several financiers are involved – and if all of them have the information provided by monitoring – then competition among these financiers will protect the entrepreneur. Anticipating this, he will choose the long-term project after all. Here it is the *lack of exclusivity* that servies to commit the financiers to the initial contract.[9]

More generally, there seems to be a certain tension between the problem of committing the firm in a long-term relation with its financiers and the problem of committing the financiers in a long-term relation with the firm. Exclusivity as a mechanism that reduces the one problem may at the same time exacerbate the other problem. At this point, we are simply in need of a more systematic study of the functioning of different commitment mechanisms, the tradeoffs between different types of commitment and the relation of these mechanisms to financial intermediation.

6   Inside finance and the emancipation of firms

To conclude this discussion, I return to the issue that separates Gerschenkron and Mayer. To what extent should a system of corporate finance based on intermediation through a 'main bank' be regarded as internally stable? Mayer (1988) seems to believe that the superior performance of such a system is a guarantee of its persistence over time. In contrast, Gerschenkron (1962) regards it as being transitory with firms depending on outside finance through banks *only* until they have enough inside finance available.

Gerschenkron's position is based on the assessment that, around the turn of the century, German industrial companies became rather less dependent on their banks than they had been during the startup phase. This assessment seems to be shared by historians (e.g. Feldenkirchen, 1979; Pohl, 1983) as well as contemporaries (Jeidels, 1905; Riesser, 1910). This development seems to have been due to two factors:

> Firms in certain industries, e.g. chemical companies, were increasingly able to finance themselves by retentions.
>
> As firms grew, banks were rather less able to bear the risk exposure associated with exclusive financing, so exclusive financing of firms by single banks was replaced by consortial financing.

The little evidence that we have suggests that these accounts of Germany at the turn of the century are still relevant today. Thus, Fischer's (1990) study of financial relations between banks and firms in Germany reaches the following conclusions:

> For all but the smallest companies, exclusive financing by a single bank is the exception rather than the rule.
>
> There is no evidence that banks have information advantages that enable them to avoid bankruptcy risks.
>
> There is no evidence that the 'main bank' relation makes for a greater willingess to aid the firm in financial distress.

According to Fischer, the market for loans to firms in Germany displays a competitiveness that belies the predictions of exclusivity given by Mayer or by his own theoretical analysis. This competitiveness is due to the following factors:

> The larger, publicly traded companies can avail themselves of organized markets for their securities.
>
> The medium-size, non-traded companies have a conscious policy of maintaining relations with a handful of competing banks.
>
> All companies have a conscious policy of making sure that reliance on outside finance does not endanger their independence.

Similar patterns can also be observed in other countries. Thus Hoshi *et al.* (1989a, b) report that in Japan, too, the larger, more profitable companies avail themselves of the newly developing organized markets to become more independent of their banks. Preliminary findings for medium-size, non-traded Swiss companies also confirm the importance of bank competition and of inside finance.

Altogether the empirical evidence suggests that the 'main bank' relationship as discussed by Jeidels (1905), Mayer (1988) and Fischer (1990) is somewhat less stable than one might have expected. There is a certain tendency for firms to emancipate themselves from such a relationship, using markets, competition among banks and, above all, reliance on inside rather than outside finance.

How are we to assess these tendencies? The emancipation of firms from close banking relationship is certainly not costless. Recall the observation of Hoshi *et al.* (1989c) that the costs of financial distress in Japan are significantly larger for firms without close banking relations than for firms with close banking relations. For firms that are not in financial distress, Hoshi *et al.* (1989a, b) report a similar observation: hence the emancipation from a 'main bank' relation goes together with a significant increase in the sensitivity of current investment to fluctuations in current earnings and liquidity. Bank loans are less used and/or less available to smooth over fluctuations in earnings.

To be sure, such increased sensitivity of investment to earnings and liquidity is to be expected when firms rely increasingly on inside finance. The problem is that investment opportunities are typically less than perfectly correlated with current earnings, so too close a relation between earnings and investment is bound to entail inefficiencies in the allocation of funds for investment. The question is whether these costs of firm emancipation can be taken to be balanced – or more than balanced – by benefits accruing elsewhere.

The basic question is really what are the mechanisms underlying the firms' reliance on inside finance and their desire to be independent from outside financiers. Given that practically *all* financial systems that we know involve a substantial reliance on inside finance (Mayer, 1988), it is remarkable how little we know about the factors behind the use of inside finance and what are its implications for the functioning of the financial system.

From the perspective of Jensen and Meckling (1976), one might argue that inside finance has priority because the agency costs of inside finance are lower than the agency costs of outside bank or market finance. This is also the explanation given by Myers and Majluf (1984) in the context of a model with asymmetric information and signalling. Inside finance is taken to have no agency costs because it represents the use of funds available to the firm on account of the firm itself. Outside finance does have agency costs (signalling costs, monitoring costs, simple inefficiencies) because information asymmetries and externalities preclude the attainment of a first-best allocation in the arrangement between the firm and its outside financiers.

From this perspective, the Hoshi *et al.* observation of investment sensitivity to current earnings should be seen as evidence for the agency costs of *outside* finance: investment projects that are expected to be profitable under internal finance are deemed to be unprofitable under outside finance when the agency costs of outside finance are added to the mere opportunity costs of funds. The inefficiency in the allocation of funds across firms that results when investment opportunities are less than perfectly correlated with earnings is nothing but an element in the overall agency cost of outside finance.

In passing, I note that Diamond (1989) gives a very similar explanation for the substitution of bank finance by market finance in the top segment of the very large and profitable companies. In his analysis, the agency costs of direct finance for such companies are low because their track records provide the market with enough information about them. Presumably one could also argue that at least some of these companies are so large and so well diversified in themselves that their debts may be considered riskless and hence free of agency costs.

The common theme of these analyses is that observed financing patterns represent efficient (second-best) solutions to given information and incentive problems. Shifts in financing patterns reflect changes in the data of the problems, e.g. reliance on outside finance decreases as more agency-cost-free inside finance is available; reliance on market finance increases as the agency cost of market finance goes down.

I am not convinced that this is the entire story. The interpretation of financing patterns as efficient solutions to given information and incentive problems is based on the presumption that the financing decision itself is not subject to such problems. Thus Jensen and Meckling (1976) consider the situation of a risk-neutral owner/manager who has not yet obtained any outside finance. For such an owner/manager, inside finance involves no agency costs because both the costs and the benefits of his choices under inside finance concern only himself, i.e. no externalities are involved.

In contrast, when there are already some outside claims to the firm, the financing decision itself may affect the interests of the outside claimants, so a new agency problem arises. In particular, when there are outside shareholders, the costs and benefits of inside finance concern these outside shareholders as well as the firm's management. To the extent that management has discretion over the financing decision, the following problems can be expected to arise:

> To the extent that management underestimates the portion of the costs of inside finance that falls on shareholders, there may be a bias towards excessive retentions (Jensen, 1986).
>
> To the extent that projects provide non-pecuniary private returns to management as well as financial returns, there may be a bias towards projects where these private returns are particularly high. Thus, management may prefer to hold 'reserves' in the form of real estate rather than financial securities because the discretion it has on the valuation of real estate and the realization of book profits provides a way to conceal fluctuations in operating earnings and thereby to reduce management's accountability to the firm's outside financiers. One typically observes that bankruptcies are declared late because, for a substantial period prior to bankruptcy, management was able to use reserves in order to conceal the substantial difficulties that the firm encountered.

Similar considerations apply to the emancipation of a firm from a 'main bank' – be it through market finance, bank competition or simply reliance on inside finance. From the perspective of Jensen and Meckling (1976), this is a response to the agency costs of 'main bank' finance, e.g. the prospect of a squeeze where the 'main bank' might use the threat of cutting off interim financing to appropriate a larger portion of the firm's returns. From the perspective of Mayer (1988), the firm's desire for independence may simply be a breach of the implicit prior contract whereby the bank provided startup or rescue finance in return for a substantial share of the firm's subsequent profits.

Here again, we encounter the need for a more systematic analysis of the relation between financing patterns and commitment mechanisms. As yet we are only beginning to understand the dynamic interactions between firms and their financiers. A more systematic analysis is likely to provide us with a rather more differentiated assessment of the role of inside finance and the tendency towards firm emancipation from close banking relationships.

NOTES

I thank Franklin Allen, Margaret Bray, Colin Mayer, Luigi Spaventa, Ernst-Ludwig von Thadden, Marie-Odile Yanelle and the IMI-CEPR Conference participants for very helpful comments. Research support from the Swiss National Science Foundation is gratefully acknowledged.
1 For a concise formulation of the problem, see Landes (1969, pp. 348ff). An up-to-date account of the debate on the role of German banks is given by Wellhöner (1989, chapter 5).
2 To be sure, Gerschenkron acknowledges the possibility of 'forced saving by the money-creating activities of banks'. However, he treats this possibility as secondary relative to the 'collection and distribution of *available* funds' (my emphasis). In contrast, when he discusses the role of the state in Russian industrialization, he emphasizes scarcity of capital at the aggregate level and the use of 'the compulsory machinery of the government . . . in directing incomes from consumption to investment'.
3 The firm's problem here is akin to that of a beginning assistant professor who has to anticipate whether his tenure committee will take a lack of output after five years as an indication of unproductiveness or an indication of productiveness in a very long-term research strategy.
4 Strictly speaking, Diamond only requires that unobservable, presumably project-specific risks be diversified away. Commonly observable, in particular market-wide risks would be unproblematic. However, it is not clear that the risk-bearing discussed by Tilly falls altogether under this category.
5 Monitoring and prevention of too competitive behaviour actually was the main purpose of the Austrian Kontrollbank at the turn of the century. I am grateful to Erisch Streissler for this information.
6 The cartelization example should make clear that the analysis presented here is entirely positive. No welfare or policy analysis of bank finance and bank relations with industry is intended. Any such normative analysis would have to distinguish rather carefully between the different types of gains that entrepreneurs and their financiers can derive from delegated monitoring.
7 A remarkably clear discussion of these issues is given by Weskamp (1989). Writing from the perspective of the Coase theorem, she tried to identify information asymmetries and bargaining costs that actually prevent efficient reorganizations when there are distributional conflicts.
8 A related problem of underinvestment due to a distributonally motivated threat of premature liquidation by the financier is discussed by Hart and Moore (1989).
9 Mayer (1988) mentions the problem of committing the financier to the provision of interim finance for a long-term project. However, he does not see that the exclusivity of the 'main bank' relation, which commits the entrepreneur to the financier, has precisely the opposite effect for the reverse commitment problem.

REFERENCES

Bolton, P. (1990) 'Renegotiation and the Dynamics of Contract Design', *European Economic Review* **34**, 303–10.

Brainard, W. and J. Tobin (1961) 'Financial Intermediaries and the Effectiveness of Monetary controls', in D. Hester and J. Tobin (eds.), *Financial Markets and Economic Activity*, Cowles Foundation Monograph 21, New Haven: Yale University Press.

Broecker, T. (1990) 'Credit-Worthiness Tests and Interbank Competition', *Econometrica* **58**, 429–52.

Diamond, D. (1984) 'Financial Intermediation and Delegated Monitoring', *Review of Economic Studies* **51**, 393–414.

(1989) 'Monitoring and Reputation: The Choice Between Bank Loans and Directly Placed Debt', University of Chicago, Graduate School of Business.

Feldenkirchen, W. (1979) 'Banken und Stahlindustrie im Ruhrgebiet – Zur Entwicklung ihrer Beziehungen 1873–1914', *Bankhistorisches Archiv* **5**, 26–52.

Fischer, K. (1990) 'Hausbankbeziehungen als Instrument der Bindung zwischen Banken und Unternehmen: Eine theoretische und empirische Analyse', Doctoral Dissertation, University of Bonn.

Gale, D. and M. Hellwig (1985) 'Incentive-Compatible Debt Contracts: The One-Period Problem', *Review of Economic Studies* **52**, 647–63.

(1989) 'Repudiation and Renegotiation: The Case of Sovereign Debt', *International Economic Review* **30**, 3–31.

Gerschenkron, A. (1962) *Economic Backwardness in Historical Perspective*, Cambridge, MA.: Harvard University Press.

Grossman, S. and O. Hart (1983) 'An Analysis of the Principal-Agent Problem', *Econometrica* **51**, 7–45.

(1986) 'The Costs and Benefits of Ownership: A Theory of Vertical and Lateral Integration', *Journal of Political Economy* **94**, 691–719.

Gurley, J. and E. Shaw (196) *Money in a Theory of Finance*, Washington: Brookings.

Hart, O. and J. Moore (1989) 'Default and Renegotiation, A Dynamic Model of Debt', Massachusetts Institute of Technology.

Hellwig, M. (1977) 'A Model of Borrowing and Lending with Bankruptcy', *Econometrica* **45**, 1879–906.

Hoshi, T., A. Kashyap and D. Scharfstein (1989a) 'Corporate Structure, Liquidity, and Investment: Evidence from Japanese Industrial Groups', Massachusetts Institute of Technology; forthcoming, *Quarterly Journal of Economics*.

(1989b) 'Bank Monitoring and Investment: Evidence from the Changing Structure of Japanese Corporate Banking Relationship', Working Paper No. 3079, National Bureau of Economic Research.

(1989c) 'The Role of Banks in Reducing the Costs of Financial Distress in Japan', Massachusetts Institute of Technology.

Ibbotson, R., J. Sindelar and J. Ritter (1988) 'Initial Public Offerings', *Journal of Applied Corporate Finance* **1**, 37–45.

Jeidels, O. (1905) *Das Verhältnis der Deutschen Grossbanken zur Industrie*, Leipzig.

Jensen, M. (1986) 'Agency Costs of Free Cash Flow, Corporate Finance and Takeovers', *American Economic Review, Papers and Proceedings* **76**, 323–9.

Jensen, M.C. and W.H. Meckling (1976) 'Theory of the Firm: Managerial Behavior, Agency Costs and Ownership Structure', *Journal of Financial Economics* **3**, 305–60.

Landes, D.S. (1969) *The Unbound Prometheus*, Cambridge University Press.

Malinvaud, E. (1972) 'The Allocation of Individual Risks in Large Markets', *Journal of Economic Theory* **4**, 312–28.

Mayer, C. (1988) 'New Issues in Corporate Finance', *European Economic Review* **32**, 1167–88.

Myers, S. and N. Majluf (1984) 'Corporate Financing and Investment Decisions When Firms Have Information that Investors Do Not Have', *Journal of Financial Economics* **13**, 187–221.

Neuburger, H. and H. Stokes (1974) 'German Banks and German Growth 1883–1913: An Empirical View', *Journal of Economic History* **34**, 710–31.

Pohl, H. (1983) 'Formen und Phasen der Industriefinanzierung bis zum 2. Weltkrieg', *Bankhistorisches Archiv* **9**, 13–33.

Riesser, J. (1910) *Die Deutschen Grossbanken und ihre Konzentration im Zusammenhang mit der Entwicklung der Gesamtwirtschaft in Deutschland*, Jena.

Tilly, R. (1966) *Financial Institutions and Industrialization in the Rhineland 1815–1870*, Madison: University of Wisconsin Press.

(1986) 'German Banking 1850–1914: Development Assistance to the Strong', *Journal of European Economic History* **15**, 113–52.

(1989) 'Banking Institutions in Historical and Comparative Perspective – Germany, Great Britain and the United States in the 19th and 20th Century', *Journal of Institutional and Theoretical Economics (Zeitschrift für die Gesamte Staatswissenschaft)* **145**, 189–209.

Tilly, R. and R. Fremdling (1976) 'German Banks, German Growth and Econometric History', *Journal of Economic History* **36**, 416–27.

Tobin, J. (1969) 'A General Equilibrium Approach to Monetary Theory', *Journal of Money, Credit, and Banking* **1**, 15–29.

von Thadden, E.L. (1990) 'Bank Finance and Long-Term Investment', University of Basel.

Wellhöner, V. (1989) *Grossbanken und Grossindustrie im Kaiserreich*, Göttingen: Vandenhoeck-Ruprecht.

Weskamp, A. (1989) 'Die Auswirkungen der Sicherungsrechte auf die effiziente Ausgestaltung von Kreditbeziehungen', Doctoral Dissertation, University of Bonn.

Yanelle, M.O. (1989a) 'The Strategic Analysis of Intermediation', *European Economic Review* **33**, 294–301.

(1989b) 'On the Theory of Intermediation', Doctoral Dissertation, University of Bonn.

Discussion

FRANKLIN ALLEN

It is some time since I have read a survey as thought-provoking and interesting as this one. The basic issue that Hellwig addresses is the role of financial institutions in the allocation of capital for investment. Historically, there are two types of institution that have been important; the first is banks and the second is stock markets.

These institutions have played varying roles in different countries at different times. For example, in Germany and Japan banks have been much more important than in the UK and US where stock markets have played a more significant role. One of the things that I particularly liked about the paper was the use of historical and contemporary evidence for assessing the various theories that have been suggested. Moreover, the theories that are considered are not restricted to those suggested by economists; the hypotheses developed by economic historians are also considered.

Why is it that different countries have such different financial institutions? As Hellwig points out, standard economic theory has little to say on this issue; the Walrasian model simply assumes a set of frictionless institutions. Until recently, the most popular explanation for the role of intermediation was based on transaction costs. Gurley and Shaw (1960) argued that financial intermediaries such as banks transformed the earnings streams generated by firms into a form that investors found desirable. For this argument to hold, the technology for issuing securities must be such that it is less costly for intermediaries to do this repackaging than for investors to hold securities directly. In this view, banks improve the efficiency of the economy relative to stock markets alone since they allow a more efficient allocation of resources.

This argument is intuitively appealing. However, the precise nature of the assumptions necessary for these results to hold is unclear since transaction costs were not formally modelled by Gurley and Shaw. In Allen and Gale (1988, 1989, 1990) the effect of incorporating the transaction costs of issuing securities is considered. Banks are not explicitly analysed. However, the results indicate that, in general, the institutions generated by the 'invisible hand' in the presence of transaction costs are not an efficient set of institutions. For example, in Allen and Gale (1990) it is shown that options markets may arise even though everybody could be better off if they did not exist. Also, the financial institutions that do arise when transaction costs are incorporated depend on the precise form of the legal system and the property rights that exist. In this view, one possible explanation for the differences in the role of banks and stock markets in different countries is due to the different legal systems in place.

The second type of explanation for intermediation which Hellwig considers is based on asymmetric information. Diamond (1984) has suggested that banks act as delegated monitors. In his model, it is inefficient for many small shareholders each to incur the cost of monitoring a firm's management. Instead, a single bank can monitor so that the cost is incurred only once. The problem faced by investors is 'Who monitors the monitor?' or in other words how do the investors ensure that the bank actually does the monitoring? In Diamond's model, there are a large number of firms with independent payoff risks. If the intermediary invests in a very large number of firms the risk is diversified away. This allows investors to observe costlessly whether or not the bank has undertaken the necessary amount of monitoring since if it did not it would not be able to pay the promised rate of return.

As Hellwig points out, there are a number of problems with Diamond's analysis. At a theoretical level, his model contains a number of special assumptions and it is not clear how robust the results are to changes in these assumptions. At an empirical level, firms tend to have relationships with many banks simultaneously. Also it appears that banks are unable to diversify away all risk; but if a bank has risky investments there remains the problem of monitoring the monitor.

As mentioned above, the starting point of Diamond's analysis is the observation that in a stock market it would be very costly for many small investors each to incur the cost of acquiring information about a firm. In actual stock markets there appears to be another mechanism for ovecoming this problem, namely a market for information. Investors do not gather information themselves but purchase it either directly or indirectly. The counterpart to 'monitoring the monitor' is ensuring that sellers of information do actually have superior information. Bhattacharya and Pfleiderer (1985) and Allen (1990) have considered this problem and show that under certain circumstances information can be gathered by a single party and sold to many investors so that the cost is shared. The analysis of the market for information is still at a very early stage. It is still unclear under what circumstances, if any, incorporating it into the analysis of stock markets leads to a superior allocation of resources compared to banks.

The third type of explanation for intermediation that Hellwig considers is that it is a mechanism of commitment to a long-term relationship as suggested by Mayer (1988) and Fischer (1990). This view stresses the difficulties lenders may have in ensuring that a firm fulfills its commitments when it borrows money. For example, if a firm has problems and requires a loan the lender may require a high interest rate to compensate it for the risk of the loan. However, once the firm is out of difficulty it has an incentive to obtain alternative financing at a lower cost. By forming a long-term relationship where the bank acquires better information about the firm than other lenders, it may be possible to mitigate this type of problem more easily than when a firm issues securities to many investors.

Hellwig's paper contains an excellent summary and critique of the literature on why banks exist and their role in the allocation of resources. It does not spend much time on the advantages of stock markets. One point that is made is that *ceteris paribus* intermediation will be more costly since it involves a chain of transactions. Also the theory of Diamond (1989) is mentioned. He suggests that the top segment of large and profitable firms will be able to finance directly in security markets because of their previous track records.

Other theories explaining the coexistence of stock markets and banks, which are not mentioned are Gorton and Haubrich (1987) and Seward (1990). Gorton and Haubrich's model is an extension of that in Diamond (1984). Firms precommit to an optimal level of monitoring by taking on an appropriate level of bank debt. This allows them to obtain the highest possible price for the securities they issue in the stock market. In Seward's model there are two types of asymmetric information. The providers of finance cannot observe the investment allocations of firms and can only partially observe cash flows. Seward shows that a firm can mitigate the problems created by these two types of asymmetric information by simultaneously issuing debt in the securities markets and taking on bank loans.

In varying degrees, these theories share the characteristic that stock markets appear to be of secondary importance. This view appears to be in sharp contrast to the apparently widely held belief in the UK and US that the stock market plays a vital role in the operation of the economy. Mayer (1988) has presented evidence that in terms of raising actual funds stock markets are fairly unimportant. What then is the role that they play?

Manne (1965) has argued that the control of corporations may constitute a valuable asset. In this view different individuals or management teams can operate firms with different degrees of profitability. The important issue in this case is for there to be mechanisms which allow control to be acquired by those most able to exercise it. In countries such as Germany, where the predominant financial institutions are banks, the amount of information that is publicly available about firms is very small. In this type of situation it is very difficult for able individuals and management teams to discover firms which they could control better than the incumbent management. However, it can be argued that in economies with active stock markets such as the UK and US there is a great deal more publicly available information about firms and this makes it significantly easier for control to flow to the individuals and management teams that are best able to exercise it. Thus, even when stock markets are unimportant in terms of raising new funds, they may nevertheless be important in terms of ensuring an efficient allocation of the control of capital.

One of the problems with this argument is that it relies on superior managers being able to acquire control of firms with inferior management. The problems of takeovers as a mechanism for acquiring control have been widely analysed (see Stiglitz, 1985, for a discussion). For example, Grossman and Hart (1980) have identified a free-rider problem. Acting individually each small shareholder has an incentive to hang on to their shares in the face of a takeover which will increase the value of the firm since they will then be able to share in the increased post-takeover value. This means that value-enhancing takeovers will not succeed unless they pay the full post-takeover value. The takeover therefore cannot be profitable and if there are any costs to mounting it will be unprofitable. Grossman and Hart argue that this free-rider problem can be overcome to some extent if the new owners can dilute the value of the firm by, for example, transferring assets to themselves. This type of dilution may be desirable if it increases the probability of a takeover which allows the firsm assets to be better managed. Even though the takeover mechanism has various imperfections, a stock market may nevertheless lead to a better allocation of control rights than a financial system where banks predominate.

In conclusion, our understanding of the role of financial institutions is still very incomplete. There are a number of theories which suggest that financial systems where banks predominate may be superior to financial systems where stock markets are important. There are also theories which suggest the reverse. However, these theories are not yet able to convincingly explain why, for example, banks played such an important role in Germany and Japan while stock markets have been more important in the UK and US. Much more work is required before we have a reasonable understanding of these important issues. Hellwig's survey is a good starting point for anybody wishing to pursue research in this area.

NOTE

Research support from the NSF (Grant No. SES-8920048) is gratefully acknowledged.

REFERENCES

Allen, F. (1990) 'The Market for Information and the Origin of Financial Intermediation', *Journal of Financial Intermediation* **1** (forthcoming).

Allen, F. and D. Gale (1988) 'Optimal Security Design', *Review of Financial Studies* **1**, 229–63.

(1989) 'Arbitrage, Short Sales and Financial Innovation', Working paper 10–89, Rodney L. White Center, University of Pennsylvania.

(1990) 'Incomplete Markets and Incentives to Set Up an Options Exchange', *Geneva Papers on Risk and Insurance* 15, 17–46. (Special issue on 'The Allocation of Risk with Incomplete Asset Markets' edited by Herakles Polemarchakis.)

Bhattacharya, S. and P. Pfleiderer (1985) 'Delegated Portfolio Management', *Journal of Economic Theory* **36**, 1–25.

Diamond, D. (1984) 'Financial Intermediation and Delegated Monitoring', *Review of Economic Studies* **51**, 393–414.

(1989) 'Monitoring and Reputation: The Choice Between Bank Loans and Directly Placed Debt', Working Paper, Graduate School of Business, University of Chicago.

Fischer, K. (1990) 'Hausbankbeziehungen als Instrument der Bindung zwischen Banken und Unternehman: Eine theoretische und empirische Analyse', Doctoral Dissertation, University of Bonn.

Gorton, G. and J. Haubrich (1987) 'Bank Deregulation, Credit Markets, and the Control of Capital', *Carnegie-Rochester Conference Series on Public Policy* **26**, 289–334.

Grossman, S. and O. Hart (1980) 'Takeover Bids, the Free-Rider Problem, and the Theory of the Corporation', *Bell Journal of Economics* **11**, 42–64.

Gurley, J. and E. Shaw (1960) *Money in a Theory of Finance*, Washington: Brookings.

Manne, H. (1965) 'Mergers and the Market for Corporate Control', *Journal of Political Economy* **73**, 110–20.

Mayer, C. (1988) 'New Issues in Corporate Finance', *European Economic Review* **32**, 1167–83.

Seward, J. (1990) 'Corporate Financial Policy and the Theory of Financial Intermediation', *Journal of Finance* **45**, 351–77.

Stiglitz, J. (1985) 'Credit Markets and the Control of Capital', *Journal of Money, Credit and Banking* **17**, 133–52.

MARGARET BRAY

This paper addresses a large and important question; what effect does the institutional form of the financial system have on the allocation of funds for investment, the way in which firms operate and more generally on economic growth?

Hellwig points out that this is not a question which can be studied in the standard Walrasian paradigm. In the Walrasian framework the role of financial markets is to provide funds for firms at one date in return for repayments at other dates, returns which may be state-contingent. This role continues when the shift is made to a non-Walrasian framework, with asymmetric information, incomplete markets and incomplete contracts, which may be costly to enforce. But in a non-Walrasian model, as in the real world, the financial system has another immensely important role, that of motivating, monitoring, and sometimes replacing the senior management of a firm. The financial system may perform well or badly both in the allocation of investment funds to firms and in facilitating the effective management of firms. It seems possible that the latter role is as or more important than the former in its effect on the performance of individual firms and of the economy as a whole.

Hellwig draws extensively on historical and institutional studies as a foundation for his discussion. This is an approach with which I have enormous sympathy. In the post-war period a large part of the empirical work of academic economists has been confined to the econometric analysis of numerical data sets, thereby giving us a very blinkered view of the world. One important fact which emerges is that there is not a single one-way trend in all sectors of the financial markets. In recent years there has been a move towards disintermediation by the very largest firms. There have also been a trend towards syndicated and securitized debt, and as Hellwig observes a tendency on the part of firms to shift from external to internal finance whenever possible. On the other hand there has been a distinct move towards intermediation as equity markets become increasingly dominated by institutional investors, pension funds, insurance companies and unit trusts.

How do these trends fit into Hellwig's three categories of explanation for financial intermediation: economies of scale in transactions costs, monitoring, or the mitigation of incentive problems? One important reason for part of the movement from bank to bond debt on the part of the very largest blue chip companies is the fact that the banks' exposure to third world debt means that the banks' credit rating is less good than that of the companies, so it is cheaper for these companies to go directly to the bond market. This does not seem to fit into any of Hellwig's categories.

On the other hand I think that the increasing institutional dominance of equity markets in the UK and US can probably be explained in terms of the Gurley-Shaw model of economies of scale in transactions costs. The costs of dealing are lower for the large institutional investor than they are for the private client. Another factor may be the belief on the part of some investors that there is an expertise in fund management which they lack and the institutional fund managers have; this is perhaps best thought of as a set-up cost in the competent management of investment, another form of economy of scale. The monitoring and incentive models of intermediation seems less relevant here. There is some direct involvement of these funds in the UK and US in the monitoring and management of the corporations whose securities they own, but it seems to be limited.

This observation suggests to me that it is as important and as interesting to contrast different forms of financial intermediation as it is to contrast intermediated and non-intermediated finance. As a very broad generalization the stake of a bank in a firm usually takes the form of debt, in which there is no active market, whereas an institutionally managed fund consists in large part of equity in which there is an active market.

Hellwig argues that the distinction between bank finance and market finance is largely independent of the distinction between debt and equity finance. I have sympathy with his point in so far as he is trying to move the focus of the study of corporate finance from financial instruments to financial institutions, but I also consider the debt-equity distinction to be very important when looked at in the context of the monitoring and incentive problems which Hellwig discusses. The holders of equity and the holders of debt have a very different set of sanctions at their disposal if they do not like what the firm is doing. In principle equity holders can directly control a company through the exercise of their voting rights. This may be an effective procedure in a closely held company, in which case a significant number of shareholders may be directly involved in the management of the company as executive or non-executive directors. It may work more dramatically, and possibly more effectively, in a family-controlled company; relatives have ways of harassing each other which are not open to outsiders. However in a widely held company the direct exercise of power by shareholders is subject to considerable organizational and free-rider problems. The power of shareholders in these companies operates largely through the equity markets, and in particular through the price of equity, which affects the company and its management through its effect on payments to management through stock options and other incentive schemes, through the cost to the firm of raising new equity should it wish to do so, and through the takeover mechanism. This is a much larger topic than I can discuss here, apart from pointing out that these sanctions work by depressing the share price when investors do not like what a company is doing, which is very much against the investors' interests if they are contemplating selling the securities, or if they are assessed and rewarded on the basis of the current value of their portfolio.

Contrast the position of a bank holding debt, in which there is no active market. This makes it much harder for the bank to get out of a relationship with a firm when it does not like what the firm is doing than it is for an institutional investor which can simply sell securities. The bank can in principle call in the debt but doing so may well force the firm into insolvency which may not be in the bank's interests. If an institutional investor can sell the securities at the market price it can get out very easily. In practice this may not be possible, particularly if the sale is taken as a signal by the market of bad news about the company. Never the less it seems plausible that because it is harder for the bank to get out than it is for an institutional investor holding actively traded equity, the bank will have a greater interest in maintaining a relationship, and thereby mitigating the monitoring and incentive problems.

Martin Hellwig argues, I am sure correctly, that debt contracts are incomplete. However debt contracts are very much more complete than equity contracts in specifying the payments to be made and information to be provided. It is much easier to be in breach of a debt contract than it is to be in breach of an equity contract, and an individual debt holder has the ultimate legal power to force a company into insolvency if it does not receive its contractually specified repayments, whereas an individual shareholder has no corresponding power. Of course it may not be in a bank's interests to force insolvency, but it surely matters to the relationship between bank and firm that the possibility exists.

The theme which recurs throughout the latter part of Hellwig's paper where he discusses monitoring and incentive-based models of financial intermediation is the possible importance of exclusive arrangements and long-term relationships. There are a variety of different considerations at play here: free-rider problems and winner's curse problems, long-term relationships reducing informational asymmetries thereby making more efficient contracts possible, and also weakening competition *ex post*, and thus allowing banks a larger share of the returns when firms do well, but also giving the bank monopoly power with respect to the firm. There are further issues which Hellwig does not mention. There may also be long-term relationships between banks, so to some degree they act cooperatively rather than competitively. This may allow banks the benefits of portfolio diversification, whilst retaining the advantages of exclusivity, so the problems of free-riding and *ex-post* competition are reduced. One of the consequences of financial deregulation, and the expansion of banks into each other's domestic markets may be the weakening of this cooperation if it exists.

Indeed the number of possibilities seems only to be limited by the ingenuity of the theorist. As Hellwig says, there is not much to conclude here except that further study is called for. Some of this work must be theoretical, but there is also a clear need for more empirical work. We know that there is sometimes, but by no means always, an exclusive relationship. We need a clearer view of when and where, and then a theory to explain what we observe.

What if anything does all this imply about policy? Hellwig is almost silent on this. He points out that the analysis which he presents is entirely positive; no welfare or policy analysis is intended. We have a number of different models, attempts to capture particular insights. Different models point in different directions. There is no unified model in which to weigh one insight against another. There is thus no secure basis for welfare and policy analysis, which is inevitably a matter of balancing one consideration against another. In the circumstances it is tempting, and perhaps right, for academics to forswear policy discussion whilst pleading for more research funds to move the analysis on. But meanwhile the world changes, policy decisions are made, and the policy debate moves on. Hellwig poses welfare questions. He asks how far the efficiency of capital markets in the US and UK serves investors who want to shuffle their portfolios, but is of little relevance to firms who want to raise outside finance. He also asks how the trend towards securitization affects incentives, suggesting that it may not be an entirely good thing. Finally he queries the efficiency of internal finance, which gives the managers of profitable firms a huge degree of latitude. We do not know the answers to these questions. But it seems clear that policy on matters such as disclosure requirements, company and insolvency law, and the structure and regulation of financial markets, needs to be made with these issues in mind.

4   How (not) to integrate the European capital markets

YAKOV AMIHUD and HAIM MENDELSON

1   Introduction

Free Europe (which, in the long run, may be all of Europe) is moving quickly to become an integrated marketplace without internal frontiers, with free movement of goods, persons, services and.capital. In particular, Europe of 1992 and beyond will approach the state of a unified market in which firms issue securities on a European-wide basis. Given the important role of liquid secondary (trading) markets for capital formation and their crucial effect on the cost of capital (Amihud and Mendelson, 1986, 1988, 1989c), the structure of the European capital markets after 1992 is of paramount importance. In this paper, we focus on the following question: how should the unified European Community integrate trading in its securities markets, especially for those firms that will raise capital on a European-wide basis?

This question is not as futuristic as it may appear at first. In a number of countries (Italy, Spain and Switzerland, to mention a few examples) there are efforts underway to integrate existing local exchanges and form national securities exchanges. Turning to the case of integration across countries, the European exchanges have looked in a variety of settings at the question of unification either on a European-wide basis or on a regional basis (e.g. establishing a Nordic stock exchange). The general sentiment so far has been against establishing a single European Community exchange and in favour of preserving the existing national (and sometimes regional) stock exchanges. However, it is expected that there will be substantial cross-listing of securities in the different exchanges, continuing the current trend. For example, Pagano and Roell (1990) report that, in the first half of 1988, trading in London's SEAQ International amounted to about half of the trading volume in the respective stocks in the Paris and Milan stock exchanges, with Frankfurt and Madrid following with 16% and 6%, respectively. All this raises concerns that the market will become *fragmented*. The question which arises, then, is what integration facilities, if any, will be beneficial for the European securities markets?

These concerns already exist to some extent today, and they will increase dramatically in 1992 and beyond. The Chairman of the ISE, Andrew Hugh Smith, outlined the Exchange's strategy towards a single European market at an International Financial Markets conference on 10 May 1989.[1] Mr Smith highlighted the value of liquidity, 'the prime and the most anxiously sought after characteristic of a securities market . . . The European secondary market of the future must be able to assure investors that they can indeed avail themselves of very substantial liquidity.' (p. 11) According to Mr Smith, the national exchanges of Europe should come together and agree to cooperate in creating a 'screen-based market' which would channel the order flow of different countries through one central exchange. But, if the national exchanges fail to cooperate, 'then in my view, the International Stock Exchange would have to seek by itself to create the sort of marketplace that I have indicated' (p. 13). If indeed the national exchanges do not cooperate in developing appropriate trading methods and standards, market fragmentation may ensue.

When changing their trading mechanisms, all of the European Stock Exchanges adopted trading systems from the US and Canada. It is therefore instructive to examine the issues of market integration from the perspective of the US, where a large number of securities are cross-listed on more than one exchange. The US response to the problem of fragmentation in the equities markets has been the establishment in 1978 of an order-routing linkage system called the Intermarket Trading System (ITS). ITS is primarily a communication facility, enabling the transmission of orders from one market to another. In this paper, we evaluate order-routing linkages like the ITS, examine their applicability to the case at hand and analyse their impact on fragmented markets. Then, we briefly present our approach to market integration.

Our approach is consistent with the approach taken recently by the European Community to the problems of technical harmonization and standardization (Pelkmans, 1987). Rather than follow the traditional approach of producing directives regarding the specific technical aspects of products and services, the new approach focusses on the promotion of standards to facilitate access. The new approach 'is an attempt to accelerate harmonization processes . . . while at the same time providing more flexibility for innovation and easier market access' (Pelkmans, 1987, p. 249). In the context of securities markets, we think the emphasis should be on creating interfaces and facilitating the development of new trading mechanisms rather than on the imposition of rules that constrain the operation of the exchanges.

In what follows, we review current research findings on market fragmentation in section 2. In section 3 we analyse how liquidity is provided to the market, and in section 4 we discuss the role of priority rules and their incentive effects on the provision of liquidity. The two sections provide a set of criteria for the evaluation of market integration facilities, which are applied in section 5 to the analysis of order-routing linkage systems. Section 6 briefly outlines our own approach to market integration, and our concluding remarks are in section 7.

2   Market fragmentation: research findings

The purpose of market integration is to mitigate the potential problems associated with fragmentation. To evaluate market integration facilities, we thus need to define what these problems are. A market is *fragmented* if the results of order executions obtained in it are different from those that would have obtained in a central auction market (Mendelson, 1987). We expect that, other things equal, consolidation should lead to a superior market structure because it allows the interaction of all the orders available in the market. On the other hand, the argument for fostering a number of competing markets is that intermarket competition should bring down execution costs and create further incentives for innovation. It follows that there is a tradeoff between the costs of fragmentation and the benefits of intermarket competition.

Both the costs of fragmentation and the benefits of intermarket competition have been evaluated by a number of studies. In a cross-section study, Branch and Freed (1977) found a negative effect of the number of exchanges in which a security is traded on its bid-ask spread, and further suggested that competition reduced NYSE spreads but did not affect AMEX spreads. Hamilton (1979) studied the effects of off-board trading on NYSE spreads, finding that 'the competitive effect tends to reduce both the NYSE specialist spreads and the daily stock variances by more than the fragmentation effects tend to increase them. Equally important, however, neither effect is large.' (p. 186)

Two SEC studies (SEC 1986a, b) found that multiple trading increases the liquidity of traded options, demonstrating the possible benefits of intermarket competition. At issue was whether to allow multiple trading in stock options. Until recently, most options on listed stocks were allocated by a lottery to the five options exchanges in the US, so that each option was traded in one market only. The SEC considered abolishing the allocation system and allowing any market to trade in any option, thus leading to competition between markets, where each tries to attract order flow. Until now, competition between the options exchanges took place in the trading of options on OTC stocks and on a small number of listed stocks. Markets competed by offering traders attractive incentives of excecuting their orders, such as low fees, fast and reliable execution, prompt clearing and high liquidity. Experience shows that, in these contests, trading tended to concentrate in one market. However, even though trading in options which qualified for multiple listing was 'mono-polized', the liquidity of multiply traded options remained higher.

The SEC attributed this to the fact that there was a constant threat of the order flow moving to another market should the 'winning' market reduce the quality of execution, suggesting that the 'contestable markets' form of competition prevails even if most of the trading in an option is concen-trated in a single exchange. This form of competition (if it indeed prevails as suggested by the SEC studies) enables the preservation of the benefits of competition without the losses due to fragmentation: it is the *threat* of entry, rather than the actual entry of competitors, that keeps the markets in line, without bearing the costs due to the fragmentation of the order flow.

The effects on market performance of internalization – a special form of fragmentation, where a broker-dealer or an automatic execution system executes orders off-board, before they reach the exchange floor – was studied by Cohen et al. (1982). They showed that there are private incentives which can favour internalization of orders, but the market as a whole will suffer. While some traders might on average do better in a fragmented environment, fragmentation would reduce overall welfare, since in a regime of internalized orders the fragmented market leads to a larger bid-ask spread and greater price volatility. Cohen et al. concluded that the best market structure is an informationally consolidated market where the best in-house quotes are exposed to the entire market.

A problem which arises in a fragmented market is not only that price-priority rules can be violated because of trade-throughs (trading in one market at a price worse than in the other market), but that, even if the price-priority rule is adhered to, there will be a violation of *secondary* priority rules, such as the time-priority rule (which gives priority to the order placed first). The effect of violation of secondary-priority rules on market fragmentation was studied by Cohen et al. (1985). They find analytically (using a queueing model) that the expected time a limit order has to wait on the book until it is executed is larger under the fragmented market regime. This is because in a fragmented market, there is less chance that the order will find an available counterpart. Studying the effects of violating secondary-priority rules, they compared two market regimes: one with time priority strictly observed, and one where a limit order is randomly selected from those tied in price. They found that a violation of time priority increases the bid-ask spread and reduces the probability that a limit order will be executed before it expires. Thus, they concluded that the quality of fragmented markets deteriorates even when price priority is strictly adhered to because of the violation of time priority. These results underscore the importance of following the *secondary* priority rules. As we show below, there are even stronger reasons – related to the incentives to place limit orders and provide liquidity to the market – to preserve the secondary priority rules.

Mendelson (1987) compares the performance of a number of consolidated and fragmented market architectures. His performance measures are the overall gains from trade, the price volatility faced by transactors, the quantity traded and the 'noise' in the reported transaction prices. Comparing a consolidated order flow sent to a central auction market to an order flow which is split between fragmented markets, Mendelson finds that fragmentation increases the volatility of transaction prices and reduces the overall gains from trade as well as the quantity traded. This is because when markets are fragmented, each order is exposed only to a subset of the order flow, and hence enjoys less liquidity. Mendelson also demonstrates how the quality of price signals produced by separate fragmented markets can be improved by creating an aggregate price index. His results show that, when markets operate without order interaction between them, the consolidation of reported prices leads to improved price signals even relative to the consolidated market regime. Finally, Mendelson's results show that the consolidation of order flow has decreasing returns to scale: the more liquid the market, the lower the added value of further integrating it, and the potential benefits of added integration are minuscule when the market is sufficiently liquid already.

Pagano (1989b) analyses an equilibrium model of entry to alternative markets. In his model, speculators decide on entry to a market by assessing its price variance, its ability to absorb excess demand or supply and its direct transaction costs. In this model, traders prefer a higher price variance because it increases their potential speculative profits; the more traders there are in a market, the lower this variance. On the other hand, when there are more traders in a market, the market impact of an individual trader's excess demand or supply is lower, creating a preference for a market with a large number of traders. Thus, a 'deep' market has advantages and disadvantages for traders. In general, there will be multiple equilibria, depending on the initial conjectures that each trader forms about the choices of others. When there are two markets with the same transaction costs, trade will concentrate in equilibrium in one of them. If the two markets have different transaction costs, trade may be either concentrated or fragmented. When direct search is compared to a consolidated market, if there is a conjectural equilibrium involving some search, there will always be another conjectural equilibrium involving trade in the consolidated market.

The question of investors' choice of a market to trade in is related to the question of understanding the distribution of stock ownership across geographical locations and, in particular, across countries. In the international context, the question is: why do investors tend to invest mostly in their home country's securities, given that simple portfolio theory tells us that this is suboptimal? Such investment policies can be motivated by costs of information as well as by transaction costs. In particular, investors have lower costs of access to information about firms in their home market, resulting in better ability to monitor their performance and act on it. In addition, the total costs of transacting are higher when trading takes place across countries because of the added costs and uncertainties due to exchange-rate fluctuations, institutional and regulatory differences and barriers and implicit costs that are due to differences in languages and customs (which are of particular importance in the case of Europe). The fast evolution of information systems and electronic communications should reduce the scope of these problems and put some of these explanations to the test.

The effects of market linkages on price dispersion was studied by Garbade and Silber (1978). Their results corroborate the proposition that such linkages have decreasing returns to scale: the trans-Atlantic cable in 1866, which substantially reduced the communication time, reduced the mean price difference between the London and New York US Treasury Bond markets by more than two-thirds. Similarly, the domestic telegraph reduced the mean price difference between the New York and New Orleans Foreign Exchange markets by almost 50%, and reduced the price differences between the New York and Philadelphia exchanges by a similar order of magnitude. The consolidated NYSE tape – a major innovation in the market for equities in 1975 – reduced the mean price difference between the NYSE and the Midwest Stock Exchange by about 6.5% for a sample of four stocks. Their results support the notion that, beyond a certain point, the returns to integration become minuscule, and that the best way to accomplish the 'right' degree of integration is to let the market decide on the issues: 'The automation of the trading process itself is the next logical step in market integration, and is currently under active consideration by the exchanges and the SEC. Will it produce significant economic benefits? Perhaps, but one of the lessons of our story is that it might be best to leave that decision to the instincts of the private sector.' (Garbade and Silber, 1978, p. 831.)

Garbade and Silber (1979) tested the price relationships between dually traded securities on the NYSE, the Midwest Stock Exchange and the Pacific Stock Exchange, finding that the regional exchanges are best characterized as satellites of the NYSE, meaning that regional exchange prices are essentially derived from NYSE prices with some time delay allowing for price adjustment. As Garbade and Silber (1979) explain, this finding is consistent with the historical evolution of the regional exchanges as well as their mode of operation. This result is directly related to the basic problem pointed out in our discussion of information externalities: we cannot expect the regional exchanges to become primary price-setters in the multiply listed securities since their pricing is NYSE based. If the NYSE becomes less liquid and its prices become more volatile, so will the prices on the regional exchanges.

In summary, market fragmentation clearly has undesirable consequences. A central auction market improves the quality of order execution as well as the quality of price signals, but it eliminates the potential benefits of competition between markets. Recent evidence suggests that trading in a single market can provide the benefits of consolidation and yet be highly competitive if traders have the *option* to divert their order flow to a competing market center. Then, the threat of losing order flow should induce the pattern of behaviour we expect in a competitive market, even though trading may be almost fully concentrated in a single market.

An important issue which deserves further attention is the effect of market structure on the incentives to place alternative order types, which are critical to the functioning of any liquid market. This subject is discussed in the next two sections.

3   Order types and their effects on market liquidity

Traders in securities markets have two primary ways of placing orders: market orders and limit orders.[2] Market orders are orders to buy or sell a given quantity of a security at *any* price. A limit order makes the execution conditional on a limit price. A *buy* limit order specifies (in addition to quantity) the *maximum* price at which the order is to be executed, and a limit *sell* order specifies the *minimum* price at which it is to be sold. If, for example, the only possible transaction price is below the specified price on a limit sell order, this order will not be executed. Only when the price rises and reaches the quoted limit sell order's price will that order be executed.

Market orders differ from limit orders (and quotes) in three important respects:

(i)   in their immediacy and certainty of execution;
(ii)   in the liquidity they provide to the rest of the market; and
(iii) in the amount of information released by the order.

The first and obvious difference between market orders and quotes/limit orders is in their immediacy of execution: while a market order is executed immediately, a limit order specifies the price at which the order is to be executed but the time and likelihood of execution are uncertain. Thus, a market order reflects a preference by the trader for reducing the time until execution while accepting the available quoted price, whereas a limit order reflects the trader's preference for determining the execution price while leaving the time of execution undetermined.

The second difference is in the liquidity provided by the order to the rest of the market. A liquid market should satisfy the requirement of *immediacy*, i.e. an incoming order can be executed immediately if the trader so wishes. Immediacy is *supplied* to the market by *limit* orders and is *consumed* by *market* orders.[3] Without limit orders, the supply of immediacy will dry up and the market will become illiquid and volatile, since market orders will necessarily result in significant price swings. The viability of a continuous market requires that there be an incentive to place limit orders which provide immediacy of execution to those who seek it.[4]

Not only is the *existence* of limit orders important to ensure a liquid market; so is their size or 'depth'. The 'market impact' cost – the decrease or increase in prices caused by a sell or a buy market order (respectively) – which is an important component of the cost of immediacy, depends on the 'depth' of the market. A sell order which is larger than the quote size at the current bid price can be executed only at a discount, resulting in a price decline (at least temporarily). We may also observe situations where the whole order is executed at a price which is worse than the best quoted bid or ask prices. This decline in the price received by the seller constitutes the market-impact cost (similarly, a large buy order can be executed only at a premium which reflects the market-impact cost to the buyer). If the existing quote sizes are small, immediacy will be available for only a small quantity and hence market liquidity will be low. The larger the quote size, the 'deeper' the market. In a 'thin' market which is lacking in 'depth', i.e. in a market where the quantity that can be sold or bought at the quoted bid or ask prices (respectively) is small, we observe a greater market-impact cost.[5]

What makes a market liquid and 'deep' is the availability of a large number of limit orders (by market-makers or by the public) with the bid and ask prices being close to each other. Then, the costs of the bid-ask spread as well as the market impact costs are smaller. It is the willingness of market-makers to stand ready to buy and sell at the quoted prices that makes markets liquid. And, to induce market-makers and the public to perform this important role by providing quotes and limit orders with sufficient 'depth', the trading system must provide them incentives to do so.

A third difference between market orders and limit orders is in the information they release to other market participants. A limit order reveals information about the trader's assessment of the value of the security for which the order is placed, and his confidence in this value (reflected in the quantity that the trader is willing to trade at this price). Market orders reveal much less. At best, they tell that the quoted price at which the market order is executed is at least as good as the value assessed by the trader who has placed the market order.

Since the provision of information is one of the important functions of the market, it should be designed so that traders will have an incentive to reveal information through their limit orders and quotes. These incentives are key to the proper functioning of the market.

The foregoing discussion has shown that the incentives to place limit orders are critical to the functioning of a liquid market. These incentives are adversely affected by two inherent (and related) problems which make limit orders costly to the traders that place them. Whenever the design of a securities market aggravates these problems, we should expect that the liquidity of the market will suffer. These problems are discussed in the next two subsections.

3.1   The liquidity externality

An investor or a dealer placing a limit order in the market is doing so to promote his own self-interest. Yet, there is a positive externality[6] associated with the limit order, since it also improves the liquidity of the market as a whole: traders on the other side of the market have the option to trade against the limit order, thus becoming better off. First and foremost, the existence of the limit order provides them with immediacy. In addition, a trader whose reservation price is better than the quoted price will gain a *surplus* by executing his order against the limit order. To illustrate, suppose that trader A places a buy order at a price of 50 or better (i.e. or lower). If trader B is willing to sell at a price of $49\frac{3}{4}$ or better (i.e. or higher), he can immediately execute his order against the limit order of trader A at A's buy price, 50. Thus, trader B gains a *surplus* of $\frac{1}{4}$ above his reservation price, whereas A will have to quote a lower price to gain a surplus.

Liquid markets require immediacy of execution, narrow bid-ask spreads and large quote sizes. A market regime which provides the proper incentives to place limit orders will be conducive to greater liquidity: limit orders will either reduce the bid-ask spread (if their prices are better than the current bid or ask prices) or increase the depth of the market. Thus, an unintended by-product of the self-motivated placement of limit orders is the addition of liquidity and depth to the market. Mendelson (1985) shows that, when more traders place orders in the market, this creates gains for *all* market participants over and above those perceived by traders that placed the orders: 'When traders join the market, they certainly gain some surplus as a result; but they also increase the surplus of all other traders by increasing the liquidity of the market (by providing traders on the other side of the market the opportunity to trade with them).'[7]

The problem is that those who place limit orders are not compensated for making the continuous market viable. As in any economic activity where the provider of a service is not fully compensated for the benefit he confers on others, the level of service provided will be lower than is optimal for society as a whole. In our case, this implies that in the securities markets, there would be too little liquidity provided by limit orders.

A related problem is that the propensity of traders to place limit orders and to quote prices is reduced because by doing so they put themselves at a disadvantage compared to better-informed traders. We call this the 'sitting-duck problem'. Suppose a trader considers the 'fair' value of a security to be x, given the information he has. If he quotes a bid price of x, he might buy the security from a 'liquidity' trader who has no specific (negative) information about it but happens to need the money. However, it could well be that the trader who sells the security to our trader is a *better-informed* one, who knows that there is 'bad news' which will drive its price down. If our trader buys the security from the informed trader, he will end up losing on the transaction.[8]

Anyone who places a limit order (either a public limit order or a market-maker's quote) is thus like a 'sitting duck', risking that his order will be hit by better-informed traders. To protect himself against this possibility, the trader in our example will quote a buying price *below* x even if, based on his information, x is the proper price. By the same argument, a seller will quote a higher ask price and, altogether, the bid-ask spread will widen. Alternatively, our trader may quote very small quantities at the narrow bid-ask spread and larger quantities at bid and ask prices which are further apart. In both cases, this 'sitting duck' problem, which is an inherent problem in any exchange, reduces the amount of liquidity provided to the market by limit orders.[9]

3.2   Information externality and 'quote matching'

When placing a quote or a limit order, a trader announces the price at which he is willing to buy or sell the security, thus releasing information on his assessment of the value of the asset, or his reservation price. In this way, those who place limit orders provide investors and dealers with valuable information which can help them assess the value of the asset without being fully rewarded for the information they provide to others. This information is thus another important externality provided by limit orders.

The information content of quoted prices has been analysed by Garbade *et al.* (1979). In a model which was strongly supported by evidence from the government securities market, they considered a market where dealers quote prices for a traded security. Each dealer has his own assessment of the 'true' value of the traded asset, but he also derives information from the prices quoted by other dealers and consequently reassesses his estimates. They show that dealers learn new information by observing the quotations of their competitors. While not treating their own information as redundant, dealers systematically update their quotes based on other dealers' quotes. And, the greater the number of dealers' quotes observed by any dealer, the greater the value of information inferred from their quotes.

It follows that participants in the securities markets receive valuable information from the quoted prices. Additional information is received by observing the quote sizes at each of the quoted prices. From any participant's viewpoint, the optimal course of action is to observe other traders' quotes without disclosing his own. In this way, he obtains information without giving his own information to others, thus taking a 'free ride' on the information provided by others. Naturally, what is optimal to one person is not optimal for the market as a whole. If *all* market participants refrain from advertising their quotes, the functioning of securities markets will be severely impaired.

A special case of this 'free riding' is the phenomenon of quote matching, which is found in some securities markets as well as in some other types of markets. It works as follows: market maker *A* in one market announces his bid and ask prices as well as the quote sizes. Market-maker *B* in another market promises traders to 'match' *A*'s quotes, i.e. he will execute their orders at the same prices quoted by *A*. This is a classical case of *B* exploiting the information provided by *A*, or 'free riding' on *A*'s quotes. If *A*'s profits are derived from executing orders, this 'quote-matching' will disadvantage *A*. Because *A* is not sufficiently well compensated, he may be reluctant to quote prices, or he will quote a wide bid-ask spread which provides less information. The result is undesirable for *all* market participants.

Quote matching is prevalent in the US equities markets that use the Intermarket Trading System (ITS) employed in the US equities. It works as follows: when a floor broker receives an order to buy or sell stock, he will compare the quotation in his market with the ITS display of quotations from other markets. If the ITS display shows that another market has a superior quote, the broker may send the order through the ITS to that market. However, the ITS plan does not require that the order be routed to the market with the better quote, and orders are often executed in the market in which they were received, with that market matching the better quote. Naturally, the market-maker in the market where the order has been received will match the best quotes only when it pays for him to do so, but will refrain from matching when market conditions have changed in an adverse way. Then, the routing of orders to the market with the best quote is more likely to take place when the person who has placed the quote is likely to lose. For example, suppose that the best bid price is $49\frac{3}{4}$, the best ask is 50, and the market is stable. Then, a market-maker may well match the best bid price if he receives an incoming sell order. But if the market has just moved downward such that the bid and ask prices should be $49\frac{3}{8}$ and $49\frac{7}{8}$, the market-maker will exercise his option not to match the best bid of $49\frac{1}{2}$. Rather, he will route the order to the 'best' quote on the competing market.

While 'quote matching' may be regarded as helping investors execute their orders at the best price, it also destroys the incentives to enter competitive quotes and openly announce the best buying and selling prices. Then the gain to investors due to competition may be offset by the loss due to the lower propensity to place competitive limit orders. As we pointed out above, the placement of limit orders is crucial to the liquidity of securities markets; without them, the markets will be quite illiquid. It is therefore necessary, in order to foster market liquidity, to establish a trading system which will provide incentives to the public and to market-makers to place limit orders and quotes and announce their best buying and selling prices and largest possible quote sizes.

4   Preservation of priorities

Ideally, a trading system which involves a number of markets should operate as if orders were routed to a central auction market and executed there according to agreed principles. These principles must be designed to provide incentives to the suppliers of immediacy and liquidity, i.e. to those who place quotes and limit orders. Otherwise, liquidity will dry up and both the members of the exchange and the investing public will suffer. An important set of exchange rules providing such incentives is that pertaining to *priorities*. Within these rules, we can distinguish between those that tend to be self-enforcing, and those that require external enforcement by the exchanges since traders and investors have no incentive to follow them.

(1) **Price priority** is a natural-priority rule: an order for a given security should be executed at the best available price. This priority rule is particularly meaningful when there are a number of dealers competing *within* an exchange, where the other attributes of the quality of execution – speed of execution, service, reliability, exchange fees – are given. Price priority tends to be *self-enforcing* since, other things equal, an investor has the incentive to execute his order at the best available price. Thus, to the extent that this rule is consistent with investors' interests, it will be enforced by the investors themselves in the process of searching for the best price.

Although this rule is intuitively appealing, strict adherence to it may *not* always be in the trader's best interest when trading in a number of markets. For example, the best bid or offer quoted in one market may be for small order quantities, while the second-best price quotes in the other market are for larger quote-size (order quantity). Strict adherence to price priority would require breaking up the order between the market with the best quote and the other market, and this may inflict additional costs on the investor, such as the cost of undesirable delays in execution.

Within a given exchange, the intangible dimensions of execution quality (in particular, speed) are relatively homogeneous, implying that strict adherence to price priority is in the investors' best interest. Across exchanges, however, there are differences in the other dimensions of the quality of execution, such as speed, service and reliability of execution. This is because of the existence of non-price elements of competition among exchanges, which influence the investor's willingness to pay, but are not reflected in the quoted prices. Thus, while price priority is highly desirable *within* an exchange, where execution efficiency and reliability are homogeneous, it is much more difficult to evaluate across exchanges.

(2) **Time priority** is an important priority rule which, not being self-enforcing, is codified in some form in the rules of most important exchanges. By this rule, two orders whose prices (and other features) are the same will be executed in the order that they have arrived to the marketplace: first in – first out. The time-priority rule gives traders a strong incentive to place limit orders. As we pointed out above, one problem with limit orders is that while the price at which they are to be executed is predetermined, their time of execution is uncertain, and thus

they are lacking in immediacy. The time-priority rule partially compensates traders for their risks and costs by letting them enjoy earlier execution. In this way, the time-priority rule induces traders to provide the liquidity needed for proper market operation.

There is an important difference between price and time priority: the investor who trades against a standing limit order has a direct (and strong) incentive to enforce price priority, since it reduces his costs. Thus, even if price priority were not externally enforced, rational investors would cause it to be the rule rather than the exception. In contrast, the investor with a market order choosing against which quote or limit order to trade has no incentive to adhere to time priority, since his cost is not affected by the time at which the limit order has been placed. It is therefore the duty of the exchange authority in the case of intramarket trading, or of the regulatory authority in the case of intermarket trading, to enforce this rule, which provides a powerful incentive for traders to place limit orders.

(3) **Size priority.** Some exchanges have rules that provide direct or indirect priority on the basis of quote size.[10] These rules both induce the supply of liquidity to the market and facilitate the trading of large orders. As we already pointed out, part of the costs of illiquidity is the market-impact cost. In a 'thin' market, the size of an incoming order is more likely to exceed the quote size, and thus to 'move' the market price beyond the best bid or ask prices in a direction which is adverse to the trader. This can also cause undesirable short-term price volatility. In a deep market, where the quote size of the best bid and ask prices is high, a relatively large transaction, and even a reasonable sequence of transactions, can be executed at the best bid or ask prices without moving the market price. Thus, large quote sizes provide liquidity to the market, and the size-priority rule helps to induce traders to offer large quote sizes.

(4) **Public order priority.** This rule provides for a priority of public limit orders over dealers' orders. It is designed to amend a fundamental disadvantage of the public in the trading process compared to professional floor traders. The reason is that traders who are right on the exchange floor enjoy an informational advantage over the outside public. A member of the public who places a limit order cannot monitor market movements as closely and as immediately as exchange members can. Thus, if he places a limit order, he stands the risk of having it executed to his disadvantage not only by someone who is better informed about the specific asset (e.g. a corporate insider), but also by anyone who watches closely the movement of market prices and can act on them promptly. Clearly, exchange members have far easier access to the trading floor and are better able to act quickly than a member of the public. The

public-order-priority rule mitigates this problem and increases the incentive for members of the public to place limit orders. In addition, public orders tend to be liquidity motivated (as opposed to informationally motivated) and hence prioritizing them is expected to increase market liquidity. Sometimes, 'small orders' serve as a proxy for 'small (or public) investors', resulting in an *inverse* size-priority rule.

Summarizing, priority rules are important in providing incentives for placing limit orders and for quoting narrow bid and ask spreads and large quantities at these prices. They are intended to partially compensate for the liquidity and information externalities provided by the limit orders which benefit the public as a whole. Thus, strict adherence to thse priority rules is paramount if liquidity in the markets is to be enhanced.[11]

So far, we have analysed the importance of the public's limit orders and the dealers' quotes in providing liquidity to the market. We have outlined the inherent problems which reduce the propensity of traders to place limit orders and quotes, and the value of these orders to the trading public at large. We further pointed out possible market arrangements which reduce market depth and the importance of establishing priorities in order to restore market depth. In the next section we shall examine the integration system which operates in the US markets in light of the above analysis.

5   Evaluation of order-routing linkage

The most common form of market integration is an order-routing linkage system such as the Intermarket Trading System (ITS) which links the US equities markets. The ITS is a computer-communication linkage among the major US stock exchanges that provides facilities for the display of composite quotation information at each participating market centre and the routing of orders between these centres. Trading through the ITS occurs as follows. When a floor broker receives an order to buy or sell a stock, he compares the best bid and offer in his market with the ITS display of quotations from other markets. If the ITS display shows that another market has the best bid or offer (BBO), the broker may either match the BBO and execute the order locally, or send the order through the ITS to the market with the BBO. This is done by sending to that market a 'commitment to trade', good for a specified amount of time (one or two minutes). If the BBO is still good at the receiving market when the commitment arrives, the receiving member will send an acceptance through the ITS. The receiving market can also respond with a 'missed market' message if the quote has changed in the meantime, in which case the order returns to the originating market. Also, if the commitment to trade is not honoured within the specified period, it expires and the originating market then has to handle the order again.

In this section we analyse the appropriateness of an order-routing linkage for market integration, using the American ITS as a model. Building on the general criteria developed in the previous section, we suggest that the European capital markets should *not* follow the US example and should not adopt an ITS-like system.

5.1   Is an order-routing linkage necessary?

The ITS was developed in the US in the 1970s, when the use of information technology by the exchanges was at its infancy. Correspondingly, quotation and information systems were just being developed, and it was quite difficult to get composite quotation information on the different markets in the brokers' offices. However, today's US systems can provide the office broker with all quotations in all markets. The office broker can thus route the order *directly* to the market of choice. At the exchange, the order is received by the floor broker and it is executed promptly. Better still, the order can be sent to the exchange's automatic execution system in which execution is instantaneous at the quoted price. Given that the order has been initially routed to the market that was deemed best given all current quotes, order-routing linkage is completely redundant, and there is no more need for the floor broker to compare quotes and use the system to route the order to the market with the BBO. In other words, the intermarket communication provided by order-routing linkage systems is unnecessary when brokers can route orders initially to the market which they consider provides 'best' execution. Note that, in addition, due to the existence of non-price attributes of execution quality, only the broker can make an informed choice on the market he is willing to trade in.

One could argue that, while some European markets actually lead the US in terms of their use of information technology, others lag and those markets will benefit from an order-routing linkage system such as the ITS. However, the implication is that the system of the future will be driven by the lowest common denominator, something which is not conducive to progress. We believe that it is better to develop the best and most efficient system rather than to try to cater to the least efficient of markets. Further, the direction of the technological evolution of the securities market is quite clear. We believe that, by the time such a system could be implemented most if not all European exchanges, being pushed by the need to compete, will have advanced their use of information technology to the efficient frontier.

5.2   Effects on timeliness of execution

One of the most important attributes of quality of execution is timeliness, because delay costs are particularly significant in the case of securities trading. These costs exist because a delay in execution may result in an unfavourable change in the price between the time an order was placed and its ultimate execution. For example, suppose that a trader wants to sell because he believes the security is overpriced. By delaying the execution time, the trader exposes himself to the risk that the price will decline, as he expected, and he will incur a loss. Investors are often willing to pay to avoid or reduce their risk of delays. For example, traders who choose to execute their orders in automated execution systems forego the opportunity to trade at a better price (a negotiated price between the current bid and ask quotations) in order to gain execution speed. The prevalence of market orders shows the importance of speedy execution and the investments made by investors in information technology testifies to the value placed by traders on timeliness.

By its very nature, the ITS increases the time elapsed between the receipt of an order and its execution. Instead of the order being executed at the market where received, it will be sent to another market. It can return from that market after one or two minutes unexecuted or executed only partially if the quote size in the market with the BBO was smaller than the order size. If, in the meantime, another market (not the originating one) posts BBO, the order may again have to be rerouted to that market. The process may continue and a relatively long time may elapse until the order is executed in its entirety.

Thus, an ITS-like order-routing system inflicts a cost on investors by prolonging the overall time to execution. *Immediacy of execution*, which is the *raison d'etre* of continuous markets, will be impaired.

5.3   Preservation of priorities and 'quote-matching'

Perhaps the most serious problem with ITS-like order-routing linkage systems is that by their design, they violate *all* secondary priority rules and hence reduce thei incentives to place limit orders that are critical to the functioning of the market. This is because orders are routed on the basis of price alone, regardless of time priority, order size (depending on implementation) and whether the order was placed by an exchange member or by the public. These systems encourage quote-matching *by design*, and hence are detrimental to the provision of liquidity in the long run. Rather than repeat here the analysis of sections 3–4, we simply note that this analysis clearly demonstrates that rather than helping liquidity,

ITS-like order-routing linkage systems are actually worse than no system at all due to their negative effects on the incentives to provide immediacy and liquidity to the market.

5.4   Conclusions

We have argued that, by their very nature, ITS-like order-routing linkage systems cannot provide a proper solution to the problems of capital market integration. But then, what system can? Our general analysis provides some positive guidance for answering this question. In the next section, we briefly outline an alternative approach to the design of trading systems, which responds to the problems raised above.

6   An alternative approach

As we have shown, any trading system must create incentives to provide liquidity to the market, primarily in the form of limit orders and quotes. This means that a proper integration facility must support and preserve the (so-called) 'secondary' priority rules which are not likely to be self-enforced by traders in the market. Rather than preserving price priority only, which is important but will be self-enforced by traders seeking the best price, a market integration facility must be based on an agreed protocol of priority rules. This protocol must include at the very least system-wide preservation of time priority, and possibly additional 'secondary' priority rules such as public-order priority.

Within each national system, a Consolidated Limit Order Book (CLOB)[12] has the advantage that it enables the preservation of both price-priority and the secondary-priority rules, and hence provides a sound integration facility. In fact, a number of European exchanges have already adopted automated trading systems which are based on a CLOB. Between markets, an automatic routing system can be used to channel investors' orders to the best market while preserving both price-priority and the secondary-priority rules. The system could also accommodate exchange-rate conversions, if necessary. As we demonstrate below, the national CLOBs should co-exist with other trading mechanisms, thus becoming modules in an integrated design which allows investors to access different trading mechanisms, competing and interacting with each other. This brings up the importance of *competition* between trading mechanisms that will function together and will enable traders to trade off attributes of execution quality, such as immediacy, price and required disclosures.

The concepts of competition and modularity are particularly important in the context of an integrated European Community market. Since the market has grown from a network of heterogeneous national markets which will continue to function, trading both single-listed national securities and multiple-listed European Community securities, it is important to allow each market to operate in its own fashion while supporting the interfaces between markets. Thus, each market should be viewed as a module which competes in the framework of a larger network. Rather than try to homogenize the markets – which is probably infeasible and perhaps undesirable – it is better to let each market offer its own unique features and facilitate competition between markets.

As we have seen, timeliness is an important performance measure for any trading system, and in particular computer-based ones. A manual interface such as the one used by the ITS is inconsistent with the level of timeliness required of today's systems. It is also inconsistent with the notion that *only the investor can make the choice between competing markets*, implying that the point of choice must be the brokers' offices or the investors' PCs rather than the floors of the exchanges. Further, to be acceptable, each component of the trading system must have well-defined and flexible computer-based interfaces with the other components. This requires an overall systems plan as well as careful design of the interfaces between subsystems, which is at the core of what integration is all about. It also requires a blueprint which defines subsystem interfaces so that subsystems can be added to the overall trading system in a modular fashion. In the next subsection we suggest that integration must start with such a blueprint.

6.1   A blueprint for integration

The key to the integration of capital markets is the development of a modular conceptual design which enables competition between market centres and defines the interfaces they must all adhere to. As we discussed in section 5, agreed interfaces are more important than physical links. Rather than build links and change them over time in reaction to a variety of pressures and demands, the effective route to integration starts with a well-thought-out vision of the future. This vision focusses on the common interfaces between systems that support trading in different countries, using different approaches and alternative trading mechanisms. In the same way that the IBM PC has been developed with an open interface that allows competing vendors to develop modules or 'cards' that serve diverse functions, and allows users to choose the functions they are most interested in, we propose that the European Community should focus on the development of common rules and interfaces between the exchanges rather than on the linkage facilities themselves. The underlying assumption must be that traders (or their agents, the brokers) are in the best position to choose what exchange and which trading mechanism is best for them, rather than have rules and regulations that make the choice *for* them. Order-linkage routing systems violate both of these requirements. First, like directly wiring parts into the PC, they harm the modularity of the system. Second, they impose their own priorities on the trader or his broker.

We have proposed (Amihud and Mendelson, 1985) an integrated approach to computerizing the trading systems, which is based on three principles:

(1) The design of interfaces to integrate three subsystems: portfolio management, execution and settlement.
(2) Competition between alternative locations *and* exchange mechanisms.
(3) Flexibility in operation and easy access.

We briefly discuss each of these principles below.

(1) **Integration**. The integration of geographically dispersed financial markets is only one aspect of integration. We think it is equally important to create interfaces that allow the integration of the *functional* components of the market in addition to the geographical ones. These functional components are naturally separable into three interfacing subsystems:

> the portfolio management subsystem,
> the order execution subsystem, and
> the settlement subsystem.

By 'integration' we refer to interfaces between the portfolio management subsystem, which is located and controlled in the brokerage house or the investor's own systems, the order execution subsystems which are decentralized to the national exchanges and the settlement system which must be centralized or at least coordinated with mutual guarantees (as in the case of interbank cheque-clearing systems). Our approach requires both setting up a community-wide settlement system and facilitating the interfaces between the three subsystems discussed above.

(2) **Competition.** Our approach enables traders to choose between competing trading mechanisms, as well as between market locations enabling them to trade-off price, volatility and probability of execution. The result will be a system that increases traders' welfare and enables the market to better adjust to intertemporally changing conditions: sometimes one mechanism or market may be more heavily used, whereas in different situations a competing mechanism or market may be superior. Investors will be able to choose between alternative ways of executing an order and

from alternative locations where execution might take place. They will be able:

> to direct market orders to market-makers or automatic quotation systems at the exchanges, to be executed at the quoted bid or ask prices;
>
> to apply a negotiating mechanism, by computer interaction (e.g. advertising a 'block' and soliciting offers) or via brokers;
>
> to enter limit orders on a 'book', with the option of having the limit order either openly displayed to solicit traders on the other side of the market or concealed; or to enter orders – limit or market – to the forthcoming clearing in a 'clearing transaction.'

The latter trading mechanism will execute *simultaneously* orders to trade various stocks at a single price for each stock, all at specified times during the trading day (see subsection 6.2).

We believe that, regardless of how much intermarket integration is accomplished, the ultimate choice on the market where execution takes place must be left to the investor (or his agent).

(3) **Flexibility and Accessibility.** Traders will enjoy significant flexibility due to the interfaces between the order execution and portfolio management subsystems. The system will enable them to process a comprehensive set of information to support their trading decisions and to condition their orders on such information. All users will have access to all publicly available information, to provide information sources to which they subscribe, and to their own order and portfolio data, all being supplied in *real time*. When an investor's order is executed, it will immediately update the state of his portfolio, possibly triggering the cancellation of existing orders and the generation of new ones. Traders will be able to program the system to generate orders conditional on a complex set of real time data. The data can be on the security to be traded, on other securities, on securities and commodities in other markets, on various macroeconomic indices, etc. This will enable investors to keep up with developments in the market and with changes in their own portfolios without requiring continuous monitoring, cancellation and reissuing of orders. In fact, some contemporary systems already provide many of these capabilities, albeit with very limited or no integration.

Under this approach, it will be possible to condition a limit order on a comprehensive set of information, such as the prices of other stocks in the same and in related industries, changes in a market indexes, trading volume, external announcements (earnings, money supply, interest rate changes, etc.). This will reduce the need to monitor the market and be continuously ready to change the limit order. Under today's system, the fact that a fast change in market conditions can render a limit order's price out of line necessitates continuous monitoring and voluminous communication with the exchange. If the limit order is not changed fast enough, it will be hit by another trader who can react more quickly. The problem is exacerbated by the unequal access of traders to the technology with the shortest reaction time. Thus, some traders are disadvantaged not only in the information they have but also in the technology they can apply in placing and removing orders. Under our approach, the limit order will automatically track the relevant market conditions and the limit price will be automatically recomputed as necessary. This will reduce traders' reluctance to place limit orders, since it will reduce the need to monitor them and the associated costs (and risks).

It follows that availing traders with on-line information about all markets and enabling a direct interface with the order execution system mitigates the problems associated with the placement of limit orders and quotes and thus increases market liquidity and 'depth'. In addition, the extent of agreement needed by the different national centres is relatively small. The emphasis is rather on a uniform method of communication and transmission of information, and on a uniform way of interacting with the system's execution, clearing and settlement subsystems.

6.2   The clearing transaction

We also propose to incorporate a *new* trading mechanism, which we call the *clearing transaction*, in the integrated system.[13] The clearing transaction will clear participating orders periodically, at specified points of time during the trading day[14] – for example, at the opening, at 1:00 p.m. and at 3:30 p.m., as well as at night (mainly in order to attract overseas investors). Orders designated for the clearing transaction will accumulate prior to these clearing times. While clearing-transaction orders accumulate, the continuous auction market will keep operating up to the clearing epoch (for mid-day clearings) and immediately afterwards without any interruption. Thus, the clearing transaction will not cause any trading halt and will not interfere with ordinary continuous trading. At clearing time, all qualifying orders will be executed simultaneously at a single price.

Two types of orders will be submitted to the clearing:

(1) Conditional orders, i.e. orders whose execution depends on a set of specified conditions, such as the price of the security for which the order is entered (which is the equivalent of limit orders entered today) or on other conditions, such as the clearing prices of *other* securities that participate in the clearing at the same time.

(2) Unconditional, or market, orders.

All orders will remain sealed until clearing time, although traders will be allowed to reveal ('advertise') them if they wish to solicit matching orders for the clearing. At clearing time, a computer system will solve the set of equations and inequalities implied by the participating orders to determine, for each security, the quantity traded and the market clearing price. This will be done by interpreting each order as a multi-commodity excess demand function and finding an equilibrium solution corresponding to these functions. All qualifying orders for all participating securities will be executed at the very same instant.

To illustrate how our proposed clearing transaction works, consider the order 'if the price of Fiat stock rises above 8 ECU and the price of BMW falls below 250 ECU and the price of Peugeot is above 114 ECU, sell 400,000 shares of Fiat and use the proceeds to buy BMW'. In the current system, it is possible to guarantee only one of these conditions, but not all three. And, although the available automated systems shorten the time lag between observation and execution, the fast changing prices make even a short response time insufficient to guarantee the desired execution. In addition, the market impact of the very order which is executed can change the market-clearing price. Even if the *observed* price of BMW falls below 250,the impact of the buy order itself may be to drive the execution price above 250, and this would be particularly so if many traders apply the same trading rules at the same time. Only in the clearing transaction can an order of the type described above, contingent on conditions which are *current* at the instant of execution, be executed.

Many exchanges employ today the call-market method, usually in the opening of the trading sessions, for actively traded stocks. While it is similar, in some respects, to our proposed clearing transaction (see Amihud and Mendelson, 1987, 1989a, 1989b; Amihud *et al.*, 1990), it is certainly not identical. In the call-market method, orders for each security are clearly separated (and not always simultaneously). The only conditional orders allowed are simple limit orders, and the unconditional ones are market orders, specified only in number of shares. Thus, these systems do not support simultaneous execution across securities, and certainly cannot allow conditioning an order in one security on the conjectural clearing prices of other securities.

Investors are clearly interested in other securities' prices when placing their orders in the call transaction. In our studies we have found that, following the call transaction, investors 'correct' prices in accordance with what they have observed regarding the prices of other stocks. This trading activity, which adds noise to the market process, would be naturally reduced under our proposed clearing transaction. The availability of the clearing transaction will also reduce the noise generated by the activity of program traders who track the markets and enter orders through automatic execution systems whenever a profitable price-gap between securities is observed. This activity can sometimes cause price oscillations and keep triggering orders which attempt to exploit the observed price gap. The probability that the price-gap will exactly close is practically zero under current trading systems. In the clearing transaction, however, orders can be designed to bring about the exact closing of the price-gap, and the prices of related securities will be kept more in line.

The simultaneous conditioning and execution also enables traders to construct exact portfolios according to their specifications, a task which is problematic under the continuous trading mechanism where orders can be conditional only on *past* information. In current systems, when an order is generated by satisfying some condition, that condition may have changed by the time of execution and the executed order may not satisfy the condition any more.

An important advantage of the clearing transaction over continuous trading mechanism is that it substantially reduces the 'sitting duck' problem. Since all qualifying orders for each security are executed at a single price, traders gain the benefit of their order being executed at a price better than their quote. This is because the execution price is determined by the intersection of the demand and supply schedules constructed by batching orders with different limit prices. This generates a surplus to traders whose orders are executed, equal to the difference between their limit price and the execution price.

We have pointed out above the problem of information externality associated with the placement of limit orders. In the clearing transaction, unless a trader chooses, there is no information revealed by his limit price or by his quote size. This is particularly useful for block trading, when the disclosure may have an adverse effect on price.

7   Concluding remarks

The evolution of capital markets around the world shows that the same securities are often traded in more than one market. Currently, US stocks are traded in London and in Tokyo, and in the US, the same stocks are traded in a major market as well as in some regional markets. This multiple-listing of securities is likely to occur to a significant degree in unified Europe. The forthcoming economic integration of the European Community is already motivating calls to integrate the European capital markets. The immediate response to such calls may be to adopt the US solution, namely, establishing an intermarket linkage system which will be used to route orders across markets.

The objective of any design of a market system should be to enhance market liquidity. We have found that the greater the liquidity, the lower the required return by investors, and the lower the cost of capital to firms. Thus, great care should be exercised in designing the future structure of the European capital markets.

We suggest that a liquidity-increasing market design should be careful to provide incentives to investors and traders to place limit orders and quotes, which are the basis for any continuous liquid market. Trading mechanisms which facilitate the exploitation of the externalities provided by limit orders should be rejected. In addition, rules should be instituted to preserve the incentives for the placement of limit orders, such as preserving 'secondary' priorities beyond price.

Finally, we have briefly outlined some of our ideas regarding the path for the integration of the European capital markets. Our approach is based on decentralization of the trading process and on allowing the current trading mechanisms as well as additional ones to compete. In particular, investors will have the freedom to place an order into a limit order book, into the markets as they operate now, or into a new 'clearing transaction' trading mechanism which will avail investors with a number of important advantages. The development of the system should be modular and enable the existing exchanges to 'fit' into it after satisfying rules of uniformity in communication and information, but not necessarily in their modes of operation. Thus, the unified capital market structure will evolve in response to market forces and competition, rather than being imposed by regulators.

Our approach to the integration of markets across countries can also be applied to the integration of different types of securities markets, such as the spot and futures markets. We discussed above the problem of market fragmentation, where the *same* security is traded in two (or more) markets. The fragmentation problem also arises when two *different* securities whose prices are closely related are traded in two different markets, as is for example the case for the spot and futures markets. The prices of both contracts, written on the same underlying asset, are very highly correlated, but their prices are determined in two separate markets. This leads to price disparities which motivate trading activity to exploit these disparities. Our proposal for a clearing transaction with a *cross-conditioning* of orders is designed to address this form of integration. Under our proposed system, it will be feasible to enter an order which is simultaneously conditional on the spot and futures prices, thus keeping them both in line and preventing the ill effects of market fragmentation across assets.

NOTES

We acknowledge helpful comments by Colin Mayer and by the discussants, Richard Levich and Marco Pagano.

1 Recorded in *International Securities Digest*, June 1989, pp. 10–14.
2 In addition, market-makers and dealers can place *quotes* which serve a similar economic function as limit orders, i.e. they are commitments to buy or sell specified quantities at specified prices within some time interval.
3 See Grabbe (1986), p. 101.
4 Pagano (1989a) shows that trading may entail a conjectural 'thin' market equilibrium and discusses transfer payment arrangements for moving away from this equilibrium.
5 The narrowest bid-ask spread represents the market-impact cost for standard small orders.
6 An externality is the effect of an economic action on the welfare of other economic agents which is not priced in the market. A positive externality occurs when an action generates an economic benefit to others without being fully rewarded for it by the market mechanism.
7 Mendelson (1985), p. 271.
8 Bagehot (1972) was the first to point out this problem, which has been modelled since in a number of papers on liquidity and asymmetric information.
9 This issue is closely related to the unsettled question of whether to provide special privileges to designated market-makers. Our approach (see section 6) is to let competition between trading mechanisms settle the issue.
10 Usually this is not a straightforward priority, but a more complex procedure.
11 In interdealer markets, dealers often develop long-term relationships that can be viewed as implicit priority rules. This can serve a useful role in activities such as block trading, where dealers' reputations help reduce costs of asymmetric information. Indeed, block trades are often arranged 'upstairs' rather than on an exchange.
12 A Consolidated Limit Order Book (CLOB) lists all the buy and sell limit orders entered by public investors and market-makers for the underlying security. Each limit order specifies whether it is to buy or to sell, the limit price and the order quantity. When displaying the orders, the limit sell orders are presented at an ascending order of their limit prices and the buy orders are presented at a descending order of their quoted prices. The lowest limit sell price and the highest limit buy price define the narrowest bid-ask spread. Each incoming order (limit or market) is either executed against the best available limit order on the CLOB or, if its specifications do not qualify it for execution, it is added to the orders already on the CLOB.
13 Mendelson (1982, 1985, 1987) calls a related mechanism 'clearing house'.
14 In our study of the Tokyo Stock Exchange (Amihud and Mendelson, 1990), we examined the performance of the mid-day openings in Tokyo, finding that its volatility and efficiency were comparable or superior to those of the closing transactions. These results strongly support our proposal to introduce a clearing transaction while the continuous market is operating.

REFERENCES

Amihud, Y. and H. Mendelson (1985) 'An Integrated Computerized Trading System', in Y. Amihud, T.S.Y. Ho and R.A. Schwartz (eds.), *Market Making and the Changing Structure of the Securities Industry*. New York: Lexington Books.

(1986) 'Asset Pricing and the Bid-Ask Spread', *Journal of Financial Economics* **17**, 223–49.

(1987) 'Trading Mechanisms and Stock Returns: An Empirical Investigation', *The Journal of Finance* **62**, 533–53.

(1988) 'Liquidity and Asset Prices: Financial Management Implications', *Financial Management* **17**, 5–15.

(1989a) 'Index and Index-Futures Returns', *Journal of Accounting, Auditing and Finance* **4**, 415–31.

(1989b) 'Market Microstructure and Price Discovery on the Tokyo Stock Exchange', *Japan and the World Economy* **1**, 341–70.

(1989c) 'The Effect of Beta, Bid-Ask Spread, Residual Risk and Size on Stock Returns', *Journal of Finance* **64**, 479–86.

(1990) 'Volatility and Trading Mechanisms: Evidence from The Japanese Stock Market', Working Paper, Graduate School of Business, Stanford University.

Amihud, Y., H. Mendelson and M. Murgia (1990) 'Trading Mechanisms and Stock Returns: Evidence from Italy', *Journal of Banking and Finance*, forthcoming.

Bagehot, W. (1972) 'The Only Game in Town', *Financial Analysts Journal*.

Branch, B. and W. Freed (1977) 'Bid-Asked Spreads on the AMEX and on the Big Board', *Journal of Finance* **32**, 159–63.

Cohen, K.J., R.M. Conroy and S.F. Maier (1985) 'Order Flow and the Quality of the Market', in Y. Amihud, T.S.Y. Ho and R.A. Schwartz (eds.), *Market Making and the Changing Structure of the Securities Industry*. New York: Lexington Books, pp. 93–112.

Cohen, K.J., S.F. Maier, R.A. Schwartz and D.K. Whitcomb (1982) 'An Analysis of the Economic Justification for Consolidation in a Secondary Security Market', *Journal of Banking and Finance* **6**, 117–36.

Garbade, K.D., Pomrenze, J.L. and W.L. Silber (1979) 'On the Information Content of Prices', *American Economic Review* **69**, 50–9.

Garbade, K.D. and W.L. Silber (1978) 'Technology, Communication and the Performance of Financial Markets: 1840–1975', *Journal of Finance* **33**, 819–32.

(1979) 'Dominant and Satellite Markets: A Study of Dually-Traded Securities', *Review of Economics and Statistics* **61**, 455–60.

Grabbe, J.D. (1986) *International Financial Markets*. New York: Elsevier.

Hamilton, J.L. (1979) 'Marketplace Fragmentation, Competition, and the Efficiency of the Stock Exchange', *Journal of Finance* **34**, 171–87.

Mendelson, H. (1985) 'Random Competitive Exchange: Price Distributions and Gains from Trade', *Journal of Economic Theory* **37**, 254–80.

(1987) 'Consolidation, Fragmentation and Market Performance', *Journal of Financial and Quantitative Analysis*, **22**, 189–207.

(November 1982) 'Market Behavior in a Clearing House', *Econometrica* **50**, 1505–24.

Pagano, M. (1989a) 'Endogenous Market Thinness and Stock Price Volatility', *Review of Economic Studies* **56**, 269–88.

(1989b) 'Trading Volume and Asset Liquidity', *Quarterly Journal of Economics*, 255–74.

Pagano, M. and A. Roell (1990) 'Trading Systems in European Stock Exchanges: Current Performance and Policy Options', *Economic Policy* **5** (10), 63–115.

Pelkmans, J. (1987) 'The New Approach to Technical Harmonization and Standardization', *Journal of Common Market Studies* **25**, 249–69.

Securities and Exchange Commission (1986a) Office of the Chief Economist, 'Potential Competition and Actual Competition in the Options Markets'.

(1986b) Directorate of Economic and Policy Analysis, 'The Effects of Multiple trading on the Market for OTC Options'.

Discussion

RICHARD M. LEVICH

As the twelve nations of the European Community (EC) advance toward 1992, the forces favouring evolution and integration of financial markets will mount. Ahead of these changes, it is useful to consider the experience of financial markets in the United States and to ask whether any lessons stand out regarding market microstructure and market organization. Yakov Amihud and Haim Mendelson have focussed their attention on several general themes (market centralization versus fragmentation, the creation of liquidity in markets and priority trading rules) and on the specific approach adopted for linking securities markets in the United States, the Intermarket Trading System (ITS). Amihud and Mendelson characterize the ITS as an order-routing system (as distinct from an order-matching system) with several serious deficiencies that make it a poor model for the European Community to follow. The authors present their own proposal that accommodates geographically dispersed financial markets by integrating them via several systems – a portfolio management subsystem, an order execution subsystem (based on a central limit order book), and a clearing and settlement subsystem that utilizes EC-wide clearing and a new mechanism for executing orders simultaneously, the 'clearing transaction'.

The authors' basic observations about geographically dispersed markets are surely correct. An industrial economy benefits by having efficient capital markets with high liquidity and low spreads. There are gains from market centralization but the centralized market needs a credible competitive threat, in this case from either inside or outside of the EC. And, as for the specifics of the trading system, I completely agree that the ITS is an anachronism that makes poor use of present day technology. Market participants need the freedom to route orders where prices are most favourable. And, as limit orders provide positive externalities, the trading system should be designed to encourage them.

1   Differences between the United States and the European Community

In my view, the paper by Amihud and Mendelson addresses the problem of the design of a trading system, once the financial market has been integrated, as in the fashion of the United States. The issues I wish to raise in this comment pertain to the transition to an integrated, US-style market. Even though the EC is committed to removing the internal barriers to the movement of goods and services and factors of production, in 1993 the EC will still confront problems unlike those in a domestic stock market such as the United States. By definition, a domestic economy already enjoys considerable integration by having a unified currency area, a single legal system, harmonized accounting principles and information disclosure rules, and a single set of federal tax rules for capital gains and dividends, plus the disclosure (to tax authorities) of dividends and interest paid and for withholding taxes on these payments. Once there is a unified economy in the above sense, the issue of stock market design (including the number of market places and the particulars of the trading system) becomes a complex, but largely technical, matter governed by parameters such as size of country, number of time zones, number of firms, number of shareholders, costs of communications, costs of information monitoring, investor demands for liquidity and investor demands for portfolio rebalancing.

It is important to note that, while the United States has two centuries of experience in the design of financial markets, it is still fine-tuning its own financial markets. For example, it is now fashionable to ask whether US financial markets might be *too* integrated and whether financial futures markets (together with program trading and index arbitrage) might be a factor contributing to greater price volatility in equity markets. The specialist system of the New York Stock Exchange (NYSE) and the possible lack of sufficient market-making capital have also come under scrutiny. Pressures are mounting to abolish the Glass-Steagall Act and to permit US commercial banks to engage in securities activities, as is the case in the EC. And similarly, pressures have been mounting for the US Securities and Exchange Commission (SEC) to allow foreign companies to issue securities in the US without following US style accounting principles or disclosure practices, again as is the case in Europe.[1] The United States therefore offers both positive and negative lessons for the EC.

Amihud and Mendelson argue (and I agree) that there are decreasing returns to scale from innovation in financial linkages. The removal of capital controls, from the abolition of investment sterling in 1979 through the abolition of intra-EC controls by June 1990, represents an important innovation. The United Kingdom, in particular, has utilized this innovation to accumulate international investment experience that ranks it as the world's largest international portfolio investor with $180.5 billion at the end of 1988.[2]

But two major innovations remain to be accomplished in the EC and it seems as though their existence has been assumed by Amihud and Mendelson. First, the EC is still some years away from having a common currency. While some officials (Monsieur Delors) are actively promoting European Monetary Union (EMU) with a common currency (perhaps the European Currency Unit [ECU]) and a European Central Bank, others (Prime Minister Thatcher) remain cautious if not strongly opposed.[3] The analysis by Rudiger Dornbusch (see this paper) suggests that the fundamentals are now inconsistent with EMU. Without a common currency, even standardizing securities quotations in terms of ECU will impose an extra exchange risk and transaction costs on EC investors with income and/or expenses denominated in a unit other than the ECU.

Second, while clearing and settlement of domestic securities transactions in Europe may be very efficient (two days for a transaction in Germany, but a month in Spain), international settlement is notorious for delays.[4] It has been estimated that as many as 90% of all international equity trades are settled by physical delivery between agent banks of the two countries involved. As national settlement systems have grown up independently, there are important differences between country practices which are compounded by differences in time zones, holidays, languages, legal and regulatory requirements, and taxation policies. Another difficulty is the lack of a common world standard identification code for securities and securities firms. Not surprisingly, only about 50% of cross-border trades are settled on time.[5]

Were these two innovations accomplished, securities trading in Europe might much more closely resemble what we observe in the United States, where a buyer in Cleveland uses a broker in Boston to buy securities of a Chicago firm on the New York Stock Exchange from a seller who lives in Florida and uses a broker based in San Francisco. Dealing in a common currency with a paperless settlement process allows for substantial trading efficiency across a large geographic region. The marginal contribution of further refinements that consolidate and integrate the market may be small, but still worth working towards given the magnitude of financial markets and the volume of transactions that they support.

2   Incentives for regional markets and multiple listings

An important theme in the design of securities markets when issuers, investors and intermediaries are geographically dispersed is the degree of centralization versus fragmentation of markets. Amihud and Mendelson focus on the competitive and efficiency aspects of this trade-off. However, other fundamental forces have led to fragmentation in the United States as well as in the EC to a greater or lesser extent. For example, consider the incentives for multiple listings at geographically dispersed markets in the United States and the EC.

Years ago, high communication costs between Chicago, San Francisco and New York were one incentive to develop the Midwest, and Pacific Stock Exchanges that still compete with the NYSE. In addition, transactions between local residents on a regional exchange would incur lower settlement costs. The same forces are more pronounced in Europe where language diversity raises communication costs, and international settlement costs are greater than inter-regional costs in the US. The existence of many time zones and the preference of agents to transact in their own time zone is another factor that has effected the US market. With four time zones in the continental United States, the Pacific Stock Exchange permits Pacific time-zone residents to extend their trading day by three hours beyond New York. Given a common currency, paperless settlement, and modern communications, the Pacific Stock Exchange also enables Eastern time-zone residents to extend their trading day in the event of late-breaking news.[6] With only two time zones, this should not be an issue for the development of multiple listings in Europe.

Segmentation of the real economy manifested by regional consumption and regional production without substantial commodity trade between regions is also an important incentive for the development of regional stock exchanges. To the extent that investment acts as a hedge against future consumption, economic agents will hold claims on those firms that produce future consumption goods. Even though the EC countries are open to trade in goods, home country consumption bias argues for tilting investments towards home country shares. As barriers to trade within the EC decline, the hedging motive suggests that investors from one European country should hold shares from a broader range of EC countries.

Segmentation of the real economy is also likely to foster expertise in regional securities. Local investors are more likely to invest in regional stocks as their relative information costs and expertise are an advantage. In the United States, many firms began with a small, primarily local investor base. Three such examples are Minnesota Mining and Manufacturing (3M) and Honeywell (both originally traded on the Minneapolis Stock Exchange), and IBP (originally Iowa Beef Packers, a small Iowa meat-packing company founded in the late 1950s) all of which now trade on the NYSE. If regional firms prosper, they gain a larger investor following and larger capital requirements which may take them to a larger national market.

Regional segmentation because of regional expertise might be more common in Europe where diversity in accounting principles and disclosure practices may act as a barrier to investment.[7] Similarly, a European firm may begin as a national company with its capital needs satisfied by the local capital market. But, if the firm expands its production and/or sales into other countries, it may be unable or undesirable to finance its expansion from purely domestic sources.[8] Firms may seek multiple listings as a marketing or promotional device.[9] Daily quotations on a local exchange published in local newspapers may be especially valued in consumer goods companies, or when the firm has a local presence and employees hold shares in the firm from bonus plans, pensions or other compensation plans.

European firms may also be interested in multiple listings as a means of regulatory arbitrage. Regulations, and the regulatory burden incurred by firms and their shareholders, may be minimized by choosing a favourable location for a new issue or secondary trading of existing shares. The Eurobond market with its minimal information disclosure requirements has been a favoured market venue since the 1970s. Variability in exchange fees, commissions, transfer taxes, stamp taxes and new trading technologies, such as London's SEAQ, suggests a range of costs and competitive market conditions for secondary market activity.[10]

3   Barriers to integration in the EC financial markets

Despite recent advances in telecommunications and computer technology and the lessening of capital controls, important barriers remain to the integration of European securities markets.[11] Tax rates on dividends, interest and capital gains differ widely across EC countries. Regulations for withholding tax and disclosure of interest and dividend payments to authorities also vary around the EC. We should expect to see these regulations converge somewhat after capital flow barriers are lifted on 30 June 1990.

Differential accounting principles and disclosure practices are another non-tariff barrier for some investors in the EC. While some institutional investors claim that their decisions are unaffected by accounting diversity, other large investors and possibly many small investors feel that accounting diversity is a deterrent to cross-border investing. Again, endogenous forces may be reducing some of these differences.[12]

The main factors differentiating the EC from the United States in terms of financial market integration are that Europeans incur the costs of (a) many currencies and (b) many and stochastic settlement times. The Spanish investor buying the DM denominated securities of a German firm faces a dual settlement problem – two-day foreign exchange delivery combined with n-day security settlement. Foreigners will necessarily face additional risks in entering local currency (e.g. Deutsche mark) limit orders, even if these local currency orders are *not* made more uncertain by accounting diversity and other factors. And, even if a centralized European securities market were to adopt ECU pricing, it would be essential to coordinate securities market and foreign exchange market settlement times.

4   Summary remarks

The developments of the last few years – lower costs of computing and communication and reduced capital control costs – imply that the geographic reach of the market can expand and the participants (investors, issuers and intermediaries) can be more closely integrated. But do these developments suggest that issuers will reach out towards investor markets (i.e. fragmentation) or that investors will find it more convenient to travel to the main market of the issuer (i.e. centralization)?

In the interviews for our study of accounting diversity and capital markets (Choi and Levich, 1990), some non-American issuers complained that small, foreign investors who utilize ADR (American Depositary Receipt) shares tended to be 'skittish'. When markets become volatile, they sell their shares, resulting in a flow-back problem. These issuers prefer long-term, sophisticated investors who understand foreign accounting conventions and who can trade for themselves on foreign markets. The issuers gain a liquid and efficient market by focussing on their home market. They avoid the costs of foreign listings while courting foreign investors to maximize the market value of their shares. This suggests centralization of trading on the home exchange. The issuer may promote a wide distribution of quotes via electronic screens and via newspapers (for consumer marketing purposes), and a central limit order book to encourage order flow. Depositary receipts may continue to trade in national or regional markets for the benefit of small investors.

While the design of a European securities system raises complex technical problems, the bigger issues are of the political and turf variety. First, where will the portfolio managers, traders, brokers and back-office personnel sit? Second, which political and regulatory body will enjoy the rents from various financial activities – clearing and settlement, brokerage and funds management, underwriting, etc.? Sometimes in the twenty-first century, when Europe enjoys a single currency, the incentives to centralize will be very great. Each nation will want to attract its share of security market activity, in an industry that will be extremely footloose. But, by that time, the rents from financial services should be very small. The net regulatory burden that can be imposed on financial services while maintaining those activities within a country will be at or near its lower limit. The technology will likely be such that investors in Milan will find the screens of Italian stocks in Milan, British stocks in London, American stocks in New York, and even Russian stocks in Moscow, equally easy to access.

NOTES

1 Until recently, foreign companies could issue securities to large institutional investors, but restrictions on resale reduced the liquidity and raised the cost of these private placements. Rule 144A, adopted by the SEC on 19 April 1990, exempts resale to large institutional investors (defined as $100 million or more under management) from the registration and financial disclosure requirements of publicly offered securities. A '144A market' for foreign securities is expected to develop with accounting and disclosure practices determined by market forces, much as in the Eurobond market. While this represents an improvement in the US private placement market, Rule 144A could be seen as perpetuating fragmentation between 144A securities and securities that are publicly traded in the United States. See Gurwitz (1989) for further discussion of Rule 144A.
2 Swiss accounts (of residents and non-residents) were second at $118.4 billion and the US third at $62.7 billion. See Howell and Cozzini (1989) for further statistics on international equity market flows.
3 The prospects for European Monetary Union are also analysed in Temperton (1989).
4 *Quality of Markets Quarterly*, London: International Stock Exchange, Summer 1988, pp. 24–5.
5 Ibid., p. 23.
6 It could be argued that the United States has a special non-traded advantage because of time zones and the International Date Line. Because the day, for example Monday, 22 February 1990, 'ends' at the International Date Line, all contracts (e.g. tender offers) that have to be cleared and settled by 22 February could be done 'at the last moment' in a US financial market. Robert Heller has argued that this advantage may preserve a special role for the US dollar and US banks in international markets.
7 The impact of international accounting diversity on capital markets is analysed in Choi and Levich (1990).

8 Firms from smaller countries may want to issue securities in larger markets to reduce their cost of capital. They may want to list their shares in a larger market to gain a higher P/E multiple. The financing strategy of Novo is a classic example of these motives. See Stonehill and Dullum (1982). Multinational firms also choose local financing as a way to hedge political and exchange risks. See Aliber (1978).

9 See Choi and Levich (1990) for further discussion of how international accounting diversity affects investor and issuer decisions in international capital markets.

10 See Levich and Walter (1990) for a discussion of the impact of transfer taxes on the location of securities trading in Europe.

11 Member EC countries agreed to abolish remaining capital controls by 30 June 1990. Some countries with controls, notably France and Italy, moved in advance of this deadline. However, countries retain the option to resume controls on a temporary basis in the event of an emergency.

12 As European firms expand and their capital requirements increase, they may be forced to utilize non-bank sources of finance. This may induce them to provide accounting information and disclosures that more closely conform to those in the United States. See Choi and Levich (1990).

REFERENCES

Aliber, R.Z. (1978) *Exchange Risk and Corporate International Finance*, London: Macmillan.

Choi, F.D.S. and R.M. Levich (1990) *The Capital Market Effects of International Accounting Diversity*, Homewood, Illinois: Dow Jones-Irwin (forthcoming).

Howell, M. and A. Cozzini (1989) 'International Equity Flows: 1989 Edition', London: Salomon Brothers, August.

Gurwitz, A.S. (1989) 'SEC Rule 144A and Regulation S: Impact on Global Fixed Income Markets', Fixed Income Research Series, New York: Goldman Sachs, September.

Levich, R.M. and I. Walter (1990) 'Tax-Driven Regulatory Drag: European Financial Centers in the 1990s', in H. Siebert (ed.), *Reforming Capital Income Taxation* (forthcoming)

Quality of Markets Quarterly (1988) London: International Stock Exchange, Summer.

Stonehill, A.I. and K.B. Dullum (1982) *Internationalising the Cost of Capital*, New York: John Wiley.

Temperton, P.V. (1989) 'A Single European Currency in the 1990s?' *Currency and Bond Market Trends*, Merrill Lynch Capital Markets, December 21.

MARCO PAGANO

In their paper Amihud and Mendelson provide a clear non-technical explanation of some key issues that are relevant to the integration of European equity markets. Their paper is very timely: as the competition among European exchanges and trading systems proceeds, it becomes increasingly important to understand whether there should be any coordination between them and what form this coordination should take.

Since 1985 – the date of birth of SEAQ International, the London market specializing in foreign equities – the main European stock exchanges have competed with increasing intensity for trading volume on European 'blue chips' (Pagano and Roell, 1990). Their efforts have been aimed in particular at the 'wholesale segment' of the market, that consists of block orders placed by large institutional investors. The result of this competitive process is that now dealers and brokers are given the opportunity to monitor and access several national markets from a single location. London dealers can already watch at the screens of the computerized CAC auction market operating in Paris, and French dealers can monitor the quotes of London dealers on SEAQ International from their Paris offices. SEAQ International is planning to install its monitors in the main German financial centres, and the German exchanges are considering exporting to London their own brand-new IBIS trading system. More recently, newcomers are adding even more spice to the competition: the US-based NASDAQ exchange is currently trying to break into the European equity market, and agencies that so far provided only price information (such as Reuters) have discovered that they can easily become the vehicle for quotation systems managed by large international banks.

So far, access to trading systems in other national exchanges has been limited to major institutional investors and securities firms. But it is likely that access will become more widespread in the near future. If no coordinated policy action is taken by the exchanges, the near future is probably well described by the words of the Vice-Chairman of the Federation of German Exchanges: 'it is possible that in two years' time every securities dealer in Europe could be surrounded by Reuters, SEAQ, CAC and IBIS monitors and would have to decide from case to case which system he should employ to buy or sell the 100 to 200 European blue chip shares and bonds' (Von Rosen, 1990).

These developments raise a few problematic issues. Amihud and

Mendelson identify two of these issues: the effects of fragmentation on market liquidity, and the design of the system to route orders for execution to one of the various exchanges. They do not address another problem of paramount importance, i.e. the danger that in this fragmented marketplace many regulations might become impossible to enforce, or that 'beggar-thy-neighbour' competition among exchanges might lower regulatory standards to the lowest common denominator (for instance, on issues such as information disclosure or takeovers). But here, following their line of argument, I shall myself focus on the issue of fragmentation and on the design of the order routing system.

1   Fragmentation

As the authors point out, fragmentation has two effects: one one hand, it reduces market liquidity, but on the other it induces competition between different exchanges, with potential benefits for the users of each exchange. Amihud and Mendelson suggest that the best point in this trade-off between liquidity and competition is achieved when most trade concentrates on one market, but traders have the option of trading on a minor, competing marketplace. This competing marketplace then provides competition mainly in the form of a threat of the order flow moving away from the main market.

It is not clear, however, if in the European situation the gravitational pull of any individual market is sufficiently strong to attract most of the trade in any given stock, leaving the other exchanges to provide competition, mostly as potential entrants. While economies of scale and positive externalities in the provision of liquidity in fact promote the concentration of trade on a single market, other factors can make for persistent fragmentation: different markets may appeal to different categories of investors, either because of differences in trading methods or location. The foothold gained by London's SEAQ International in the continental European markets in the late 1980s shows that competition can lead to substantial and rather persistent fragmentation of the order flow across markets. So it may be quite hard to avoid the costs of fragmentation, and retain only the beneficial effects of competition. On the other hand, the benefits that traders can expect from the competition between exchanges are not negligible, as shown not only by the US evidence, but also by the European experience.[1]

2   Order routing and execution

In fact, Amihud and Mendelson's proposal for the order routing system of the 'integrated' European market is aimed precisely at capitalizing on the beneficial effects of competition among markets, while accepting fragmentation as a datum of the problem. Their realistic view is that one should retain the existing trading systems, and try to devise a system by which traders could easily monitor and access any of the existing market-places at each instant of time. In this sense, their proposal goes in the same direction in which things are spontaneously evolving – that of giving traders simultaneous access to the various existing trading systems. Moreover, it is sufficiently flexible to accommodate future additions to the current set of exchanges and trading systems.

Their proposal is also quite different from that often vaguely aired by several authorities of European exchanges, who have been talking for some time of the need to coordinate the disparate trading systems existing in Europe from an integrated continental equity market. Although views on this integrated equity market diverge considerably, integration is often meant to imply the joint creation of a brand new trading system by stock exchange authorities. The German authorities, for instance, propose that this trading system should build on the computer network called PIPE – a continental network that is currently being created by the main EC exchanges to disseminate price information from 1991 onwards, and historical price and turnover data starting from 1992 (von Rosen, 1990). This proposal is aimed at eliminating the costs of fragmentation, and as such it presupposes that all or most of the order flow will be attracted by the new facility. It is not clear, however, what would force trade to concentrate into this common European trading system, once it were operative. How could one prevent the stocks designated to be traded in this integrated system from being traded also elsewhere – and maybe more actively? If the existing trading systems are retained, the new 'common' trading system will just be one more system adding to the plethora of existing ones; if instead they are scrapped – admitting that this is feasible – one would lose the beneficial effects from competition associated with them.

Clearly, both the proposal of a common European exchange and that by Amihud and Mendelson are still too general and vague to be discussed in detail. However, their basic ideas are sufficiently different to be thought-provoking. The plan of a common European stock exchange aims at replacing the existing variety of competing systems with a new single trading facility, thus minimizing the costs of fragmentation but also the associated benefits from competition. Amihud and Mendelson's plan 'not to integrate' the existing systems (except by standardizing their interface with their final users) is instead predicated on the merits of competition and the benefits from the variety of trading mechanisms already existing in Europe, and implicitly gives lesser weight to the costs of fragmentation.

At the very least, each of these two opposite proposals teaches us something about the shortcomings of the other.

NOTE

1 See Pagano and Roell (1990), pp. 102–5.

REFERENCES

Pagano, M. and A. Roell (1990) 'Trading Systems in European Stock Exchanges: Current Performance and Policy Options', *Economic Policy* **5** (10), 63–115.
von Rosen, Rudiger (1990) 'The Future of the European Stock Exchanges – the German Perspective', paper presented at Financial Markets Group Conference on 'The Future of the European Stock Exchanges', London School of Economics, 8 May.

5 European financial regulation: a framework for policy analysis

COLIN MAYER and DAMIEN NEVEN

The wages of labour vary according to the small or great trust which must be reposed with the workman. The wages of goldsmiths and jewellers are everywhere superior to those of many other workmen, not only of equal, but of much superior ingenuity, on account of the precious metals with which they are entrusted. We trust our health to the physician; our fortune and sometimes our life and reputation to the lawyer and attorney. Such confidence could not safely be reposed in people of a very mean or low condition.

(Adam Smith, *An Inquiry into the Nature and Causes of the Wealth of Nations*, p. 105.)

1 Introduction

The regulation of financial services is normally associated with banks. Banks transform short-term deposits into long-term loans. This leaves them exposed to withdrawals that necessitate the premature liquidation of long-term assets. If the net realizable value of assets falls below deposits, then banks are unable to service withdrawals in full and insolvency may result. Perceiving this risk, investors may be induced to withdraw their deposits from financially sound banks in anticipation of similar behaviour by others. Investment decisions by investors can therefore impinge on others and banks are prone to runs (Diamond and Dybvig, 1983). Furthermore, if a run on one bank can prompt a run elsewhere then there is a risk of contagion. In particular, if the ability of other banks to launch rescues of troubled banks is dependent on their own financial condition then investors may correctly infer information about the soundness of the financial system from bank failures (see Aghion, Bolton and Dewatripont, 1988). There are therefore externalities between investors and between institutions that justify regulation.

Systemic risks are not in general a feature of other financial institutions. Investment managers such as mutual funds and private client investment businesses do not usually offer debt contracts that guarantee particular rates of return. Instead, they act as agents for investors who delegate portfolio selection and administration to an investment manager. Likewise, brokers merely effect transactions on behalf of others. In neither case are there similar externalities between investors to those that exist in banks. Furthermore, financial collapse is less contagious in some segments of the financial sector than in banks. There is little reason why the failure of one investment manager should have repercussions elsewhere particularly if portfolios under management can be transferred at low cost from one manager to another (see Franks and Mayer, 1989). In the case of brokers and market-makers, failure can be of wider significance since client assets are closely associated with those of the firm. The collapse of a counterparty to a financial transaction can endanger others. There is therefore stronger justification for protection against systemic failure in brokers and dealers than in investment managers but in neither case is it as compelling as it is in banks.

What then is the rationale for the elaborate system of regulation of non-bank financial institutions that exist in many countries? The market failure that is most commonly associated with non-bank financial institutions is imperfect information on the part of investors. It is costly for investors to establish the quality of firms offering financial services and, in the presence of a large number of small investors, there will be free-riding in the collection of information. As a consequence, there will be poor discrimination between low- and high-quality firms and prices charged for financial services will reflect some perceived average quality of financial institutions as a whole. This price may not provide high-quality firms with adequate compensation for the expensive services that they provide and the average quality of financial institutions may therefore decline. In addition, firms may choose to provide service of lower quality than is recognized by consumers. There are, therefore, problems of adverse selection (Akerlof, 1970) and moral hazard.

In the context of financial institutions, poor quality can be associated with negligence, incompetence or dishonesty in the provision of services. Firms may have poor systems for managing client accounts or they may transact with low-quality brokers and dealers. In addition, there may be a high incidence of employee fraud or, still more seriously, the firm may have been set up to defraud clients.

Most financial regulation outside of banks is concerned with investor protection and not the prevention of systemic failure. In this regard, the regulation of non-bank financial institutions has greater affinity to the regulation of the professions than banks. The regulation of accountants, doctors and lawyers is usually discussed in relation to imperfect information (Shaked and Sutton, 1980 and Shapiro, 1986). As a consequence, the form that regulation of non-bank financial institutions takes may be expected to be very different from that of banks.

The approach that different countries take to the regulation of financial services varies appreciably. In the UK, until 1986, the regulation of non-banks was very rudimentary. The principle statute governing securities investments was the Prevention of Fraud (Investments) Act of 1958. With some exceptions, this required dealers in securities to be licensed and to be subject to certain rules regarding the way in which they conducted their business. However, the Act did not address broader questions concerning competence rather than honesty and following the collapse of several investment businesses at the end of the 1970s and the beginning of the 1980s, a comprehensive system of legislation was introduced (the Financial Services Act, 1986). This requires those who wish to establish an investment business to be screened and to be subject to rules regarding their conduct of business, the holding of clients' funds and their financial reserves.

In the US, the Securities and Exchange Commission is responsible for most protection of investors in non-banks. In the case of investment managers, there is little attempt to screen individuals or to require them to hold capital. Instead, most emphasis is placed on the monitoring of firms and the punishment of fraud. Brokers and dealers are required to hold capital but even here the primary concern is with detection and correction of fraud rather than prevention of incompetence.

The regulation of financial services on the Continent of Europe is a product of the close association of the provision of financial services with banks. This is most starkly exemplified by Germany where any institution involved in the managing or handling of securities is classified as a bank even if it is acting in a purely agency capacity. Financial institutions in general are therefore subject to the onerous regulation of banks irrespective of the nature of the services that they provide. This regulation includes capital requirements, rules governing the conduct of business, as well as initial screening of agents.

There is one other important difference in financial services regulation between countries. In the UK financial regulation is a distinctive blend of statutory and self-regulation. The Financial Services Act (FSA) established a supervisory body known as the Securities and Investments Board (SIB) which formulated a set of rules regarding the conduct and operation of investment businesses. However, unlike most regulators, the SIB does not in general regulate businesses itself. Instead, it delegates this function to a group of five Self-Regulating Organizations (SROs) that comprise members from different parts of the investment business. The power of the SROs derives from their ability to sanction and ultimately expel members. The significance of this stems from the fact that, under the FSA, membership of an SRO or direct certification by the SIB is required of all investment businesses.[1] However, unlike other countries, the SROs regulatory rules are not enshrined in statute and the SROs themselves, not some agency of government, are responsible for their enforcement.

The advantage of self-regulation is perceived to be a higher degree of flexibility in the formulation and enforcement of rules than statutory regulation permits. Flexibility has been regarded as an important characteristic of the regulation of an industry in which there has been rapid product innovation. On the other hand, there is concern that self-regulation does not provide adequate investor protection. The SROs may be prone to regulatory capture by their members and may not in any event have had adequate powers conferred upon them.

The appropriate design and implementation of financial regulation is of particular concern to European countries that at present employ very different forms of regulation. The European Commission is currently trying to establish common minimum standards of regulation of financial services. These will involve the imposition of statutory requirements that are sometimes widely divergent from existing regulations in force in member states. For example, current proposals do not require investment businesses that merely provide advice to hold capital. All other firms do: 50,000 ECUs if they do not handle clients' monies, 100,000 ECUs if they do, and 500,000 ECUs if they take positions on their own account. That compares with a minimum absolute capital requirement on investment managers of the UK of £5,000.

This paper is an examination of the regulation of financial services. It is concerned with the appropriate design and implementation of regulation. Section 2 examines the market failures that can arise in the provision of financial services. It reviews the existing literature on imperfect information and the regulation of the professions and examines the role of reputation in limiting abuses associated with imperfect information.

In section 3, a model of the regulation of financial services is presented. This model is used to analyse the design of a regulatory framework for financial services. It contrasts capital requirements and the imposition of penalties as methods of discouraging abuse of investors by investment businesses. In section 4, the implementation of regulation is examined. Statutory legislation is contrasted with the self-regulatory organizations in which a desire on the part of members of the organization to maintain the value of invested capital encourages expulsion of deviant firms and restrictions on entry of new firms.

Section 5 uses the analysis of sections 3 and 4 to evaluate different regulatory systems and recent proposals from the European Commission. In particular, it considers the role of self-regulation in providing investor protection.

Section 6 concludes the chapter.

2   Moral hazard and adverse selection with respect to product quality

The economics literature distinguishes between three classes of goods: 'search goods' whose quality can be ascertained in advance of purchase, 'experience goods' whose quality can only be deterined after purchase and 'credence goods' whose quality may never be established (see Nelson, 1970 and Darby and Karni, 1973). Examples of search goods are consumer durables, such as clothes and furniture; examples of experience goods are such non-durables as wine and tobacco; and examples of credence goods are the quality of advice that a consumer receives regarding the timing of a car repair or a surgical operation. Evaluation of such advice may involve answering counterfactuals of the form of what would have happened if the advice had not been taken.

By their very nature financial services involve investments whose quality cannot be evaluated *ex ante*. At the very least, financial services therefore constitute experience rather than search goods. However, even *ex post* it may not be possible to establish whether a high-quality service was provided. There are two reasons for this. First, it is difficult to evaluate financial performance. Performance measures are sensitive to the benchmark against which they are compared. For example, risk premia on portfolios depend on the chosen asset-pricing model, the securities that are included in benchmark portfolios and the period over which risk is computed. Secondly, investors will typically not be able to disentangle the effects of bad luck on the one hand and incompetence, negligence or dishonesty on the other on portfolio performance. A high return may be earned from a lucky, dishonest firm and a low return from a competent, honest but unlucky firm. Financial services may therefore be best classified as credence goods.

The implication of financial services being experience or credence goods is that investors are susceptible to risks of adverse selection and moral hazard. The dishonest and incompetent can pose as the honest and competent; the negligent cannot be distinguished from the conscientious. As a consequence, as Leland (1979) demonstrates, markets with informational asymmetries supply suboptimal quality levels. The prices that suppliers receive reflect average, not marginal, levels of quality offered in the market. Thus, so long as average quality exceeds marginal, there is an incentive to entry to occur which further depresses the average level of quality supplied.

Leland argues that this justifies regulation that imposes minimum standards. However, if regulation is set by the professions, Shaked and Sutton (1980) demonstrate that they have incentives to impose barriers to the entry of new members. Rents thereby accrue to existing members at the expense of consumers. Allowing for quality choices by the agents, Shapiro (1986) shows that licensing of professionals through the implementation of a minimum level of human capital investment leads to excessive training by providers of low quality. This is to the benefit of consumers seeking high-quality services but to the detriment of those who wish to purchase low-quality services at a low price. By contrast, where certification is used as a method of regulating entry, high-quality sellers undertake excessive training to signal their quality. This raises the price of high-quality services.

In seeking to correct distortions, regulation may therefore curtail competition, limit the range of quality offered to consumers and modify the trade-off between quality and price. Instead of regulation, reliance may be placed on mechanisms which provide information on quality and discourage deceptive supply of low quality. Guarantees will diminish uncertainty consumers face about product quality and reduce returns that firms earn from deceptively producing low quality. But guarantees are only effective if they can be enforced and where there is a risk of bankruptcy their value is limited.

Incentives may be improved by repeat purchases. First, adverse selection may be diminished if high-quality firms are able to distinguish themselves from low-quality firms by initially charging low prices and it is not in the interests of low-quality firms to mimic them (Nelson, 1970). Secondly, moral hazard will be reduced if firms wish to establish reputations for providing high-quality services.

Two mechanisms for establishing reputations have been suggested. Shapiro (1983) describes a model in which high-quality firms identify themselves by initially selling their products below cost. Consumers repeat purchases while quality is maintained and firms continue to provide high quality so long as the value of maintaining reputation exceeds costs saved by cutting quality. This requires a consumer to pay a premium for high-quality products.

In the models of Kreps and Wilson (1982) and Milgrom and Roberts (1982) [KWMR] consumers experiment with different products. They entertain the possibility (however small) that firms have an incentive to supply high quality even in a 'one-shot' game but cease purchasing if deceived about quality. Firms might then choose to supply high quality to avoid being classified as low-quality firms. This strategy is profitable if the value of the reputation of being high-quality exceeds the cost saving associated with deceiving consumers about quality.

Unlike the Shapiro model, the KWMR theory does not rely on firms having an infinite horizon. They still opt to supply high quality in periods preceding the terminal one to take advantage of high-quality demand. In the Shapiro model, since firms cheat in the terminal period, they cheat in the penultimate period and therefore in the one before that; they therefore always cheat unless horizons are infinite.

Reputation therefore plays an important role in rectifying market failures created by asymmetric information. Financial services are no exception in this regard. Yet, there are reasons why reputation may be less effective in financial services than in other industries. Where firms handle clients' monies and assets, the losses that they can impose on investors are large. They can steal principal payments as well as the returns that they are supposed to earn for investors. Thus incentives to cheat are high, and few firms will have the reputation required to make it not seem worth while to cheat.

Reliance on reputation may also create barriers to entry. Reputation takes time to acquire and requires experimentation on the part of investors (Diamond, 1989). Risk-neutral or risk-averse investors whose wealth can be appropriated by dishonest firms are unlikely to engage in experimentation. This suggests that a primary function of the regulator should be to reinforce incentives created by reputation and to diminish barriers to entry that exist in its absence.

In addition, the low prices that high-quality firms charge in the Shapiro model may threaten their viability and encourage fraud.[2] This is similar to the moral hazard and adverse selection problems that high interest rates create in Stiglitz and Weiss's (1981) model on bank lending. Finally, the incentives to cheat may increase as reputations improve. For example it has been said that it was Johnson Matthey's strong reputation as a bank in the UK that allowed its irregular activities to remain undetected for so long.

This last point acts as a reminder that financial services may not only be experience but also credence goods whose quality is unobservable *ex post* as well as *ex ante*. Reputations may therefore be inadequate to sustain good behaviour. Conversely, reputations are vulnerable to incorrect assessments by markets; unless markets can perfectly evaluate quality, firms may suffer from unwarranted loss of reputation. For these reasons, reputation may have to be supplemented by regulation. The subsequent analysis adopts a framework that encompasses monitoring by both regulatory authorities and markets.

In the next two sections, the paper considers the design and implementation of regulations. Beyond screening, a regulator of a financial firm typically has powers to require it to hold capital and to impose penalties (both civil and criminal). The next section considers the appropriate balance between these forms of regulation.

3 Regulatory design

The purpose of this section is to set out a framework for analysing the design of regulation, i.e. the balance between capital requirements, penalties and quality control. The next section deals with the implementation of regulation. It investigates the alternatives of statutory or self-regulation.

We consider a market for financial services in which there are firms of varying quality $x \in (x^-, x^+)$. Quality relates to the ability of personnel, their work–leisure preference and corporate organization. Quality affects the performance of firms as measured by their profits $\pi(x)$ where $\pi' > 0$ and $\pi'' < 0$. However, instead of supplying services honestly, firms can cheat investors and earn $\pi_d > \pi(x)$ for all $x \in (x^-, x^+)$. This higher return is earned entirely at the expense of investors. Firms can earn a return (or a present value of earnings) of V outside the industry.

Firms have capital of an amount C where $0 \le C \le C^+(x)$ and $C'^+ \ge 0$. $C^+(x)$ is the least upper bound on the capital of firms with quality x. It increases with x, reflecting the greater value of high quality firms *ceteris paribus*. There is a uniform density of firms below $C^+(x)$, between x^- and x^+. In this context, capital refers to net worth of firms at market value. It comprises not only the liquid and physical assets which are traditionally included in capital measures but also the goodwill associated with reputation and industry-specific training. However, it excludes assets which cannot be appropriated by regulatory authorities and whose value is not affected by expulsion from the industry. In other words, the definition of capital that is relevant here is the sum of collateral provided by firms and sunk costs.

A regulatory framework is composed of a capital requirement CR and an *ex post* penalty U. The penalty could be a fine or imprisonment. It is presumed in this section that misbehaviour is observed, so that, if firms are caught, they incur the penalty and lose their capital. However, there is a probability $(1 - \alpha)$ $(0 \le \alpha \le 1)$ that honest firms are deemed to have misbehaved. This reflects possible misconceptions on the part of regulators and investors about dishonesty in firms. For example, an announcement by regulators that enquiries are underway into the conduct of firms may in itself adversely affect public perception of their quality. As a consequence, firms' reputation may suffer even when enquiries subsequently fail to uncover evidence of misdemeanours. The problem of public reaction to regulatory conduct is recognized in the area of

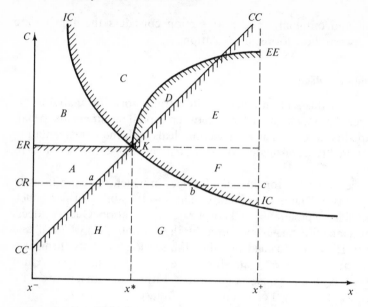

Figure 5.1   The constraints

banking where risk of runs can be exacerbated by the intervention of regulators. That firms in financial services are also worried about public perceptions is suggested by their reluctance to disclose internal enquiries into employee fraud.

The converse problem of failure by the regulator to uncover fraud is not pursued here. It is shown in the appendix that it can be offset by an increase in the penalty U, without altering capital requirements. In other words, a change in probability of detection merely affects the *ex post* penalty and not *ex ante* screening through capital.

In what follows we describe firms' behaviour and the way in which regulation affects the set of active firms and their behaviour. The first condition determines which firms supply honestly. Firms will not deviate provided the following incentive compatibility condition is satisfied:

$$\pi(x) - (1 - \alpha)(U + C) \geq \pi_d - (U + C)$$

i.e.

$$\pi(x) \geq \pi_d + \alpha(U + C) \qquad\qquad IC$$

In figure 5.1, all firms to the right of *IC* supply honestly.

Assuming that they supply honestly (*IC* is satisfied), firms will decide to enter if and only if:

$$\pi(x) - (1 - \alpha)(U + C) \geq V \qquad\qquad EE$$

All firms to the right of *EE* (and *IC*) in figure 5.1 will decide to enter. *EE* assumes that firms that are erroneously deemed to have misbehaved still earn a profit $\pi(x)$.

Next, we introduce the least upper bound on firms' capital ($C^+(x)$):

$$C \leq C^+(x) \qquad\qquad CC$$

This condition delineates the population of firms in the range $[x^-, x^+]$. It is shown as *CC* in figure 5.1.

The last condition relates to the case where the incentive compatibility condition is not satisfied. Firms will then enter provided:

$$\pi_d - (U + C) \geq V \qquad\qquad ER$$

Firms below *ER* in figure 5.1 (and to the left of *IC*) enter and cheat.

These four conditions describe the behaviour of firms for given conditions ($C^+(x)$, V, U, α, $\pi(x)$, π_d). The interplay between the various constraints can be described as follows. The minimum quality (x^*), which is consistent with both *IC* and *EE*, is associated with a level of capital C^*, such that:

$$C^* = \pi_d - U - V \qquad\qquad (I)$$

Accordingly, $x^* = \pi^{-1}[(1 - \alpha)\pi_d + \alpha V]$ \qquad (II)

Since the level of capital associated with firms that are on the margin of entering and deviating (from *ER*) is the same as the level of capital associated with x^*, *ER*, *IC* and *EE* have a unique common intersection (as shown in figure 5.1). This level of capital increases in π_d and falls with V. At the same time, x^* is increasing in π_d and V and decreasing in α (given that since $\pi_d > \pi(x)$, $\pi_d > V$ from *EE*).

The behaviour of firms in figure 5.1 can be summarized as follows. As *CC* has been drawn, there are no firms in the areas, *A*, *B*, *C* and *D*. However, if there were, firms in area *A* would enter and cheat; firms in area *B* would cheat but choose not to enter; firms in area *C* would behave honestly but would not have adequate incentive to enter; and firms in area *D* would like to enter, and would behave. Firms in areas *E* and *F* enter and are honest. Firms in areas *G* and *H* enter and cheat.

A capital requirement condition *CR* is now introduced. This states that:

$$C \geq CR \qquad\qquad CR$$

It is shown as a dashed line in figure 5.1.

The capital requirement prevents some firms in areas *G* and *H* in figure 5.1, which would otherwise cheat, from entering. However, some honest firms in area F are excluded. There is therefore a trade-off between allowing dishonest firms to enter and excluding honest firms. Define the width ac in figure 5.1, corresponding to firms with capital CR, as, the quality width and bc, corresponding to quality levels over which firms do not cheat, as the acceptable width. If equal weight is attributed to cheating and inappropriate exclusion of firms.[3] CR will be set so that the acceptable width corresponding to that level of capital is half the quality width. An increase in the ratio of the acceptable to quality width reflecting either a steeper IC or CC schedule (for a given ER) reduces the optimum level of CR. A reduction in the relation between quality and capital of either the population of firms (a steeper CC schedule) or the acceptable sample of firms (a steeper IC schedule) thus reduces the optimal capital requirement CR, for a given ER.

Furthermore, an upward shift of CC for a given set of IC, EE and ER schedules reduces the ratio of the acceptable to the quality width and thus raises CR at the expense of increased exclusion of honest firms. Conversely, as the penalty U falls, IC and ER shift vertically upwards. From equations (I) and (II), the intersection of IC and ER is also displaced vertically upwards. As a result, the ratio of the acceptable to the quality width falls. CR is therefore increased but by less than the fall in U. The trade-off between the admission of dishonest firms and the exclusion of honest ones is thus assisted by the association of capital resources with firm quality.

If the intersection, K, of EE and IC rises above CC, then minimumn quality x^* has to increase. However, up to that point, avoidance of cheating does not require a sacrifice of low-quality firms, in contrast to the results on regulation discussed previously. For the remainder of this section, it is assumed that the optimum point of intersection falls on CC.[4] In what follows, we consider how the intersection, K, of ER, EE and IC is affected by exogenous parameters.

(i)   A decline in α

A reduction in α shifts EE to the right (to EE') reflecting the lower incentive to enter on account of the higher risk of a random penalty (figure 5.2). IC shifts up (to IC') because of the reduced incentive to good behaviour as the incremental penalty over the random risk of loss diminishes. From equations (I) and (II), this is associated with a horizontal shift of the intersection K to K'.

At the initial position K, the capital constraint on the population of firms is binding. As the intersection between IC and EE is shifted to K', the capital constraint is relaxed. As a result, the trade-off between admitting honest and dishonest firms can be improved by lowering U. This raises IC

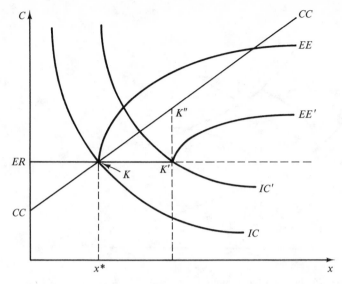

Figure 5.2 The effect of lowering α

and *EE* and, from equations (I) and (II), has the effect of shifting their intersection vertically from K' to K''. *CR* also rises since an upward shift of *IC* reduces the ratio of acceptable to quality width for any level of capital.

(ii) An increase in V
An increase in *V* raises the minimum quality of firms entering the industry (x^* rises, see equation (II) as *EE* shifts to *EE'* in figure 5.3) and from equation (I), $U + C$ falls at the intersection of *IC* and *EE*. However, the capital constraint is not binding and, as before, the trade-off between excluding honest and dishonest firms can be improved by lowering the penalty *U* until K''' is reached. Again, the upward shift in *IC* raises *CR*.

(iii) An increase in π_d
An increase in π_d worsens the incentive compatibility condition (it shifts from *IC* to *IC'*) and elicits a higher penalty at the intersection of *IC* and *EE* (see equation I). As shown the capital constraint is not satisfied at K''. This can be avoided by raising *U*, thereby pushing *IC'* and *EE* downwards and shifting the intersection from K'' to K'''. The *IC* corresponding to K''' still lies above the initial *IC*, so that *CR* rises.

Table 5.1 summarizes the influences on regulatory design. The level of capital requirement in relation to other penalties will be highest where (a)

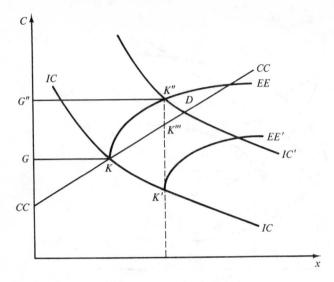

Figure 5.3   The effects of raising $\bar{V}$ and π_d

there is low precision in imposing penalties on firms and (b) the opportunity cost of entering an industry is high. Both capital and other penalties are high where the rewards to cheating are large. As previously noted, capital requirements are also highest where there is a close correspondence of actual and acceptable quality levels with capital.

Table 5.1 also reports the determinants of the minimum quality of honest firms and a measure of the cost imposed on honest firms by the regulatory system. The cost is the wedge between the returns that have to be offered to an honest firm to induce it to enter the industry and the return that it can earn elsewhere. From EE this is equal to $(1 - \alpha)(U + C)$, the expected value of the penalty that is incorrectly imposed on firms. Table 5.1 records that greater imprecision in imposing penalties and greater incentives to cheat raise both the minimum quality of honest firms and the cost imposed on honest firms. A higher opportunity cost of entering the industry raises the minimum acceptable quality of firms (because fewer honest firms want to enter) but reduces the cost of operating the system (because dishonest firms are also discouraged from entering). By allowing capital requirements to be reduced at a lower cost to quality, a weaker relation of quality to capital reduces the cost of regulation, for given x^*.

4   Statutory versus self-regulation

The previous section has noted a trade-off between exclusion of honest firms and inclusion of dishonest firms. Of course, more sophisticated

Table 5.1. *Some determinants of the design of financial regulation*

Parameter	U	C_R	x^*	Cost of regulation
Weaker relation of capital resources to acceptable and actual firm quality	Unchanged	Falls	Unchanged	Falls
Less precision in imposing penalties	Falls	Rises	Rises	Rises
Better opportunities elsewhere	Falls	Rises	Rises	Falls
Greater rewards to cheating	Rises	Rises	Rises	Rises

legislation than that considered above could be enacted that stipulates the class of firms to which minimum capital requirements apply (i.e. $x < x^*$), or imposes more severe penalties (U) on just this group of firms. But legislation can only refer to verifiable parameters (see Hart and Moore, 1989) and many of the determinants of quality (such as organizational structure and conduct of business) are unlikely to be readily observable by third parties. The reason that statutory legislation is limited in this way is that it has to adjudicate between conflicting interests of investors and investment businesses.

On the one hand, it has already been noted that some investment services are credence goods, whose quality cannot be readily established *ex post*. In that case, there is a risk of rogue firms (in area G) escaping punishment. In response, investors may seek the assistance of private auditors in policing investment businesses. On the other hand, as agents of investors, auditors may be over-zealous in their pursuit of misdemeanours. They may fabricate evidence, provoke too high a rate of prosecution or extract side payments from firms wishing to avoid risks of public exposure.

A statutory system of legislation therefore has to strike a balance between the interests of investors and firms. Rules have to be formulated regarding the conduct of both investment businesses and those responsible for their monitoring and application have to be open to judicial enquiry. Since these rules have to be observable by third parties, it is not possible to make them a function of firm quality.

This raises the question of whether there is a self-enforcing mechanism that has the desired effect merely through the pursuit of self-interest. Section 2 described models in which conflicts between *ex ante* and *ex post* can be resolved through a desire to preserve reputations. As an alternative to recourse to intertemporal considerations, cross-section aggregation across firms may assist.

The idea is as follows. Suppose that there is a group of firms, called a club, that comprises N identical honest members. Each member puts up the same capital C and agrees to the following rules. New members will only be admitted if they too subscribe capital C. If they cheat, they forego their capital and are subject to an additional penalty U. As before, there is a probability $(1 - \alpha)$ that honest firms will be penalized (this risk being uncorrelated across firms).

Investors can call upon the capital of other members of the club to supplement a shortfall in the capital of any deviant member or a failure of the club to impose a full penalty U.[5] Other members' capital thus provides coinsurance for the risk that inadequate capital is required of new members or insufficient penalties are imposed on existing members.[6]

Does the club enforce its rules? Consider a two-period model where firms apply for membership in the first period and in the second period either provide services honestly or cheat. If they cheat, then clubs may impose penalties. Consider first the second period and suppose an existing member cheats. By imposing a penalty the club collectively loses $U + C$. In contrast, if it fails to penalize, it loses up to αNC (granted that by assumption it anyway imposes a capital cost of expected value $(1 - \alpha)C$ on honest firms). Thus it will respond to the incidence of cheating by imposing the appropriate penalty if (and only if):

$$U + C \le \alpha NC \qquad\qquad CI$$

Now consider the first period and suppose a deviant firm has applied for membership. Assuming CI and that there is no discounting, it is willing to pay up to $\pi_d - V - (U + C)$ for the privilege of entry to the club. If U and C are set at such a level that ER is not satisfied, then entry is discouraged. However, if the club fails to impose the full capital requirement entry may occur. As before the club has to make good any shortfall up to αNC but can be bribed unless:

$$\pi_d - V \le \alpha NC \qquad\qquad CR$$

From the ER condition, CR implies that there is an upper bound to the incentives to cheat that the club can credibly correct through selection of members. Furthermore, from equation (I), conditions IC and EE, and the fact that $\pi'(x) > 0$, if CR is satisfied then CI is satisfied over the relevant range of IC. In figure 5.1, if $ER \le \alpha NC$ then IC will be implemented as well as entry of dishonest firms refused.

The strength of self-regulation comes from the fact that there is no requirement that *IC* or *ER* conditions be verifiable by third parties. However, self-regulation is only effective for a restricted class of problems. It is more effective the greater the capital that members have invested in the club and which is at risk from deviant behaviour. Thus large clubs containing firms of high repute will be able to police more serious crimes than small groups of poorly established firms. The effectiveness of clubs is also undermined by the risk that invested capital is involuntarily extinguished (low values of α).[7]

No attention has been given here to the dynamics of club formation or the equilibria that will prevail if free entry of clubs is permitted. For example, the club's criteria for selecting honest firms will only coincide with *EE* if the earnings of existing members are unaffected by a new entrant, i.e. the demand for the club's services is elastic. Otherwise, the club will impose unduly demanding requirements on new entrants to ensure that sufficiently large rents can be extracted to compensate for more intense competition. The effect is similar to the club imposing a (shadow) increase in *V* in the *EE* condition; in terms of figure 5.3, the club wishes to raise quality to the equivalent of *K'* and does this by increasing capital requirements from *G* to *G''*, thereby excluding (honest) firms in the area *KK' K''*.

Of course, competition between clubs may help to avoid the imposition of unwarranted barriers to entry. However, by reducing returns to honest members of a club, intensified competition exacerbates risks of cheating (shifts *IC* out) and by reducing invested capital (*C*) diminishes incentives on clubs to police effectively. Furthermore, the formation of clubs is impeded by problems in the initial identification of the quality of firms (recall that above it was simply assumed that the *N* initial members were honest). In practice, therefore, the development of clubs raises similar problems to reputation building by firms and creates similar barriers to the entry of new clubs.[8]

5   Financial regulation in practice

Considerable care is required in attempting to draw policy conclusions from a simple model. However, the above analysis does suggest some relevant considerations.

First, both the appropriate design and form of regulation are sensitive to the structure of the industry. The financial sector undertakes a wide range of activities. Even leaving aside the distinction between banking and non-banking to which reference was made in the introduction, investment businesses differ in form, function and the risks that they pose to investors. It is thus unlikely that the same type of regulation will be appropriate for all investment businesses.

In particular, the parameters discussed in section 3 differ markedly between firms. Firms that merely provide advice to clients on how to invest their portfolios without directly managing them pose comparatively few risks to investors. In comparison, firms that make markets in stocks handle large amounts of money and securities. Their risks of default are significantly diminished by holding capital. Thus investment advisers have relatively low and market-makers high values of π_d. From table 5.1, market-makers should therefore be subject to more onerous capital requirements than investment advisers. Instead, greater reliance should be placed on the imposition of other penalties (U) on investment advisers. This is precisely the design of both EEC and US requirements: brokers and dealers are required to hold quite substantial amounts of capital; investment advisers are not.

Secondly, it may be possible to structure firms in such a way as to facilitate the imposition of certain regulatory systems. Investment managers that act on a discretionary basis can put investors' assets at risk. However, if the assets and monies of clients are separated from those of the firm and managed by a custodian then the risk of this occurring is substantially diminished. Since there is a poor relation between the quality of investment managers and the capital at their disposal ($C'^{+}(x)$ is high) (Franks and Mayer, 1989, report cases of where capital has been accumulated *at the expense of* clients), according to table 5.1, investment managers should not be required to hold much capital. Furthermore, a reduction in risks of fraud diminishes capital requirements. If investment managers were reuqired to separate clients' funds from their own then capital requirements on investment managers in general could be eliminated. That again is closer to the US system of regulation and is reflected in the European Commission's proposed capital rules.

Turning to the form of regulation, the prevous section concluded that self-regulation will be feasible where potential investor losses are modest and where clubs containing several firms with large amounts of invested capital can be formed. It is least suited to investor protection where there is a serious risk of fraud and where there are few well-established firms. In the case of the UK, self-regulation is therefore least suited to the case of the Financial Intermediaries, Managers and Brokers Regulatory Association (FIMBRA) which draws its membership from independent investment brokers, managers and advisers. It is much better suited to the membership of the Investment Management Regulatory Organization (IMRO) which mainly comprises investment managers that are part of larger companies. Even in the case of IMRO, self-regulation would be less open to abuse if the possibility of client losses could be diminished by separating client funds and the positions that firms take on their own accounts.

Where investors are vulnerable to certain types of abuse then it may be possible to combine self- and statutory regulation. For example, statutory legislation and public policing of fraud and theft may be combined with self-regulation of negligence and incompetence. To a certain extent this is already commonplace where personal indemnity insurance is used to provide protection against negligence. There would appear to be considerable scope for clubs to extend this function.

Furthermore, a greater degree of competition between clubs could be entertained if the risk of self-regulatory organizations being captured by their members was diminished by public policing of fraud. At one extreme, free entry of clubs could be permitted provided that investors were aware of the quality of service being offered by members of a club (see Kay and Vickers, 1988). Competition between clubs would not then be very different from competition between firms.

Unfettered competition is not appropriate where externalities exist in the form of risks of contagious failure. Harmonization of regulation is therefore still required for banks and possibly brokers and dealers whose financial failure can have widespread consequences for the operation of a financial system (see Mayer, 1989a, b). Elsewhere, attempts by the European Commission to establish common minimum levels of protection over and above the prevention of fraud are probably misguided. If investors are aware of the quality of service being offered by members of a club and, if there is no risk of clubs defaulting on their obligation, countries or groups of firms within countries should be free to choose the quality of service that they supply.

A hierarchical system of regulation therefore emerges with international organizations being responsible for the coordination of regulation of systemic risks, national regulators being concerned with the prevention of fraud and self-regulatory organizations correcting negligence and incompetence. While this method of implementation is similar to that in the UK, the appropriate design is closer to that of the US.

6   Conclusions

This paper has investigated the design and implementation of financial regulation. It has noted that the rationale for the regulation of financial services is different from that of banks. Instead of systemic risks, market failures created by asymmetric information between investors and firms lie at the heart of concerns about financial services. Investors are unable to distinguish honest from dishonest, competent from incompetent and negligent from conscientious firms.

Reputation provides some correction for imperfect information. But a distinctive feature of financial services is the large penalty that misconduct by investment businesses can impose on investors. That risk creates a significant barrier to the entry of new firms.

Regulation of financial services is therefore in large part concerned with reducing barriers to entry. It does this by extending the set of penalties that can be imposed on firms. Two classes of incentives were considered: capital requirements and direct penalties. The former has an advantage over the latter where there is a relation between the capital available to a firm and its quality.

However, capital requirements that are unable to distinguish between firms' quality exclude some honest firms. As a consequence, there is a trade-off: capital requirements will be more onerous where there is a close relation between capital and quality and where there is less precision in imposing penalties.

The trade-off reflects the limitations of statutory legislation. In resolving disputes between investors and firms, legislation is restricted to activities and outcomes that are verifiable by third parties. Quality of individuals and organizations may not fall into this category.

Instead, control may be best self-administered. Self-regulatory organizations can be granted powers to impose capital requirements and penalize deviant firms, if only by expulsion from an industry. The question that self-administration raises is whether clubs have adequate incentives to enforce capital requirement rules and impose penalties. The paper suggests that such incentives do exist where firms have sufficient capital at stake, in the form, for example, of industry-specific assets and where benefits from cheating are limited.

The implications of this paper for policy are that, (i) forms of regulation should differ between classes of investment services (e.g. investment management and broking), (ii) capital requirements should be limited in investment management where there is a poor relation between capital and quality, (iii) possible abuses in investment management should be reduced through the separation of clients' accounts to allow low capital requirements to be imposed, (iv) there is more opportunity for self-regulation by well established firms (such as members of IMRO rather than FIMBRA in the UK) and (v) in the absence of systemic risks, there is little justification for the harmonization of regulatory rules on clubs whose quality can be identified. Competition between clubs may be an important way of avoiding monopoly abuse.

APPENDIX

The purpose of this appendix is to examine the effect of a failure to detect misbehaviour. Let β denote the probability that a dishonest firm is caught and assume that no honest firm is wrongly penalized ($\alpha = 1$).

The four conditions can then be rewritten as:

$$\pi(x) \geq \pi_d - \beta(U + C) \qquad\qquad IC$$

$$\pi(x) \geq V \qquad\qquad EE$$

$$C \leq C^+(x) \qquad\qquad CC$$

$$\pi_d - \beta(U + C) \geq V \qquad\qquad ER$$

Since EE is independent of β, there is a unique value at (x, C) such that EE and CC are binding. Thus for IC and ER to intersect EE and CC at the same point $\beta(U + C)$ must be constant. With C fixed:

$$(\beta/U)dU/d\beta = (- U + C^+(c))/U$$

so that for $C^+ > 0$, a rise in β is offset by a more than proportional fall in U.

NOTES

This paper draws on work that Colin Mayer has done with Julian Franks in the past. As part of that work numerous discussions have been had with financial institutions and regulators in various countries. We are grateful to Tony Courakis, Julian Franks and John Vickers and participants at the CEPR/IMI Conference on European Financial Integration.

This paper is part of the Centre for Economic Policy Research 'International Study of the Financing of Industry'. The CEPR study is being financed by the Anglo-German Foundation, the Bank of England, the Commission of the European Communities, the Economic and Social Research Council, the Esmée Fairbairn Charitable Trust, the Japan Foundation and the Nuffield Foundation. The second author is grateful to INSEAD for financial support under grant No. 2172R.

1 Members of certain professional organizations (such as accountants) and firms authorized under the Insurance Companies or Friendly Societies Acts are exempted.

2 See Franks and Mayer (1989) for evidence that fraud has often been a response to financial crises.

3 The relative weighting of cheating and excessive exclusion depends on (a) the effects of cheating on investment, (b) the distributional consequences of cheating and (c) the levels of competition. Little insight is provided by explicit modelling of the social welfare function.

4 If there is an area D between CC and EC where the intersection of EE and IC meets CC, then the optimal value of U may exceed that associated with this point.

5 To provide clubs with appropriate incentives to discourage cheating, the cost of the club of drawing on other members' capital has to be fractionally in excess of amounts raised. The cost of administering the scheme may account for this.

6 In general, only partial insurance is provided. As shown below, to deter entry of dishonest firms the capital that the club guarantees has to be merely in excess of $\pi_d - V$. However, if all of a dishonest firm's profits are earned at the expense of investors, then full compensation requires the payment of π_d.

7 Essentially a shortfall of α below unity introduces discounting of future returns even in the absence of an explicit discount factor.

8 There are further questions associated with relaxing the assumption of homogeneous members of a club. What happens when the quality of firms can vary and clubs can initially contain both well-established and unknown firms?

REFERENCES

Aghion, P., P. Bolton and M. Dewatripont (1988) 'Interbank lending and contagious bank runs', mimeo, Delta, Paris.

Akerlof, G. (1970) 'The market for "lemons": qualitative uncertainty and the market mechanism', *Quarterly Journal of Economics* **84**, 488–500.

Darby, M. and E. Karni (1973) 'Free competition and the optimal amount of fraud', *Journal of Law and Economics* **16**, 67–88.

Diamond, D. (1989) 'Reputation acquisition in debt markets', *The Journal of Political Economy* **97**, 828–62.

Diamond, P. and D. Dybvig (1983) 'Bank runs, deposit insurance and liquidity', *Journal of Political Economy* **91**, 401–19.

Franks, J. and C. Mayer (1989) *Risk, regulation and investor protection: the case of investment management*, Oxford: Oxford University Press.

Hart, O. and J. Moore (1989) 'Incomplete Contracts and Renegotiation', *Econometrica* **56**, 755–86.

Kay, J. and J. Vickers (1988) 'Regulatory reform in Britain', *Economic Policy* **3** (7), 285–351.

Kreps, D. and R. Wilson (1982) 'Reputation and imperfect information', *Journal of Economic Theory* **27**, 253–79.

Leland, H. (1979) 'Quacks, lemons and licensing: a theory of minimum quality standards', *Journal of Political Economy* **87**, 1328–46.

Mayer, C. (1989a) 'The appropriate level of regulation in Europe: local, national, or community-wide? A roundtable discussion. The case of financial services', *Economic Policy* **4** (9), 473–6.

(1989b) 'The regulation of financial services; lessons from the UK for 1992', in J. Dermine (ed.), *European banking after 1992*, Oxford: Blackwell.

Milgrom, P. and J. Roberts (1982) 'Predation, reputation and entry deterrence', *Journal of Economic Theory* **27**, 280–312.

Nelson, P. (1970) 'Information and consumer behavior', *Journal of Political Economy* **78**, 311–29.

Shaked, A. and J. Sutton (1980) 'The self-regulating profession', *Review of Economic Studies* **48**, 217–34.

Shapiro, C. (1983) 'Premiums for high quality products as rents to reputation', *Quarterly Journal of Economics* **98**, 659–80.

(1986) 'Investment, moral hazard and occupational licensing', *Review of Economic Studies* **53**, 843–62.

Stiglitz, J. and A. Weiss (1981) 'Credit rationing in markets with imperfect information', *American Economic Review* **71**, 393–410.

Discussion

JOHN VICKERS

There are two market failure rationales for investor protection regulation: the negative externalities of systemic failure (e.g. bank runs) and the fact that many buyers are much less well informed than sellers about the quality of the services that they are buying. This asymmetric information problem has been recognized in a number of contexts, at least since the classic 'lemons' article by Akerlof (1970), and it is the focus adopted by Mayer and Neven in their analysis of European financial markets. They note that the problem for investors can be particularly acute, because it may be impossible to judge 'quality' – the honesty and skill of advice, dealing, fund management, etc. – even *after* purchse. Such services are known as 'credence' goods; other examples are professional services.

The asymmetric information perspective taken by Mayer and Neven is in my view very apt and much needed. Their analysis also leads them to conclusions that I support. My comments are in two parts – first, a few questions about the model, and second, some further discussion of the incentives of self-regulatory organizations to detect and expose wrongdoing.

A somewhat curious feature of the model in the text is that dishonest firms are caught with probability 1 (but will nevertheless cheat unless the fine plus their capital foregone outweighs the immediate gain) and that honest firms are deemed to have misbehaved with probability $1 - \alpha$ $(0 < \alpha < 1)$. Higher capital requirements drive away both types of firms, but improve the trade-off between honest and dishonest firms because capital and quality are associated. A combination of lower fine and higher capital requirement can therefore have merit. However, I find at least as plausible the different assumption in the brief appendix: that no firm is wrongly penalized and that a dishonest firm is caught with probability β $(0 < \beta < 1)$. Higher fines are then the straightforward answer, though they could be limited by bankruptcy. They have no cost in terms of driving away honest firms but they deter cheating. The analysis of clubs that is offered, which builds on the observation that self-regulators are better informed, also hinges on the assumption in the main model (the 'α case'). I suspect that the results here would also vary significantly in the 'β case' of the appendix. The general lesson seems to be that the information structure can make quite a difference to the implications for policy. An overarching framework, in which both type 1 and type 2 errors could occur, might be worth examining. The model is not designed to address endogenous investment decisions, or the effects of policy intervention on competition and prices, and there is no explicit welfare framework. While these elements would complicate matters, they are necessary to trace through all the influences that might be at work. Mayer and Neven offer a suggestive partial approach, but there is clearly scope for much more work to be done on the question at hand.

Now let me turn to a question about statutory versus self-regulation that Mayer and Neven do not develop. How much incentive does a self-regulatory organization have to detect and expose wrongdoing by its members? The following framework could apply to an SRO whose members are financial firms, or to a firm whose members are its employees. (Indeed a firm can be viewed as a type of SRO, though of course there are differences, for example in respect of how much competition is faced.) Assume that the profit or payoff of the SRO depends on the reputation it has for honesty, skill, etc. Suppose that the SRO can invest effort in detecting wrongdoing (fraud, say) by its members. Detected fraud can be punished in two ways – privately ('behind closed doors') or by public exposure. To make the point as simply as possible, assume that fraud is effectively penalized, and hence deterred, only if there is public exposure.

Exposure will improve the SRO's reputation insofar as it is a positive signal about the SRO's level of vigilance, and perhaps because it means that the average quality of remaining members is high – the 'bad apple' (lemon?) having gone. On the other hand, exposure might be a negative signal about the general quality of members in the first place, and could have *negative* implications about the level of vigilance by the SRO. The reason for this last effect derives from members' decisions whether to engage in fraud. Members are likely to have better information than outsiders about the level of SRO vigilance, i.e. the chance of getting caught and exposed. Exposure of a fraudulent member is, among other things, a sign that the member thought that vigilance was low enough for there to be a reasonable chance of getting away with it. To an extent, therefore, it is a bad signal about SRO vigilance.

It would be interesting to build a model that was able to capture all these effects (and more). A version that emphasizes the last effect mentioned runs as follows. Suppose that all members are the same – they will engage in some fraud if the chance of being exposed is low enough. There are two types of SRO, which insiders can, but outsiders cannot distinguish between. Honest SROs are maximally vigilant always. No member of such an SRO would find it worthwhile to engage in fraud. The other type – the optimizing SRO – will expose fraud if and only if that improves its reputation. Suppose that a fraud comes to light in such an SRO. Would it be exposed (given the framework at hand)? No, because exposure would be a sure sign that the SRO was not the honest type. Exposure could only worsen the SRO's reputation. But if an optimizing SRO would not expose fraud, members of such an SRO will be correspondingly undeterred from engaging in it. This is rather an extreme set-up, but it shows that concern about the incentives of SROs to expose fraud might have coherent underpinnings.

A more general model would have different member types, (Nash) equilibrium fraud and vigilance choices, Bayesian updating of beliefs by consumers, and so on. It could also be extended to the case of 'parallel regulation', i.e. the possibility of statutory and self-regulation in tandem. Although the statutory regulators might be less well informed than the SRO, they might have better incentives to expose fraud. In particular, the competition in regulation that they provide could considerably enhance the incentives of the SRO itself. These last remarks are somewhat speculative, but they suggest a perspective, complementary to that given by Mayer and Neven, which could be worth exploring.

6 Corporate mergers in international economic integration

RICHARD E. CAVES

This paper addresses the corporate mergers and reorganizations likely to be involved in the further integration of the European Community identified as 'Europe in 1992'. Speculation on the future is as cheap as it is unreliable. However, the past contains lessons about mergers and international economic integration clearly relevant to the European Community's prospects. The process of international economic integration has been proceeding slowly but steadily throughout the industrial world since the Second World War, as falling relative costs of international transportation, travel and communication have enlarged the internationally traded proportions of tradable-goods outputs and promoted multinational enterprises and transnational corporate alliances and contracts. These trends have been accompanied by changes in the organization of international markets through the expansion of intraindustry and intracorporate trade. They may also be associated with the increase in the 1980s of transnational mergers and acquisitions within international industries. The interpretation of these mergers is the focus of this paper. If the recent wave of international horizontal mergers can be associated with aspects of international economic integration, we can hope to predict merger activity associated with closer integration in the European Community and anticipate any problems for public policy that integration may entail.

The economic analysis of horizontal mergers is in an unsettled state, and one goal of this paper is to provide an untraditional explanation. Two classic explanations exist. Mergers between direct rivals can give rise to monopoly rents even if entry is not blockaded. Recent research has, however, emphasized the limitation on capture of this gain because the consolidating firms must contract their outputs.[1] Attainment of scale economies is the other classic goal for mergers. Why should firms exist that have failed to exploit economies otherwise but can do so by means of horizontal mergers? Suppose that an increase occurs exogenously in the

136

scale economies in some stage of an industry's production/distribution process. Subject to the constraint of sunk costs, a merger can increase the scale of this activity in the combined firm whilst leaving unaltered other activities whose efficient scales are unchanged.

This paper conjectures that these standard models may capture little of the forces promoting international horizontal mergers. We provide an alternative strategic interpretation and compare it to a version of the efficient-scale hypothesis related to foreign direct investment. Data on recent international horizontal mergers involving US enterprises support a limited test of these two models and lead to conclusions about the prospects of transnational corporate integration in Europe.

1   Complex firms, heterogeneous market opportunities and corporate mergers

Reports of international horizontal mergers in the business press leave two sharp impressions: they are numerous, and clusters occur within short periods of time in industries such as pharmaceuticals, processed food products, book and magazine publishing and domestic appliances.[2] Leading firms in these industries offer diverse lines of product: they are only moderately concentrated at the global level, yet the extension of their activities through international mergers seems to involve parallel and imitative strategies.

These merger waves may have a non-strategic explanation: some change in cost or demand conditions reveals to all competitors new payoffs to deploying configurations of assets attainable through international mergers. A more subtle, strategic explanation, however, competes with this simple hypothesis based on Nash behaviour. The strategic hypothesis rests on distinctive views of both firms' organization and their profit opportunities. The elements of the analysis are not new but their assembly may be. To sketch the argument, we assume a world market with sellers highly concentrated at the national level and substantial international trade. The output is not homogeneous and may involve diverse lines of products further differentiated between national markets. The firms that serve this market are large, complex coalitions of inputs including not just physical assets but also assorted skills or technologies that adhere in teams of specialized employees attached to the firm by informal long-run contracts. Conditions facing the industry are not static. Nature periodically reveals new transaction opportunities or configurations. Each has its own technology of execution, so the firm that would grasp an opportunity must be ready to deploy the right set of assets. The internationalization of markets involves a changed distribution of opportunities from which Nature draws, tilting towards those grasped only by means of the multinational deployment of specific assets. International mergers bring enlarged stocks of such assets under unified entrepreneurial control. International economic integration (or its anticipation) then can lead to international mergers, undertaken either to gain access to options of seizing new opportunities or to avert or limit the diversion of profits when rivals seize such opportunities. We examine these components of the analysis in sequence.

1.1   The firm as a complex organization

The model of the firm used here seems to originate with Penrose (1959) and has seen active service to explain corporate diversification (for example, Montgomery and Hariharan, forthcoming).[3] Its main elements are:

(1) The inputs utilized by the firm (needed to produce its output) consist of a set of heterogeneous specialized assets. These include physical capital but also, and more importantly, skills and technologies that are shared among teams of employees. These employees are organized into functional departments of the firm, and each department's members share as a team a repertory of response capabilities to various problems or tasks. They also share bodies of intangible knowledge that depend for their effective use on team-possessed know-how and capabilities of adaptation, even if subject to legal property rights (patents).

(2) These heterogeneous assets are attached to the firm by contracts of varying but substantial formality and duration. The firm can enlarge or shrink its stock of these assets but always subject to adjustment costs. The adjustment costs embrace not only the direct transaction cost of recruiting or laying off such assets but also the organizational cost of integrating new ones into the firm or reorganizing those that remain when some are dropped.[4] These assets are discrete and lumpy. Those that are proprietary intangibles by definition incur zero marginal costs when put to additional uses. In general, each asset's current cost entails a fixed component and a marginal cost well below the average cost of its services up to some capacity constraint.

This characterization of the firm has many corollaries. It implies that the ongoing firm always operates in a short run (that is, with some fixed factors). The actions that it can undertake within any given time period are constrained by the sufficiency and competence of the stock of assets in hand to meet the action's input requirements.

1.2 Ambient market structure

The input coalition for a pure single-market firm follows directly from the production function for its output.[5] Traits of actual markets, however, mandate important properties for the organization of inputs not evident in a static production function. These traits include unpredictability concerning the timing and intensity of the use of inputs. Specifically, assume:

(1) The industry serves a market that is fissured to some degree into niches or segments by distinctions of product attributes, quality levels, or geography. The industry's product varieties are assumed generally good substitutes in production and/or use within whatever niches and segments may exist (pharmaceuticals or electric household appliances provide examples).

(2) Nature periodically injects disturbances by revealing (as common knowledge) new configurations of product attributes (in the broadest sense, including distribution, information for customers, auxiliary services, etc.) that can be profitably supplied by a firm possessing the right set of specific assets. These disturbances stem from changes in tastes, changes in technologies or pure innovations (so long as the innovations are non-proprietary and inappropriable). The 'rightness' of the asset bundle is a matter of degree; the point is that firms with suboptimal qualifications can expect lower rates of return. These opportunities may either be temporary or entail sustaining first-mover advantages.

(3) When a new opportunity arises and is seized by one competitor, profits are reduced for rival firms in affected segments of the industry's product space.[6] The assumption of adverse effects on rivals' profits makes the firm's inventory of specific assets significant for competition. These assets are strategic complements and carry option values, so that their revenue productivity to the firm embraces not only cash flows generated by their current uses but also the possibility of seizing opportunities yet to be revealed.[7] The significance of these options for rivals' reactions to mergers, underlined by the third assumption, will be considered below. Overall the assumptions imply that competition in the industry occurs not only as price-quantity rivalry among producers of close substitutes but also rivalry to pre-empt emerging niches or opportunities.

These assumptions about the firm's organization and the market's technology and demand have mutually consistent implications for the conventional elements of the industry's market structure. The lumpiness of the specialized assets creates scale economies for the firm and economies of scope among product varieties and/or the geographic segments in the market. Such economies of scale and scope, driven by common-multiple problems with the firm's lumpy specialized assets, give rise to a cogent if non-standard scale-economy barrier to entry. Vernon (1970) characterized this barrier in a different way in terms of the hazard of failure in assembling the necessary complex coalition of inputs, and Lippman and Rumelt (1982) modelled the implied industry structure in which firms with successful coalitions obtain rents, although the potential entrant expects only a normal rate of return after allowing for the chance of failure.

Because the number of incumbents depends mainly on entry barriers and the size of the market, the presence of few firms in such a market is a deduction rather than an assumption. The assumption that products are differentiated and the product-line complex is consistent (given any economies of scope) with the assumed complexity of the firm's coalition of specific assets. Product differentiation rests empirically on either the number and range of the attributes bundled into the product or the buyer's cost of acquiring relevant information to guide selection of the product; either foundation makes the seller employ a set of diverse specialized assets to install the attributes or transmit the producer-supplied component of the buyer's information.

1.3   *Changes in opportunites and horizontal mergers*

Horizontal mergers and their strategic significance can now be examined in this context of a mutually consistent structure of market and incumbent firms. A horizontal merger enlarges the bundle of specific assets in the hands of a single management. The assumed structures of firm and industry imply that firms may be direct market rivals but nonetheless possess different bundles of specific assets and offer sets of products (attributes) that do not overlap completely.[8] When two firms in such a market combine, the successor holds a more diverse stock of specific assets than did either partner. Other things being equal, the combined firm can seize more of Nature's opportunities.

Not only does the merging firm gain (no doubt at some cost) a set of option values from its merger, but also it enjoys an enhanced capacity to reply when its profits suffer from the seizure of an opportunity by its rival. When a rival seizes a newly emergent opportunity, will the firm's best response be to do nothing, to retreat or to make some countermove? We shall call a positive response 'imitation', although the best-reply deployment of its specific assets need by no means be a me-too version of the rival's action. Theory does not establish the predominance of any type of response, but there clearly exist broad sets of circumstances in which imitation beats the alternatives.[9] Best-reply imitative responses, like

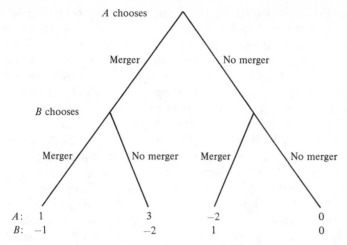

Figure 6.1 Consequences of merger choices by asymmetrically placed rival firms after Nature reveals a new opportunity

initial moves to seize opportunities, are reasonably assumed to require the deployment of complex bundles of specific assets. A merger that expands the firm's inventory of specific assets also enlarges its repertory of responses. Therefore mergers may supply valuable options to defend as well as to innovate.[10]

Consider these relations a bit more formally in light of the game structure shown in figure 6.1, which focusses on the payouts obtained by rivals after Nature reveals an opportunity. Decisions to merge are made before Nature acts, but they anticipate Nature's action. Think of these payouts as the players' expectations based on their knowledge of the probability distribution from which Nature's moves are drawn; the payouts include any non-strategic consequences of the mergers for the firms' net cash flows. The rivals are assumed to be asymmetrically positioned to undertake a merger, reasonable if international mergers may be regarded as strategic innovations: A has the greater gain and also the first choice. A gains from the merger, whether or not B imitates, and also wards off the adverse effect of leaving open the opportunity for B. B chooses to imitate, although (in the numerical illustration shown) B is worse off than if Nature's opportunity never provided a merger inducement, and indeed industry profits are not enhanced.[11]

The analysis thus explains why an international merger by one market competitor can provoke imitative mergers by competitors. It does not explain why the acquisition of international assets is valuable for capturing strategic opportunities, which remains an assumption. Various corollaries follow. The expanded set of options for the combined firm makes the acquirer's reservation price exceed that of the independent target firm's shareholders and explains an acquisition premium.[12] If the same target firm were the preferred international merger partner of both A and B, the assumed asymmetry of the acquirers' positions would still leave A with a potential surplus after meeting B's best offer for the target. The mechanism does not assume that mergers yield any monopolistic gains and indeed is inconsistent with them in presuming that A's acquisition reduces B's expected profits.[13] On the other hand, it supplies no presumption that horizontal mergers are efficient. The imitative merger in figure 6.1 creates benefits only because it curbs profit-shifting. The social cost due to horizontal mergers may stem from rent-seeking rather than monopoly. At the same time mergers that appear mindlessly imitative could be privately rational (if not socially optimal), and purchases of assets that yield no direct profits to the acquirer could pay for themselves in options to be exercised in strategic interactions.

The literature on foreign investment in fact contains a substantial forerunner of the strategic model just outlined – Knickerbocker's (1973) analysis of the timing of foreign-investment decisions by US multinational enterprises. He observed that their moves seemed to cluster, with several firms based in the same US industry establishing subsidiaries in a given nation abroad within a short period of time. As with horizontal mergers, a cluster could occur simply because some exogenous shift raised the payoff to foreign investment for all competitors. Knickerbocker established, however, that new investments clustered more in industries with certain traits: they were not yet mature oligopolies; their firms did not already have extensive networks of foreign subsidiaries; and concentration was high enough in the US market to induce the rivals to maintain parity in their oligopolistic interactions. Knickerbocker posited that any one oligopolist expects its rival's foreign investment to yield some discovery or advantage that would not only shift profits to the rival in the foreign market but could also favour the rival back in the shared US domestic market (and perhaps other shared markets).[14]

2   Non-strategic foreign investment

The strategic explanation for international horizontal mergers relies on a rather specific industrial context. Before testing the model's explanatory power we look for competing explanations. The fact that international mergers are vehicles for foreign direct investment provides a simple non-strategic explanation why they occur. An international merger is one way (along with new plant construction and joint venture) for a firm to implement its decision to initiate or extend its multinational activities. Multinational companies arise in response to structural forces that cause production activities in an industry to be dispersed internationally whilst supplying advantages based on transaction costs for common ownership of these far-flung facilities. If these structural factors explain the level of multinational corporate development, their changes (or the general growth of markets, given their presence) induce increases in transnational linkages among business units and thus in the incidence of international mergers. We now consider more closely some components of this non-strategic interpretation.

2.1 Foreign investment and international mergers

Over the past half-century international mergers have grown greatly in importance (relative to new-plant investments) as the vehicle by which foreign-investment decisions are implemented (Curhan, Davidson and Suri, 1977, p. 21), and in the 1980s they came to assume a dominant role. The cause of this shift is unknown, although the choice between acquisitions and new assets nowadays rests on profit-related considerations (Caves and Mehra, 1986). Not all foreign investments bear a horizontal relation to the principal activity of the investor, of course: vertical and (increasingly) diversified transactions are also involved (Hisey and Caves, 1985). Although mergers serve to implement diversifying more than horizontal foreign investments, they are common for all types.

2.2 Foreign investment and trade liberalization

If expansion of the equilibrium stock of foreign investment gives rise to international horizontal mergers, and such mergers accompany increased international economic integration, we need to confirm the implied positive association between expanding foreign investment and increased integration. The evidence is mixed but quite interesting. The standard market-equilibrium story holds that the relation between foreign investment and economic integration is negative, not positive, because foreign investment substitutes for exports as the least-cost way to supply an overseas market. Tariff increases promote foreign investment, and so trade liberalization should reduce it (Horst, 1971).

Nonetheless, the empirical evidence has repeatedly shown the growth of exports and foreign investment to be complementary.[15] Complementarity is consistent with the conditions assumed in the strategic model of international mergers. It has been attributed to a dynamic process by which exporting activities reveal or develop bases for profitable foreign investments, or a foreign subsidiary supplies a marketing arm for exported components of the firm's product line not produced by the subsidiary. The pattern is consistent with the assumptions that markets are continually exposed to new states of nature, and that a firm's ability to grasp opportunities depends on its existing configuration of activities.[16]

2.3   Foreign investment and intraindustry trade

Foreign investment and exports emanating from a given country and sector might be complementary. Whether the multilateral liberalization and expansion of trade is associated with the multilateral expansion of foreign investment is a question that requires bringing intraindustry trade into the picture. The evidence (which will not be reviewed here) seems supportive. At least in sectors congenial to intracorporate trade, the partial-equilibrium complementarity of trade and exports within a sector does seem to extend to and be linked with complementarity of intra-industry trade and intraindustry foreign investment for the set of trading nations.[17]

The theory and evidence on foreign direct investment thus supply a coherent non-strategic explanation for international horizontal mergers. Mergers occur when and where the equilibrium stock of multinational-enterprise capital is increasing. They should appear only in those industries whose structures support multinational forms of corporate organization. In such industries their frequency should be related to changes in the determinants of the equilibrium prevalence of multinational companies.

3   Empirical patterns: US international mergers, 1978–88

The strategic and non-strategic models of international mergers can be tested in various ways. The strategic model is best tested on selected international industries to determine whether the occurrence of firm i's merger is related to the mergers recently completed by its rivals, with the indicators of the direct profitability of i's merger controlled. Another approach would be to ascertain whether rival firms making international acquisitions about the same time are more similar than randomly drawn competitors in the sets of assets they possess and the market segments they occupy.

An ideal test of the non-strategic version would involve fitting a model of the structural determinants of the prevalence of foreign direct investment (across industries and/or countries) at some point in time, observing the changes in those structural determinants over a subsequent interval of time, and testing for correspondence between the predicted changes in the prevalence of foreign investment and the occurrence of international horizontal mergers.

Neither of these tests is complex conceptually, but both entail onerous efforts to collect data: standardized data on international horizontal mergers are lacking, and reconciling the standard industrial data collected by different countries is tedious. The modest statistical analysis that follows merely sheds some light on the prevalence of behaviour matching these two models and thus the prospective role of mergers in international economic integration. The interindustry distribution of international horizontal mergers involving US corporate assets provides a cheap site to test the relative explanatory power of the strategic and non-strategic models of international mergers offered above. The shortcoming of US mergers for this analysis is their lack of evident connection with international economic integration.

3.1   Interindustry patterns

We collected data on international horizontal mergers involving firms in US manufacturing industries during the ten years from the fourth quarter of 1978 through the third quarter of 1988. The apparent abundance of such mergers during the 1980s suggested this time period. The starting date was dictated by the first appearance in *Mergers and Acquisitions* of annotated lists of international mergers identifying the companies, their national domiciles, their product lines, the month of the transaction, and (sporadically) other information that will be mentioned below.[18] A merger was defined as a transaction in which control of the target firm changed hands, with the acquirer coming to hold more than 50% of its equity. The acquirer might have held a minority interest previously. The acquired business might have been sold by a domestic company, but the sale could not involve an international disinvestment. The legal acquirer might be an existing subsidiary operating in the same nation as the target, so long as the acquisition was horizontal with respect to the parent's overseas activities but *not* horizontal with respect to its target-nation subsidiary. An international merger might be deemed horizontal because of activities of the parent in countries other than its home or that of the target firm (such cases were rare).

It would of course have been desirable to cover international acquisitions involving all industrial countries, not just the United States. Neither the strategic nor the non-strategic model advocates restricting the sample to transactions involving one country. Indeed, the strategic-behaviour model suggests that for a broadly internationalized industry

Table 6.1. *International horizontal mergers by year of occurrence and origin of acquiring firm, 1978–88*

Year	Total	Foreign acquirer	US acquirer	US percentage
1978[a]	36	0	36	100
1979	68	36	32	47
1980	51	27	24	47
1981	52	37	15	29
1982	67	34	33	49
1983	51	17	34	67
1984	75	46	29	39
1985	70	37	33	47
1986	66	46	20	30
1987	92	54	38	41
1988[a]	81	67	14	17

Note: [a]Numbers of mergers for 1978 (fourth quarter) and 1988 (first three quarters) are blown up to annual rates, for comparability to other years.

the restriction could introduce important noise. The only defence of this feasibility-based constraint is that the size of the US market and the prominence of US firms in most substantially international industries make it likely that US business units would be involved in any significant international strategic interactions.

A crucial step was to determine whether a given international merger is indeed horizontal. The criterion used was that acquirer and target both manufacture products classified to the same four-digit industry in the US Standard Industrial Classification (SIC). With about 450 categories, the four-digit level of the SIC is fine enough that included companies are likely to employ the same technologies or serve the same types of customers, even if they offer goods that are not very close substitutes. The major problem was to distinguish between horizontal mergers and what are called product-line extensions. The distinction in practice is one of degree, in that in few cases are the acquirer's and target's outputs clearly perfect substitutes. The four-digit SIC criterion seemed to provide a reasonable dividing line. We presumed that doubtful cases should be excluded.[19]

This procedure yielded a total of 662 merger transactions distributed over time as shown in table 6.1.[20] The annual count shows an erratic upward trend, as does the proportion representing acquisitions of US business units by foreign enterprises. For the whole period 58% of the acquisitions involved the purchase of US assets. The distributions by country or region of acquisitions are reported in table 6.2. These distributions correspond roughly to the historical distribution of foreign-investment activity involving the United States, with the United Kingdom

Table 6.2. *Distribution by country or region of businesses acquired by US companies and US businesses acquired by foreign companies*

Country or region	Acquisitions by US Companies		Acquired US businesses	
	Number	%	Number	%
Canada	41	15	71	18
Great Britain	58	21	121	32
France	28	10	30	8
West Germany	30	11	33	9
Italy	19	7	4	1
Other Europe[a]	49	18	76	20
Japan	4	1	29	8
Australia/New Zealand	16	6	16	4
All other	33	12	4	1
Total	278		384	

Note: [a]Includes Israel.

and Japan active net acquirers and Italy and the rest of the world net targets.

The distribution of acquisitions among industries is particularly important to this study. They are strikingly dispersed among four-digit industries, with at least one transaction occurring in no less than 230 sectors. The average per industry is less than three, so most industries had only a few. Ten or more transactions occurred in only five industries, and only twenty-four reported five through nine. This pattern puts a damper on the strategic-behaviour hypothesis, suggesting that only a handful of industries experienced enough transactions that strategic interactions might be revealed. On reflection, the finding is perhaps no surprise. The strategic-interaction model requires that producers in the international market be few enough, either overall or in well-defined market niches, for strategic interaction to be important. Concentration is much lower than this in most industries.

Some simple statistical tests were performed to explain the numbers of mergers classified to each industry (including, where appropriate, industries with no mergers). The hypotheses and the variables embodying them were:

(1) The non-strategic hypothesis indicates that international mergers implement the normal expansion of foreign investment in growing industries in which it is prevalent. The number of international mergers should (*ceteris paribus*) be proportional to the initial stock of foreign investment in the industry. We used three measures of this stock, the proportion of sales by US multinational enterprises that are made by their foreign

subsidiaries (*FDI*1), the proportion of shipments made by US producers accounted for by subsidiaries of foreign enterprises (*FDI*2), and the sum of these proportions (*FDI*3). The relative maturity of US foreign investment suggests a preference for *FDI*1 or *FDI*3 over *FDI*2.

(2) If the foreign-investment stock is a significant explanatory factor, we should control for how closely national markets are linked to each other through international trade. Strongly linked markets should show greater scope for strategic interactions involving the players' international business assets. What matters here, we assume, is not the overall importance of international trade to national markets but the extent to which existing multinational enterprises transfer goods internationally (either between their affiliates or to independent parties). The variables employed are the exported proportion of sales of foreign affiliates of US enterprises (*FDX*) and imports by US affiliates of foreign enterprises as a proportion of their total sales (*FDM*). If FDI exerts a positive influence on the merger count, we expect a positive influence of *FDX* and/or *FDM*.[21]

(3) Producer concentration is a necessary condition for international mergers involving strategic interaction, although not for mergers that implement expansions of non-strategic foreign investment. The concentration measure used, the proportion of shipments by the four largest US producers, should be a reasonable proxy for concentration in foreign markets as well, on the basis of Pryor's (1972) findings.[22] The variable is designated *C*4.

(4) Although few companies are actually involved in international mergers, the number of transactions is ultimately constrained by the number of companies large enough to be likely candidates. Although international acquisitions of small targets are common, the probability of involvement surely increases with the size of firm. Again relying on US data to approximate the international industry, we used the logarithm of the number of companies (*LNCOMP*),[23] on evidence that the average size of companies decreases with an industry's number of producers.

(5) Studies of foreign direct investment indicate that whatever advantages arise from the transborder coordination of economic activity they must be traded off against the costs and disadvantages faced by a managerial unit operating in an alien national environment. The smaller are the advantages, the more likely are foreign investors to stick to countries that are similar in language, legal system, culture, etc. For industries that experienced some international mergers, therefore, we assumed that the total would be smaller, the larger the proportion of

mergers taking place across the US-Canada border ($CANADA$), where the elevation of coordination costs should be minimal.

To summarize, the number of international mergers observed in an industry (M) should increase with each of these variables except $CANADA$. The following two models indicate the results for the 412 industries for which data were available (including those with no mergers):

$$M = -1.85 + 4.43 \; FDI3 + 0.44 \; LNCOMP \qquad \bar{R}^2 = 0.075$$
$$\quad (2.57) \; (5.17) \qquad (3.82)$$

$$M = -3.25 + 4.37 \; FDI1 + 0.02 \; C4 + 0.60 \; LNCOMP$$
$$\quad (2.58) \; (4.46) \qquad (1.72) \quad (3.74) \qquad \bar{R}^2 = 0.067$$

For the 230 industries with $M > 0$ (for which the variable $CANADA$ is defined) we obtain:

$$M = -1.55 + 4.05 \; FDI3 + 0.01 \; C4 + 0.58 \; LNCOMP$$
$$\quad (0.84) \; (3.81) \qquad (0.35) \quad (2.45)$$
$$\quad -0.01 \; CANADA \qquad\qquad\qquad \bar{R}^2 = 0.085$$
$$\quad (1.10)$$

All signs are as expected, and the control for the company population ($LNCOMP$) performs properly. The base stock of foreign investment clearly has a strong influence ($FDI3$ more than its components).[24] Concentration is significant only for distinguishing between industries with some and no international mergers – not encouraging for the strategic hypothesis. Although each model is significant overall, explanatory power is obviously weak. The trade-intensity variables FDX and FDM do not appear because missing observations cost many degrees of freedom, and when included their coefficients are not at all signficant.

3.2   Temporal concentration of international mergers

Despite the poor performance of the strategic hypothesis about international mergers, we proceeded to investigate the corollary of temporal concentration of strategic mergers. The measurement of this concentration could be approached in various ways. Suppose that an industry's potential international mergers exhibit a rectangular distribution over time. M mergers are observed over T months. The expected rate is M/T per month, or tM/T over any given subperiod of arbitrary length t. Judgementally we selected periods of 20 and 40 months for t^*, the period in which temporal concentration of mergers is presumed to reveal itself (the total observation period is 120 months). For each industry with five or more mergers during the 120-month period, we identified the 20- (or

40-) month subperiod in which the largest number of mergers (m^*) actually occurred and calculated $MCON = (m^* - t^* M/T)/(t^* M/T)$. It can be regarded as the proportional excess of actual over predicted mergers in the period of their greatest concentration.

Merger concentration appears high, with 50% of M occurring in the busiest 20-month period and 60% in the most active 40-month period for the median industry. It would require a Monte Carlo analysis, however, to determine whether these values are significantly outside statistical expectation. Our concern is rather with the differences in this concentration among industries. $MCON$ was accordingly treated as a dependent variable and regressed on models including the exogenous variables introduced above. The number of companies ($LNCOMP$) is no longer relevant, but $MCON$ should on a random basis decline with the number of mergers observed in an industry. We assumed that the relation can be controlled by $MINV = 1/M$, a functional form suggested by a plot of the data.

The results are decidedly negative. $MINV$ wields a significant positive effect, as expected. With $MINV$ controlled, no other variable significantly influences $MCON$, and the signs of the non-significant variables generally differ between the versions of $MCON$ based on 20- and 40-month intervals. Temporal concentration may or may not be abnormal, but it shows no behaviour predicted by the strategic model of mergers.

3.3   Incidental results

The data base yielded a few incidental conclusions that conform to the non-strategic model based on expanding foreign investment. The data source on international mergers reported when available the annual sales of both acquiring and target company, the price paid for the target and whether the target was a free-standing company or a business unit sold by another firm. For each industry we calculated the average of each variable for such observations as are available. They yielded the following conclusions:

(1) Excepting Canada, the average sizes of non-US acquiring companies are a little larger than those of US-based acquirers. This fact probably reflects the greater maturity of the leading US firms as multinational enterprises.

(2) As in domestic mergers the target firm is typically much smaller than its acquirer. Foreign acquirers bought US firms on average 6.4% their own size, one-half larger than the average relative size of foreign firms bought by US companies (4.3%). The sizes of acquirers and their targets are highly correlated (0.29).

(3) A substantial proportion of the transactions involved the purchase of a business unit from another firm, with the transferred business's activity more closely related to those of its new than its old parent. The proportion of transactions involving the purchase of sold-off business units was smaller for US acquirers (26%) than for foreign acquirers (35%), probably because diversified US companies were shedding many 'unrelated' business units during the 1980s. Firms based in the continental European countries were particularly active buyers.

Aside from their general interest, these results are relevant to the preceding findings for their consistency with known behaviour patterns of multinational enterprises, and thus with the interpretation of international mergers as a normal part of the expansion of these enterprises.

4   Strategic mergers: a realm of application?

If statistical evidence fails to support application of the strategic model to manufacturing industries at large, it could still pertain to sectors with congenial market structures – highly concentrated worldwide and carrying out activities that require irreversible investments in diverse, lumpy and specialized assets. Waves of international acquisitions that have recently swept through such industries may show the strategic model at work. As a suggestive exercise this section sets out some patterns inferred from the business press in the guise of hypotheses capable of analysis and more formal testing.[25]

A number of industries display the appropriate market structures and histories of similar international mergers clustered tightly in time. They include pharmaceuticals, major home appliances, processed food products, automobile tyres, motion-picture production and distribution, music recording and distribution, luxury automobiles and electronic information services. We advance a series of propositions bearing on the situations of the merging firms, their stated objectives and ambient industry conditions:

(1) The combining firms seldom produce close to identical products. Rather, they tend to offer product lines that are subject to close rivalry in certain product segments or geographic areas, but much of their competition is potential rather than actual.

(2) A stated reason for merging is to achieve full utilization of the lumpy, multiuse asset. An example is a merger between pharmaceutical companies, one having excess capacity in its distribution and promotion system, the other with products that this sales force can market. This

motive for merger is simply an application of a standard theoretical basis for corporate diversification (Montgomery and Hariharan, forthcoming). It calls into attention the wobbly line between horizontal and diversifying acquisitions and points out that such mergers need not be strategic. However, lumpy, multipurpose assets with high fixed and low marginal costs clearly offer options for unanticipated future uses, strategic or otherwise. Related to this pattern are indications that mergers occupy in response to increases in important types of fixed costs (of developing a new pharmaceutical or preparing and distributing a motion picture with worldwide popularity). Models of two-stage competition (fixed costs are incurred, then competition occurs) imply that increases in fixed costs will reduce the equilibrium number of sellers in the long run, regardless of their mode of competitive interaction.

(3) Races to make acquisitions are frequently set off by the perception that potential targets are few in number and may soon all be acquired (major motion-picture studios, small-volume luxury automobile producers). Acquirers pay high prices in order to complete deals quickly and avoid being left out. These races confirm strategic interaction and the assumption by acquirers that failing to maintain parity in assets with major rivals leads to severe penalties.

(4) Besides parity in asset structures acquirers often seek to maintain or achieve parity in total size. It is hard to explain this objective for a value-maximizing firm except as a way to maintain options or to sustain capacity to make and reply to threats, consistent with the strategic approach to international mergers.[26]

(5) Firms making international horizontal acquisitions assign value to having an intangible 'presence' in the target's national market. Equally intangible are objects of maintaining a listening post or learning from the foreign environment. These goals seem inconsistent with seeking the most efficient use of resources in a static context and demand an interpretation in terms of options – strategic options insofar as the intangible objectives relate to competitive positions.

(6) Stated objectives of mergers are often linked to 'Europe in 1992' and other changes in regulations and transaction costs expected to increase the geographic scope of close product-market competition. Acquirers seem to assume that economic integration carries with it enlarged opportunities and threats, thereby raising the option values of holding farflung portfolios of assets (Markides, Oyon and Ittner, 1990).

(7) International horizontal mergers sometimes occur along with otherwise similar transactions between domestic firms (the pharmaceuticals

and publishing industries supply examples). The strategic model applies equally to domestic mergers insofar as the national market is fissured and subject to localized disturbances and opportunities.

(8) Some options sought through international horizontal mergers pertain to bargaining advantageously with suppliers and customer whose scopes of activity are expanding. International mergers in branded food products, for example, have been explained by the enlarged scales and increasingly international organization of both grocery chains and advertising media in the European countries. The model may apply to strategic moves in bilateral contracting as well as horizontal competition.

The preceding generalizations are only impressionistic. Still, they both suggest a realm of validity for the strategic model and offer hints about its testing and elaboration.[27]

5   Summary and conclusions for integration in Europe

We now collect the implications of this paper for 'Europe in 1992', taken to mean significant reductions in various types of non tariff and administrative protection within the European Community. That this integration should promote corporate mergers is a commonplace in the business press, but the reasons are far from transparent to economists. If mergers would increase firms' efficiency and hence their ability to withstand increased competition from abroad, why should the mergers await the threat of more competition? If, despite this caveat, mergers respond to anticipated increases in competition, what types of benefits do the acquiring firms expect to obtain?

This paper has approached these questions by focussing on international mergers, presenting two models capable of explaining such mergers as a response to increased economic integration. The more stylish ('strategic') model imputes them to firms' attempts to recruit assets valuable for capturing the changed and enlarged set of opportunities that the more integrated European market will bring. This model implies that such mergers will be bunched in time, because they are strategic complements for firms that regard each other as international oligopolistic rivals.[28] A parallel but non-strategic model identifies international mergers as simply the vehicle for implementing an increase in the equilibrium level of multinational-company capital. The non-strategic model is a special case of the efficient bases for mergers stressed in the finance literature. It rests on the assumption – surprising but empirically supported – that the expansion of trade and foreign investments are complements rather than substitutes. It is also consistent with waves of mergers occurring due to some change in optimal business organization, but (unlike the strategic model) it does not associate the bunching with competitive strategies.

Organizing appropriate data to perform high-quality statistical tests of these models is dauntingly costly. This paper offers only an exploratory analysis of international horizontal mergers across the US border during 1978–88. These mergers were not necessarily the result of increased international economic integration – indeed, no specific cause of their upsurge is assessed here. Nonetheless, they clearly shed light on the prospective European experience. The evidence supports the non-strategic but not the strategic model for a broad sample of manufacturing industries. These mergers were scattered among many industries. Their number is strongly related to an industry's initial stock of foreign investment but not (in an appropriate way) to the concentration of its producers. The temporal bunching of mergers in those industries exhibiting five or more is unrelated to variables indicated by the strategic model.

These data do not so much reject the strategic model as suggest its applicability may be confined to a small subset of industries. A review of business-press reports of mergers in industries with appropriate structures (concentrated internationally, with structurally complex markets and diverse specialized assets) yields a series of empirical observations that both confirm and extend the strategic model's implications.

Overall, the analysis supports the expectation that further integration in Europe will be preceded or accompanied by a wave of mergers. Many of these will implement foreign-investment plans of EC-based firms that are changing the scale and scope of their activities in response to more integrated markets and of non-EC firms responding to a shifted balance of advantage between exporting to the Community and producing within it. These non-strategic choices do not pose normative problems with regard to market competition, but of course they can implement general-equilibrium distortions (trade diversion) identified in the theory of customs unions.

If we assume that structural conditions in some important industries provide scope for strategic mergers, they pose specific threats to the efficient organization of business activities. Increased integration within the EC is now promoting and will continue to promote waves of mergers in such industries induced in part by opportunities for strategic threat and deterrence rather than for non-strategic value-maximization. It has been suggested that stepped-up mergers among European firms are now responding to the perceived superior strategic positions for the post-1992 period of the large US multinationals, with their trans-European networks of facilities already in place (Lipsey, 1990). It is not easy to identify these costs of rent-seeking, let alone write rules to limit them. But the possibility of important resource misallocations ('business misorgani-zations') from this source should certainly be kept on the policy agenda. Of course, the possibility of international horizontal mergers for mono-poly is not denied by this paper's emphasis on other motives for mer-gers.[29] In short, integration will bring many international horizontal mergers, and they will make up a dauntingly mixed bag for policy-makers seeking to secure good market performance.

NOTES

I am grateful to the Division of Research, Harvard Business School for support, to Denise Neumann for assistance, and to conference participants for helpful suggestions.

1 Although recent studies of stock-market valuations of horizontal mergers have not fully confirmed monopoly rents as an inducement to horizontal mergers, there is little doubt that many industry-wide consolidations under-taken at the beginning of the twentieth century were profitable (on the US experience see Caves, Fortunato and Ghemawat, 1984). For recent theoretical discussions see Perry and Porter (1985) and Farrell and Shapiro (1988).

2 On the home-appliances ('white goods') industry, see Bianchi and Forlai (1988), especially pp. 291–3.

3 It is closely related to the 'Carnegie' view of the firm as a lateral contract among functional specialists, advanced by Cyert and March (1963).

4 Prescott and Visscher (1980) formally developed Penrose's idea that the growth of the firm is constrained by the need to expand organizational capital in parallel with the growth of its total asset stock.

5 Representing the firm as an organizational coalition pays off best in the model of diversified firms, based on the assumption that the lumpy, specialized assets attached to the firm have uses in more than one industry. Their lumpiness then supplies a basis for diversification when such an asset is not optimally used to capacity in the activity for which it was first recruited (because the firm faces a downward-sloping demand curve for that activity). The diversifier's profit from entering an activity that fully utilizes the partly idle asset exceeds the profit of a specialist firm that must incur the asset's full cost. See Rubin (1973) and the empirical evidence of Lemelin (1982) and Montgomery and Hariharan (forthcoming).

6 This assumption brings us close to the 'product selection' problem of product differentiation and the theoretical literature on brand proliferation. However, models of the Judd (1985) variety are not automatically relevant because assumptions made above imply that economies of scale and scope place entry barriers before 'niche' entrants.

7 The asymmetries in firms' qualifications to seize market opportunities pre-clude the extinction of rents that occurs when symmetrical rivals race to obtain an innovation. Also relevant is the model of Mills (1988), showing that rents are preserved when it is costly to threaten pre-emption. Mills' model implies that the best-qualified firm can stake a claim that preserves nearly the mono-poly value from exploiting the opportunity, whatever rivals exist or appear.

8 This condition underlies the theory of strategic groups (Caves and Porter,

1977) and the literature on business strategy that stresses not only the qualitative differences among competitors' asset bundles but also differences in the quality or competence of a given specific asset relative to its counterpart held by competitors (the firms' 'strengths and weaknesses').

9 The theory of innovation under rivalry illustrates these points. The pursuit of any given innovation is modelled as a race in which symmetrical rivals spend ontil one gains the prize and the others quit. During the race 'flow' costs are strategic complements. After the race imitation can equally well be the loser's best reply, and a 'fast second' strategy can have advantages (Scherer, 1967; Baldwin and Childs, 1969).

10 A similar conclusion can be reached by a different but related route. Bernheim and Whinston (forthcoming) showed that when multimarket firms meet each other in several markets, shares of sales in excess of the minimum needed to sustain cooperative behaviour in one market can help to stabilize it in other markets. That model yields the same conclusion reached below that one firm's merger in a set of closely related markets can increase the payout for merger by its rival by bringing the conditions for multimarket cooperation closer to fulfillment.

11 A formal model with some affinity for the one sketched here is Flaherty and Raubitschek (1987). For them the advantage of holding offshore production facilities lies in their favourable effect on local demand.

12 The use of option values in this context may be contrasted to recent applications of the concept to irreversible expansions of capacity (Pindyck, 1988). In that setting investment exercises an option, closing off the opportunity to invest later under better circumstances. Here a merger opens opportunities for short-run deployments without necessarily involving a completely irreversible decision (although the sunkenness of such a merger is an important question).

13 This approach seems consistent with the somewhat confusing evidence on capital markets' valuations of the effects of horizontal mergers on the profits of both the merging firms and their competitors (Eckbo, 1985, and papers cited therein). Although rivals do obtain positive abnormal returns when their competitors merge, these abnormal returns tend to decrease with the market's level of seller concentration. Also see McGuckin, Warren-Boulton and Waldstein (1988).

14 Another relevant analysis of strategic interaction concerns intraindustry foreign investment (analogous to intraindustry trade), which has been seen in strategic terms as challenge and best-reply or as a mutual exchange of hostages. Either interpretation is consistent with the model of strategic international mergers proposed above but more restrictive; the strategic model is nonspecific about the national locations of acquiring and target companies. The hypothesis of international horizontal mergers as an exchange of threats or hostages will not be pursued in this investigation for reasons that emerge below. See Erdilek (1985), especially the papers by Graham and by Nelson and Silvia.

15 While complementarity cannot hold in general equilibrium (because both activities draw on the source-country's stock of resources), it can hold in partial equilibrium.

16 On the complementarity of exporting and foreign investment see Bergsten, Horst, and Moran (1978, chapter 3). Also relevant is evidence of the growth of intracorporate trade in intermediate components and complementary product-line items.

17 Telling evidence comes from an econometric study of short-run adjustments to international disturbances by Canadian manufacturing industries. In the typical industry increased import competition promotes responses by domestic producers (temporarily increased capital expenditures, increased labour productivity) that actually result in increased exports. The sizes of the adjustments and the inducement of intraindustry trade are greater, the more active are multinational companies in a sector. The study did not, however, analyse induced changes in foreign investment. See Caves (1990).

18 We spot-checked the lists in *Mergers and Acquisitions* against other sources that claim to cover international mergers. Discrepancies in information on mergers covered by more than one source were minor for our purposes, and *Mergers and Acquisitions* seemed to provide the most complete and systematic coverage. That source was therefore assumed to be generally accurate.

19 Where *Mergers and Acquisitions* is insufficiently specific about product lines, especially that of the acquirer, we sought information in business directories such as *Kompass*. The limitation of this procedure is that directory information can seldom be obtained at the ideal date – shortly prior to the acquisition.

20 One industry, newspapers, was excluded from the tabulation at the outset, because the large number of individual acquisitions of small-circulation US newspapers by a major Canadian chain were thought noncomparable to other transactions in the sample. Only later was it recognized that the same enterprise had made a similarly large number (18, included in the 662) of acquisitions of specialized US magazines.

21 The years used for these variables were 1980 for variables involving US investment abroad and 1977 for variables involving foreign investment in the United States. Selecting a date for observing these variables (from the limited choices available) posed a dilemma. The structural conditions should predate the transactions that they propose to explain. With the transactions spread over ten years, however, and at most one or two relevant observations available on the regressors, a compromise was necessary. We settled for years near the beginning of the mergers period (1978–88) rather than demanding that they precede it.

22 The year chosen was 1982, for reasons mentioned in the preceding footnote. Preparing this series was complicated by the fact that a major revision of the US Standard Industrial Classification was announced in 1984 to take effect for the 1987 Census of Manufacturers. We used the new SIC to classify mergers to industries, because it embodies a number of obvious improvements, but we therefore had to estimate the concentration ratios that would have been reported in 1982 for industries defined as in 1987. Although a few industries were lost, it seemed possible to make a close approximation in most cases because the four-digit industries redefined in 1987 can usually be described in terms of pre-1984 five-digit product classes, for which 1982 concentration ratios were published.

23 The variable pertains to the year 1982 and like $C4$ (see note 22) was constructed on the basis of the 1987 SIC. Going back to the 1977 Census for $C4$ and $LNCOMP$ would have involved more difficulties transforming to the revised SIC as well as a year remote from the mid-1980s merger boom.

24 The data support a very rough test of the directionality of the influence of the underlying stocks of foreign investment: was the proportion of acquisitions by US firms in total mergers correlated with the ratio of our proxy for the US

initial stock of international investment ($FDI1$) to the measure of the total stock ($FDI3$)? This correlation is 0.085, positive as expected but not statistically significant.

25 These patterns are inferred from a broad if casual reading of business newspapers and periodicals. Specific documentation will not be offered. For other descriptive treatments see Khoury (1980) and Grey and McDermott (1987).

26 Large absolute size of course may also provide managerial utility and serve the organizational goals of maintaining attractive challenges and promotion opportunities for employees.

27 Indirect statistical support can be found for the strategic model. Its assumptions about market structure are consistent with the hypothesis that concentrated industries are fragmented into strategic groups, which enjoys wide statistical support. Quantitative studies of corporate diversification confirm the importance of irreversible investments in lumpy, multi-use assets for related diversification and the mergers that sometimes implement it (Lemelin, 1982). The literature on market valuations of international mergers offers some support, as in the finding that positive value is attached to a multinational firm's first entry into a national market but not to an acquisition made in a national market where it has previously operated (Doukas and Travlos, 1988).

28 The analysis has been confined to mergers, but it can be applied as well to less sweeping types of alliances among firms, such as joint ventures and cooperative agreements.

29 From recent theoretical analyses of horizontal mergers (based on Cournot behaviour), it is not clear that an increase in the cross-elasticities of demand among firms (the natural way to interpret greater international economic integration) raises the incentives for mergers for monopoly. Integration would, however, increase the incentive for mergers that bring an international industry's concentration to a level that sustains cooperative rather than Nash behaviour. It is not clear whether international mergers for monopoly would be clustered. They would cluster if large-share firms can agree to acquire all competitors with shares not large enough to deter their cheating on a collusive agreement. They will not if, following a 'leading' merger, other firms choose to free-ride on the rents that will flow from the acquiring firm's subsequent contraction of output.

REFERENCES

Baldwin, W.L. and G.L. Childs (1969) 'The Fast Second and Rivalry in Research and Development', *Southern Economic Journal* **36**, 18–24.

Bergsten, C.F., T. Horst and T.H. Moran (1978) *American Multinationals and American Interests*, Washington: Brookings Institution.

Bernheim, B.D. and M.D. Whinston (forthcoming) 'Multimarket Contact and Collusive Behavior', *Rand Journal of Economics*.

Bianchi, P. and L. Forlai (1988) 'The European Domestic Appliance Industry, 1945–1987', in H.W. de Jong (ed.), *The Structure of European Industry*, 2nd edition, Dordrecht: Kluwer Academic, 269–96.

Caves, R.E. (1990) *Adjustments to International Competition: Short-Run Relations of Prices, Trade Flows, and Inputs in Canadian Manufacturing Industries*, Ottawa: Economic Council of Canada.

Caves, R.E., M. Fortunato and P. Ghemawat (1984) 'The Decline of Dominant Firms, 1905–1929', *Quarterly Journal of Economics* **99**, 523–46.

Caves, R.E. and S. Mehra (1986) 'Entry of Foreign Multinationals into U.S. Manufacturing Industries', in M.E. Porter (ed.), *Competition in Global Industries*, Boston: Harvard Business School Press, pp. 449–81.

Caves, R.E. and M.E. Porter (1977) 'From Entry Barriers to Mobility Barriers', *Quarterly Journal of Economics* **91**, 241–61.

Curhan, J.P., W.H. Davidson and R. Suri (1977) *Tracing the Multinationals: A Sourcebook on U.S.-Based Enterprises*, Cambridge, MA: Ballinger.

Cyert, R.M. and J.G. March (1963) *The Theory of the Firm*, Englewood Cliffs: Prentice-Hall.

Doukas, J. and N.G. Travlos (1988) 'The Effect of Corporate Multinationalism on Shareholders' Wealth: Evidence from International Acquisitions', *Journal of Finance* **43**, 1161–75.

Eckbo, B.E. (1985) 'Mergers and the Market Concentration Doctrine: Evidence from the Capital Market', *Journal of Business* **58**, 325–49.

Erdilek, A. (ed.), (1985) *Multinationals as Mutual Invaders: Intra-Industry Direct Foreign Investment*, New York: St. Martin's Press.

Farrell, J. and C. Shapiro (1988) 'Horizontal Mergers: An Equilibrium Analysis', Olin Program Discussion Paper No. 17, Princeton University.

Flaherty, M.T. and R.S. Raubitschek (1987) 'The Impact of Local Manufacturing Presence on International Manufacturing Configurations and Global Competition', presented at Econometric Society.

Grey, S.J. and M.C. McDermott (1987) 'International Mergers and Takeovers: A Review of Recent Trends and Developments', *European Management Journal* **6**, 26–43.

Hisey, K.B. and R.E. Caves (1985) 'Diversification Strategy and Choice of Country: Diversifying Acquisitions Abroad by U.S. Multinationals, 1978–1980', *Journal of International Business Studies* **16**, 51–64.

Horst, T. (1971) 'The Theory of the Multinational Firm: Optimal Behavior under Different Tariff and Tax Rules', *Journal of Political Economy* **79**, 1059–72.

Judd, K.L. (1985) 'Credible Spatial Preemption', *Rand Journal of Economics* **16**, 153–66.

Khoury, S.J. (1980) *Transnational Mergers and Acquisitions in the United States*, Lexington: Lexington Books.

Knickerbocker, F.T. (1973) *Oligopolistic Reaction and Multinational Enterprise*, Boston: Division of Research, Harvard Business School.

Lemelin, A. (1982) 'Relatedness in the Patterns of Interindustry Diversification', *Review of Economics and Statistics* **64**, 646–57.

Lippman, S.A. and R.P. Rumelt (1982) 'Uncertain Imitability: An Analysis of Interfirm Differences in Efficiency under Competition', *Bell Journal of Economics* **13**, 418–38.

Lipsey, R.E. (1990) 'American Firms Face Europe: 1992', Working Paper No. 3293, National bureau of Economic Research.

Markides, C.C., D.F. Oyon and C.D. Ittner (1990) 'The Valuation Consequences of International Acquisition', Working paper, Harvard Business School.

McGuckin, R.H., F.R. Warren-Boulton and P. Waldstein (1988) 'Analysis of Mergers Using Stock Maret Returns', U.S. Department of Justice, Antitrust Division, Discussion Paper No. EAG 88-1.

Mills, D.E. (1988) 'Preemptive Investment Timing', *Rand Journal of Economics* **19**, 114–22.

Montgomery, C.A. and S. Hariharan (forthcoming) 'Diversified Expansion by Large Established Firms', *Journal of Economic Behavior and Organization*.

Penrose, E.T. (1959) *The Theory of the Growth of the Firm*, Oxford: Basil Blackwell.

Perry, M.K. and R.H. Porter (1985) 'Oligopoly and the Incentive for Horizontal Merger', *American Economic Review* **75**, 219–27.

Pindyck, R.S. (1988) 'Irreversible Investment, Capacity Choice, and the Value of the Firm', *American Economic Review* **78**, 969–85.

Prescott, E.C. and M. Visscher (1980) 'Organizational Capital', *Journal of Political Economy* **88**, 446–61.

Pryor, F.L. (1972) 'An International Comparison of Concentration Ratios', *Review of Economics and Statistics* **54**, 130–40.

Rubin, P.H. (1973) 'The Expansion of Firms', *Journal of Political Economy* **81**, 936–49.

Scherer, F.M. (1967) 'Research and Development Resource Allocation under Rivalry', *Quarterly Journal of Economics* **81**, 359–94.

Vernon, R. (1970) 'Organization as a Scale Factor in the Growth of Firms', in Jesse W. Markham and Gustav F. Papanek (eds.), *Industrial Organization and Economic Development: In Honor of E.S. Mason*, Boston: Houghton-Mifflin, 47–66.

Discussion

GÜNTER FRANKE

What role do mergers play in international economic integration, or, more specifically, in European integration? Richard Caves presented a stimulating paper on international mergers which provokes many thoughts. Let me structure my discussion into three parts. First, I shall comment on the theoretical part of his presentation, second, on the paper's empirical findings, and, third, let me say something about recent merger activity in the European community.

1   On the theory of mergers

Caves extends the theory of horizontal mergers by adding a hypothesis on the options value of horizontal mergers. His hypothesis is that, under certain conditions, a horizontally merged firm can adjust faster to random disturbances and exploit new opportunities more profitably than separate, non-merged firms. Support for this hypothesis can be gained from two lines of thought.

The first line has emerged in the 1980s, primarily in the finance literature. According to this theory, the market value of the firm, V, can be split into two components, the market value of the assets in place, V_{iP}, plus the market value of options to be exercised in the future whenever this is profitable, V_0

$$V = V_{iP} + V_0$$

This approach has been promoted by various researchers, most notably by Pindyck (1988). Although the distinction between assets in place and options is arbitrary to some extent, it points to the importance of future adjustments to random disturbances. The disturbances may be technological, such as innovations of new products or new production technologies, or they may arise from changes in the markets for factors of production or in the product markets. If no adjustment takes place, then no options are exercised so that the option value disappears.

The market value of the options depends on the structure of the industry in which the firm operates and on the characteristics of the firm as compared to those of its rivals. In a perfectly competitive environment, options can be exploited by everybody so that the option value will be zero. Thus industrial economics as the second line of thought becomes important to analyse the conditions under which these options are valuable.

In a broad sense, some barriers to entry must exist in order to make these options valuable. Caves defines these barriers by the following scenario. The national product market is highly concentrated with only a few sellers. These sellers have substantial international trade and their output is not homogeneous. Their firms are large and use complex coalitions of inputs. Specialized assets are used in long-run contractual arrangements. Skills and technologies are shared among teams of employees. Any adjustment in the composition and in the size of this production system is costly and thus it may be viewed as a barrier to entry.

Under this scenario it is not possible to set up an efficient production system within a short period of time. Moreover, the setup is costly. One possibility to set up such a system is a horizontal merger to combine various skills which are not identical but are related to similar products. Thus a horizontal merger would enhance the value of options to be exercised in the future.

Although one can imagine that a horizontal merger creates positive synergy effects with respect to future business options, it is not at all clear what is required for such synergies. The empirical evidence on the efficiency of research and development in large versus small firms is quite mixed. There is no general superiority of large firms. Moreover, small firms are said to react faster and adjust better to new opportunities, which is very important for the option value.

Thus, in order to find superiority for large firms, one has probably to assume some economies of scope. It is conceivable that firms which produce different, but related products, can combine their knowledge for the production of a hybrid product more efficiently within a merged firm than through market transactions.

This reasoning has some support from the observation that markets for technological information appear to be quite imperfect. Thus, according to the internalization hypothesis, firms prefer to communicate this information internally instead of trading it in markets.

But do we have convincing empirical evidence to support this hypothesis? In the computer industry, for example, it seems that some small firms have given the big firms a hard time. Rapid technological changes appear to have favoured at least some small firms at the expense of the big firms.

If economies of scope are a necessary condition for high option values of horizontal mergers, how can we distinguish between Professor Caves' hypothesis and the conventional economies of scope hypothesis for mergers? In fact, it appears that both hypotheses are very closely interrelated. Presumably they will be empirically indistinguishable. It might be possible, however, to test whether horizontal mergers are more frequently observed in industries with high uncertainty in technology and market conditions than in industries with small uncertainty. If this were true, then it would support the option value hypothesis of Professor Caves.

A casual observation pointing in the opposite direction is the merger activity observed in the European financial services industry. Many managers in this industry feel that horizontal mergers create substantial economies of scope. I consider the financial services sector a sector with low uncertainty in technology and market conditions. Thus, in this example, economies of scope do not depend on uncertainty. On the contrary, if the economies of scope are fairly certain, then their expected present value is high so that a strong motive for a horizontal merger exists.

The focus of analysis should not be narrowed down, however, to the comparison of horizontal mergers and firms operating independently. We observe other approaches to reaping synergy effects. Cross-national cooperation agreements in research and development are often observed, supplemented by licensing agreements. Joint ventures are another route to follow. We know little about the advantages and disadvantages of such agreements relative to mergers.

Caves elaborates on the strategic aspects of horizontal mergers, too. If the national market is served by a few large firms, then strategic aspects play an important role. If one firm merges with another cross-border firm, then the national rivals are afraid that the newly merged firm will seize additional profit opportunities at their expense. I consider this an important argument although two qualifications appear necessary:

(1) This fear is justified only if a horizontal merger really does create additional profit opportunities.

(2) We know that many horizontal mergers have failed, or, at least, did not live up to expectations. Hence it appears safe to assume that there exists substantial uncertainty about the effects of a merger. High uncertainty creates the desire to protect or insure oneself against potential adverse events. Therefore the rivals of a merged firm may imitate the merger just for insurance purposes. Even if the merger turns out to be unprofitable, the competitive position of a firm within its industry stays the same if all firms behave the same. This would also explain temporal concentration of mergers.

An analogy is known from the capital market. Every trader spends money on information collection to insure himself against being exploited by better-informed traders. In the end, the capital market may be informationally efficient so that, in the aggregate, the traders do not reap an advantage from information collection. A similar insurance hypothesis could explain part of the observed mergers.

2   Remarks on the empirical findings

Caves adds some empirical findings. They are, however, not related to his option-value hypothesis on international mergers. Instead, he tests whether mergers are positively related to a firm's international involvement. This is measured by the proportion of sales of US multinationals made by their foreign subsidiaries, and by the proportion of sales of US producers to subsidiaries of foreign firms. Professor Caves finds the expected positive relation. Thus international mergers appear to be one form of international involvement which is positively related to other forms.

This finding is interesting and supports the hypothesis that firms first test their potential for international success by sales and, if successful, go ahead by foreign direct investments some of which are mergers.

Table 6A.1. *Cross-border purchases of firms in the Common Market in the first three quarters of 1989*

	Jan.–March 1989	April–June 1989	July–Sept. 1989	Jan.–Sept. 1989
Number of purchases	235	341	377	953
Volume of purchases (billion DM)	10	20	36	66

Purchases by (billion DM)		Purchases in (billion DM)	
US firms	20.0	United Kingdom	31.0
French firms	15.0	Germany	9.6
German firms	5.8	Italy	7.6
British firms	9.8	France	6.6
Japanese firms	2.2	Spain	4.0

Source: Translink's *European Deal Review* (1989b).

A second test concerns the impact of strategic motives on international mergers. Professor Caves does not find significant relations, but he finds a high temporal concentration of mergers within industries which is consistent with the insurance motive. The reason why Professor Caves does not find significant relations may be that he primarily uses sales proportions as independent regression variables. Thus profitability considerations are at best implicit although they should also play a major role in strategic mergers.

3   Mergers and European integration

The big discussion about business strategies for the European Market started suddenly in 1987–8. We do not know why it became such a big issue in these years. The discussion evolved like a nuclear chain reaction. Cross-border merger activity is expanding quite fast as table 6A.1 shows.

The table shows very distinct patterns across countries. Almost half of the purchases are purchases in the United Kingdom, but British firms spend much less on cross-border purchases. Apart from US firms, French firms spend most on cross-border purchases, but purchases in France are low. This is, perhaps, due to the strong public sector in France which is resistant to takeovers. Purchases in Germany are constrained since most corporations are closely held so that unfriendly takeovers have no chance.

German firms themselves spend little on cross-border purchases, apart form the Siemens-Plessey deal. Thus it appears that nationality plays a strong role in cross-border merger activity.

A special situation for German firms has been created by the recent radical political changes in Eastern Europe, especially in East Germany. This may completely change their investment behaviour. If East Germany implements strong economic reforms, then West German firms will invest a lot of money there. They have important advantages over firms from other Western countries in terms of language, culture and geographic distance. Then we may see even less West German takeover activity in other EC countries. At the same time, the ensuing capital shortage in West Germany may make it easier for foreign firms to take over West German firms.

One important concern of European integration for managers appears to be cost reduction. Therefore a major approach is to improve cost effectiveness at the home base. This concerns most firms, independent of size. According to an inquiry of 15,000 German firms by the Deutsche Industrie- und Handelstag in 1989 the first emphasis is placed on: cost reduction (35%), improving marketing (31%), improving the product mix (23%), cross-border production (8%). Cost effectiveness may be promoted by mergers since they may achieve substantial economies of scale in industrial mass production. Synergism from horizontal integration is by far the most important motive for cross-border acquisitions of firms in Europe (Translink's *European Deal Review*, 1989a, p. 17). But takeovers are usually too capital-intensive for small firms. Takeovers may be a powerful strategy for big firms. Thus the overall significance of cross-border mergres for European integration appears to be limited, despite some spectacular events.

Economies of scope currently play an important role in mergers of the financial services industry. The so-called financial supermarket is viewed as the best strategy by many banks. Again, only a few very big banks have enough capital to take over other financial services firms on a European scale. The other banks try to cooperate with supplementary financial services firms.

Finally, let me mention the well-known protectonist merger motive for firms with their home base outside the Common Market. They are afraid of being hurt by a 'Fortress Europe'. This would make it difficult for outsiders to sell in the Common Market, but at the same time they would be threatened by import competition of Common Market-based firms. Therefore purchasing a firm in the Common Market is considered insurance against this worst case scenario.

REFERENCES

Pindyck, R.S. (1988) 'Irreversible Investment, Capacity Choice, and the Value of the Firm', *American Economic Review* **78**, 969–85.

Translink's *European Deal Review* (1989a) First Six Months, 1989.

Translink's *European Deal Review* (1989b) First Nine Months, 1989.

JULIAN R. FRANKS

1   Introduction

The paper provides a model for horizontal mergers to explain the bunching of European cross-border merger activity arising from the process of harmonization in the EEC.

It is assumed that economic disturbances take place, for example changes in tastes or new non-proprietary technical innovations. These alter the opportunities available to an oligopolistic firm, in relation to the existing investment set and growth options. Importantly, those firms operating with less than optimal bundles of assets or which do not have first-mover advantage incur lower returns as a result of the changes revealed by nature. The strategic theory, as it is called, tells us that the disturbance initiates a rent-producing merger by firm A which results in losses for firm B; the latter enters into a defensive merger so as to minimize the loss of value brought on by A's move.

The model predicts (i) that there are no gains in aggregate from merging even though each party appears to be profit maximizing and (ii) that the bunching (or wave-like behaviour) of mergers stems from the interactive nature of A and B's investment sets. This strategic model is contrasted with a non-strategic model where firm B does not lose as a result of A's merger, but may still imitate A because a merger is a profitable activity in itself, given the shock produced by nature.

The strategic model is reminiscent of Shleifer and Summers' (1989) argument that mergers may improve shareholder returns but only at the expense of other stakeholders, although in their case the loss to other stakeholders involves the breach of implicit contracts or a breach of trust, whereas Caves' model makes no such (explicit) assumption.

Using a time series of data on cross-border acquisitions involving US companies, Caves' results reject the strategic theory in favour of the more traditional thory. The test, however, does not measure the wealth gains arising from mergers.

2   The model

The model assumes a highly concentrated industry at the domestic level, and substantial organizational specific value, arising from rent-producing physical assets and from employees that are bound to the firm by strong long-term implicit contracts. Harmonization or integration of markets alters the set of opportunities available which can best be taken advantage of by international transactions. An example might be mergers in the financial services sector initiated by harmonization of regulation, allowing a single firm to operate in all jurisdictions without the prior authorization of the host country.

The change in the opportunity set may relate to assets in place or to growth opportunities, referred to loosely in the paper as options. As nature reveals itself one competitor seizes the opportunity by way of a merger, and as a result makes its competitors worse off. The latter, in order to minimize but not eliminate their losses, mimic the behaviour of the firm with first-mover advantage. Thus, the author forecasts the bunching of mergers (or wave-like behaviour), where aggregate gains from merging are zero even though all mergers are, at least in an incremental sense, profitable. This result is readily understood from figure 6.1 in the paper, rearranged below in the form of a matrix.

| | | Firm A (First Mover) | |
		Merger	*Non-Merger*
	Merger	$Va = 1$ $Vb = -1$	$Va = -2$ $Vb = 1$
Firm B			
	Non-merger	$Va = 3$ $Vb = -2$	$Va = 0$ $Vb = 0$

where Va is the gain for firm A

According to the paper the strategy chosen is for A to merge first with B's optimal reaction being to merge as well, the net gains of both parties being zero. However, a better strategy would be for A to make side payments to B and for B not to merge, producing an overall gain of 1. Alternatively, A might contemplate the acquisition of B. It is not altogether clear that, if the payoffs were changed so that net gains in this second strategy were zero, the structure of the model would remain the same.

The author contrasts this model with a non-strategic model where there are net gains to merging. Here A merges but the merger does not necessarily affect the profitability of B. B may still mimic A and merge, but only because this is perceived as a profitable activity in itself. Obviously the policy consequences of the strategic model are very different from the non-strategic one.

3   Comments

Readers will find this paper interesting because of the interactive and mimicing nature of A and B's behaviour, and because of the prediction that particular types of merger activity may be profit-maximizing for individual firms, but result in no net gains for shareholders in aggregate and in losses for society (if there are adjustment costs to merging).

Although the author confines the model to horizontal mergers, a case could be made for extending it to vertically integrated mergers. Similarly, while the author uses the model to explain cross-border mergers, I see little reason why it cannot be used to explain domestic mergers. For example, takeover activity in the brewery industry was considerable throughout the 1960s and 1970s. This bunching of takeovers was caused by a series of shocks ranging from new technology and economies of scale to changes in tastes. More recent changes in regulation have disrupted the very close relationship between brewers and their tied retail outlets. Thus if one can explain bunching or wave-like behaviour internationally one can probably explain it domestically.

Wave-like behaviour has long been thought of as a feature of the UK and US economies; for example, in the UK the value of domestic takeover activity has ranged from 0.2% of the capital stock to 4.5% over the period 1969 to 1988. There are few theories which account for this behaviour, although King's (1988) tax and Q motivated explanation is an intriguing one, albeit one that has yet to receive much empirical support.

It is clear that some horizontal (and some vertical) mergers do not fit into the strategic model. For example, mergers motivated by the managerial failure of the target may produce net gains for the firms as well as society, but not result in mimicing behaviour. It is an interesting question as to what proportion of mergers fall into the strategic category, as described by Caves.

It may be worth considering how one would construct an event study to test the strategic model's central prediction – that is, when firm A merges so does its rival, and aggregate gains are zero. Let us sketch out a few of the ideas and some interesting problems associated with the test:

(i)   Using a sample of horizontal mergers by industry, we must consider how to distinguish between strategic and non-strategic mergers.

(ii) We would then have to confront the question as to when the stock market anticipates the gains and losses to the disturbance. Suppose the takeover announcements of A and B constitute the events. When A merges its share price should rise by 1, using the example of figure 6.1. If the market fully anticipates events B's share price will immediately decline by 1 upon A's announcement; the merger by B will be fully anticipated and there will be no price effect on its announcement. Let us now assume the market does not anticipate B's defensive merger. In this case there may be a price fall for B of say 2 when A announces the bid, reflecting the losses inflicted by A. When B announces its own bid its price rises by 1.

(iii) An important issue is the degree of competition in the acquisitions market. The example in figure 6.1 appears to assume that all the gains from merging accrue to the bidder, because there is a scarce supply of bidding firms and a plentify supply of targets. As a result there is no bid premium for the target. The evidence in fact suggests a plentiful supply of bidders and a shortage of targets. If the acquisitions market is perfectly competitive then the target will receive all the benefits accruing to A, i.e. 1; the gains of the bidder will be zero. This is an important point to test for, and to bear in mind in constructing the experiment and measuring the gains to each party.

4   Empirical evidence

Although we do not have a study that tests the current model we do have a large number of event studies using stock market data that give us some clues. The main conclusion for both the UK and the US, is that there are net gains from mergers for shareholders around the announcement date. Most if not all of those gains accrue to the target, although the relatively large size of the bidder to the target makes it difficult to know whether to attribute the bidder's gains to merging or to assets in place. In addition, even if the gains from merging are large they may not be significant statistically because of the very large size of the bidder.

However, in an unpublished paper Harris and Ravenscraft (1989) have completed an event study of the wealth gains arising from 159 US cross-border acquisitions for the period 1970 to 1987, and compared these wealth gains with those arising from a sample of more than 1,100 US domestic acquisitions over a similar period. In almost three-quarters of the cross-border acquisitions the buyer already had operations in a line of business closely associated with the target, thereby indicating that many of the acquisitions may be classified as horizontal. They found bid premiums to targets in cross-border acquisitions to be 50% higher than in domestic acquisitions. They conclude that their results are consistent with a view that cross-border acquisitions produce higher value gains to shareholders than domestic acquisitions.

In another study, Doukas and Travlos (1988) measure wealth gains to US buyers of overseas firms. They find (i) buyers gained from an expansion of their existing multinational network, (ii) those gains were greater when the acquisition took place in a country in which the company was already operating and (iii) the gains were greater when the acquisition was in a related industry.

One response may be that whatever share price studies show, accounting studies comparing the pre- and post-accounting rates of return suggest that mergers do not add value. Meeks' (1977) UK study and that of Ravenscraft and Scherer (1987) suggest that post-merger returns on investment are lower than pre-merger returns, indicating a lack of added value in mergers. However, beside the usual criticisms of measuring economic values using accounting data, there is one additional difficulty raised by Caves. His strategic theory suggests that the value added in the merger may lie in the increased options available to the firm resulting from the merger. The value of option-like investments is contingent on specific events in the future taking place. They are unlikely to happen immediately. Thus, accounting data that measures returns one year or two years after takeover will fail to capture this added value for the simple reason that it has not yet taken place. Attempts to capture the longer-term benefits by examining returns three or more years beyond the merger become increasingly difficult because of benchmark problems. Providing the market is fully informed and prices the benefits properly the stock market capitalization should capture the expected gains around the announcement date.

REFERENCES

Doukas, J. and N.G. Travlos (1988) 'The Effect of Corporate Multinationalism on Shareholders' Wealth: Evidence from International Acquisitions', *Journal of Finance* **43**, 1161–75.
Harris, R. and D. Ravenscraft 1989) 'The Role of Acquisitions in Foreign Direct Investment: Evidence from the US Stock Market', Working Paper 89–27, University of Virginia.

King, M. (1988) 'Takeover Activity in the United Kingdom', in J. Fairburn and J. Kay (eds.), *Mergers and Merger Policy*, Oxford: Oxford University Press.

Meeks, G. (1977) 'Disappointing Marriage: A Study of the Gains from Merger', Occasional Paper 51, chapter 3. London: Cambridge University Press.

Ravenscraft, D. and F. Scherer (1987) 'Life After Takeover', *Journal of Industrial Economics* **36**, 147–56.

Schleifer, A. and L. Summers (1988) 'Breaches of Trust in Hostile Takeovers', in Alan Auerbach (ed.), *Corporate Takeovers: Causes and Consequences*, Chicago: University of Chicago Press.

7 Capital flight and tax competition: are there viable solutions to both problems?

ALBERTO GIOVANNINI and JAMES R. HINES Jr

1 Introduction

The history of European capital taxation is one of 12 disparate systems, competing for revenue not only with each other but also – and sometimes dramatically – with their own taxpayers. With the imminent arrival of 1992 the fiscal landscape will change significantly: if current capital tax systems are left untouched, European governments are likely to find it very hard to collect revenue from internationally mobile capital. Indeed, Europe may transform itself into a single (large) tax haven.

In this paper we perform an exercise in applied positive economics: we design a model of residence-based corporate taxation that, while preserving national tax sovereignties, minimizes the distortions arising from international capital mobility. This type of exercise is in our view especially useful because in the current debates over tax reform in Europe there is much confusion between administrative problems and political constraints.[1] Analysis of models of taxation like ours can help clarify where administrative issues end and political issues begin.

To motivate our study, we begin in section 2 with a look at the data on revenue from capital income taxes and a brief discussion of the role of the history of capital taxation in shaping the fiscal institutions and private practices that are visible today. After listing in section 3 the (often unintended) distortionary incentives embodied in current tax treatments of international income, we analyse in section 4.1 a plan for a system of corporate income taxation that is consistent with the goal of minimizing the distortions arising from the international mobility of capital. The plan is inspired by the full application of the residence principle of taxation of international capital income. The plan is further discussed in section 4.2 and 4.3.

172

Table 7.1. *The revenue from capital income taxes, 1987*

Country	Revenue from capital income taxes as % of					
	Income taxes		Total tax revenue		GDP	
Belgium	34.4	(29.1)	13.5	(11.4)	6.2	(5.3)
Denmark	17.0	(8.0)	9.6	(4.5)	5.0	(2.3)
France	55.4	(29.1)	10.0	(5.2)	4.5	(2.3)
Germany	24.2	(14.7)	8.2	(5.0)	3.1	(1.9)
Greece	40.8	(25.9)	7.0	(4.1)	2.6	(1.7)
Ireland	20.6	(9.0)	7.8	(3.4)	3.1	(1.4)
Italy	37.2	(30.0)	13.4	(10.6)	4.9	(3.9)
Luxembourg	56.5	(40.4)	23.9	(17.1)	10.5	(7.5)
Netherlands	44.7	(31.4)	12.2	(8.6)	5.9	(4.1)
Portugal	58.4	(48.0)	11.3	(9.3)	3.6	(2.9)
Spain	35.2	(22.7)	10.4	(6.7)	3.4	(2.2)
United Kingdom	66.3	(30.7)	24.7	(11.4)	9.2	(4.3)
EC Average	40.9	(26.6)	12.7	(8.1)	5.2	(3.3)
United States	51.3	(28.3)	22.7	(12.5)	6.8	(3.8)

Note: Figures in parentheses represent calculations in which capital tax revenues exclude revenues from wealth taxes.

Source: Authors' calculations based on data in OECD (1989).

2   Capital income tax revenue: international comparisons and their interpretation

Table 7.1 reports the revenue from capital income taxes in the 12 EC countries and in the United States, for the year 1987. These revenues include those of the central government and of state and local governments. Capital income taxes are defined as the sum of corporate income taxes, of taxes on capital gains to individuals and, when available, any other taxes on capital income accrued to individuals,[2] plus taxes on net wealth, property, inheritance and gifts, and financial transactions ('wealth taxes' in the OECD classification). The latter have been included since they might stand for taxes on certain types of capital income that are different to estimate in practice such as the value of owner-occupied housing (hence authorities use welath as a basis to compute the tax due). The numbers in parentheses contain the same computations when wealth taxes are excluded. The revenues from capital income are reported as a fraction of total incomes (excluding wealth), total tax revenue, and gross domestic product, respectively.

Table 7.1 reveals a number of important facts. As a percent of GDP,

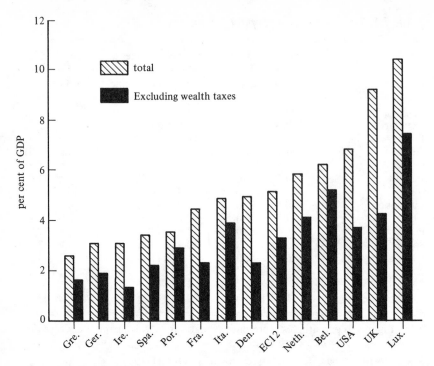

Figure 7.1   The revenue from capital income taxes

capital income taxes are relatively low in Europe, despite the fact that the ratio of taxes to GDP is higher in the EC than in the United States (40.6% versus 30% in 1987). This is further highlighted by figure 7.1, reporting the revenue from (the two definitions of) capital income taxes as percent of GDP. The ratio of capital income taxes to GDP is equal to 6.8% in the US, but only 5.2% on average in the 12 members of the EC. Excluding Luxembourg and the UK, the only two countries with a ratio of capital income taxes to GDP higher than the US, the European average falls to 4.2%. Among the countries with less capital income tax revenues than the US (and Luxembourg and the UK), Belgium and the Netherlands both exceed 5.5% of GDP, Denmark, France and Italy are in the 'middle tier' from 4 to 5%, while Portugal, Spain, Ireland, Greece and, surprisingly, the Federal Republic of Germany are all below 4%.

Since in the United States property taxes are an important source of revenue to local authorities, we repeat the calculations subtracting all wealth taxes (results in parentheses). In this case the ratio of capital income taxes to GDP decreases to 3.7% in the United States, and to 3.3% in the EC12. The average for the EC excluding the UK and Luxembourg

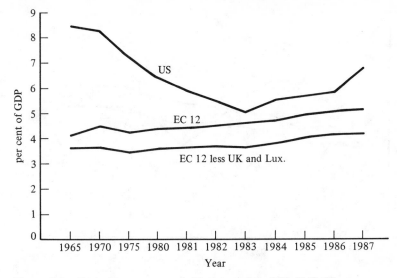

Figure 7.2   Capital income taxes in Europe and the US, 1965–87

is only 2.8% of GDP. The distribution of the revenue across EC countries (also reported in figure 7.1 in the black histogram) broadly resembles the one obtained by including wealth taxes.

The first column of table 7.1 reports the ratio of capital income taxes to total income taxes. It shows that the menu of taxes on income is not uniform across the EC12 countries. Capital income taxes account for as much as 66% of income taxes (31% when wealth taxes are excluded) in the United Kingdom, as little as 17% of income taxes in Denmark. The second column, reporting capital income taxes as a fraction of total tax revenue, highlights the important role of taxes on goods and services in European countries. In the US the ratio of capital income taxes to total tax revenue is almost twice as large as in Europe.

Figures 7.2 and 7.3 show the historical trends in capital income tax revenue, and in the revenue from corporate income and capital gains taxes, respectively. The difference between the UK and Luxembourg and the other European partners is highlighted by the plots of both the average across the 12 EC countries and the one excluding the UK and Luxembourg. Both figures indicate the presence of a positive but small trend in Europe and wide fluctuations in the United States, even though, on average from 1965 to 1987, the US revenue from capital income taxes exceeds that in Europe. When wealth and property taxes are included, we find that the revenue in the US starts as high as 8% of GDP to drop to 5%

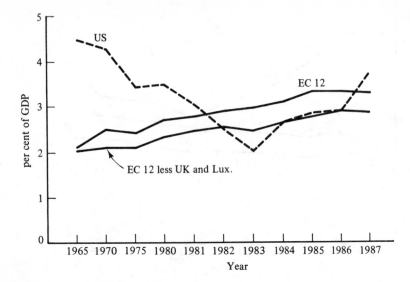

Figure 7.3   Capital gains and corporate income taxes in Europe and the US, 1965–87

of GDP in 1983 and end at roughly 7% of GDP. In Europe, there is a stable and small growth from 4% in 1965 to 5% in 1987. Corporate income taxes and capital gains taxes (in figure 7.3) start in the US at 4.5% in 1965, relative to just 2% in Europe. The figure shows that the fluctuation of capital income tax revenue in the US is due to the fluctuation of corporate tax revenue, while property taxes and wealth taxes are, as a percent of GDP, relatively stable over the sample.

In summary, the data presented in ths section suggest that the revenue from capital income or wealth taxes is, and has been, significantly lower in Europe than in the United States. In countries like West Germany, the revenue from capital income taxes is only a fraction of that in the US. Of course, the revenue from capital income taxes is the product of average tax rates times the assessed tax bases. The lower European numbers could be either due to lower effective rates, or to lower assessed bases, or to both. Except for specific cases like Luxembourg – whose economy relies heavily on the business of financial intermediaries, and whose high revenue from capital income taxes is due mostly to the high fraction of capital income in total income – the data we present cannot, by themselves, tell us what exactly determines these differences.

Knowledge of the political preferences of European governments can, however, help to interpret the evidence. Socialist and social democratic ideologies that influenced economic policy-making in Europe after the Second World War should have favoured heavier taxation of capital income than would US administrations. It seems safe to rule out explanations of lower European capital income taxes based solely on the political inclinations of governments facing the same elasticities of capital income to taxes. This leaves us with two alternatives:

(a) Effective tax rates are high but assessed bases are low because of higher avoidance or evasion than in the US.
(b) Both effective rates and assessed bases are low because the high elasticities force governments to keep rates low, both to ensure some tax revenue collections and to prevent large distortions.

Cases (a) and (b) both point to the following, related, phenomena:

In Europe the costs of administering or enforcing capital income taxes are higher than in the United States (this might explain the data for Greece, Spain, Portugal and Ireland);
In Europe the elasticities of capital income tax bases to tax rates are higher than in the United States.

These phenomena find a likely explanation both in the geographical structures of European countries and in the historical experience of capital income taxation on the two continents. Consider the geographical constraints first: the fraction of population living close to national borders is much higher in Europe as a whole than in the US. European residents are thus more aware of the potential for tax avoidance offered by international transactions. Furthermore, the cost of exporting capital abroad, both legally and illegally, are likely to be lower in Europe, since proximity increases the frequency and the ease of border crossings and lowers the probability of detection.

The historical experience provides additional potential explanation for the apparently higher elasticity of capital flows to capital income taxes in Europe.[3] The financial burden of the First World War was proportionately much higher in Europe than in the United States, because of the difference in the size of the war effort. As a result, government indebtedness grew so much in Europe that in the immediate postwar period a large fraction of the public opinion, including leaders of the middle-class liberal parties, favoured extraordinary taxation of capital – a capital levy – to restore the public finances.

Capital levies have been fiercely debated in the United Kingdom and France, and were actually imposed, with mixed success,[4] in Italy, Germany, Austria, Hungary and Czechoslovakia. There is to date no systematic study of the effects of these capital levies on international capital flows, and the way the private sector attempted to avoid these extraordinary taxes, in part because good data on balance-of-payments transactions in the capital account are very difficult to obtain. Indirect evidence together with descriptive accounts, however, suggest that capital flight in response to the announcement of the capital levies could have been significant.[5]

Rearmament further increased the fiscal burden on capital income. These demands were met by higher taxes in most countries and by new capital levies in Italy (1937 and 1938) and in Hungary (1938). Furthermore, in other countries capital levies were contemplated but not implemented.[6]

Finally, the two world wars had additional, and more dramatic, differential effects on private welath: they were fought on European soil, not in North America. European savers had to bear extraordinary taxes not only from their governments, but also from the armies of occupation; they had to escape political persecution and deportation; and they suffered directly from deterioration and destruction of their investments in physical capital.

In conclusion, the geography of the European continent, the two world wars and the extraordinary taxes that they brought along, are likely to have left profound markings on the attitudes of savers towards tax authorities. They suggest the presence of higher responsiveness of European savers to current or anticipated taxes on capital income, and explain their demand for privacy, and the attendant success of European tax havens. At the same time, the evolution of national tax systems also reflects recent history. National tax systems are characterized by provisions designed to avoid double taxation, and tax authorities have created a number of bilateral tax treaties designed to grant reciprocal advantages in the imposition of withholding taxes on interest and dividend payments. Yet, as we show in the following section, in view of substantial international capital mobility, the current regime is characterized by almost non-existent cooperation among tax authorities, and in fact, by its very nature, it exerts on them strong pressures to compete with each other.

3   Capital income taxes in Europe

In this section we briefly sketch the current regime of taxation of capital income, paying special attention to the treatment of foreign-source income. The purpose of this exercise is to highlight the way the current regime introduces distortions in the allocations of international investment and in the level of taxation.

Table 7.2. *Statutory corporate tax rates, 1989 (in per cent)*

	Central government	Central and local government[1]
Belgium	43	43
Denmark	50	50
France	39	39
Germany	56/36/[2]	62/45/[2]
Greece	35[3]	35[7]
Ireland	10[4]	10[4]
Italy	36	46
Luxembourg	37[5]	43
Netherlands	35	35
Portugal	36.5	40
Spain	35	36[6]
United Kingdom	35	35

Notes:
[1]Net rates.
[2]Split rate system: first rate applies to retained earnings, second rate to distributed earnings.
[3]Rate for industrial companies quoted on the Athens Stock Exchange.
[4]Rate for industrial companies, to remain into effect until the end of the year 2000. The standard rate for other companies is 43%.
[5]Including a 2% surcharge (deductible) for the employment fund.
[6]Includes the surcharge for the chamber of commerce.

Source: Tanzi and Bovenberg (1989).

3.1   Corporate taxes

3.1.1 Tax rates
The countries of Europe currently tax corporate income at different rates; table 7.2 summarizes the statutory corporate income tax rates in the 12 EC countries. The table suggests that there is considerable variation in these rates; differences in corporate income *bases*, discussed below, further complicate the analysis of investment incentives in different European countries.

An interesting phenomenon observed in the recent past is a weak tendency of corporate tax rates to converge. In 1977 the average corporate rate in the EC12 was 43%, while the standard deviation of corporate rate was 8%. In 1989 the average rate was 40%, and the standard deviation 6.5%. This convergence towards lower rates is in the direction advocated by the 1975 draft directive on corporate income taxes (a

Table 7.3. *Depreciation methods currently applied by EC countries*

Country	Straight-line	Declining-balance
Belgium	allowed for all assets	allowed for all assets purchased after 1 January 1977 (maximum rate twice the straight-line rate)
Denmark	normally applied to buildings and intangible property	normally applied to other fixed assets (on a pool basis)
France	normal method	optional for most assets (except for buildings – other than hotels – automobiles, telephones and typewriters)
Germany (Fed. Rep.)	allowed for all assets	not available for buildings (unless specifically elected by the 'Bauherr') and for intangible assets; if available, the maximum rate is three times the straight-line rate with a maximum of 30%
Greece	normal method	not available
Ireland[1]	normal method for buildings	normal method for other fixed assets
Italy	normal method	not available
Luxembourg	allowed for all assets	not allowed for buildings and intangible property
Netherlands	allowed for all assets	allowed for all assets except buildings other than hotels
Portugal	allowed for all assets	allowed, subject, however to the approval of the tax authority
Spain	allowed for all assets	only allowed for certain new, qualifying assets
United Kingdom[2]	available for buildings	available for plant, machinery and patents

Notes:
[1] Intangible assets are depreciable in Ireland.
[2] A 100% first-year allowance is available for capital expenditure on scientific research.

Source: Kuiper (1988).

directive that was not passed by the European Parliament), and might also have been prompted by the worldwide tendency towards reduction in corporate rates, documented, for example, by Whalley (1989).

3.1.2 Tax bases

Prior to taxing income governments must define it, but all governments face the difficulty that there is seldom such thing as well-defined annual corporate income, even by their own national accounting standards. In addition, accounting methods all differ.

The most important differences arise in the depreciation of capital expenditures for tax purposes. Table 7.3 reports differences among EC countries in depreciation practices for fixed investments. As the table indicates, there is considerable variation among countries in the acceptability of declining-balanced depreciation methods (generally more favourable for investors) in place of straight-line methods. In addition, there is considerable variation even within countries but especially between them in the depreciable lifetimes of new investments, differences that are not easy to summarize in simple tables.[7] Some of these differences reflect variation in nominal interest rates (depreciation allowances are seldom indexed), and some may be related to historical differences in usable capital lifetimes, but more generally they reflect differing desires on the part of central governments to encourage investment through tax incentives.

Other differences in tax bases have more obscure origins. EC countries differ in the number of years tax losses can be carried forward and back, in the treatment of inventory gains and losses, and in the rules that govern transactions between related parties.[8] There are also very substantial discrepancies in the treatment of foreign-exchange gains and losses, the most important turning on distinctions between short-term and long-term, and realization and accrual. Again, the choice of tax base definition reflects partly the historical experience of a government and partly a contemporaneous decision of which activities to encourage and which to discourage.

There are three types of problems created by the failure of governments to harmonize their concepts of tax basis. The first is straightforward: base differences encourage tax-avoiding behaviour that may be inefficient. Countries offering accelerated depreciation of new investment expenditures attract investment capital away from countries that do not. Differences in effective tax rates on new investments summarize these incentives.[9]

The second problem concerns the coordination of tax systems for taxing international income. For example, when British multinationals claim

Table 7.4. *Tax treatment of intercompany dividends*

Country	Tax treatment
Belgium	Dividends subject to 25% w/h tax. The tax is refunded or deductible from corporate income tax of the firm receiving the dividends. 90% of gross dividend is not subject to corporate income tax.
Denmark	Tax exempt if company has owned at least 25% of total share capital during the year.
France	95% of gross dividends from subsidiaries excluded from computation of income tax.
Germany	Dividends are taxed as normal income, but credit is granted on the full underlying imputation tax (36%) and on the 25% withholding tax. Tax exempt if shareholder holds more than 10% of share capital.
Greece	Unquoted shares: dividends taxed at the source at 47% (registered shares) and 50% (bearer shares). Quoted shares: the corresponding rates are 42% and 45%.
Ireland	Dividends not liable to tax.
Italy	No special provisions exist. Dividends are not subject to local corporate income tax.
Luxembourg	Deductible from taxable income if participation exceeds 10% of share capital or LF 50 million.
Netherlands	'Participation exemption' rule: all income from a company held by at least 5%, including cash dividends, dividends in kind, bonus shares and hidden profit distributions are exempted from the corporate income tax.
Portugal	95% of gross dividends received deducted from corporate income tax. Tax withheld can be credited if holding exceeds 25% of share capital.
Spain	All dividends included in calculation of corporate income. Withholding tax is credited. 50% of dividends can be credited in general, 100% if share capital held exceeds 25%.
United Kingdom	All dividends are excluded from the taxable income of the recipient company. Intragroup dividends may be paid without advanced corporation tax.

Source: Price Waterhouse (1989).

Table 7.5. *Tax treatment of foreign-source dividends*

Country	Taxation principle	Credit/deduction
Belgium	W	Deduction
Denmark	W	Credit
France	T[d]	Both[a][d]
Germany	W	Both[a]
Greece	W	Credit
Ireland	W	Credit
Italy	W	Credit[b]
Luxembourg	W	Both[a]
Netherlands	W[c]	Exemption
Portugal	W	Credit
Spain	W	Credit
UK	W	Credit

Notes: 'W' stands for 'worldwide' and 'T' stands for 'territorial'.
(*a*) Taxes paid abroad in excess of the allowable credit are deductible as expenses.
(*b*) Taxpayer is entitled to a refund of the excess foreign tax credit.
(*c*) Resident corporations often receive proportionate relief for taxable income in other countries granted by way of unilateral relief (see discussion of the 'participation exemption').
(*d*) In general France does not allow any tax credits against foreign income taxes paid on the business income of foreign permanent establishments. This does not apply to foreign-sourced dividends or interest, which are subject to French corporate tax when realized, and for which a foreign tax credit may offset French taxes.

Source: Price Waterhouse (1989); Giovannini (1989).

foreign tax credits for taxes paid by their French subsidiaries to the French government, it is necessary for those companies to establish exactly how much income they earned in France, when it was earned, what French taxes were paid on that income, and when it was paid. The mechanics of this computation typically affect the attractiveness of real and financial decisions of the French (and other) subsidiaries. Unusual incentives typically emerge due to the differences between home-definition and host-definition of taxable income.[10]

The third problem stems from the inability of governments to coordinate intermediate charges between multinational parent companies and their related affiliates; the partial solutions that governments adopt create incentives for firms to respond inefficiently to national tax differences. Enforcement of transfer-pricing regulations is often imperfect; cognizant governments have introduced *ad hoc* measures in response. This phenomenon is particularly acute in the cases of cross-border charges for intangible goods such as patent royalties and interest charges, but is not limited to these; if the post-1992 regime in Europe in fact involves porous and unmonitored borders between countries, then international trans-actions between related parties will offer opportunities for tax arbitrage.

3.1.3 Measures to avoid double taxation

Table 7.4 reports the tax treatment of intercompany dividends from domestic sources: all countries have provisions to avoid double taxation of group income. The treatment of income from the same firms' foreign subsidiaries is, however, quite different.

Table 7.5, reporting the treatment of income from foreign susidiaries, shows that all countries except France follow the worldwide (or resi-dence) principle. This is in accordance with the OECD Model Double Taxation Convention (1977), which aims at achieving a sort of 'capital export neutrality'. Since foreign income becomes taxable both by the authorities of the host country (where the income is produced), and by the authorities of the country of residence of the parent company (or the individual owner), taxes paid to foreign authorities are *credited* against domestic taxes by most countries that follow the residence principle.

In practice, foreign taxes are credited by computing domestic taxes owed on foreign-source income *grossed up* by foreign taxes, and then subtrac-ting foreign taxes paid. In some countries, like the F.R. of Germany and Ireland, investors have the option of *deducting* from taxable income foreign taxes paid.

Double taxation relief can take other forms. Some of the countries applying the residence principle allow exemptions of special kinds of foreign-source income. In Belgium, if a foreign corporation is a 'per-manent investment' of a domestic corporation, 95% of its dividend income is exempted from the Belgian tax.[11] In the Netherlands, dividends of companies that qualify for the 'Participation exemption'[12] are exemp-ted from Dutch taxes: this rule extends the treatment of group income to foreign-source income.

The application of the residence principle, however, is subject to two important exceptions:

> Countries impose a *limitation* on foreign tax credits. The calculation of tax credit limitations varies significantly across European coun-tries. In Belgium, the foreign tax credit for 'non-permanent' invest-ments is 15%. In Denmark, the limit is either 50% of the Danish income tax attributable to the net income of the foreign affiliate (in the case where the parent is jointly taxed with the subsidiary) or the

equivalent of the Danish tax rate applied to foreign income (in the case where the parent is not jointly taxed with the subsidiary). In Germany the tax credit is 36% of the foreign income. In Greece and Spain the limitation is based on the domestic corporate tax rate. In Luxembourg, any foreign taxes in excess of the domestic rate are deductible as expenses. As a rule of thumb, the limitation is normally equal to the domestic tax rate applied to foreign-source income. It is justified by governments' reluctance to subsidize foreign investments by domestic residents, by paying their foreign taxes in excess of the domestic rate applied to foreign-source income. The limitation has two effects: (a) whenever investors accumulate excess tax credits (foreign taxes paid exceed the credit limitation)[13] income from domestic and foreign investments is taxed at different rates (domestic and foreign investments end up being taxed at the domestic and foreign tax rates, respectively); (b) whenever excess credits in some countries[14] can be offset against excess limitations in other countries, the allocation of foreign investments among high- and low-income-tax countries can also be distorted.

The concept of foreign-source income differs from the one used in the computation of the corporate income tax. Most countries require that domestic taxes be levied when the dividends are paid by the foreign subsidiary to the parent company, and not when the dividend income is produced. Hence, the deferral of dividend payments amounts to a deferral of the payment of domestic taxes, while foreign taxes are regularly paid as income is produced. Deferral – when allowed – defeats the main purpose of the worldwide principle: foreign subsidiaries pay only the foreign tax as long as dividends are not repatriated.

For these reasons, the treatments of foreign subsidiaries' incomes differ significantly from those of domestic subsidiaries. These differences affect corporate financial policies, the cost of capital, and investment decisions. Deferral and the tax credit limitation are the two features that, despite the formal adoption by most EC countries of the residence principle, make the current regime look more like a regime of territorial taxation.

As long as corporate income is taxed in the location in which it is earned, the tax rates differ, then corporations have incentives to manipulate the prices they use to record international transactions. In particular, firms can be expected to declare that income was earned in low-tax locations rather than high-tax locations. Two problems result. The first is that European governments as a whole fail to collect the taxes they would otherwise be due on income truly earned in Europe. Those taxes actually collected may accrue to the 'wrong' governments; that is, tax havens rather than the governments in whose country income actually was earned.

The second problem is that the course of facilitating transfer price manipulation can involve resource misallocation by firms attempting to cover trails of fictitious trades. This problem already faces European tax systems. It is, however, likely to grow in magnitude as cross-border trades become easier with the removal of customs barriers.

One manifestation of this problem is very real yet generally ignored in analyses of the inefficiencies that accompany current European tax systems. As just mentioned, the treatment of transfers of intangible goods like patents is especially problematic: intangibles typically have unique features that make them hard to price on a world market and difficult to value even within a firm.[15] The nature of regulation seems to be that governments are able only in extreme cases to enforce their arm's-length pricing legislation.

As a result, most governments have adopted rule-of-thumb requirements for allocating some intangible costs and profits. But rules like the one applied by the US – according to which US multinationals with foreign sales are not allowed to deduct 100% of their research and development costs against domestic-source income – end up discouraging productive activities like research and development. This occurs because foreign governments, in turn, do not permit their resident US-owned subsidiaries to deduct the remaining part of the research and development expenditures.

International differences in taxation also create incentives to locate productive and financial activities in low-tax countries. This encourages national governments to lower their taxation of internationally mobile capital in order to attract it from abroad. Indeed, countries can attract foreign capital by subsidizing foreign residents' tax avoidance and tax evasion. In equilibrium this process leads to under-taxation of capital income.[16]

3.2   The integration of corporate and individual taxes

Table 7.6 illustrates the taxation of corporate income accruing to individual shareholders, in the form of dividends and capital gains. As far as dividend taxation is concerned, countries adopting the *classical* system tax income both at the firm level and at the individual level. Countries adopting the *split rate* system tax distributed profits at a lower rate than undistributed profits. Finally, countries adopting the *imputation* system provide individuals with credits for the taxes paid by the corporations they own. Table 7.6 shows that, even though many countries provide some credit for corporate taxes paid by firms, perfect integration between individual and corporate taxes is not achieved. Capital gains receive preferential tax treatment at the individual level in almost all countries.

The treatment of corporate income from abroad accruing to individuals, however, is again different. In this case governments are unwilling to grant credits for taxes paid to foreign governments by corporations owned by domestic residents. This reluctance stems in part from the reporting burden that crediting would impose on corporations. If individuals were eligible for credits on the taxes paid by the corporations whose shares they own, then it would be necessary for those corporations to calculate the appropriate credits, since individuals do not have access to firms' detailed financial and tax records. But, given the current hodge-podge of national accounting rules, European corporations would have to compute credits with 12 different methods to accommodate just European shareholders' needs; many more such calculations would be necessary throughout the world. Instead European governments deny individuals the credit, thereby making multiple complicated calculations unnecessary, and discouraging (relative to a credit system) individual ownership of foreign shares.

The absence of perfect international integration of individual and corporate taxes would induce, in the current regime, an additional distortion, even if the worldwide principle were perfectly applied at the level of the corporation. Multinational corporations would have an incentive to locate their parent companies in low-tax countries in order to minimize double-taxation of their own shareholders. In this case the location of investments by corporations would not be affected by differences in tax rates, but tax revenues would be affected, compelling governments to rely on alternative sources of funds.

3.3 Withholding taxes

Withholding taxes are the most typical sign of the inefficiencies of the current tax regime. They are levied at different rates by the *source* country, depending on the country of residence of the payees, and on the nature of the investment income (see tables 7.7 and 7.8). Withholding taxes arose in part due to governments' (in some cases well grounded) lack of faith in their own ability to enforce their domestic tax laws against clever international avoidance and capital flight; by taxing capital income as it leaves the country, governments feel that they limit their exposure to avoidance. The lack of uniformity of withholding taxes across European

Table 7.6. *The integration of corporate and personal taxes in EC countries*

Country	Corporate taxes	Taxation of dividends	Taxation of capital gains	Regime
Belgium	Basic rate 43%	NA	NA	Imputation
Denmark	50% (state income tax)	Marginal ind. rate	50% on short-term gains.	Imputation
France	42% on distributed profits: 39% on undistributed profits.	Marginal rate less tax credits (= 50% of cash div. received)	16% if gains > F288,400 or shares held > 25% firm cap.	Imputation
Germany	36% on distributed profits; 50% on undistributed profits.	dividends grossed up and credit is granted on full 36% corpor. tax.	long-term gains (> 6 months) untaxes. Short-term gains taxed.	Split rate
Greece	35–46% depending on the nature of business.	dividends of < Dr. 50,000 (per shareholding) or < Dr. 200,000 (overall) not taxable.	Not taxable.	Imputation
Ireland	43% basic rate.	Tax credit on div. (28/72nds of dividends received)	s.t. (< 1 yr) 60%	Imputation
Italy	Basic tax 36% plus 56.25% 'excess' dividend distributions[1]	Dividends received grossed up by 56.25%. Credit granted at 36%. Also w/h tax 10%.	Not taxable unless arising from spec. intent.	Imputation
Luxembourg	Progressive schedule 20% to 34%.	Withholding taxes on dividends credited.	Taxed at ord. rate if < 6 months.	Classical
Netherlands	35% basic rate.	Fully taxed.	Not taxable unless vendor has held 'substantial interest'.	Classical
Portugal	36.5% basic rate.	Taxed at 25%.	On shares held for more than 24 months: 10%.	Split rate

Table 7.6. (cont.)

Country	Corporate taxes	Taxation of dividends	Taxation of capital gains	Regime
Spain	Basic rate 35% assumed w/h rate if profits distributed.	Receipts grossed up and withholding credited.	Taxed as 'irregular income'.	Imputation
United Kingdom	35% basic rate.	Receipts taxed at individual rate.	Taxed at individual rate.	Imputation

Note:
¹Dividend distributions exceeding 64% of taxable income.

Sources: Corporate taxes, taxation of dividends, taxation of individual capital gains and, for Spain, integration regime: Price Waterhouse (1989). Local income taxes not included. Integration regimes: Alworth (1988), except for Spain.

Table 7.7. *Withholding taxes on dividends* (%)

Paying country	Recipient country											
	Belgium	Denmark	France	Germany	Greece	Ireland	Italy	Luxembourg	Netherlands	Portugal	Spain	UK
Belgium	—	15	10-15	15	15	15	15	10-15	5-15	15	15	15
Denmark	15	—	0	15	30	0	15	15	15	10	10	15
France	15	0	—	0	25	10-15	15	15-25	15	15	10	15
Germany	10-25	10-25	10-25	—	25	10-20	25	10-25	10-25	15	15	10-25
Greece	25	42-53	42-53	25	—	42-53	25	42-53	35	42-53	42-53	42-53
Ireland	0	0	0	0	0	—	0	0	0	0	0	0
Italy	15	15	15	30	25	15	—	15	0-30	15	15	5-15
Luxembourg	10-15	5-15	5	10-15	15	5-15	15	—	2.5-15	15	15	5-15
Netherlands	5-15	0-15	5-15	10-15	5-15	0-15	0	2.5-15	—	25	5	5-15
Portugal	12	10-12	12	12	12	12	12	12	12	—	10-12	10-12
Spain	15	10	10	10	18	18	15	18	10	5	—	10
UK	*	*	*	*	*	*	*	*	*	*	*	*

Note:

*For the UK, tax treaties have been renegotiated. No withholding taxes are normally levied on dividends. The exact treatment can vary depending on the type of treaty.

Sources: Price Waterhouse (1989); Giovannini (1989).

Table 7.8. *Withholding taxes on interest* (%)

Paying country	Recipient country											
	Belgium	Denmark	France	Germany	Greece	Ireland	Italy	Luxembourg	Netherlands	Portugal	Spain	UK
Belgium[a]	—	15	15	0–15	10	15	15	0–15	0–10	15	15	15
Denmark	0	—	0	0	0	0	0	0	0	0	0	0
France[b]	10–15	0	—	0	0–10	0	15	10–45	0–10	10–12	10	10
Germany[c]	0–15	0	0	—	10	0	25–50	0	15–50	0–15	10	0
Greece	15	25	10	10	—	25	10	25	10	25	25	0
Ireland	15	0	0	0	35	—	10	0	0	35	35	0
Italy	12.5–25	12.5–25	12.5–25	0–25	10	10	—	0–10	12.5–25	12.5–25	12	12.5–25
Luxembourg	0	0	0	0	0	0	0	—	0	0	0	0
Netherlands	0	0	0	0	0	0	0	0	—	0	0	0
Portugal	15	15	10–12	10–12	30	30	15	30	30	—	30	10
Spain	15	10	10	10	18	18	12	18	10	15	—	12
UK	15	0	10	0	0	0	27	0	0	10	12	—

Notes:
(a) No withholding tax on interest due on commercial debts and interest paid by banks established in Belgium to foreign banks or to certain non-residents.
(b) The lower rates generally apply to income from bonds and other negotiable securities. No tax withheld on interest on foreign currency deposits with French banks. The rate may also be reduced to 10% for interest paid on loans granted to French companies by foreign banks. Luxembourg holding companies are not entitled to any of the benefits of the France–Luxembourg treaty.
(c) Interest payments on normal loans and publicity issued bonds are not subject to withholding tax.

Sources: Price Waterhouse (1989); Giovannini (1989).

countries is due to a number of bilateral tax treaties, whereby countries grant reciprocal lowering of rates. Differences in tax rates then lead naturally to their own distortions in the pattern and magnitude of capital flows.

Withholding taxes are often fully credited by domestic tax authorities, since strictly speaking they represent the obligation of the payee and not the payer, the payer being merely the withholding agent.[17]

3.4   *Summary*

This brief description of European tax systems suggests a general conclusion: there is a wide gap between the general tax principles that most countries agree with, and the imperfection of day-to-day practice. This gap is mostly due to the lack of cooperation among tax authorities, as well as to inconsistencies in the tax systems that slowly evolve behind the rapidly changing international financial markets. In particular, three main points stand out:

> Countries rely on territorial taxation and withholding taxes in order to ensure some tax revenue in the presence of high international capital mobility. In particular, the corporation tax is the typical territorial tax, and, in the presence of integration between corporate and individual income taxes, it works as a withholding tax on individual incomes. This situation has evolved partly because of the remarkable absence of cooperation among tax authorities in industrialized countries, mirrored by strategic use of bank secrecy laws to attract foreign tax evaders.
>
> The application of the worldwide principle at the firm and at the individual level is ineffective in the presence of deferral, tax-credit limitations, and imperfect integration of corporate and individual income taxes. This gives rise to distortions in the geographical allocation of investment.
>
> The increased integration of goods and assets markets increases the difficulties in administering such a system, which requires a determination of the territorial distribution of income produced by multinational corporations.

4   Reforming capital income taxes

The advent of 1992 will be accompanied by a number of contemplated and proposed reforms in European practices of taxing capital income. It appears that the various reform movements draw their impetus from two

sources. As the argument in section 3 illustrates, those who seek efficiency
in the taxation of capital income have every reason to be dissatisfied with
current practices, and, while these inefficiencies are not new, the general
spirit of reform and agreed goal of intra-European efficiency in 1992 offer
the opportunity to repair a system long in need of fixing. The second
source concerns the harmonization of value-added taxes in view of the
elimination of border controls. In the absence of these controls 1992 is
likely to bring a flood of tax arbitrage unless new measures are taken.

The European Commission as long ago as 1975 proposed a scheme of
corporate tax harmonization throughout Europe that envisioned uniform
tax rates and integration of corporate and personal taxes. More recently,
the Commission in 1988 prepared an 'avant projet' for a draft directive to
harmonize definitions of tax bases for corporate income. Both proposals
have attractive features, though the first foundered in practice on its
implied reduction in overall tax revenue and the removal of countries'
abilities to set tax rates at whatever level they choose. In the absence of
coordinated actions such as those potentially provided by the Commission, the EC countries find themselves engaging in *de facto* uncoordinated
harmonization via corporate tax reductions. The question facing Europe,
then, is whether there is an efficient and acceptable coordinated alternative.

There are several alternatives on the table. After reviewing many of the
possible tax arrangements, Devereux and Pearson (1989) argue in favour
of corporate taxation on the basis of residence of parent companies, or,
failing that, corporate taxation at source.[18] McLure (1989) reviews the
experience of unitary state-level corporate income taxation within the
United States, and, while careful not to offer unitary taxation as a
panacea for Europe, at the same time urges its consideration as an
alternative to other schemes that fail to address more directly problems
related to cross-border trade after 1992. Tanzi and Bovenberg (1989)
favour harmonization of tax bases around an agreed reasonable standard,
along with at least partial uniformity in statutory tax rates. Musgrave
(1987) and Cnossen (1989) also recommend base harmonization and rate
equalization in view of firms' abilities to transfer profits to low-tax
jurisdictions; in addition, Musgrave favours harmonization on the
grounds of interjurisdictional equity, while Cnossen fears the alternative
of intergovernmental tax competition.

Any proposal for reform must confront the reality that raising revenue
distorts resource allocation. The direction of reform consistent with the
goals of recent EC proposals is one that minimizes revenue loss over the
transition, preserves the double taxation of corporate income, offers
incentives that are as efficient as possible and at the same time permits a

wide degree of national tax sovereignty. We analyse one such scheme: a plan providing for international corporate taxation under the residence principle and with no deferral. In particular, we consider a system in which each country collects tax revenue on the *corporate* income earned by its *individual* residents. The system is effective if the definition of this income is harmonized among states of Europe and if the appropriate coordinating practices are adopted. Fortunately, many of the necessary apparatuses are similar if not identical to those already contemplated.

4.1   A model corporate tax system

4.1.1 Corporate tax rates
Under this plan corporations would be taxed throughout Europe at a uniform high rate, such as 50%. Taxes would be due on a territorial basis, to the government of the country where earned. There would be no distinction for the purposes of this tax between a local branch of a foreign corporation and a separately incorporated entity.

A separate system of country-specific rebates would apply to owners of corporate shares. Individual governments would set their own tax rates on corporate income, subject to the constraint that every country's rate must be not more than the overall European rate (50% in the previous example). Owners of corporations would receive rebates from their home governments for the difference between 50% and their local rate.

4.1.2 Tax basis
The definition of taxable corporate income would be for each country the outcome of mutual agreement. The presumption is uniformity of tax basis according to Haig-Simons principles as practically implementable. Hence, corporations investing in plant and equipment would deduct from their taxable income depreciation allowances that reflect (as closely as possible) actual capital lifetimes and decay patterns. Expenditures on research and development and on advertising would be deductible quickly, but in a manner consistent with the capital nature of these investments. Inventories would be treated for tax purposes in LIFO fashion and indexed for inflation. International transactions between related parties would be recorded at arm's-length prices.

Host governments would be permitted to subsidize firms, industries, and particular industries (such as investments in new structures or in research and development), but the subsidy would be includable in the tax base. Thus, if the UK government were to offer a 5% investment incentive for new manufacturing structures, the total value of the incentive payment (since it is a part of before-tax profits) would be taxable at the overall European rate (e.g. 50%). Subsidies could of course take the indirect form that governments collect taxes at rates lower than the European rate; those subsidizing governments would then be responsible for making up the difference between what all European firms must pay (e.g. 50% of profits, inclusive of subsidies) and the taxes they collect from the firms they subsidize.

4.1.3 Measures to avoid double taxation
Foreign income within Europe would be exempt from direct corporate taxation by the country of corporate residence. The profits of a French subsidiary of an Italian parent company would be taxed at the corporate level only once, by the government of France; there would be no additional tax due to Italy. Of course, if the shareholders of the parent company were Italian, then they would be eligible for rebates from Italy as described in section 4.1.1.

Foreign income outside Europe would be taxed at the full 50% rate, but a credit allowed for foreign income taxes paid directly by European owners or indirectly by their subsidiaries. The credit would be subject to a limitation represented by the 50% rate applied to extra-EC income.

4.1.4 Corporate/personal integration
Corporate income would be attributed to individual shareholders without deferral, and therefore subject (potentially) to taxation at the individual level and the corporate level. Governments would have great flexibility in choosing the rate of personal and corporate taxation, subject only to the restriction that the rate of residence-basis corporate taxation not exceed the European maximum (e.g. 50%).

Individuals would receive rebates from their home governments equal to the difference between the taxes paid by the corporations they own and the individuals' national tax rate on corporate income. It would be incumbent on individuals to file for their own rebates; this process is facilitated by vouchers provided for shareholders at yearend by corporations.

4.1.5 Withholding taxes
Governments would not be permitted to impose withholding taxes on corporate financial flows between European countries.

4.1.6 A clearing system
A clearing system would be established to reallocate corporate income taxes from source countries to the countries of shareholder residence. For

example, suppose that the corporate tax rate in Denmark is 30%, and consider the case of a Greek company 50% owned by Greek citizens and 50% by Danish citizens, earning profits of 200 in Greece. The firm pays 100 in taxes to the Greek government, and the Danish shareholders receive 20 [200 × 0.5 × (0.5 − 0.3)] in rebates from the government of Denmark. The clearing system then reallocates 50% of the tax revenue collected by the Greek government to the Danish government. The clearing mechanism can be based on corporate records, and can use the vouchers submitted by individuals to their national governments as an indirect check and a mechanism to identify non-compliance. Notice that this type of clearing system would be much less burdensome than the one envisioned for value-added taxes by the Cookfield plan (draft directives presented in August 1987), which required a record for every transaction subject to the tax. Under this plan, there is a set of records for every corporation's annual income statement: the whole system of tax clearing is unlikely to exceed, every year, a few hundred thousand entries.

There are several alternative modes of operation for the tax clearing system, each of them consistent with its general purpose. The system could be either destination-based or source-based. In the former case countries compute the difference between rebates paid and taxes received, thus obtaining the net credit position *vis-à-vis* the clearing fund. In the latter case corporations provide information to their tax authorities about their foreign ownership during the tax year, thus enabling tax authorities to compute their net debit position *vis-à-vis* the clearing fund. The two systems could of course work in parallel.

The clearing system would be likely to face severe demands from stocks that are heavily traded. There are a few methods that might be used to handle multiple short-term ownership of stocks during reporting periods. One method would require individuals who file for rebates to declare the dates of their ownership and prorate corporate tax payments during, say, that quarter. Alternatively, governments could establish *de minimis* rules for ownership − stocks must be held for whole quarters in order for owners to be eligible for rebates, for example. The *de minimus* approach purchases administrative simplicity at the expense of 'throwing sand in the gears' of financial markets by locking investors into their stocks in order to get rebates; but a number of commentors have recently proposed such measures in order to reduce volatility in stock markets.[19] Alternatively, tax payments could be assigned to particular (quarterly) dates and the owners on these dates; while such an approach is likely to create short-term clienteles for stock ownership in low-tax countries, the problem seems unlikely to be any more severe than the rather mild problem that already exists with stock ownership on dividend days.

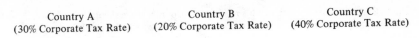

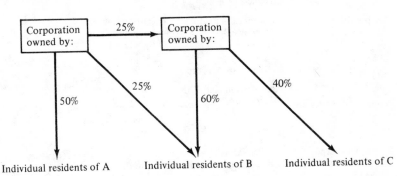

Figure 7.4   The application of residence-based taxation: an example of a chain of international corporate ownership

The clearing system would retain source taxation of corporate income earned by non-Europeans. Suppose an American company owns an Italian subsidiary that in turn has a 100%-owned second-tier French subsidiary, and the French subsidiary earns 150 in profits; which government would collect the 75 in tax revenue? It is envisioned that the tax revenue would be divided according to arm's-length principles, but these are subject to agreement.

4.1.7 Openness to other governments

Whatever an 'ideal' system of international taxation is considered, it is necessary to tackle the issues raised by its adoption only by a limited group of countries, while in the rest of the world tax havens and other loopholes survive. We envision a structure in which only the rules that do not require changes in foreign laws are extended to the rest of the world. This system maintains the general regime currently in place: foreign tax credits and tax-credit limitations would be applied using the 50% rate and foreign corporations are taxed at the 50% rate on the income they produce in Europe. However, foreign source income produced in the rest of the world would be taxable when produced and not only when remitted (deferral is eliminated).

At the same time, every country willing to join this system would be allowed to do so. In other words, it should be possible to extend the exemption of income produced by investors residing in a country, in exchange for the same privilege allowed on income produced by

Country A's residents	Country B's residents	Country C's residents
(30% Corporate Tax Rate)	(20% Corporate Tax Rate)	(40% Corporate Tax Rate)

(Owners of B's corp.)

Corporation paid 25	Corporation paid 7.5	Corporation paid 5
They owe 15	They owe 3	They owe 4
Rebate = 10	Rebate = 4.5	Rebate = 1

(Owners of A's corp.)

Corporation paid 12.5
They owe 5
Rebate = 7.5

Notes: The corporation in A has earned 100.
The corporation in B is exempted for income from A.

Figure 7.5   Calculation of rebates

investments in that country that are owned by domestic residents, and the application of the 50% rate and the system of clearing and rebates.

Figures 7.4 and 7.5 illustrate the practical working of this system. Figure 7.4 shows an example of a structure of cross-country investments owned both by corporations and individuals. The source of income is the corporation in country A. That corporation is taxed at the 50% rate, and pays after tax profits to a corporation in B, and to direct owners in A and B. The corporation in B is in turn owned by country B's residents and by residents in country C. The calculation of tax rebates is performed by computing the difference between the taxes paid by the corporation in A pro-rated to the individual owner, and the taxes owed (obtained by applying the tax rate in the country of residence). Since the corporation in B is exempted from taxes income received from the corporation in A, indirect ownership shares are computed by multiplying the shares of ownership in the various corporations in the chain. Hence the residents of C, owning 40% of the corporation in B which owns 25% of the corporation in A, end up owning $(0.4) \times (0.25) = 0.10$ of the corporation in A. Hence the tax payments to country A attributable to country C's residents are 5 (50% of 10% of the total profits of the corporation in A) and the calculation of the rebate follows directly.

4.2   Why residence-based taxation of international corporate income?

The scheme described in section 5.1 permits European governments to tax twice the returns to corporate capital investments: once at the corporate level, and a second time at the individual level. What could possibly be the rationale for such a system?

It is not our intention to consider carefully the full range of questions raised by the taxation of corporate income. These questions include issues of whether and to what degree the corporate income tax really is a tax, by whom the burden of the tax is borne, what distributional effects the tax has, what are its effects on incentives to invest, and what is the likely magnitude of its efficiency cost.[20]

Instead, we start from the observation that every European country taxes the income of its resident corporations. These taxes serve the function of taxing the savings of individual residents, if they own domestic corporations, and also taxing foreign residents on their shares of corporate ownership. The scheme described in section 4.1 satisfies the first of these functions, and not the second: in return for excluding foreign-owned corporations from the tax base, home governments would tax the foreign earnings of their domestic residents.

Classical public finance theory offers two governing principles of tax design: taxation according to ability to pay, and taxation according to benefits received.[21] The first concept views taxation as the government's primary redistributive instrument and may justify progressive taxation, while in the second governments act as might firms that sell public goods and may or may not be consistent with taxes falling more heavily on the rich. In addition to these general goals of the tax system, it is necessary to incorporate the incentive effects of tax rates and tax enforcement; governments that raise tax revenues with anything other than lump-sum instruments distort the economy. The existence of these distortions need not change the goals of taxation, though it must change their implementation.

On what basis, then, do governments justify their corporate taxes? The corporate tax imposed at source is sometimes viewed as a benefit tax.[22] corporations use resources in the jurisdictions in which they have profitable operations; their profits may arise in part from the characteristics of those locations. Since government activities constitute important attributes of a location, and governments make (costly) expenditures on intermediate goods like roads and port facilities, the corporate tax is, in this framework, fair exchange for the profit opportunities provided to corporations without charge by the government.

This benefit tax interpretation of corporate income taxation is, however, troubling in its implication that in the absence of corporate taxation countries would prefer that corporations not locate business operations within their boundaries. What, after all, is the social cost of corporate business activity? While externalities no doubt limit the attractiveness of hosting some businesses, the benefits of employment, indirect and wage tax revenue, and raising the general level of economic activity impel most governments to welcome new corporations, even if they need to offer generous tax holidays to do so.[23]

The benefit interpretation of the corporate income tax further requires a specification of why only incorporated businesses are subject to this tax. The benefit of incorporation is, of course, the limited liability that corporate shareholders enjoy. This is a crucial aspect of certain businesses. But incorporation is not particularly costly to governments, or at least the cost of providing it is certainly not equal to 35% of annual corporate profits.

One might argue that the benefit principle underlies corporate taxation even though governments can provide incorporation at relatively little cost: corporations earn profits through operations they could not undertake without limited liability, and governments in providing that opportunity are entitled to some of its rents. This argument, which is not compelling even in a domestic context, offers little support for systems of source-based international corporate taxation. Since multinational firms can in many cases choose their own countries of residence, the benefit of country-specific incorporation *per se* is limited to the difference in profitability with the next most desirable corporate home. This is unlikely to represent 35% of profits.

Taxation according to ability to pay offers weaker support for source-based corporate taxation. This application of the ability to pay principle requires that the incidence of corporate taxation falls on high-income individuals. Without evaluating the merits of this empirical argument, accepting it is only the first step in evaluating international source-based corporate taxation as a redistributive tax. Do tax collections from foreigners further the redistributive goals of a national tax system? A positive conclusion would take the usual understanding of redistributive taxation far beyond its boundaries. If redistribution is understood literally, then residence-based corporate taxation is clearly more consistent with this goal. Source-based taxation of foreigners looks much more like rent extraction than redistribution; in contrast, the proposed system redistributes income only among the residents of the country.

There remains another possibility: that the corporate income tax satisfies neither principle, but instead represents a compromise with the practical reality of the excess burden of taxes. Given the efficiency cost of tax collections, the corporate tax may offer an attractive method of raising (at least some) revenue. But there is no agreement on this view, either. In particular this view does not explain why corporate income should be taxed differently than non-corporate business income, and if corporate income is to be taxed, why it is not better to offer corporations efficient investment incentives with a cash-flow tax instead of a classical income tax.

The efficiency argument for corporate income taxation relies on the existence of some form of rents to incorporation. Certain businesses earn pure profits, of course, and these businesses if large may require the liability protection available to corporations. By taxing the rents governments avail themselves of distortion-free tax revenue.

The corporate income tax typically does not, however, tax only pure rents. Corporate taxes discourage investment by taxing incomes without allowance for the opportunity cost of equity capital; for equity-financed investments this lowers the after-tax rate of return on new investments. By contrast, the cash-flow tax represents an alternative scheme that taxes only pure rents.[24] Under this system the tax base is corporate profits calculated as cash-flows; firms deduct 100% of their investment expenditures immediately, but are not allowed deductions for interest payments or dividends. It is straightforward to show that the cash-flow tax does not discourage investment; the base of the tax in present value is simply abnormal returns earned in the corporate sector. These abnormal returns are rents to incorporation, and by taxing them the government obtains a fraction τ of them in revenue. From the standpoint of efficiency this tax may be very attractive indeed.[25] The flip side of its efficiency is, however, that the cash-flow tax may not raise very much in revenue.

The attractive features of the cash-flow tax illustrate a limitation at the same time. If the cash-flow tax really taxes only rents, then its optimal level presumably is 100%, or nearly so. But as the tax rate approaches 100% one would hardly expect very many businesses to stay incorporated, or many new firms to incorporate. Put differently, the benefits of incorporation are limited. These benefits may, hwoever, be related to firm size: the larger is the firm, the greater the monitoring costs of each owner and the more (potentially) costly the unlimited liability of individual owners. Larger and more profitable firms might therefore be willing to endure higher corporate taxes in return for the corporate protection. Hence the taxation of corporate income may offer just the kind of differentiation that optimal tax theory recommends.

The plan we describe contains a number of features that are consistent with the efficiency goals of current national tax efforts while at the same time preserving, and even, in some instances, reinvigorating, the national sovereignty of some tax systems that are drained by competitive pressures currently. Corporate taxation on the basis of residence of ownership rather than location of income immediately removes tax incentives to locate business in one European country versus another. It also removes the incentive to *claim* that income was earned in European locations in which it was not; since tax rates are the same whether income was earned in Germany or in Luxembourg, firms have no incentives to misrepresent the prices at which international transactions take place. Naturally, there will still be ordinary business reasons to locate plants in particular places. And one of the factors affecting such decisions will be the (pre-tax) wages firms are required to pay indigenous labour, wages that may be influenced by local income tax policies. Other government policies such as expenditures on complementary goods are likely to affect the desirability of various locations, but not to distort location decisions any more than subsidies that governments are free to make would distort them.[26]

Furthermore, if governments set tax rates independently in a residence-based corporate tax system like the one we describe, the distortions arising from non-cooperative policies are likely to be much smaller than those in a system – like the present one – of source-based taxation. In the latter system, the high responsiveness of the tax base to the tax rate, due to international capital mobility and the opportunity to shelter income by exporting capital, forces governments to set tax rates that are too low. In the former case, by contrast, the distortion arises from the effect of these taxes on the rate of interest prevailing in the system, and on investments. But these effects, which depend on the elasticity of saving to the rate of interest, are likely to be very small.[27]

There is a separate issue concerning the common level of the 'notional' European corporate tax rate, which was set at 50% in the exposition of the scheme in section 4.1. In practice governments might want to set this rate at a level higher or lower than 50%. This common rate represents the tax rate that non-European corporations must pay; setting a high rate yields one-time revenue from their capital already in place, making high rates potentially attractive to European governments. This revenue comes, however, at the cost of possibly discouraging new investments from non-European sources.[28] In addition, the managers of European corporations are likely to be disquieted by high 'notional' rates, since the differences between the common rate and national rates represent distributions to shareholders that corporate managers might not otherwise choose to make.[29]

The choice of 'notional' tax rate might also depend on the proclivity of European taxpayers to evade taxes on their capital income earned within Europe. One method of doing so currently is for individuals simply not to declare income from their ownership of shares of corporations based in foreign countries; the magnitude of this type of evasion is unknown.[30] Under the system described in section 4.1, individuals would of course still be able to evade taxes in this way, but their inclination to do so would diminish sharply since they lose the rebate to which they would otherwise be entitled. Hence individuals purchase anonymity in their foreign holdings at prices that rise with the 'notional' tax rate, and governments, which cannot in any case eradicate tax evasion, would at least be able to tax it by imposing high common rates.

4.3   Revenue effects

The plan described in section 4.1 removes countries' ability to tax directly the corporate income earned within their borders by firms owned by non-domestic Europeans. This represents a significant break from the current practice and is potentially a serious stumbling block for governments inclined to do exactly that. It is worth considering, then, the consequences of this limitation along three lines: what are the efficiency consequences, the distributional consequences, and the implications for national sovereignty that would ensue from the scheme?

Efficiency and distribution are linked by the allocational consequences. The scheme retains the current double taxation of corporate income, so that old capital already in place can be expected to generate rents that governments will continue to capture.

A more fundamental question is whether location-specific rents that accrue to individuals from ownership of corporate shares represent a sufficient basis for double taxation of corporate income throughout Europe. Indeed, under the proposed plan the application of the same corporate rate to distributed and undistributed profits could, in the absence of corrections in tax rates, result in heavier taxation of corporate profits. This induces two effects: on one side a generalized tendency towards bond financing on the part of firms, and on the other side increased pressure on governments to compete for corporate ownership by lowering the corporate tax rate, that is, decreasing the extent of double taxation of corporate income. Put concretely, would the emergence of a European haven for corporate ownership – say if the UK declared corporate income to be untaxed at the individual level – undermine the system by concentrating all corporate ownership in Britain? Such an outcome appears unlikely. As it currently stands individuals within countries face different marginal tax rates on different investments, and yet one never observes anything like the kind of tax clienteles that a tax-arbitrage story would predict.[31] Diversification and possibly the existence of heterogeneous expectations are forces that consistently overwhelm pure tax considerations for all but very specialized financial instruments. As long as individuals have strong desires to hold corporate shares, the government can successfully exploit their demands with corporate taxes.

The plan envisions that governments would voluntarily forego their

Table 7.9. *Significance of foreign multinationals to host governments*

	% of industrial workforce employed by foreign multinationals		% Foreign capital stock/GNP (year)	% Foreign capital from Europe
	manufacturing	all industries (year)		
Belgium	33.0	18.0 (1975)	11.8 (1982)	37.5
Denmark	14.8	3.5 (1984)	3.0 (1983)	38.8
France	20.2	— (1982)	2.8 (1982)	54.7
Germany	15.8	8.3 (1982)	4.8 (1983)	29.6
Greece	21.3	— (1977)	4.0 (1980)	33.1
Ireland	34.6	— (1981)	21.7 (1981)	37.3
Italy	8.3	6.5 (1981)	2.9 (1984)	45.8
Netherlands	19.2	7.5 (1980)	13.2 (1983)	31.5
Portugal	12.9	8.2 (1981)	3.1 (1984)	58.9
Spain	—	46.6 (1977)	2.9 (1982)	48.6
United Kingdom	14.8	— (1981)	12.6 (1981)	15.4

Note: Data are compiled from tables in Dunning and Cantwell (1987); countries differ somewhat in the bases for these calculations. Figures for percent of foreign capital from other European countries are derived from data in table 7.10, and are not measured in a consistent fashion with all of the capital stock data.

rights to retain corporate tax revenue from foreign shareholders; is this a politically viable scenario? It should be recalled, of course, that governments simultaneously obtain the right to tax in full their own citizens' non-domestic corporate income, a right they currently cannot exercise effectively. Furthermore, governments as a whole are likely to enrich themselves from this scheme since taxes are less distortionary and the current pressure to lower capital tax rates is likely to abate significantly. Governments can still, if they want, encourage investment or employment through direct subsidies (though some of the subsidy is lost to foreign tax authorities). But nonetheless the plan requires governments to relinquish a power they currently hold. Their willingness to do so would seem to depend on the relative benefits and costs.

The important positions of foreign multinationals in some European economies makes the benefits and the costs of tax system reform potentially quite large. Table 7.9 presents some indicators of the extent to which host countries are currently affected by the multinationals of other European countries. Belgium, France, Greece, Ireland (and presumably Spain) owe more than 20% of their employment in manufacturing to foreign multinationals (though not all of the employing firms are

European). These governments as well as others might be concerned about any reforms that could reduce their abilities to use various tax incentives to attract and retain investment from abroad. Alternatively, these governments might welcome reforms along the lines of the tax system described in section 4.1, since greater capital mobility might promise additional investment and employment even in the absence of costly incentives.

Table 7.10 presents a rough picture of government tax revenue exposures under the reform presented in section 4.1. Absent all the allocational effects that would be likely to ensue from the tax change, the treasuries of governments that are currently capital exporters to the rest of Europe would be likely to benefit in the reform relative to other EC members, while capital importers would lose revenue. Examination of what figures are available in table 7.10 suggests that the gainers would be Germany, the Netherlands and the United Kingdom; the losers would be France, Italy and Spain.[32] One way to reconcile all parties to the reform would be, therefore, a system of reallocating some of the corporate tax revenue in early years to those countries that sustain revenue losses from the switchover; alternatively, the capital-importing EC states could be assigned greater-than-source-basis shares of the non-EC-corporate tax revenue collected by member states.

There remains the potentially dangerous problem posed by tax competition among EC members: what happen to this system under unbridled competition or even secession from the system? This issue turns on governments' abilities to enforce the true concept of individual residence. As long as every European owner of capital cannot declare the lowest-tax jurisdiction to be his home, then countries can compete for their residence in the same way that they do now: by offering the most attractive package of taxes and benefits. Under residence-based capital taxation there is no inconsistency between the interests of different governments, and all could ultimately share the benefit of more efficient allocation of capital.

NOTES

We are grateful to Julian Alworth, David Bradford, Roger Gordon, Glenn Hubbard, Mauro Maré, Colin Mayer, Gilbert Metcalf and Anne Sibert for helpful comments on an earlier draft.

1 For analyses of administrative problems associated with current tax systems and proposed reforms, see the discussion in Tanzi and Bovenberg (1989) and Schlesinger (1989).

2 For example, in the case of Belgium, the pricompte immobilier and the pricompte mobilier have been added.

3 We do not examine carefully the historical American experience with capital taxation. In the more restricted realm of corporate taxation, Auerbach and

Table 7.10. *Revenue exposures under capital tax reform*

	units	year(s)	inward investment from Europe	(% of total inward investment)	outward investment to Europe	(% of total outward investment)
Belgium	b BF	1959–81	89.52	(37.5)	—	—
Denmark	m DKr	1974–83	6,636	(38.8)	5,680	(41.0)
France	m F Fr	1975–83	49,056	(54.7)	29,443	(26.6)
Germany	m DM	1983	23,851	(29.6)	36,356	(34.3)
Greece	m US$	1953–78	387.8	(33.1)	—	—
Ireland	m Ir £	1981	843.9	(37.3)	—	—
Italy	b L	1984	8,258	(45.8)	4,100	(29.1)
Netherlands	m N Fl	1983	16,319	(31.5)	46,263	(38.6)
Portugal	m Esc	1983	22,639	(58.9)	—	—
Spain	b Pta	1960–83	410.21	(49.6)	61.73	(21.6)
United Kingdom	m £	1981	2,606.1	(15.4)	5,910.2	(20.7)

Note: Data are compiled from tables in Dunning and Cantwell (1987). Investment figures for single years represent capital stocks (as best they can be measured); investment figures for multiple-year periods represent cumulative investment flows (and are presented because stock data are not available).

Poterba (1987) find that secular declines in the share of corporate in overall taxation over the period 1959–85 were due more to changes in corporate profitability than to statutory tax changes, suggesting in fact that the US corporate income tax base responds inelastically to tax changes.

4 See Eichengreen (1989).

5 Giovannini (1988) argues that a large fraction of the dramatic devaluation of the lira in 1919 and 1920 could be explained as a reaction to the announcement of the levy. Italian observers of the time suggest that the greatest effect of the levy was capital flight to countries like Switzerland.

6 See Hicks *et al.* (1941). There are, of course, many ways to tax capital in place other than through explicit capital levies. For example, raising the rate of tax on sales or on value added serves in part as a capital levy. (Though a VAT that is constant over time does not tax capital, and for that reason VATs are not included in capital income taxes in table 7.1 and in figures 7.1–7.3.) We do not include in our calculations these and certain other taxes the incidence of which may be partly on owners of capital.

7 Devereux and Pearson (1989) and Tanzi and Bovenberg (1989) offer some summary statistics on asset lifetimes in EC countries.

8 See Kuiper (1988) for a brief summary of some of the important differences.

9 See, for example, King and Fullerton (1984).

10 Problems also arise if home governments explicitly accord foreign investments ungenerous tax basis treatment, as is standard. See Hines (1988a, 1989) for details of the likely impact of this aspect of the US system on international investment incentives.

11 This proportion is 90% if the Belgian parent company is a holding company.

12 See table 7.3.

13 And whenever these credits cannot be offset against future or current taxes.

14 In the United Kingdom, however, the tax credit limitations are based on averaging within countries, but not across countries. See Alworth (1988).

15 Hines (1988b) suggests a new method of appropriately valuing intangible goods provided by affiliates of the same firm.

16 For formal elaborations of this process see Giovannini (1989) and Razin and Sadka (1989).

17 And hence the name withholding taxes. Part of the idea behind the design of such taxes is to maximize the available foreign tax credit, which is obtained by making the payee liable for the tax, while enforcing the tax in the payer's country, which is obtained by making the payer responsible for withholding the taxes.

18 They describe altogether seven different approaches to reforming European corporate taxation, including taxation on the basis of shareholder residence. The method they choose to implement residence-based taxation is, as they note, administratively cumbersome and they reject it partly on that basis (and also because they feel it too greatly reduces national sovereignty). Another serious problem with the scheme they describe is that European firms would continue to face incentives to invest (and reinvest) in low-tax European locations, since their tax accounts are settled only upon payment of dividends from corporations to their shareholders.

19 See, for example, Summers and Summers (1989).

20 While an exhaustive list of references on these and related questions would fill a paper rather than a footnote, recent contributions to understanding these

questions include Auerbach (1979, 1983), Auerbach and Hines (1988), Bradford (1981), Gravelle and Kotlikoff (1989), Harberger (1962), King (1977), Krzyzaniak and Musgrave (1963), McLure (1979), Sinn (1988) and Stiglitz (1973, 1976).
21 See, for example, Musgrave (1959).
22 See, for example, the arguments surveyed in Musgrave and Musgrave (1972).
23 Consider, for example, the tax holiday (until the year 2000) offered by the government of Ireland to all new manufacturing firms.
24 For a recent description and analysis of this tax see King (1987).
25 As, for example, Hubbard (1989) has argued before a wide audience.
26 Gersovitz (1987) analyses the incentives governments face currently to tax subsidize foreign investors only with indirect and possibly inefficient means, in order to exploit the foreign tax credit mechanism. This type of consideration lead Tanzi and Bovenberg (1989) to argue that tax harmonization should be accompanied by restrictions on government expenditure levels and patterns. An efficient alternative is residence-based corporate taxation.
27 See Giovannini (1989) for an elaboration of this argument.
28 Governments might want to adjust the common 'notional' tax rate over time, and they could do so, subject to the restriction that the highest national tax rate should not exceed the common rate. This restriction could prove to be important, since as Gordon (1986) argues, the optimal tax rate on foreign direct investment is zero for a small country. Europe is not small, but could in some instances face very elastic foreign investment schedules. Another important feature of the 'notional' tax rate is that it represents the foreign tax credit limit for European corporations investing outside of Europe; the choice of appropriate limit may be complicated by the circumstances of individual firms and the bilateral nature of relations between home and host countries.
29 The desirability of forced distributions depends on what firms would do with undistributed cash. For the view that internal funds stimulate corporate investment, see Fazzari et al. (1988) and Hoshi et al. (1990). For a more sanguine view of the likely uses of free corporate cash flow, see Jensen (1986).
30 See OECD (1987) for a general discussion of issues and practices related to international tax evasion.
31 See for example the evidence presented in Feldstein (1976); while he finds individual tax rates to influence the types of assets individuals hold, a great deal of the variation in individual portfolios is unexplainable just on the basis of taxes.
32 Available sketchy evidence suggests that the other EC countries, Belgium, Greece, Ireland and Portugal, are all net capital importers from the EC as well and therefore likely to lose revenue.

REFERENCES

Alworth, J. (1988) *The Finance, Investment and Taxation Decisions of Multinationals*, Oxford: Basil Blackwell.
Auerbach, A. (1979) 'Share Valuation and Corporate Equity Policy', *Journal of Public Economics* **11**, 291–305.
　　(1983) 'Corporate Taxation in the United States', *Brookings Papers on Economic Activity* **2**, 451–513.

Auerbach, A. and J. Hines (1988) 'Investment Tax Incentives and Frequent Tax Reforms', *American Economic Review* Papers and Proceedings, **78**, 211–16.

Auerbach, A. and J. Poterba (1987) 'Why Have Corporate Tax Revenues Declined?' in L. Summers (ed.), *Tax Policy and the Economy*, vol. 1, Cambridge, MA: MIT Press.

Bradford, D. (1981) 'The Incidence and Allocation Effects of a Tax on Corporate Distributions', *Journal of Public Economics* **15**, 1–22.

Cnossen, S. (1989) 'On the Direction of Tax Harmonization in the European Community', mimeo, Erasmus University.

Devereux, M. and M. Pearson (1989) 'Harmonizing Corporate Taxes in the European Community', mimeo, Institute for Fiscal Studies, London.

Dunning, J. and J. Cantwell (1987) *Directory of Statistics of International Investment and Production*, New York: New York University Press.

Eichengreen, B. (1989) 'The Capital Levy in Theory and Practice', in R. Dornbusch and M. Draghi (eds.), *Public Debt Management: Theory and History*, Cambridge University Press.

Fazzari, S.M., R.G. Hubbard and B.C. Petersen (1988) 'Financing Constraints and Corporate Investment', *Brookings Papers on Economic Activity* **1**, 141–95.

Feldstein, M.S. (1976) 'Personal Taxation and Portfolio Composition: An Econometric Analysis', *Econometrica* **44**, 631–50.

Gersovitz, M. (1987) 'The Effect of Domestic Taxes on Private Foreign Investment', in D. Newbery and N. Stern (eds.), *The Theory of Taxation for Developing Countries*, New York: Oxford University Press.

Giovannini, A. (1988) 'Capital Controls and Public Finance: The Experience in Italy', in F. Giavazzi and L. Spaventa (eds.), *High Public Debt: The Italian Experience*, Cambridge University Press.

(1989) 'National Tax Systems versus the European Capital Market', *Economic Policy* **4** (9), 345–86.

Gordon, R.H. (1986) 'Taxation of Investment and Savings in a World Economy', *American Economic Review* **76**, 1086–102.

Gravelle, J.G. and L.J. Kotlikoff (1989) 'The Incidence and Efficiency Costs of Corporate Taxation When Corporate and Noncorporate Firms Produce the Same Good', *Journal of Political Economy* **97**, 749–80.

Harberger, A. (1962) 'The Incidence of the Corporate Income Tax', *Journal of Political Economy* **70**, 215–40.

Hicks, J.R., U.K. Hicks and L. Rostas (1941) *The Taxation of War Wealth*, London: Oxford University Press.

Hines, J. (1988a) 'Taxation and U.S. Multinational Investment', in L. Summers (ed.), *Tax Policy and the Economy*, vol. 2, Cambridge, MA: MIT Press.

(1988b) 'Multinational Transfer Pricing and Its Tax Consequences: Where the Profits Are', mimeo, Princeton University.

(1989) 'Credit and Deferral as International Investment Incentives', mimeo, Princeton University.

Hoshi, T., A. Kashyap and D. Scharfstein (1990) 'Corporate Structure, Liquidity, and Investment: Evidence from Japanese Industrial Groups', mimeo, MIT.

Hubbard, R.G. (1989) 'Tax Corporate Cash Flow, Not Income', *Wall Street Journal*, February 16.

Jensen, M.C. (1986) 'Agency Costs of Free Cash Flow, Corporate Finance, and Takeovers', *American Economic Review*, Papers and Proceedings, **76**, 323–9.

King, M. (1977) *Public Policy and the Corporation*, London: Chapman and Hall.
  (1987) 'The Cash Flow Corporate Income Tax', in M. Feldstein (ed.), *The Effects of Taxation on Capital Accumulation*, Chicago: University of Chicago Press.
King, M. and D. Fullerton (1984) *The Taxation of Income from Capital*, Chicago: University of Chicago Press.
Krzyzaniak, M. and R.A. Musgrave (1963) *The Shifting of the Corporation Income Tax*, Baltimore: Johns Hopkins University Press.
Kuiper, W. (1988) 'EC Commission Proposes a Directive on the Harmonization of Rules for the Determination of Taxable Profits of Enterprises', *European Taxation* **28**, 319–29.
McLure, C. (1979) *Must Corporate Income Be Taxed Twice?*, Washington, D.C.: Brookings Institution.
  (1989) 'Some Lessons from the U.S. Experience', *European Taxation* **29**, 243–50.
Musgrave, P.B. (1987) 'Interjurisdictional Coordination of Taxes on Capital Income', in S. Cnossen (ed.), *Tax Coordination in the European Community*, Deventer: Kluwer.
Musgrave, P.B. and R.A. Musgrave (1972) 'Inter-Nation Equity', in R. Bird and J. Head (eds.), *Modern Fiscal Issues*, Toronto: University of Toronto Press.
Musgrave, R.A. (1959) *The Theory of Public Finance*, New York: McGraw-Hill.
OECD (1977) *Model Double Taxation Convention on Income and Capital*, Paris: OECD.
  (1987) *International Tax Avoidance and Evasion* Paris: OECD.
  (1989) *OECD Tax Revenue Statistics*, Paris: OECD.
Price Waterhouse (1989) *Corporate Taxes – A Worldwide Summary* and *Individual Taxes – A Worldwide Summary*, New York: Price Waterhouse.
Razin, A. and E. Sadka (1989) 'International Tax Competition and Gains from Tax Harmonization', NBER Working Paper No. 3152.
Schlesinger, H. (1989) 'Capital Outflow and Taxation – The Case of the Federal Republic of Germany', mimeo, Deutsche Bundesbank, December.
Sinn, H.W. (1988) 'The Vanishing Harberger Triangle', mimeo, University of Munich.
Stiglitz, J.E. (1973) 'Taxation, Corporate Financial Policy and the Cost of Capital', *Journal of Public Economies* **2**, 1–34.
  (1976) 'The Corporate Tax', *Journal of Public Economics* **5**, 303–11.
Summers, L.H. and V.P. Summers (1989) 'When Financial Markets Work Too Well: A Cautious Case For a Securities Transactions Tax', *Journal of Financial Services Research* **3**, 261–86.
Tanzi, V. and A.L. Bovenberg (1989) 'Is There a Need for Harmonizing Capital Income Taxes Within EC Countries?' mimeo, International Monetary Fund.
Whalley, J. (1989) 'Foreign Responses to US Tax Reform', mimeo, University of Western Ontario.

Discussion

JULIAN S. ALWORTH

Giovannini and Hines' paper (GH) is divided into three broad sections: (i) a discussion of the differences in the average burden of capital income taxes in Europe and the United States; (ii) an overview and evaluation of the corporate and personal income tax systems in the various countries in the European Community; (iii) a series of reform proposals and more general considerations on the desirability of corporate income taxation. My comments will be subdivided accordingly but will not address the issue of the desirability of a corporate tax.

1   The historical experience

GH start from the observation that the ratio of capital income taxes to GDP has been lower in the 12 EC countries taken together than in the United States although the ratio of total tax revenues to GDP is higher in Europe. In Germany, the major EC country, the tax revenue from capital income and wealth taxes is only a fraction of the amount levied in the United States. Unfortunately the authors have been unable to disentangle the proportion of capital income taxes paid by the corporate sector from that paid by individuals. Nor have they taken account of transfers by the government sector to industry or of the reduction in tax revenue resulting from savings incentives. If such diverse elements were excluded from the taxes on capital income recorded by the authors, the differences between the United States and Europe and across European countries would probably be even more pronounced.

According to GH the reasons for the differences in tax burden across countries are to a large extent rooted in European geography[1] – the nearness of borders – and the historical experience of these countries during the interwar period. They note that a number of extraordinary capital levies were employed to pay back the debt burden accumulated by many European countries at the end of the First World War. These capital levies (which were often narrowly applied to government debt) as well as the loss in material wealth caused by the two world wars had profound effects on savings behaviour and resulted in a more pronounced elasticity of the tax base to the imposition of taxes on capital.

This argument, which Giovannini (1988) has explored in detail elsewhere, is quite appealing[2] but should be supplemented by other aspects of European tax history.

First, progressive and personal income taxes have had somewhat less of a following in continental Europe than in the Anglo-Saxon world, especially in the interwar period. Many economists – particularly of the 'Italian school of public finance' – rejected utilitarian principles: the concept of individual satisfaction related to a stream of income was not widely accepted, nor was the principle of equal marginal sacrifice one which encountered many adherents. Moreover, governments were not viewed as benevolent redistributors of income. Einaudi (1938), for example, after a long critical attack on the utilitarian principles, states in *Miti e paradossi della giustizia tributaria* (Myths and paradoxes of tax justice):

> Personality and progressivity are just ordinary things, neither good nor bad, without any theoretical foundation. They are manifestations of sentiments. They are welcome if they strengthen social cohesion – if solidarity pushes individuals to pay more for the common good. Wretched if they destroy the social fibre when envy pushes the poor to spoliate the more affluent. Source and proportional taxes are also expressions of sentiments, particularly that of certainty. Taxes on real assets or their return are an assurance against arbitrariness and privilege; and can encourage savings and work.[3]

Administrative problems were the second reason why many countries appeared reluctant to adopt a progressive and personal income tax. The assessment of income from capital was difficult because the corporate form was not widespread, appropriate accounting standards were seldom followed and tax evasion was quite common. Under these circumstances the distribution of the tax burden under a progressive personal tax was viewed as being potentially very inequitable.

These two considerations were particularly instrumental in Italy but also in other countries in leading to a system of taxing capital income based for the most part on source. Taxation at source is undoubtedly more elastic than taxation on the basis of individual income because highly subsitutable assets are taxed often at different rates even within the same jurisdiction.

2 The present corporate tax system in the European Community

The present tax treatment of *domestic* corporate income in the EC countries can be described as follows:

(a) Excluding on the one hand the very low rates of tax in Ireland and southern Italy, and on the other the high rates in Denmark and

Germany, corporate tax rates vary between a very narrow band (35–40%) and a marginally wider one if local levies on company income are included.

(b)   There are more pronounced differences in depreciation allowances and investment incentives (straight-line versus declining balance; tax holidays, etc.). Statutory provisions such as those presented by GH understate the actual degree of variation because governments have allowed themselves a wide degree of discretion, both in respect of what they accept as appropriate depreciation charges and in the definition of the base. Moreover, there have been numerous changes over time to accommodate economic circumstances. For example, in periods of inflation some countries have provided *ex-post* indexation (such as Italy) or a much higher level of depreciation rates (expensing in the United Kingdom, higher declining balance rate in Germany, etc.).

It is difficult to assess the effect which the differences in *corporate* tax rates and taxable income have had on the size and location of invetment in Europe. To be sure, cost-of-capital based investment demand equations have shown some impact of taxation on investment expenditures, and location in some areas has surely been influenced by regional incentives. But it is impossible to say whether effective tax rates on corporate income have been reflected in differences in the structure of interest rates across countries and whether cross-border portfolio investments have responded accordingly. It is also difficult to argue that firms have been more or less competitive because of differences in 'effective tax rates' and to measure the extent to which effective tax rates have served merely to offset other factors, such as lower growth rates.

One reason why the variations in tax rates have not stirred much debate is probably to be found in the foreign-exchange experiences of the late seventies and early eighties: in all likelihood, variations in exchange rates (for other than tax reasons) had a more pronounced impact on competitiveness than differences in tax rates.

Another reason for the little attention paid to tax factors is that differences in financial systems tend to obscure or modify the impact of taxes. For example, in comparison to other countries tax allowances in Italy are particularly generous but inefficiencies in the banking sector are also greater as exemplified by the fact that interest rates tend to be higher (Jappelli and Pagano, 1989) than elsewhere. In Germany, where banks and companies have had close relationships, debt finance has been more prevalent than elsewhere (at least up to the early eighties), thereby allowing firms to reduce part of their tax burden, which in theory is amongst the highest in the EC.

The segmentation of financial markets and other differences amongst EC countries (including the heavy involvement of governments in private sector investments) are likely to diminish significantly in the future and tax considerations will become more important as the element differentiating countries. However, under the present constellation of tax rates it is unlikely that many companies having purely *domestic* facilities will consider relocating to other jurisdictions or for that matter that many firms will shift the location of their original incorporation and cross borders.

The real problems arising from 1992 and which justify the title of the paper are of two other sorts:

The first, which GH examine carefully, arises because of the existence of companies that straddle jurisdictions and the imperfect application of the worldwide principle of taxation. They note correctly the great sensitivity of multinational financing decisions to tax differentials, spell out the distortions resulting from tax arbitrage, and draw attention to the problem of transfer pricing particularly in respect of intangibles. More stable exchange rates combined with access to wider sources of finance are likely to increase the impact of these differences much more than in the case of purely domestic companies.[4]

The second set of problems arising from 1992 concerns the treatment of portfolio investments. Here, unlike the case of multinationals, the distortions arising from the application of territoriality rather than residence are connected with tax evasion and the different tax status of various investors in different countries. In this connection, one area that the authors do not mention but which is likely to become increasingly important is the position of financial intermediaries, typically banks but also pension funds, insurance companies and mutual funds, whose tax status varies markedly according to whether they invest domestically or abroad (for example, in respect to the tax credit received under the imputation system). In addition, individuals may find it increasingly profitable to shift their investments out of their home country to a third conduit country with a wide beneficial set of tax treaties.

3   Corporate tax in the European Community

There are two reasons for preferring the worldwide principle as a basis for the taxation of capital income, i.e. on the basis of the residence of the taxpayer. Firstly, it can be easily shown under a variety of differing sets of assumptions that double taxation relief by way of a credit without deferral is 'less distortionary' to locational decisions and conforms to the maximization of world welfare more than other methods of double taxation relief. Secondly, in the case of multinational companies the credit system without deferral drastically reduces the incentive for tax arbitrage (Alworth, 1988). In spite of these advantages the implementation of the worldwide principle has encountered many difficulties: some have argued that it would penalize direct investments in less-developed countries; according to others income from a separate legal entity should be included in the parent company's profits only upon receipt of dividends.

Much of the novelty in the GH paper results from an ingenious attempt to reconcile the worldwide principle and the need to achieve tax harmonization within the European Community with the desire to preserve the tax sovereignty of individual EC member countries. Under their proposal, individual countries would be forced to adopt a common tax base and tax rate, but allowed to choose different effective rates of tax through a system of rebates at the individual taxpayer level. Hence, a 'harmonized' territorial system would operate at the corporate level but all of the company income in the European Community would be imputed to individuals in their country of residence. A clearing system would operate at the Community level to balance out the revenue gains and losses amongst member countries. Neutrality in respect of companies' financial policy would be achieved if all income were distributed because the personal and corporate tax system would be fully integrated.

I presume that one of the main advantages of this system would be to eliminate the need of placing a tier of domestic company taxes between those paid by foreign affiliates and the ultimate domestic shareholders. Whilst generally sympathizing with the authors' attempts at finding a system which could meet many diverse requirements, I wonder whether implementation would be as simple as they suggest.

First the proposal requires that the *underlying* profits of the foreign affiliate be included on a pro-rata basis in the domestic company's profits and in turn in the personal income of an individual shareholder. In effect this amounts to a full see-through integration at an international level, a system which has never been tested domestically. With the exception of the thorny questions of the distribution of tax revenues between countries – which the authors solve by way of creating a clearing house – GH address none of the administrative problems which have hitherto blocked the implementation of a fully integrated system of company and personal taxes. For example, if individual countries adopt a territorial system (or some hybrid system) for taxing personal income, how could this system be made to fit with the GH proposal? What is the tax treatment of company losses: are they passed on to shareholders? If some sections of the multinational produce losses and others are profitable, what measures will be implemented to avoid transfer pricing between the various entities, or how will divided distributions to shareholders be treated?

My second remark is that most problems, in the case of multinationals, arise when there are very wide differences in tax rates and, to a lesser extent, tax bases. If the rates of company tax with the EC continue to converge, as appears to be the case, most of the financial distortions and transfer pricing problems which concern the authors would be minimized even for multinationals.

Finally the authors do not consider the taxation of other forms of capital income – such as cross-border interest payments – which have been the subject of much discussion within the Community. There is no agreement on a common EC withholding tax or on a system of cooperation amongst the fiscal authorities. Moreover, not all countries implement a progressive personal income tax on capital. If broad segments of capital income are treated differently, it is difficult to see how it would be possible to achieve neutrality by applying the residence principle to dividend income alone.

NOTES

1 In the light of widespread capital flight from Latin American countries to the Caribbean financial centres proximity of border crossings seems a rather weak argument supporting the high tax elasticity of savings.

2 However, it should be noted that the capital levy was basically aimed at reducing the interest burden on outstanding government debt rather than the confiscation of savings in private assets.

3 Own translation of the following Italian text. 'Personalità e progressività sono due cose qualunque, né sentimenti. Buoni, ossia tali da rinforzare la compagnia socile, se si tratta del senso di solidarietà che spinge quei che possono a pagare di più per il bene comune. Pessimi, ossia tali da distruggere la società, se l'individa spinge il povero a spogliare con la progressività colui che sta al di sopra. Anche la realità e la proporzionalità dell'imposta sono la espressione di sentimenti soprattutto di quello della certezza. L'imposta la quale colpisce le cose per sé, ugualmente in rapporto al loro frutto e valore, assicura gli uomini contro arbitri e privilegi; e può incoraggiarti grandemente a risparmiare ed a lavorare.' Einaudi (1969), p. 171.

4 With regard to intangibles the new common European Community patent laws under discussion, which amongst other things reduce the length of patent protection, are likely to heighten the sensitivity of firms to the locations in which they can write off their R&D expenditures against tax.

REFERENCES

Alworth, J.S. (1988) *The Finance, Investment and Taxation Decisions of Multinationals*. Oxford: Basil Blackwell.

Einaudi, L. (1938) *Miti e Paradossi della Giustizia Tributaria* as reprinted in vol. 2 of *Opere di Luigi Einaudi*, Torino: Einaudi Editori, 1959.

Giovannini, A. (1988) 'Capital controls and public finance: the experience in Italy', in F. Giavazzi and L. Spaventa (eds.), *High Public Debt: the Italian Experience*. Cambridge University Press.

Jappelli, T. and Pagano, M. (1989) 'Consumption and capital market imperfections: an international comparison', *American Economic Review 79*, 1088–106.

R. GLENN HUBBARD

This paper addresses some important issues in the policy debate over capital taxation in Europe. The title belies two problems of historical significance in Europe – the quick responsiveness of capital to tax changes ('capital flight') and non-cooperative behaviour in setting tax rates on real investments ('tax competition'). Much of the discussion extends previous work by Giovannini on the need for stricter application of the 'worldwide principle' or ('residence principle') of taxation.[1] A focus on eliminating impediments to the worldwide principle is a useful one, as it shifts the focus of policy debates away from 'harmonization' *per se*.

The Giovannini–Hines paper is not an exercise in optimal taxation, it constitutes a specific policy proposal. I shall frame my remarks accordingly, though, at points, I shall question the merits of specific aspects of the plan as against obvious alternatives.

The basic idea is as follows. Let us suppose that we want a corporate-level tax. Suppose also that we want to mitigate distortions (e.g. avoid 'tax competition'), but, at the same time, raise revenue. Three issues arise in designing such a tax in the context of present institutions for taxing multinational corporations: (i) problems of deferral; (ii) the lack of integration of corporate and individual taxes; and (iii) defining the appropriate tax base. After reviewing briefly parts of the background discussion in the paper germane to the policy proposal, I shall discuss these issues.

1   The context: distortions in European capital taxation

Giovannini and Hines begin by noting that capital tax revenues as a percentage of gross domestic product are lower in the EC than in the US. Such comparisons are inevitably difficult, owing to measurement issues (e.g. difference in measuring proprietors' income or taxes on interest income). A reasonable goal here is to determine whether 'enforcement costs' or 'behavioural responses' explain this 'pattern'.[2] Giovannini and Hines note the wide scope for varying definitions of 'annual income' (including differences in the measurement of inventories, advertising, patents, goodwill and depreciation deductions). I return to this problem below.

At the most basic level, European countries do try to limit 'double taxation' of multinationals' foreign-source income. Relief is limited, however, owing to limitations on foreign tax credits, and to differences in the concept of 'foreign source income' from the concept used in the computation of 'corporate tax' (i.e. stemming from deferral). Moreover, in most countries, integration of 'corporate' and 'individual' taxes is very imperfect. That is, there would be significant tax distortions even if the worldwide principle were perfectly applied at the 'corporation' level.

We are left, then, with three central problems, those of (i) measuring income flows within a multinational firm (e.g. transfer pricing complications); (ii) coordinating tax systems for taxing foreign-source income when definitions of income vary; and (iii) avoiding at least some of the problems in measuring income in the current system. The Giovannini–Hines plan (hereafter GHP) addresses some of these concerns, and provides for international corporate taxation under the residence principle and with no deferral.

The mechanics of the GHP are as follows. There is a uniform ceiling corporate tax rate for all European countries. Taxes are due on a territorial basis (i.e. to the government of the country in which the income is earned). A separate system of country-specific rebates applies to owners of corporate shares. The definition of 'taxable corporate income' is for each country the outcome of mutual agreement.

Avoidance of double taxation is ensconced in the GHP. Foreign-source income within Europe is exempt from direct corporate taxation by the country of corporate residence; foreign-source income outside of Europe is taxed at the full European rate, but a credit is allowed for taxes paid. Withholding taxes are proscribed. Importantly, GHP provides for tax integration. Corporate income is attributed to individual shareholders without deferral. Individuals then receive rebates from their home governments (equal to the excess of taxes paid by the firms they own over the product of their home corporate tax rate and their corporate income). A clearinghouse system reallocates corporate income from source countries to countries of shareholder residence.

Corporate income tax systems have been under attack in academic and public policy circles. Why consider such a system here? Giovannini and

Hines review 'ability to pay' and 'benefits received' rationales for corporate taxation. The former is unconvincing in this context. Taxing foreigners on a source-based basis in all likelihood redistributes rents. The latter presumes a benefit to incorporation. Even here, convincing arguments are difficult to find. For example, large-scale enterprises have emerged in the US under partnership governance in recent years. Realistic motivations for a corporate-level tax are more likely to centre on the need for revenue (e.g. to the extent that revenue is more difficult to collect at the individual level).

Perhaps the most significant problem with corporate income taxes is that associated with measuring income (recall the significant differences internationally in this respect noted by the authors). One corporate-level tax alternative which circumvents many of these problems is a 'cash flow' tax.[3] A corporate cash-flow tax falls ultimately on rents associated with monopoly power, ideas, entrepreneurial skill, etc. The tax avoids both investment and financing distortions. In addition, at the margin, there is no need for crediting foreign taxes paid (since the government is effectively a partner in firms' equity). Raising revenue is, of course, an important consideration. Studies for both the UK (by Mayer, 1982) and the US (by Aaron and Galper, 1985) have estimated that the cash flow tax could raise similar revenue as that under an income tax at lower rates.

Giovannini and Hines argue that, under a cash flow tax, there is a temptation towards high rates (presumably to confiscate rents). This seems disingenuous. Time-inconsistency problems are common to a host of fiscal reforms. The point would have equal force applied to a true income tax. Drawbacks of switching to cash flow taxes have more to with difficulties in designing transitional arrangements. Some transitional arrangements will also be required in the implementation of the GHP.

2   The Giovannini–Hines plan as a reform

The GHP is a well-reasoned attempt to reform the system of capital taxation in Europe. The critical question, of course, is to what extent it mitigates the significant distortions in the present system. My two reservations here are as follows. First, we are given no evidence on how large the distortions under the present system actually are. Such an omission is noteworthy in a 'practical corporate tax' proposal. Second, it is not clear that the GHP addresses the significant underlying problems of measuring income required in any corporate-income-tax systems.

I would like to see the authors expand their analysis of the proposal to consider questions like the following.

What are the efficiency gains from the new system?

Suppose such gains are large. How would the gainers compensate the losers (presumably significant for political viability)?

The GHP takes away the ability of countries to tax directly corporate income earned within their borders by firms owned by non-Europeans. Are their implications for 'outsiders' (in particular, US firms) with respect to corporate takeovers, etc.?

There are limits on the ability to subsidize domestic investment. What happens in response to a shift in investment incentives in the US?

Since Europe is not the world, there presumably must be adjustments in European rates in response to major shifts in capital tax systems in the US. How would renegotiation of the European ceiling rate occur?

These questions notwithstanding, Giovannini and Hines have done an excellent job in presenting the issues and suggestions for reform. The paper should draw attention both from academic researchers assessing the efficiency costs of alternative systems and from policy-makers balancing the need for reform with national political concerns.

NOTES

1 See Giovannini (1989).
2 Of interest here as well is Giovannini's (1988) previous research suggesting that, historically, there may have been large behavioural responses to capital levies associated with wartime finance in Europe.
3 Alternative corporate cash flow bases are reviewed in King (1986).

REFERENCES

Aaron, H. and H. Galper (1985) *Assessing Tax Reform*, Washington, D.C.: The Brookings Institution.
Giovannini, A. (1988) 'Capital Controls and Public Finance: The Experience in Italy', in F. Giavazzi and L. Spaventa (eds.), *High Public Debt: The Italian Experience*. Cambridge University Press.
   (1989) 'Capital Taxation', *Economic Policy* 4(9), 345–86.
King, M. (1987) 'The Cash Flow Corporate Income Tax', in M. Feldstein (ed.), *The Effects of Taxation on Capital Accumulation*, Chicago: University of Chicago Press.
Mayer, C. (1982) 'The Structure of Corporation Tax in the U.K.', *Fiscal Studies* 3, 121–41.

8 Reflections on the fiscal implications of a common currency

WILLEM H. BUITER and
KENNETH M. KLETZER

1 Introduction: sense and nonsense in the Delors Report

The much increased likelihood of significant advances in European monetary integrations – and even of European monetary union in the medium-
term future – has not surprisingly shifted the spotlight onto the need for
coordination of fiscal policies as a complement to monetary unification.
The Delors Report (1989) made much of the fiscal implications of the
movement towards a greater degree of rigidity of nominal exchange rates
among participants in the exchange rate arrangements of the European
Monetary System (EMS).

> A monetary union would require a single monetary policy and responsi-
> bility for the formulation of this policy would consequently have to be
> vested in one decision-making body. In the economic field a wide range
> of decisions would remain the preserve of national and regional authori-
> ties. However, given their potential impact on the overall domestic and
> external economic situation of the Community and their implications for
> the conduct of a common monetary policy, such decisions would have to
> be placed within an agreed macro-economic framework and be subject
> to binding procedures and rules. This would permit the determination of
> an overall policy stance for the Community as a whole, avoid unsustain-
> able differences between individual member countries in public sector
> borrowing requirements and place binding constraints on the size and
> the financing of budget deficits.   (Delors Report, 1989, p. 18)

1.1 No deficits, please

There are frequent further references in the Delors Report to the need to
control national public sector deficits and in a number of places the
Report becomes rather specific about the constraints to be imposed on
national budgetary policy. The passage quoted below (and similar ones
scattered through the Report) make this clear:

221

> In the budgetary field, binding rules are required that would: firstly, impose effective upper limits on budget deficits of individual member countries of the Community, although in setting these limits the situation of each member country might have to be taken into consideration; secondly, exclude access to direct central bank credit and other forms of monetary financing while, however, permitting open market operations in government securities; thirdly, limit recourse to external borrowing in non-Community currencies. (Delors Report, 1989, p. 24)

Space constraints do not permit an exhaustive analysis of this rather unusual statement. Note however, in the first proposed binding rule, the startling asymmetry of the constraints on the public sector deficit: upper limits but no lower limits. Such an asymmetry can only be rationalized through a belief that absent these constraints there would be a bias towards government deficits that are too large rather than too small. The reader of the Report is provided neither with a criterion for measuring excess or deficiency in public sector deficits nor with a hint of the evidence on which the empirical judgement is based. The statement appears to represent the typical Pavlovian conditioned reflex of fiscally conservative central bankers when faced with any and all government deficits.

1.2   An independent European Central Bank: form and substance

The second proposed binding rule only makes sense if one believes that it is possible that the new 'independent' European System of Central Banks (ESCB) could still be forced (at any rate under extreme circumstances such as those represented by a very high public debt overhang) into inflationary monetization. Such a situation could come about either because the ESCB would lack formal independence or because, despite formal independence, the ESCB would choose to lose a game of chicken with the budgetary authorities rather than cause a monetary and financial crisis by not giving in. In what follows the wisdom (or lack of it) of having an independent Central Bank will not be considered. There are good arguments both for and against it. The discussion is limited to the meaning of 'independence' and the means of achieving it.

An effectively independent ESCB is one which cannot be forced, either by law or by circumstances under the control of the budgetary authorities (be they member state governments or an emerging central fiscal authority) to monetize deficits, to engage in open market operations or to engage in foreign exchange market interventions (especially non-sterilized interventions).

Even if it were possible to identify any given change in the stock of base money either as additional money issued 'to finance the government deficit', or as money issued as the counterpart of an open market purchase or as money issued as the counterpart of a non-sterilized purchase of official foreign exchange reserves, the distinction would be behaviourally meaningless unless the different ways in which an additional ECU gets into the system somehow convey different signals about the future actions of the monetary authority. In any case, monetary deficit financing, money injected through open market purchases and money injected through non-sterilized purchases of foreign exchange cannot be separately identified from the data. The three sources of base money growth are also operationally equivalent.

Consider for example the case of an accounting period during which the government deficit excluding borrowing from the Central Bank is, say, ECU 100, the monetary base and the Central Bank's holdings of public debt each increase by ECU 100 and the stock of foreign reserves remains unchanged. This could be interpreted as representing ECU 100 of monetary financing of the government deficit with no net open market purchase of government debt by the Central Bank and no unsterilized or sterilized foreign exchange market intervention. Alternatively it could be interpreted as the outcome of zero monetary financing of the deficit, ECU 100 of open market purchases of government debt by the Central Bank and zero unsterilized and sterilized foreign exchange market intervention. A third possible interpretation is to view it as the outcome of the following set of financial operations. First, ECU $-$ 100 of monetary financing of the deficit. The Treasury is 'overfunding' the deficit by borrowing ECU 200 from the non-Central Bank public (ECU 100 more than the government deficit) and thus increase its balance with the Central Bank by ECU 100. This corresponds to an ECU 100 reduction both in the monetary base and in Central Bank holdings of government debt. Second, ECU 300 of open market purchases of public debt by the Central Bank (that is an ECU 300 increase in the monetary base and an equal increase in Central Bank holdings of public debt). Third, ECU 100 of sterilized purchases of foreign exchange (that is an ECU 100 increase in foreign exchange reserves and an equal reduction in Central Bank holdings of public debt) and fourth, ECU 100 of non-sterilized sales of foreign exchange reserves (that is an ECU 100 reduction in reserves matched by an equal reduction in the monetary base). There is no natural benchmark or counterfactual. There are too many degrees of freedom.

If a Central Bank is formally independent but can easily be manoeuvred by the fiscal authorities into a position where, given the Central Bank's own objectives, the optimal thing to do is to create money to a much greater extent than it would have chosen to do if the fiscal authorities could have been induced to act differently, then Central Bank independence is an empty shell. Substantive independence presupposes a non-trivial domain over which choice can be exerted. Even if every inhabitant of Bangladesh were formally free to buy a Rolls Royce (which owing to import restrictions in that country is actually unlikely to be the case) the budget constraints of most Bangladeshis make this formal freedom an empty one.

One can easily imagine a formally independent Central Bank with a strong (but not an absolute) aversion to inflation, confronting a fiscal authority that is persistently unwilling (even though technically able) to cover current outlays with current revenues. Assume that, if the Bank does not provide accommodating monetary growth and the Treasury does not reduce the deficit, the public debt-GDP ratio will increase steadily. If the debt were to grow persistently faster than the rate of interest, eventual insolvency of the Exchequer would result. Even if there is no threat of insolvency, the increasing debt burden will, if there is no 'first-order' debt neutrality, put upward pressure on real interest rates and crowd out interest-sensitive categories of private spending or increase the external current account deficit.

Sargent (1986, pp. 19–39) contains an interesting description (attributed by Sargent to Neil Wallace) of this game of 'chicken' between a Central Bank and a Treasury. 'Chicken' is a non-cooperative game in which both players promise that they will adopt the strategy of Stackelberg leaders. For each of the players, of course, the announced strategy is feasible only if the other player acts as a follower. This struggle for dominance between the monetary and fiscal authorities represents a situation of Stackelberg warfare (Sargent, 1986, p. 37). To complicate matters, in the USA the game is between the Central Bank and a rather more Balkanized set of fiscal authorities, i.e. it is a three- or more-sided game of chicken.

The Central Bank asserts that, come hell or high water, it will not engage in inflationary monetization, in the hope of forcing the fiscal authorities to take steps to reduce the deficit. A unified fiscal authority counters by asserting that it will under no circumstances reduce its deficit, hoping to convince the Central Bank to monetize the deficit in order to prevent a steep rise in real interest rates, financial distress etc. Alternatively, with a Balkanized fiscal authority, the Central Bank may (mixing metaphors) suffer the fall-out from an unresolved game of chicken between two or more fiscal warlords. The White House fiscal warlord may threaten to veto any tax increase ('read my lips') in the hope of forcing one or more of the Capitol Hill fiscal warlords to accept spending cuts. Blocking coalitions of Capitol Hill warlords may veto cuts in certain spending categories ('not in my constituency') in the hope either of directing the spending axe elsewhere or of securing a tax increase.

Unpleasant things tend to happen when an irresistible force meets an immovable object. While no one likes to be caught bluffing, the resolve of the Central Bank may well weaken as it sees the debt burden rising. If it believes the fiscal authority is unlikely to mend its ways, it may rationally opt to be chicken rather than risking a head-on collision. The dilemma is resolved through monetization and inflation.

In a recent paper Ben Friedman (1990) has argued that in the years to come the rising corporate debt burden in the USA may play the role attributed to public debt in the Sargent-Wallace scenario: tough anti-inflationary monetary policy is not credible given the financial exposure and fragility of the US corporate sector. In the British context Buiter and Miller (1983) have identified a similar game of chicken during the 1970s between the trade unions on the one hand and the monetary and fiscal authorities on the other hand (in Britain the Central Bank is formally and effectively subordinate to the Treasury). Unions submitted inflationary wage demands (and often succeeded in imposing inflationary wage settlements) in the expectation that demand management would be accommodating. No government would be willing to live with the unemployment consequences of non-accommodating monetary and fiscal policy. Governments talked tough about not validating inflationary wage and price developments. During most of the 1970s it was the governments that blinked and lost the game. The new Conservative administration that came to power in 1979 changed the rules of the game (at any rate during its early years) and broke the inflationary momentum with the deepest recession since the 1930s.

One way to increase the likelihood that the Central Bank will win the game of chicken with the fiscal authorities is by convincing the latter that the Central Bank is implacably, irrevocably and unalterably opposed to any and all inflation. This could be achieved by the founding fathers and mothers of the Central Bank appointing someone (or a group of people) to head the Central Bank who is known to possess extreme, perhaps even irrational or pathological, inflation-aversion. (The appointment procedure for the first and subsequent heads of the Central Bank will of course be crucial for this to work.) It is not wise for anyone to play a game of chicken with an adversary who may be slightly insane. Believing it is dealing with an anti-inflationary fanatic of doubtful rationality, the Treasury may prefer to give in rather than to test the resolve of the Central Bank. The possible rationality of choosing an agent who does not exactly share one's objectives (or who may even be irrational) is explained very clearly in Schelling (1960)

> The use of thugs and sadists for the collection of extortion or the guarding of prisoners, or the conspicuous delegation of authority to a military commander of known motivation, exemplifies a common means

of making credible a response pattern that the original source of decision might have been thought to shrink from or to find profitless, once the threat had failed. (Just as it would be rational for a rational player to destroy his own rationality in certain game situations, either to deter a threat that might be made against him and that would be premised on his rationality or to make credible a threat that he could not otherwise commit himself to, it may also be rational for a player to select irrational partners or agents.)   (Schelling, 1960, pp. 142–3)

This idea has recently been taken up again, amongst others by Rogoff (1985b).

While formal independence is not sufficient to rule out the possibility of the ESCB being forced into accommodating inflationary monetization, it is a necessary condition. It is important to stress that formal independence requires that the ESCB have control over all sources of money creation: monetization of public sector deficits, monetization through open market purchases and monetization though (non-sterilized) purchases of foreign exchange. If, say, foreign exchange market intervention were to continue to occur at the initiative of the national Treasuries (or the central European Community (EC) fiscal authority) and if the ESCB were not to be free to engage in sterilizing sales or purchases of public debt, there would not even be a formally independent monetary authority. What this means in practice is that for the Central Bank to be independent, the exchange rate of the ECU with non-EC currencies must be under the control of the Central Bank, and not of the national or supranational fiscal authorities.

In principle it is of course possible for the Central Bank to have control over all sources of money creation and yet for the Treasury to have control over the exchange rate. This would be the case if fiscal instruments could be used to influence the various arguments in the money demand function. Even with perfect capital mobility between the EC and the rest of the world, international interest taxes or subsidies could enforce departures from uncovered interest parity. Since the EC is large in the world economy, fiscal policy could be used to influence the world level of real interest rates and (given the stance of monetary policy) also the level of nominal interest rates, which is one of the arguments in the money demand function. If nominal interest rates affect EC money demand differently than money demand in the rest of the world, this would be a further channel through which the exchange rate could be influenced through fiscal policy. In addition, various spending and tax instruments could be used to influence the 'scale variables' in the money demand function such as income or (financial) wealth. Given the rather severe limitations in practice on the flexible use of fiscal instruments and their uncertain effects on money demand and on the exchange rate, at least the day-to-day management of the exchange rate would have to be the province of monetary policy.

The post-Delors Report consensus that is emerging in and around Brussels appears, fortunately, to have been purged of the Report's rather obsessive concern with upper limits on national public sector budget deficits. However, there also appears to be agreement that the determination of the common EC external exchange rate should not be the exclusive province of the 'Eurofed', but should be determined by the appropriate political budgetary authority (or authorities) in the new Community. We sympathize with the view that the exchange rate is too serious a matter to be left to the Central Bank. The unavoidable implication of that view is, however, that the Central Bank cannot be independent.

The authors of the Report may well be right in their lack of confidence (implicit in the – now apparently discarded – budgetary recommendations of the Report) in the independence of the proposed ESCB. The recent embarrassing (to Central Bank pride) subjugation of the Bundesbank by Chancellor Kohl in connection with the latter's 'out of the blue' proposal for instant monetary union between the FRG and the GDR makes it clear that in the last resort even the most independent Central Bank will give in to the political authorities. It is however, somewhat ironic to find side by side in the Delors Report a statement about the need to create an independent ESCB and an implicit admission that there are identifiable contingencies when independence is bound to be an empty phrase.

As regards the last of the triad of proposed binding rules, it is very hard to make sense of the curious concern with the currency composition of external borrowing. If a European national fiscal authority or an emerging Federal European fiscal authority can borrow externally in US Dollars, Japanese Yen or inconvertible Rubles, why shouldn't it? Where is the externality?

2   Exchange rate unification, monetary unification and fiscal coordination

If phases 2 and 3 of the Delors Report's scheme for exchange rate unification and monetary union are eventually implemented, a single European Central Bank and a single European currency will emerge. The long-standing opposition to this scheme by British Prime Minister Thatcher (and the less vocal but probably no less determined opposition of the Bundesbank and part of the current West German political leadership) make it unlikely, however, that full exchange rate and monetary union for the European Community are imminent. The recent

preoccupation of the West German authorities with the monetary, financial and fiscal consequences of their take-over of the bankrupt East
German economy is likely to create further delays in the implementation
of the Delors monetary agenda.

How robust is the proposition that exchange rate unification and monetary union create greater need for fiscal policy coordination than would
prevail under greater exchange rate flexibility?

With a high degree of international capital mobility and a fixed nominal
exchange rate (and *a fortiori* with a full single-currency, monetary union
with pooled international reserves), individual national fiscal authorities
will lose control over national seigniorage as a means of financing
national public sector deficits. The total amount of seigniorage that can
be extracted by the fixed exchange rate zone or the monetary union as a
whole and its distribution among the members of the union (and between
the member governments and a strengthened and enlarged central authority in Brussels) remain objects of choice and potential bones of contention.

In the case of the European Community, the currencies of two of the
intended members of the monetary union (The D-Mark and the Pound
Sterling) have been used and continue to be used both as official international reserves and as components of private working balances by
agents outside the proposed monetary union. The ECU, when it emerges
as a full-fledged currency can be expected to play a similar international
reserve and vehicle currency role. We can therefore anticipate bargaining
over the distribution of both the external and the internal seigniorage.

Changes in the degree of national control over seigniorage revenue will
have implications for the rest of the budget, if only because government
solvency constraints must be met. The concept of solvency used by
macroeconomists and public-finance specialists only makes sense in a
dynamically efficient economy. In a non-stochastic world, dynamic efficiency rules out the possibility that the real rate of interest be for ever
below the growth rate of real economic activity. In a dynamically efficient
economy, a solvent government is assumed not to be able to play Ponzi
games with its debt: the value of the outstanding national debt can be no
greater than the sum of the present discounted value of anticipated
primary (non-interest) public sector financial surpluses and the present
discounted value of anticipated future issues of high-powered money.[1]

There are large differences in primary surpluses (as a proportion of
GDP) between the members of the European Community. For the ten
countries listed in tables 8.1–8.4 the general government primary surplus
as a percentage of GDP/GNP in 1988 ranges from + 4.6% for Denmark
to − 6.3% for Greece. For the nine countries for which net public

Table 8.1. *Net public debt, 1981–8*
percentage of GNP/GDP

	1981	1984	1988[a]
Germany[b]	17.4	21.5	23.7
France[b]	14.2	21.1	25.2
Italy	57.8	74.4	92.3
UK	42.8	43.5	33.7
Belgium	83.5	108.6	123.7
Denmark	16.6	37.2	21.2
Netherlands[b]	27.3	39.9	54.8
Spain	11.8	23.2	30.9

Notes:
[a]Partly estimated.
[b]Financial assets exclude corporate shares.

Source: OECD Economic Outlook.

debt-GDP ratios are given in table 8.1, the range in 1988 is from 21.2%
for Denmark to 123.7% for Belgium. There is no systematic tendency
over the past decade for primary surplus-GDP ratios to be positively
correlated with debt-GDP ratios. The arithmetic consequence is a very
wide range of public sector financial balance-GDP ratios, from + 0.8%
for the UK to − 14.5% for Greece in 1988.

Table 8.2. *General government primary balance, 1981–8*
Surplus (+) or deficits (−) as a percentage of GNP/GDP

	1981	1984	1988
Germany	− 2.1	+ 0.4	+ 0.1
France	− 0.7	− 0.9	+ 0.7
Italy	− 6.1	− 4.1	− 3.1
UK	+ 0.8	− 0.5	+ 3.4
Belgium	− 6.1	− 0.4	+ 2.5
Denmark	− 5.1	+ 1.7	+ 4.6
Netherlands	− 2.1	− 1.4	− 0.1
Greece[a,b]	− 7.7	− 5.4	− 6.3
Ireland[b]	− 8.3	− 3.2	+ 3.9
Spain[a]	− 3.6	− 4.1	− 0.4

Notes:[a]OECD estimates and projections.
[b]Net property income paid rather than net interest payments is used as the latter is
not available.

Source: OECD Economic Outlook.

Table 8.3. *General government financial balance, 1981–8*
Surplus (+) or deficits (−) as a percentage of GNP/GDP

	1981	1984	1988
Germany	− 3.7	− 1.9	− 2.1
France	− 1.8	− 2.8	− 1.3
Italy	− 11.9	− 11.6	− 10.6
UK	− 2.8	− 3.9	+ 0.8
Belgium	− 13.4	− 9.3	− 6.8
Denmark	− 6.9	− 4.1	+ 0.2
Netherlands	− 5.5	− 6.3	− 5.0
Greece[a,b]	− 11.0	− 9.9	− 14.5
Ireland[b]		− 10.1	− 2.7
Spain[b]	− 3.9	− 5.5	− 3.1

Notes:
[a]OECD estimates and projections.
[b]Net property income paid rather than net interest payments is used as the latter is not available.
Source: OECD Economic Outlook.

Recourse to seigniorage has been relatively small in most European Community member states (see table 8.5). Exceptions to this rule are Italy (before 1986) and Portugal, Greece and Spain.

Monetary policy can be an important policy instrument even if the use of base money as a source of seigniorage is negligible. If the right kind of nominal stickiness or inertia in wages or prices is present in an economic system with imperfect international capital mobility, real economic

Table 8.4. *Average annual percentage growth rate of real GNP/GDP, 1981–8*

Germany	1.7
France	1.9
Italy	2.2
UK	2.8
Belgium	1.5
Denmark	1.9
Netherlands	1.4
Greece	1.4
Ireland	1.1
Spain	2.6

Source: OECD Economic Outlook.

Table 8.5. *Seigniorage in the EC countries, 1984–8*
Annual change in reserve money as a percentage of nominal GDP

	1984	1985	1986	1987	1988
Germany	0.3	0.3	0.6	0.8	1.0
France	0.8	0.1	− 0.2	0.3	0.8
Italy	1.9	2.4	1.1	1.2	1.3
UK	− 0.5	0.2	0.3	0.1	0.2
Belgium	0.1	− 0.1	0.4	0.2	0.1
Netherlands	0.4	0.3	0.3	0.7	0.9
Denmark	0.3	4.6	− 2.4	− 1.1	0.8
Ireland	0.7	0.7	0.3	1.0	0.3
Greece	5.0	1.1	2.9	3.8	n.a.
Spain	0.9	0.8	1.5	5.0	1.4
Portugal	0.6	1.1	1.6	2.8	2.2

Source: IMF, *International Financial Statistics.*

activity can be influenced by both the systematic and the unanticipated components of the monetary rule. With a fixed exchange rate and perfect international capital mobility national monetary stabilization policy has national effects only to the extent that it influences the world rate of interest. With a monetary union national monetary policy exists only through national influence on the decisions of the union's Central Bank.

3   National solvency without national monetary policy

The public sector budget identity for any country i can be written as follows:
First line

$$\dot{d}_i \equiv (r_i - n_i)d_i - \pi_i - \sigma_i$$

Here d is the debt–GDP ratio, r the instantaneous real interest rate on the non-monetary public debt, n the growth rate of real GDP, π the primary surplus–GDP ratio and σ seigniorage as a proportion of GDP (the ratio of changes in the stock of base money to nominal GDP). International reserves are netted out against public debt.

With the abolition of all remaining capital controls within the European Community, full covered interest parity can be expected to prevail among the member states. With complete and credible exchange rate unification, uncovered nominal interest rate parity will also be established among the members. Whether or not this leads to greater convergence of real interest rates is a question that is theoretically and empirically open. With complete instantaneous purchasing power parity (PPP) nominal interest equalization implies real interest equalization. The behaviour of national producer and consumer price indices is far from being well characterized by PPP. Mean-reverting tendencies appear to be weak or even absent for a number of key real exchange rate indices so, even as a long-run characterization of the data, PPP leaves a lot to be desired.

It is true that real exchange rate volatility and uncertainty have been statistically associated very strongly with nominal exchange rate volatility and uncertainty. If this statistical association survives the Lucas critique when a further move towards reduced nominal exchange rate flexibility occurs, there will be a reduction in those components of national real interest differentials that reflect nominal exchange risk premia. No such presumption exists for the contribution to national real interest differentials due to anticipations of real exchange rate appreciation or depreciation. For the sake of argument, however, consider the case in which, following nominal exchange rate unification, national real interest differentials on the public debt vanish, except of course for differentials due to market perceptions of differences in national public debt default risk.

With similar primary surpluses π_i, similar seigniorage σ_i and similar real interest rates r_i, countries with high current debt–GDP ratios d_i will have more rapidly rising debt–GDP ratios unless higher GDP growth rates n_i come to the rescue of the high debt countries. There is little evidence to support the view that high debt countries are high growth countries (see tables 8.1 and 8.5).

The pure version of the solvency constraint does not rule out the possibility that a forever rising (and eventually unbounded) public debt–GDP ratio is consistent with solvency. As long as the growth rate of the debt–GDP ratio is less than $r_i - n_i$ (which in a dynamically efficient economy will eventually or in the long run be some non-negative number), d_i can rise without bound with the government's solvency intact.

This surprising fiscal feat is possible because the government is assumed to have access to lump-sum taxes which, without distortions or enforcement costs, enable it to appropriate (and to use for debt service) any amount of resources less than or equal to the sum of GDP and the interest on its debt. Allowing for distortionary taxation and/or for tax compliance costs is sufficient to establish a finite upper bound for the public debt-GDP ratio. While these bounds need not be the same for all countries, it is likely that the current high-debt countries will encounter their barriers before the less indebted countries. Countries like the UK may already be in the position that a continuation of current primary deficits and seigniorage patterns implies a steadily declining debt-GDP ratio.

With a currency union (or even just a credible fixed exchange rate system) a country headed for insolvency no longer has the option of unilaterally determining the extent to which it uses the inflation tax. Neither seignio-rage narrowly defined (high-powered money creation), nor the rest of the 'anticipated inflation tax') the effects of anticipated inflation on the primary deficit through fiscal drag or through the Tanzi effect and the Tobin effect of expected inflation on the real interest rate), nor the 'unanti-cipated inflation tax' on holders of long-dated nominally denominated fixed-interest government debt are national policy instruments any longer. It also seems unlikely that any single member country will have enough influence on the Community's Central Bank to allow it to assign the com-munity-wide inflation rate to the solution of its national fiscal problems. That leaves cuts in its primary public sector deficit and/or default on its debt as the only two policy options. The perception by the market of the existence of default risk will, by adding a default-risk premium to the inter-est rate on the public debt, exacerbate the fiscal problem and bring forward the moment when actual default becomes inevitable.

All this is likely to be painful for the inhabitants (and the government) of the heavily indebted country. The question is, should it be of concern to the other members of the Community? Are there efficiency or equity arguments for constraining the member states' public sector financial deficits, primary deficits or even spending and revenue-raising separately; that is, is there a case for coordinating budgetary policy among the member states?

4   National public sector deficits and Community-wide interest rates: pecuniary versus technological externalities

The arguments frequently made in favour of international coordination of fiscal policies, both in the scholarly literature and in non-technical policy debate, appear to apply with equal force regardless of the exchange rate regime. They often rely on *fiscal externalities or spillovers* that are present whenever domestic and foreign government debts are traded internationally or indeed when any form of international transmission is present. A representative example of this kind of argument in contri-bution to the policy debate can be found in the following quotation from Professor Casella's response to an editorial opinion in *The Economist* which had stated that there was 'no economic reason why the members of a common monetary system should not run budget deficits as they see fit'. Referring to a common monetary system she writes:

> Suppose first, in accordance with standard economic theory, that national governments with tax-raising powers could be considered safe borrowers (in contrast to private corporations). National debts in a common currency would be perfect substitutes and would therefore earn a common interest rate. A spending spree by one member state (Italy?) could be accommodated with a small increase in the interest rate – given the absence of exchange rate risk – but it would be an increase in the interest rate on the debt of *all* member states. In other words, the value of government bonds everywhere would fall, and the capital losses in the foreign portfolios would indirectly help to support the Italian deficit. Of course, the possibility of exporting the cost of financing government expenditure would distort incentives in the conduct of economic policy, in general leading to excessive deficits in all countries. Some form of coordination would be required.   (Casella, 1989, p. 4)

Even when (small) spreads between national borrowing rates (reflecting differential risks of *de jure* or *de facto* repudiation) are possible, the story just told could still hold. Quoting again,

> In a world with few borrowers, it may still be possible for one state to influence the value of the other states' debt if rates move in the same direction.   (Casella, 1989, p. 4)

Frenkel, Goldstein and Masson (1988) in their survey of international coordination of economic policies state (emphasis added)

> . . that economic policy actions, particularly those of larger countries, create quantitatively significant spillover effects or *externalities* for other countries, and that a global optimum requires that such externalities be taken into account in the decision-making calculus. Coordination is then best seen as a facilitating mechanism for **internalizing** these externalities.   (Frenkel *et al.*, 1988, p. 3)

They go on to stress the non-competitive behaviour of larger countries who 'exercise a certain degree of *influence over prices* including the real exchange rate'.

No doubt the authors of these quotes are, like other professional economists, fully aware of the distinction between efficiency-based and distribution-based arguments for policy intervention (including international policy coordination) and know the conditions under which international spillovers can have important efficiency or distributional consequences. In policy-oriented economic writing aimed at a wider audience it is especially important to be clear and explicit (albeit non-technical) about the economic reasoning underlying key assertions and propositions. The subject of spillovers, international transmission and interdependence involves subtleties that make it mandatory to cover all bases when addressing the intelligent lay person.

Since the late nineteenth century economists have recognized what are now called 'technological externalities' as possible reasons for market failure and as possible grounds for government intervention in the market mechanism. As Laffont (1987) states succinctly, a

> technological externality [is], the indirect effect of a consumption activity or a production activity on the consumption set of a consumer, the utility function of a consumer or the production function of a producer. By indirect, we mean that the effect concerns an agent other than the one exerting this economic activity and that this effect does not work through the price system.'   (Laffont, 1987, p. 263)

Such technological externalities (positive or negative) will upset the first fundamental theorem of welfare economics and create a *prima facie* case for intervention.

During the 1920s and 1930s another kind of externalities or external economies labelled '*pecuniary* external economies' by Viner (1931) was the subject of much confused debate. The classic article 'Two Concepts of External Economies' by Scitovsky (1954) settled many of the central issues (see also Bohm, 1987).

Pecuniary externalities work through the price system and refer to the effects of producer or consumer activities on the input or output prices of other producers, consumers or suppliers of factor services. It should be clear that, when all the assumptions required for competitive equilibria to be Pareto optimal are satisfied, pecuniary externalities have no *efficiency* implications. They are merely another word for general market inter-dependence. When a consumer, alone or together with many other con-sumers, shifts his consumption bundle towards bananas and the price of bananas increases as a result, all those who were 'long' in bananas (i.e. the net banana exporters) will benefit, and all those who were 'short' in bananas (the net banana importers) will suffer a welfare loss. There may be important distributional issues involved, but there is no efficiency or market failure argument for intervention.

At its simplest, the example developed by Professor Casella can be interpreted as describing an '*international* pecuniary externality'. Unless there are other departures from competitive efficiency, the higher foreign interest rate that results from increased domestic borrowing need not involve any efficiency. There are interesting distributional issues (inter-national and intergenerational) which we have analysed in a number of papers (Buiter and Kletzer, 1990a, b).

Much (though by no means all) of the work on international policy coordination uses national objective functions or social welfare functions that are not easily rationalized as utilitarian aggregators of underlying individual preferences. That need not pose any problems if one is inter-ested in a *positive* theory of policy design. The objectives pursued by those actually in command of the instruments of economic policy may reflect narrow sectional or group interests rather than the utilitarian ideals of the philosopher kings that motivate many of the *normative* approaches to policy design. Even for many of the positive or descriptive approaches to economic policy design it remains true, however, that it is not easy to rationalize the policy-makers' objectives in terms of the self-interest of any group, however broad or narrow.

When a utilitarian national objective function is optimized, it is important for a full appreciation of the meaning of statements such as 'cooperation increases (or reduces) national social welfare', to go behind the national (or global) social welfare functions and to verify what happens to the welfare of the individual consumers or households.

In Buiter and Kletzer (1990b) we show that, in a two-country overlapping generations[2] world with perfect international capital mobility, policy cooperation is not required to achieve equilibria that are Pareto efficient in terms of the underlying private preferences. With only non-distortionary lump-sum taxes and transfers (and with government borrowing constrained only by the requirement that solvency be maintained), cooperation is required to achieve Pareto optima with respect to the two national social welfare functions. Cooperation and international transfers (or side payments) are required to achieve optimality with respect to a global social welfare function that can be seen as a utilitarian aggregator of the two national social welfare functions. In this case, the gains in national or global social welfare are purely distributional: some lose and some gain. A national social welfare function represents a specific weighting of the welfare of (successive generations of) a nation's residents. The global social welfare function represents a further specific weighting of the welfare of the residents of the two nations. Cooperation does not achieve a Pareto improvement with respect to the underlying individual preferences.

When distortionary taxes or subsidies are added to the instrument arsenal, it can easily happen that the achievement of a Pareto optimum with respect to the two national social welfare functions (or the achievement of an optimum for the global social welfare function) requires the use of the distortionary instruments. This will certainly be the case if there is no mechanism for effecting lump-sum international redistribution. For example, investment taxes and subsidies can be used to influence the distribution of income between the two countries' fixed factors (labour in Buiter and Kletzer, 1990b). In that example national social welfare Pareto optima and global social welfare optima will not be Pareto optima with respect to the underlying individual preferences. The cooperative pursuit of national social welfare here means that some efficiency is sacrificed in order to achieve preferred distributional outcomes.

There obviously is nothing wrong with knowingly trading off efficiency for equity. It is, however, not always obvious that this is what is being done when national social welfare functions are plonked down and optimized. It is also not hard to think of other examples in which cooperation can lead to efficiency gains as well as improved distribution or, in the spirit of Rogoff (1985a) and Kehoe (1986), to efficiency losses and worse distribution. The moral of all this is that it is wise to stand back and reflect a bit when confronted with a finding that cooperation does (or does not) improve social welfare. Careless use of a national social welfare function for optimal policy design in an otherwise sensible model of the economy may create the misleading impression that one is dealing with a representative agent model, the nadir of macroeconomic analysis. Redistribution and conflict are swept under the carpet and what may well be the major obstacles of cooperative international policy design are ignored.

Returning to the problem of international interest rate spillovers, it is indeed likely that, in a financially integrated Europe, borrowing by any government (or private agent) will put upward pressure on interest rates everywhere. If a government borrows to the point that its ability to service the debt becomes questionable, a default-risk premium will be added to its borrowing costs and it may face credit rationing. Neither a community-wide increase in interest rates nor the market's response to a perception of sovereign risk need create an efficiency based argument for intervention or for coordination aimed at preventing these contingencies.

Higher interest rates will have international distributional consequences that are a legitimate concern of policy-makers. Higher interest rates redistribute income from borrowers to lenders. This is true within national economies and between national economies. Within a national economy higher interest rates redistribute income towards rentiers and away from labour and the owners of other real resources. It also tends to be associated with intergenerational redistribution from the young to the old. In the international context, the major resource transfer from debtor to creditor countries following the sharp increase in real interest rates in the early 1980s is a dramatic example of the redistributive implications of interest rate changes.

Sovereign default risk affecting one of the member states may create externalities for the other member states that may be pecuniary or techno-logical in nature. Asymmetric information and/or limited rationality may give rise to bandwagon or contagion effects that can cause default-risk premia and credit rationing to spread to member countries for whom the fundamentals do not warrant such penalties. Such occurrences are, however, by no means certain. In the private sector we observe the coexistence of firms with very different credit ratings and conditions of access to credit markets. Default and bankruptcy of one firm, or even of a number of firms, need not result in panics and market seizures.

Some of the concerns expressed about the high-debt countries in the Community seem to be born from the fear that the Community as a whole will be compelled (or feel compelled) to socialize part or all of their debt. While one cannot rule out categorically this or any other unusual future policy action by the new Community, there seems to be no compelling economic or political logic to support it. Even within existing nation states, provincial and local governments don't act as if they assume that the higher government tiers will routinely assume their liabilities. When city governments go into (the public sector equivalent of) receivership, as New York City did in the 1970s, the costs in terms of financial and economic disarray, loss of autonomy etc. appear to be sufficiently high to discourage emulation and repeat performances.

We can therefore safely assume that, even with a common European currency and unrestricted capital mobility, the Italian public debt will remain the Italian public debt, to be serviced out of Italian primary surpluses and out of whatever amount of seigniorage Italy manages to get from the ESCB. International intra-Community transfers may well grow in significance as the Community matures. Among the criteria government such transfers the relative magnitudes of the various national debts can be expected to play at most a very minor role. The total (private and public) international indebtedness of a country will, as one of the components of the wealth of the nation, play a role in future games of distribution, but the national public debt *per se* can be expected to remain a national responsibility.

Summarizing, international interdependence and international spillovers do not by themselves imply market failure and do not create an automatic efficiency case for any form of intervention including international policy coordination. Interdependence or spillovers reflecting the transmission of policy through competitive markets and prices (be they commodity prices or asset prices and rates of return) do not create an efficiency-based case for policy coordination unless there are other distortions or sources of market failure in the economy. This is true even if the policy authorities are 'large' and deliberately try to influence market prices in the pursuit of national advantage.

5   Non-Walrasian equilibria, pecuniary and technological externalities

When the economy has 'preexisting' distortions or when the instruments the government manipulates in the pursuit of national advantage create inefficiencies or distortions, an efficiency-based case for coordination may exist. Among the preexisting distortions that may make policy transmission through market prices inefficient are: distortionary taxes; technological consumption or production externalities; non-competitive behaviour; incomplete markets; and Keynesian market failure reflecting insufficient or excessive effective demand.

Even when markets are competitive, policy-induced distortions are absent and conventional technological consumption and production externalities are absent, a role for policy coordination may exist. As pointed out by Laffont (1987), when we move away from competitive equilibria in which all the assumptions for Pareto optimality are satisfied, market prices may do more than equate supply and demand and distribute income:

> In economies with incomplete contingent markets, prices span the subspace in which consumption plans can be chosen. In economies with asymmetric information, prices transmit information. When agents affect prices, they affect the welfare of the other agents by altering their feasible consumption sets or their information structures.
>
> (Laffont, 1987, p. 264)

In such economies the distinction between pecuniary and technological externalities vanishes because changes in prices do more than create or destroy rents.[3] It is quite possible that the arguments in favour of the coordinated international management of international pecuniary fiscal externalities are (implicitly) based on such a non-Walrasian world view. It is of course always desirable to bring out explicitly either the reason(s) for the breakdown of the first fundamental theorem of welfare economics or the distributional criteria that support the cooperative fiscal policy description.

With monetary policy emasculated as an instrument of national economic policy, the large differences between the debt burdens of Community member states foreshadow significant differences in the paths of future primary surpluses. While current and future primary surpluses are a very imperfect measure of the impact of fiscal policy on aggregate demand, there is a presumption that countries saddled with the need for relatively large future primary surpluses will have a relatively contractionary stance of fiscal policy.

If demand-deficient Keynesian equilibria are likely to result from contractionary fiscal policy actions, a *prima facie* case for policy intervention, including international coordination of policies, exists. In a Keynesian unemployment equilibrium the value of output foregone exceeds the value of the extra leisure 'enjoyed' by the unemployed. This holds even in a closed economy. In addition, in an open economy, part of any demand contraction (fiscal or private) will spill over to the rest of the world through the deflating country's demand for imports and supply of exports. This will create a non-pecuniary externality to the extent that goods and labour are not priced properly. If nominal wage stickiness (or the combination of nominal wage stickiness and price stickiness) is the key link in the transmission mechanism that causes demand-deficient equilibria to result from a contraction of demand, the magnitude of the international spillover will actually be smaller (given perfect international capital mobility) with any credible fixed exchange rate regime than with a floating exchange rate regime. The payoff from international coordination is correspondingly reduced.

It goes without saying that the efficient use of policy instruments such as exhaustive national public spending with international technological externalities will in general require international policy coordination (see, e.g. Kehoe, 1986, 1987). Public expenditure for the abatement of pollution of rivers, oceans and the air is one example. Defence expenditures and expenditures on law enforcement (given the increasingly transnational nature of major criminal activities) are another. The same holds for the efficient use of distortionary taxes and transfers, even when the activities that are taxed or subsidized do not have direct international technological externalities. When there are such international externalities (think of the taxation or regulation of national activities producing acid rain, ozone holes or greenhouse effects) the case for international coordination of taxation, subsidization and regulation is of course reinforced.

6   Conclusions

This paper studies only a few among the very large number of important fiscal policy issues facing the members of the European Community as they move along the road towards further economic and political integration. The new Europe will be characterized by greater (and increasing) mobility of factors of production, of owners of factors of production, of beneficiaries of transfer payments and of consumers of local, regional, national and Community-wide public goods. Interesting issues arise when the domain of mobility of rational private agents and the span of fiscal control or the size of the regulatory jurisdictions do not coincide. Issues like tax harmonization and tax competition (see, e.g. Giovannini, 1988; Giovannini and Hines, 1990; Razin and Sadka, 1989; Sinn, 1990a) become central issues in addition to (or even rather than) concerns about the stabilization function of national fiscal policy. The application of destination versus origin principles of commodity taxation and residence versus source principles of (capital) income taxation will have major effects on competitiveness and the location of economic activity (Dixit, 1985; Slemrod, 1988; Krugman and Feldstein, 1989: Sinn, 1990b). Internal transfer pricing by multinational corporations poses formidable challenges to the ability of national governments to tax multinationals' profits. The theory and practice of fiscal federalism will be required reading for European public finance scholars. Suitably modified versions of the theory of local public goods and of the theory of clubs will have to guide the design of efficient and fair tax and public expenditure systems in the new Europe.

For distributional reasons and, given the myriad departures from the competitive Walrasian and Tieboutian ideal types, for efficiency reasons also, coordination of national fiscal policies will be desirable in the new Europe (as it was in the old). There is no good argument why such coordination should give high priority (or indeed any priority) to binding agreements on public sector budget deficits. It is well known that the public sector deficit (level, change or share of GDP, 'raw', structural, operational, full employment, demand-weighted, inflation-corrected, permanentized or otherwise transformed or transmogrified), is not an adequate measure of the impact of fiscal policy on aggregate demand or on aggregate supply (short-run or long-run), nor an index of financial crowding-out pressure. In Buiter and Kletzer (1990a) we also show that any real effects of public sector deficits can be reproduced with a balanced budget and flexible taxes and transfers. It is very hard to come up with any reasonable argument for giving this statistic the attention it gets (see also Blinder and Solow, 1974; Buiter, 1983, 1985; and Kotlikoff, 1988).

There is no royal road to fiscal policy coordination. Agreements on contingent rules for the various tax, spending and financing instruments will have to be struck in the face not only of uncertainty about the exogeneous environment, but also of 'model uncertainty', i.e. uncertainty about the effects of policy instruments and exogenous events on key endogenous economic variables. Policy cooperation can at least ensure that strategic uncertainty does not complicate the task of economic management even more.

The desire for maximal scope to respond flexibly to new contingencies will have to be balanced against the need for simplicity and transparency in the cooperative policy rules. The success of any common strategy depends on its credibility with the private sector inside and outside the Community. Unless the private sector knows and understands the policy rules and is capable of monitoring and verifying the adherence of the various governments to the cooperative strategy, credibility will be wanting and the strategy will fail.

NOTES

1 For this solvency constraint to be non-trivial, the public debt should be valued gross of any discount reflecting a perceived risk of default, and the interest rates used to discount future primary surpluses and seigniorage should be net of any default-risk premium. When the market value of the debt is variable (and potentially different from its issue value, par value or redemption value) even without the presence of any default risk (as is for instance likely to be the case with long-dated debt), the calculation of what the value of the public would be in the absence of default risk is a non-trivial matter.

2 Examples of the use of the two-period OLG model in two-country models are Buiter (1981), Buiter and Eaton (1983), Kehoe (1986), Hamada (1986) and Sibert (1988). The Yaari-Blanchard OLG model has been applied to two-country models in Frenkel and Razin (1987), Obstfeld (1989) and Buiter (1989).

3 van Huyck (1989) eliminates the central auctioneer and price-taking behaviour from the Walrasian model. In the resulting model of 'decentralized competition', pecuniary externalities have efficiency consequences.

REFERENCES

Blinder, A.S. and R.M. Solow (1974) *The Economics of Public Finance*, Washington DC: The Brookings Institution.

Bohm, P. (1987) 'External Economics', in J. Eatwell, M. Milgate and P. Newman (eds.), *The New Palgrave, Vol. 2*, London: Macmillan, 261–63.

Buiter, W.H. (1981) 'Time Preference and International Lending and Borrowing in an Overlapping Generations Model', *Journal of Political Economy* **89**, 769–97.

(1983) 'The Theory of Optimum Deficits and Debt', in Federal Reserve Bank of Boston, Conference Series No. 27, *The Economics of Large Government Deficits*, pp. 4–69.

(1985) 'A Guide to Public Sector Debt and Deficits', *Economic Policy* **1** (1), 13–79.

(1989) *Budgetary Policy, International and Intertemporal Trade in the Global Economy*, Amsterdam: North-Holland.

Buiter, W.H. and J. Eaton (1983) 'International Balance of Payments Financing and Adjustment', in G.M. von Furstenberg (ed.), *International Money and Credit: The Policy Roles*, International Monetary Fund, Washington, DC, pp. 129–48.

Buiter, W.H. and K.M. Kletzer (1990a) 'Fiscal Policy, Interdependence and Efficiency', mimeo, Yale University.

(1990b) 'The Welfare Economics of Cooperative and Noncooperative Fiscal Policy', mimeo, Yale University, forthcoming in the *Journal of Economic Dynamics and Control*.

Buiter, W.H. and M.H. Miller (1983) 'Changing the Rules: Economic Consequences of the Thatcher Regime', *Brookings Papers on Economic Activity*, **2**.

Casella, A. (1989) 'Letter to the Editor', *The Economist* 22–8 July, p. 4.

Delors Report (1989) 'Report on Economic and Monetary Union in the European Community', Committee for the Study of Economic And Monetary Union, Commission of the European Community, Brussels.

Dixit, A. (1985) 'Tax policy in open economies', in A. Auerbach and M. Feldstein (eds.), *Handbook of Public Economics*, Amsterdam: North-Holland.

Frenkel, J.A., M. Goldstein and P. Masson (1988) 'International Coordination of Economic Policies: Scope, Methods and Effects', NBER Working Paper, No. 2670, July.

Frenkel, J.A. and A. Razin (1987) *Fiscal Policies and the World Economy, An Intertemporal Approach*, Cambridge, MA.: MIT Press.

Friedman, B.M. (1990) 'Implications of Corporate Indebtedness for Monetary Policy', NBER Working Paper No. 3266.

Giovannini, A. (1988) 'International Capital Mobility and Tax Avoidance', mimeo.

Giovannini, A. and J.R. Hines (1990) 'Capital flight and tax competition: are there viable solutions to both problems?', mimeo.

Hamada, K. (1986) 'Strategic aspects of International Fiscal Interdependence', *Economic Studies Quarterly* **37**, 165–218.

Kehoe, P.J. (1986) 'International Policy Cooperation May be Undesirable', Federal Reserve Bank of Minneapolis Research Department, Staff Report No. 103.

(1987) 'Coordination of Fiscal Policies in a World Economy', *Journal of Monetary Economics* **19**, 349–76.

Kotlikoff, L.J. (1988) 'The deficit is not a well-defined measure of fiscal policy', *Science* **241**, 791–5.

Krugman, P. and M. Feldstein (1989) 'International Trade Effects of Value Added Taxation', NBER Working Paper No. 3163.

Laffont, J.J. (1987) 'Externalities', in J. Eatwell, M. Milgate and P. Newman (eds.), *The New Palgrave, Vol. 2*, London: MacMillan, pp. 263–5.

Obstfeld, M. (1989) 'Fiscal Deficits and Relative Prices in a Growing World Economy', *Journal of Monetary Economics* **23**, 461–84.

Razin, A. and E. Sadka (1989) 'International Tax Competition and Gains From Tax Harmonization', NBER Working Paper No. 3152, October.

Rogoff, K. (1985a) 'Can international monetary cooperation be counterproductive?' *Journal of International Economics* **18**, 199–217.

(1985b) 'The optimal degree of commitment to an intermediate monetary target', *Quarterly Journal of Economics* **100**, 1169–89.

Sargent, T.J. (1986) *Rational Expectations and Inflation*, New York: Harper and Row.

Schelling, T. (1960) *The Strategy of Conflict*, Cambridge, MA; Harvard University Press.

Scitovsky, T. (1954) 'Two Concepts of External Economies', *Journal of Political Economy* **62**, 70–82.

Sibert, A. (1988) 'Taxing Capital in an Open Economy', Research Papers in Theoretical and Applied Economies, Department of Economics, University of Kansas, 1988–10.

Sinn, H-W. (1990a) 'Tax harmonization and tax competition in Europe', NBER Working Paper No. 3248, January.

(1990b) 'Can direct and indirect taxes be added for international comparisons of competitiveness?', NBER Working Paper No. 3263.

Slemrod, J. (1988) 'Effects of Taxation with International Capital Mobility', in H. Aaron, H. Galper, and J.A. Pechman (eds.), *Uneasy Compromise: Problems of a Hybrid Income-Consumption Tax*, Washington, DC: The Brookings Institution, 115–48.

van Huyck, J.B. (1989) 'Decentralized Competition, Pecuniary Externalities and Allocative Efficiency', mimeo, Department of Economics, Texas A&M University, March.

Viner, J. (1931) 'Cost Curves and Supply Curves', *Zeitschrift für National Ökonomie* 3, 23–46.

Discussion

ROGER H. GORDON

To what degree do the EC countries need to coordinate their fiscal policies as a result of their decision to create a monetary union? An effective monetary union eliminates each country's discretionary use of inflationary finance of any budget deficits. But should use of debt finance of budget deficits also be restricted? The Delors Commission report recommends that the Community impose an effective upper limit on the budget deficits of individual member countries, and occasionally suggests further restrictions. This paper by Buiter and Kletzer (hereafter BK) expresses substantial scepticism about the economic justification for any such restrictions. They examine a number of potential justifications for coordination of budget deficits, and dismiss each in turn. In this comment, I will examine each of these arguments.

1   Interest rate effects

To begin with, Casella (1989) among others argues that extra borrowing by one country raises the interest rate faced by all other countries, creating externalities which should be taken into account. BK respond that these spillovers are merely pecuniary externalities, with distributional but not efficiency consequences. They argue that this is 'true even if policy authorities are "large" and deliberately try to influence market prices in the pursuit of national advantage'. But a pecuniary externality exists only when all decisions are made facing competitive prices. Certainly exercise of monopoly power has efficiency consequences.[1] If a country can affect the world interest rate, then it has the incentive to reduce its net demand for loans, or its net supply of loans, in order to move the interest rate in a favourable direction. Creating a monetary union, thereby leading to the further integration of capital markets, should increase the degree to which capital flows across borders, potentially increasing a country's incentive to intervene to its advantage in the capital market. However, the countries participating in the monetary union would collectively have the incentive not only to eliminate the misallocation of capital among the member countries, due to each country's separate incentive to make use of any market power it has, but also to make effective use of the monopoly power the union as a whole has in the world capital market. Either objective requires policy coordination.

Buiter and Kletzer (1990a, b) find that any attempt to take advantage of this market power has no efficiency consequences, but this occurs only because they impose the restriction that governments can attempt to exploit this monopoly power only through use of debt, or lump-sum intergenerational transfers. Yet, as they note in passing, the Pareto optimal response from the national perspective is to equate the interest rate faced by domestic savers and domestic investors with the country's marginal cost of funds on the international capital market. Just because of the country's market power, this cost differs from the world interest rate. For example, when the US borrows more in the world capital market, it presumably bids up the interest rate to attract funds from other uses, thereby raising the interest rate it must pay on its existing debt as well. In order to induce savers and investors to act in the national interest, it must increase the interest rate received by US savers, and paid by US borrowers, above the world interest rate to reflect the effects of extra savings/borrowing on the interest paid on existing debt. While use of intergenerational transfers will affect interest rates, this approach still implies non-optimal individual savings and investment decisions from the national perspective.

Is this monopoly power sufficiently important to justify imposing constraints on each country's fiscal policy within the EC? After the monetary union, the EC should be roughly as important in the world capital market as the US, or perhaps Japan, has been in the past. To what degree have these countries acted to take advantage of their market power? In doing so, each would reduce the flow of capital across its borders, in order to move the world interest rate in its favour. In particular, Japan should attempt to maintain an internal interest rate below the world rate to encourage investment at home, while the US should raise its domestic interest rate above the world rate. Certainly Japan has traditionally maintained low domestic interest rates, and discouraged foreign lending, though this may not be the best explanation for these policies. It is difficult to point to specific policies in the US which raise its domestic interest rate above the world rate. This would involve, for example, a subsidy to foreign lending, rather than a tax. Yet the direction of policy changes, particularly in the 1986 tax reform, has been to try to raise the tax on US investments abroad.

Summers (1988) proposes that countries in practice use fiscal policies rather than tax policies to try to restrict net capital flows. Use of tax policies, for example, could be restricted by tax treaties, as occurs with withholding taxes on interest and dividend payments made to foreigners, or by the difficulty of changing these policies frequently in response to changes in the country's net capital position. If the US attempted to make use of its fiscal policy to reduce net capital flows, it should be increased government savings during the 1980s. Yet, to the contrary, the large government deficits arguably caused the large net inflows of capital during this period.

The case does not therefore seem very convincing that other important participants in the world capital market have gained much from taking advantage of their market power in this market. In any case, such coordination would take the form of ceilings on budget deficits only if the EC were a net borrower on the world capital market and as a result wished to reduce any further borrowing. Yet, on net, the EC is a net lender in the world capital market, implying pressures in the opposite direction.

2   Implications of existing tax distortions

Given the presence of domestic taxes, the opportunity cost of goods can differ from their market prices. From an EC perspective, the opportunity cost of funds borrowed within the EC would consist either of the foregone return on investment or else the return required to compensate individuals for increased savings. Due to corporate taxes, the foregone return on investment should exceed the market interest rate, assuming investments are mainly financed through equity. However, due to personal taxes, individuals receive a rate of return on their savings below the market interest rate, implying in equilibrium that their marginal time preference rates are also below the market interest rate.

To the degree to which a government's deficit crowds out investments elsewhere in the EC, then the opportunity cost is above the interest rate paid on the debt, potentially justifying some attempt to internalize this extra cost. In contrast, if the deficit is financed by extra savings elsewhere in the EC, then the externality has the opposite sign. Trying to forecast the degree to which a larger deficit is financed through extra savings or less investment within the EC would be a very difficult exercise. The answer hardly seems clearcut enough to justify intervention.

3   Distributional effects

An increase in a country's deficit should raise the interest rate within the
EC, helping net savers and hurting net borrowers. The general equilibrium response would likely also involve a net drop in the real wage rate.
These distributional effects would clearly be of concern in other countries, implying a welfare externality created by a country's deficit. In
principle, these externalities could justify policy intervention. Traditional
perceptions that countries favour redistribution towards labour and away
from capital-owners would imply a preference for reducing budget deficits
in other countries.

BK, however, are reluctant to grant the government 'preferences' that
result from the distributional conflicts rely solely on efficiency arguments
for or against policy coordination. They could cite Buchanan as well as
Rogoff or Kehoe in defending such scepticism. Buchanan, for example,
has argued in many places that government officials, acting in their
private self-interest, will attempt to expand the size of government excessively. Borrowing, at the expense of future tax payers who do not vote in
current elections, provides an easy way to do so. In this case, limits on
their ability to finance expenditures through debt may lead to reduced
expenditures, and a welfare gain.

When governments are denied one mechanism for financing expenditures, however, they may well resort to even more costly ways. Forecasting the effects of any such restriction on government behaviour, and the
implied welfare consequences, is not easy.

4   Strategic use of debt

A government, by developing substantial foreign debts, may hope to
induce other EC governments to redistribute funds in its favour. If these
expectations were justified, a country would have the incentive to borrow
excessively. Would it be plausible that other EC governments would bail
out a member country with heavy debts? BK think not. To ensure this,
however, may require the type of 'no-bail-out' provision now under
discussion within the EC.

Even if the EC were to promise never to transfer funds to a member
debtor country, it may still want to act as the lender of last resort, just as
the Federal Reserve Bank does for member banks within the US banking
system. Without this backup, there would be the possibility of panics, in
which lenders suddenly fear that a country will not repay its debts and so
refuse further loans, resulting in the country's inability to borrow to repay
existing debts, and thereby confirming the fears. Such a default could

occur even when the country would have no problem eventually raising enough in taxes to more than repay existing claims.

Governments that develop large foreign debts may also be tempted eventually to default on these debts – the gain from not repaying existing claims may outweigh the cost of any penalties imposed on the country by these lenders. This could occur even when the borrowing country has the incentive *ex ante* to promise credibly not to default. This is a standard type of time-consistency problem. The EC may hope to provide the credible promise that default will never occur by forbidding member countries from ever developing such a large foreign debt that default would be a serious temptation.[2]

When EC countries differ substantially in their debt levels, they are likely also to disagree substantially concerning the appropriate inflation rate within the EC. The policy implications of such disagreements depend on the degree of independence of the Central Bank. Even if extra debt does not directly impose an externality on other countries, the extra debt may lead to a policy shift towards a higher inflation rate which could create externalities. This again is a type of time-consistency story – *ex ante*, inflation raises little revenue since lenders will demand an inflation premium in the interest rate they charge, but *ex post* inflation does collect substantial revenue. Countries would therefore hope to make a credible commitment not to impose such a tax unexpectedly in the future. It would seem easier to do this by ensuring yet more carefully the independence of the Central Bank rather than restricting use of debt finance.

However, countries may also have the option to withdraw from the monetary union. If a country has accumulated large debts, then it may be tempted to do so in order to use inflation to reduce its real liabilities. Again, it has the incentive *ex ante* to promise credibly not to do so. But will withdrawals from the union be forbidden? How? If withdrawal remains feasible, then debt limits may be an effective way to provide a credible commitment that a country will never face such a temptation.

5   Individual mobility

One type of effect of government deficits not mentioned in the paper arises from the mobility of individuals. Through deficits, a country redistributes its overall tax burden from the present to the future. As a result, the country is a more attractive location at the present, and a less attractive location when the taxes are imposed to repay the debt. In response, there should be a net in-migration to the country while the deficits occur, and a net out-migration later. Similarly, the country may initially be a more attractive location for at least short-term capital investments, whose return is received before tax rates go up, and a less attractive location later when tax rates are high. If enough firms and individuals leave the country later to avoid higher taxes, then those who remain would face even higher per capita liabilities, potentially leading to massive out-migrations.

To what degree do these migration patterns impose externalities on other countries? From a fiscal perspective, this depends on how much these migrants pay in taxes relative to the costs of the extra public services they recieve. Certain types of individuals, e.g. the poor, the young and the old, impose net fiscal costs, while others provide a net fiscal surplus. Each country has an incentive to bid for those who create a net fiscal surplus, and encourage out-migration of those who impose a net fiscal cost. This can be done whether or not the country has a budget deficit or surplus.

Should there be any tendency for a deficit to lead to the migration of one type over another? In general, little can be said. The outcome depends on whose taxes are cut now, and whose taxes are increased later. A common form of restriction on deficit policy among US states is to require that debt be used to finance only capital projects, not current expenditues. Doing so limits the amount of intertemporal transfers through the fiscal sytem, since debt-financed capital projects create future benefits as well as future costs. This restriction thereby limits fiscal pressures favouring migration.

6   Asymmetric information

If foreigners have less information about the investment opportunities in a country, then this asymmetric information may lead to reduced capital flows across borders. This phenomena may provide the most plausible explanation for the lack of international capital flows pointed out in Feldstein and Horioka (1980).[3]

The misallocation created by asymmetric information may well justify policy intervention. For example, if a country is a net capital importer, private borrowers may find it difficult to raise funds abroad, since foreign lenders cannot distinguish good from bad projects. However, foreign lenders may be much more ready to lend to the government. In that case, there would be an efficiency gain if the government cut domestic taxes, allowing informed domestic individuals to use the freed funds to finance good domestic projects, then itself borrowed abroad to replace the lost tax revenue. It is in fact common in countries with substantial foreign debt to have the government at least guarantee private debts.

Given the degree of economic integration contemplated within the EC, information should flow virtually as easily between countries as within a country. As a result, there should be little justification for individual government backing for within-EC debt. At best, there seems a weak case for EC backing of outside debt.

Another implication of asymmetric information is that an increased risk of default in one country may affect the risk premia demanded on the debt of other countries. BK are sceptical of the empirical importance of such arguments, since default by private firms is not presumed to impose important externalities on other firms. But the fewer the number of parties involved, the larger should be the impact of any one event on investor expectations, making it unclear that these spillovers would remain small in an EC context.

7   Keynesian spillovers

Economists have also argued that deficits have Keynesian style macro-economic effects which spill over from one country to the rest of the world economy. While BK grant this effect, they argue that such spillovers are reduced in a monetary union, so that there is no more justification now for fiscal coordination than in the past. How they conclude this is not clear to me. With increased economic integration, demand spillovers should become more important than in the past. If the EC wishes to use Keynesian-style fiscal policy, then either this must be done centrally or fiscal policies must be coordinated among member countries – decentralized decision-making will not lead to the desired outcome. Of course, the effectiveness of Keynesian fiscal policy is still much debated.

8   Administrative difficulties in coordinating policies

Even if some of the arguments favouring fiscal coordination were not so easily dismissed, BK still argue, following Kotlikoff (1988), that the 'deficit' is such a slippery economic concept that no substantive agreement should be based on its value. Capturing all forms of intergenerational transfers within a working definition would certainly seem difficult, though a workable approximation may still seem possible.

Even if so, how would any controls be administered? If they are administered at the beginning of a fiscal year, as under Gramm-Rudman in the US, then the process of forecasting revenues and expenditures must be closely monitored. If instead they were adminstered *ex post*, then a country would face substantial uncertainty concerning the size of the deficit implied by its existing policies, with insufficient time to respond to new information. What penalties would be imposed for any violations? Would these penalties in fact be paid if they became large?

9   Conclusions

Given this disparate set of arguments, BK conclude that there are far more important fiscal coordination issues to worry about than attempting to impose restrictions on the debt issues of member countries. Certainly there are many other important fiscal issues that need addressing. However, to support their conclusion that restrictions on debt issues are inappropriate, they would need to dismiss each of these many arguments made in support of some sort of restrictions. Very little is known about the empirical magnitude of many of these stories to draw any firm conclusions, however. The strongest argument that BK make may simply be that inaction is best in the face of such uncertainty.

NOTES

1   See Gordon and Varian (1989) for a discussion of the various types of monopoly power that a country might have in international capital markets, and the types of policies they might use to exploit this power.
2   In theory, simply restricting the size of government debt would not be sufficient if a government has the option to nationalize private firms which have substantial foreign debts, then default on these debts. The risk may be a remote one, however.
3   See Montgomery (1988) for a formal analysis of this phenomena.

REFERENCES

Buiter, W.H. and K.M. Kletzer (1990a) 'Fiscal Policy, Interdependence and Efficiency', mimeo.
    (1990b) 'The Welfare Economics of Cooperative and Noncooperative Fiscal Policy', mimeo.
Casella, A. (1989) 'Letter to th Editor', *The Economist*, July, pp. 22–8.
Feldstein, M.S. and C. Horioka (1980) 'Domestic Savings and International Capital Flows', *Economic Journal* **90**, 314–29.
Gordon, R.H. and H. Varian (1989) 'Taxation of Asset Income in the presence of a World Securities Market', *Journal of International Economics* **26**, 205–26.
Kotlikoff, L.J. (1988) 'The Deficit is not a well-defined Measure of Fiscal Policy', *Science* **241**, 791–5.
Montgomery, J. (1988) 'Financial Intermediation, Contracts and International Capital Mobility', mimeo.
Summers, L.H. (1988) 'Tax Policy and International Competitiveness', in J.A. Frenkel (ed.) *International Aspects of Fiscal Policy*, Chicago: University of Chicago Press.

ASSAF RAZIN

This is a comment on comments (or reflections) on the Delors Report (1984) provided by Willem Buiter and Kenneth Kletzer. They present an interesting discussion of some key fiscal implications of the proposal of a three-stage process towards a single currency and a unified monetary body in the European Community.

The first issue addressed is whether a European System of Central Banks (ESCB) could be independent from the fiscal authorities within the EC. An independent ESCB must be able to resist monetization of deficits, to engage in open market operations or in foreign-exchange interventions and to control the exchange rates of the ECU in terms of non-EC currencies. However, one can imagine a formally independent European Central Bank confronting a national fiscal authority that is (a) persistently unwilling to cover current expenses with current tax revenues; or (b) taking the initiative in foreign-exchange interventions. Under such circumstances monetary and exchange-rate policies cannot be harmonized.

The authors remind us also that the economic motivation to engage in *national* monetary and exchange-rate policies looms large even if the use of base money as a source of seigniorage is negligible. To the extent that factor mobility (especially labour) is imperfect, and a degree of price stickiness prevails in regional factor-price contracts, a national exchange-rate policy is an important policy instrument that influences real regional economic activity and will not easily be sacrificed. Consequently, there may be circumstances in which intercountry conflicts within the supernational central bank may undermine the institution.

A key precondition for a viable ESCB is the narrowing of the intercountry gaps in tax rates, provision of public services and government debt commitments within the European Community. At the same time a key to the sustainability of a single currency area is labour mobility within Europe, which is still imperfect.

In the second part of the paper the authors look in more detail into fiscal policy issues facing members of the European Community. The two pillars of European integration are free trade in goods and free movement of capital within the community. As a consequence the intercountry disparities in tax rates on both commodities and capital income imply that significant adjustments in the VAT and capital income tax bases are likely

Table 8B.1. *Corporate tax systems in the European Community, 1989*

	Statutory corporate tax rate (%)	Investment incentives	Taxation of foreign-source income
Belgium	43	13% reduction*	Exemption
Denmark	50	—	Exemption or credit[1]
France	39	—	Exemption
Germany	56	—	Deduction or exemption[2]
Greece	35	—	Credit
Ireland	43	—	Credit or deductions[3]
Italy	36	—	Credit
Luxembourg	36	12% credit	Credit or exemption[4]
Netherlands	35	—	Credit
Portugal	36	—	Credit
Spain	35	5% credit	Deduction credit or exemption[5]
United Kingdom	35		Credit or deduction[6]

Notes:
[1]Exemption is from France, Germany, Ireland, Portugal and Spain.
[2]Exemption under treaty.
[3]Credit.
[4]Exemption under treaty.
[5]Credit on exemption under treaty.
[6]Deduction under treaty.

Source: Lans Bovenberg and George Kopits, 'Harmonization of Taxes on Capital Income and Commodities in the European Community', IMF, October, 1989.

to take place, on the one hand, and major shifts in regional market shares are expected on the other hand. Tables 8B.1 and 2 describe the large disparity in VAT rates and in the corporate tax systems which exists within the community today. Narrowing of these gaps implies tax revenue gains or losses. These revenue changes will necessitate significant tax restructuring. The fiscal adjustments may slow down the move towards the establishment of the ESCB.

Another issue that requires attention on the fiscal front is the tax treatment of foreign-source income. A fundamental distinction which exists in the context of the international taxation of capital income is that between the source principle and the residence principle. In the following passages I outline the main distinction between these two forms of international taxation.

According to the *residence* principle, residents are taxed on their world-wide income equally, regardless of whether the source of income is

Table 8B.2. *VAT rates in the European Community, 1989*

Country (year of VAT introduction)	Statutory Rates (%)				Revenue contribution as percentage of total tax revenue (1986)	Revenue contribution as percentage of GDP (1986)
	Reduced rate	Standard rate	Higher rate			
Belgium (1971)	1, 6 and 7	19	25 and 33		15.5	7.0
Denmark (1967)	0	22	—		19.5	9.9
France (1968)	5.5 and 7	18.6	28		19.2	8.5
Germany (1968)	7	14	—		15.3	5.7
Greece	3 and 6	18	36		. . .	. . .
Ireland (1972)	0, 2.2 and 10	25	—		20.8	8.4
Italy (1973)	2 and 9	18	38		14.5	5.0
Luxembourg (1970)	3 and 6	12	—		13.3	5.7
Netherlands (1969)	6	19	—		16.5	7.5
Portugal (1986)	8	17	30		17.6	5.7
Spain (1986)	6	12	33		. . .	. . .
United Kingdom (1973)	0	15	—		15.5	6.9
Commission proposal						
A:	4 to 9	14 to 20	abolished			
B:	4 to 9	minimum rate	abolished			

Sources: Table 2.1 in Cnossen and Shoup (1987) and Table 3.5.1 in *European Economy* (March 1988), *EC: The Evolution of VAT Rates Applicable in the Member States of the Community*, Inter-tax, 1987/3, pp. 85–8, and OECD, *Revenue Statistics of OECD Member Countries*, Paris, 1988, and Jacob Frenkel, Assaf Razin and Steve Symanski, 'International VAT Harmonization: Economic Effects', IMF, September 1989.

domestic or foreign. A resident in any country must earn the same net return on her savings, no matter to which country she chooses to channel them (rate-of-return arbitrage). If a country adopts the residence principle, taxing at the same rate capital income from all sources, then the gross return accruing to an individual in that country must be the same, regardless of which country is the source of that return. Thus, the marginal product of capital in that country will be equal to the world return to capital. If all countries adopt the residence principle, then capital income taxation does not disturb the equality of the marginal product of capital across countries which is generated by a free movement of capital. However, if the tax rate is not the same in all countries, then the net returns accruing to savers in different countries vary and the international allocation of world savings is distorted.

According to the *source* principle, residents of a country are not taxed on their income from foreign sources and foreigners are taxed equally as residents on income from domestic sources. Now, suppose that all countries adopt this principle. Then a resident of country H earns in country F the same net return as the resident of country F earns in country F. Since a resident in country H must earn the same net return whether she channelled her savings to country H or to country F, it follows that residents of all countries earn the same net return. Thus, intertemporal marginal rates of substitution are equated across countries, implying that the international allocation of world savings is efficient. However, if the tax rate is not the same in all countries, then the marginal product of capital is also not the same in all countries. In this case the international allocation of the world stock of capital is not efficient.

Although there are two extreme principles of international taxation, in reality, of course, countries adopt a mixture of the two polar principles using credit, deductions and exemptions procedures to avoid double taxation on foreign-source income. Accordingly, in practice, countries partially tax foreign-source income of residents and domestic-source income of non-residents, in which case both the international allocations of world savings and of world investments are distorted. In Razin and Sadka (1989) we demonstrate the world equilibrium with tax competition and the welfare ranking of these principles of taxation.

Suppose first that tax policies are not harmonized internationally, so that the two countries are engaged in tax competition. However, some minimal degree of coordination among the two countries and the rest of the world prevails, so that they can effectively tax their residents on foreign-source income. It can be shown that it is not optimal from the individual country's standpoint to tax foreigners on their income from capital invested in that country. Each one of the competing countries would tax its residents uniformly on their capital income from all sources, domestic as well as foreign. Thus, tax competition leads each country to adopt the residence (or worldwide) principle for the taxation of income from capital. Furthermore, there are no gains from tax harmonization.

In order to implement effectively a policy of taxing world-wide income, a considerable degree of coordination among countries is required, such as, for example, an exchange of information among the tax authorities, withholding arrangements, relaxing bank secrecy laws, etc. This seems a rather interesting and realistic case which captures the essence of a problem hindering European integration, that of capital moving to low-tax countries in the rest of the world. The full implications require much further research.

REFERENCES

Cnossen, S. and S. Shoup (1987) 'Coordination of Value Added Taxes', in S. Cnossen (ed.), *Tax Coordination in the European Economy*, Antwerp: Kluwer Law and Taxation Publishers.

Razin, A. and E. Sadka (1989) 'International Tax Competition and Gains From Tax Harmonization', Working Paper No. 37–89, Foerder Institute for Economic Research, Tel Aviv University.

9   Currency competition and the transition to monetary union: Does competition between currencies lead to price level and exchange rate stability?

MICHAEL WOODFORD

The United Kingdom (HM Treasury, 1989) has recently proposed an 'evolutionary' approach to European monetary union, intended as an alternative to the recommendations of the Delors Report. In addition to generally urging a more gradual and cautious approach to fundamental institutional reforms, the UK proposal argues in particular that it is undesirable to move to a single European currency, primarily because of the extent to which this would place both monetary and fiscal policy in the hands of supranational agencies (such as the proposed European System of Central Banks). Instead, it argues, the objective of 'stable prices and currencies' can be achieved, while preserving national control over monetary and fiscal policy, by 'allow[ing] currencies to compete to provide the non-inflationary anchor in the European Monetary System'. The existing European Monetary System's 'reliance on many currencies' is said to be its 'strength' rather than a liability, because of the need for 'competition' between currencies to force convergence of member states' monetary policies on low rates of money growth; 'by eliminating both competition and accountability from members' monetary policies' it is argued that 'the Delors Report version of monetary union risks producing a higher inflation rate in Europe (p. 9).'

The UK statement argues that the removal of barriers to trade in financial services, as part of Stage 1 of the process of economic and monetary union agreed to by the European Council, will greatly further the extent of competitive pressures towards coordination on non-inflationary policies, by 'increas[ing] the amount of currency substitution. Greater use will be made of low inflation currencies at the expense of high inflation ones in both transactions and deposits' (p. 3).[1] However, it also calls for additional steps to further this process. These include 'the complete removal of all unnecessary restrictions . . . on the use of all currencies throughout the Community', such as regulations requiring

257

German pension funds to invest mainly in Deutschmark assets, and the removal of legal impediments to the development and diffusion of information-processing technologies that would reduce 'the costs and inconvenience of changing between Community currencies', such as simplified cheque-clearing systems and electronic funds transfer networks (p. 5). The outcome of this 'evolutionary' process is envisioned as a Europe in which 'all Community currencies would become effectively interchangeable' and 'the European Monetary System could evolve into a system of more or less fixed exchange rates' (p. 5), although it would have come about through the invisible hand of the market rather than through 'administrative fiat' (p. 7).

It is not clear how seriously the UK proposal should be taken as an actual prescription for 'practical monetary union' in the near future, given the rather insignificant degree to which currency substitution seems to occur in Europe, even in the absence of legal prohibitions on the use of foreign currencies in many kinds of transactions. If, as experience tends to suggest, the cost advantages of using a local currency for payments within local markets are such as to deter currency substitution except in the case of extremely large (Latin American-style) inflation differentials, it is not clear how much discipline upon Community monetary policies can be expected from this channel. Still, an investigation of what the effects of increased currency substitutability ought in principle to be would seem to be timely.[2] In this paper I argue that it is not at all clear that movement towards markedly greater substitutability of currencies would favour stability of nominal price levels and exchange rates. Instead, it would seem likely to increase the scope for speculative instability in exchange rates and corresponding speculative fluctuations in price levels. Insofar as 'competition' between currencies resulted in lower rates of money growth in all countries, as argued in the UK proposal, this fact in itself could produce greater exchange rate and price level instability, owing to the greater scope for the existence of 'sunspot equilibria' in the case of contractionary policies. And finally, rather than resulting in a natural, unplanned evolution towards a system of fixed exchange rates, as suggested in the UK proposal, too great a degree of currency substitutability seems likely to make a fixed exchange rate system more difficult to manage, if not impossible. Hence insofar as Stage 1 of economic and monetary union were expected already to bring with it greatly increased currency substitution, this might be a reason to regard the adoption of a single currency as not only not unnecessary, but actually essential to the preservation of even the degree of monetary stability presently achieved by the European Monetary System.

1   Currency substitution in a cash-in-advance framework

The model I describe here generalizes in some respects the cash-in-advance models of Lucas (1982) and Lucas and Stokey (1987).[3] I assume the existence of a finite number of infinite lived households. Household h seeks to maximize an infinite horizon objective of the form

$$V^h = \Sigma_{t=0}^{\infty} \beta_h^t U^h(c_t^{h1}, \ldots, c_t^{hn}; n_t^{h1}, \ldots, n_t^{hn}) \tag{1}$$

Here c_t^{hi} denotes consumption by household h of goods of type i in period t, and n_t^{hi} denotes that household's supply of the same type of goods. The single-period utility function U^h is a concave function, increasing in its first n arguments, and decreasing in its last n; the discount factor β_h lies between zero and one. Here the n 'types' of goods represent goods that must be purchased with each of n distinct currencies. It may be wondered why it is necessary to introduce endogenous supply as opposed to simply positing an exogenous endowment of goods as in Lucas (1982). An important reason is that in a framework like that of Lucas (1982), the exogenous supply of goods of the various types implies an exogenous demand for real balances of each of the types of currencies, so that interest rate variations do not affect the demand for the various currencies. Use of such a simple framework would accordingly prevent us from discussing the way in which currency substitution should be related to the way in which foreign as well as domestic interest rates should enter money demand functions – an approach that has often been used in empirical investigations of the phenomenon (Thomas and Wickens, 1989). The model presented here is still too simple to be empirically realistic; money demand can vary only insofar as a household varies the value of its transactions, rather than through variations in cash management practices that would result in variation in the 'velocity' of money. Nonetheless, it allows for at least one way in which money demand can vary in response to market conditions, which is a minimum requirement for a useful framework. Furthermore, as is discussed below, I propose to model currency substitution not as a change in the degree to which goods of the same type are purchased using different currencies, but instead as substitution between the 'types' of goods purchased; this would not be possible, in equilibrium, unless substitution in supply were possible.

Household h seeks to maximize V^h subject to the sequence of budget constraints

$$\Sigma_i[M_t^{hi} + (B_{t+1}^{hi}/R_t^i)]e_t^i \leq \Sigma_i[W_t^{hi} - p_t^i \tau_t^{hi}]e_t^i \tag{2}$$

$$p_t^i c_t^{hi} \leq M_t^{hi} + \alpha^i p_t^i n_t^{hi} \tag{3}$$

$$W^{hi}_{t+1} = (M^{hi}_t - p^i_t(c^{hi}_t - n^{hi}_t))I^i_t + B^{hi}_{t+1} \tag{4}$$

$$\lim_{T \to \infty} [e^i_T \Pi^{T-1}_{s=0} R^i_s]^{-1} \Sigma_i W^{hi}_T e^i_T \geq 0 \tag{5}$$

as well as the non-negativity constraints $c^{hi}_t, n^{hi}_t \geq 0$, where (2)–(4) hold for each period $t = 0, 1, 2, \ldots$, and where W^{hi}_0 is given as an initial condition. We suppppose, as in Lucas and Stokey, that each period t consists of two subperiods in which different markets are open. In the first subperiod, the n different currencies can be exchanged for one another and for one-period riskless bonds denominated in any of the n currencies, which bonds mature in the first subperiod of the following period. Condition (2) represents household h's budget constraint for these financial exchanges in period t. Here M^{hi}_t denotes the quantity of currency i held at the end of the first subperiod of period t, and B^{hi}_{t+1} denotes the nominal value at maturity of the bonds denominated in currency i that are held at the same time. The price of currency i in the period t foreign exchange market is denoted e^i_t, where we adopt the normalization

$$\Sigma_i e^i_t = 1 \tag{6}$$

and R^i_t denotes one plus the nominal interest rate on currency-i bonds. Finally, W^{hi}_t denotes the nominal value of wealth denominated in terms of currency i (whether in the form of currency or bonds) carried into period t, τ^{hi}_t denotes the real lump sum taxes paid by household h to government in i in period t (assumed to be collected during the financial market subperiod), and p^i_t denotes the period t price of type i good in terms of currency i.

  In the second subperiod, goods are purchased using currency, in n distinct markets, each with a separate budget constraint (3). It is the presence of the 'cash-in-advance' constraints (3) that results in a demand for the various currencies in this model. As noted earlier, 'type i' goods may be purchased only using currency i. The parameters α^i, satisfying $0 \leq \alpha^i < 1$, indicate the relative efficiency of the payments system using the n different currencies. If one sets $\alpha^i = 0$, one has the standard cash-in-advance constraint, according to which only currency held at the end of the financial market subperiod can be used to purchase goods, and currency received for goods supplied in that same subperiod cannot be used until the financial market subperiod of the following period. This implies that currency can be used to purchase goods only once per period. An undesirable feature of this specification for our present purposes is that the assumed synchronization in time of all financial market trading and goods market trading implies that the payments lag (the time between when money is spent and when it can be spent again) must be of equal length whichever means of payment is used. I wish to be able to consider differences in the efficiency with which different payments systems are operated (in terms of, for example, the amount of time taken for cheques to clear) as one of the grounds for currency substitution, and so would like to be able to impose different payments lags for the different currencies. In order to stay within the discrete-time framework that is proposed here (and that is standard in the cash-in-advance literature), I substitute for a variable payment lag the notion that a fraction α^i of the currency i received from sales can be spent again immediately, while fraction $1 - \alpha^i$ cannot be spent until the following period. Larger values of α^i correspond to more efficient payments systems, and to higher transactions 'velocities' of the currencies in question.

Equation (4) indicates how the wealth denominated in terms of currency i at the beginning of period $t + 1$ is determined, as the sum of currency not spent in the previous period, currency received from sale in the previous period, interest payments on currency held at the end of the previous period, and bonds purchased in the previous period. The innovation here relative to standard cash-in-advance models is the allowance for interest on currency holdings; I_t^i denotes one plus the nominal interest payments (by government i) on holdings of currency i at the end of period t. Interest payments on currency are introduced to allow consideration of differential interest rates on monetary assets as another motive for currency substitution, and indeed one that has been frequently discussed in previous analyses, both theoretical and empirical. The timing chosen here for the interest payments (interest payments at the end of period t rather than at the end of the financial markets subperiod) is selected so as to preserve the simple and familiar form of first-order condition (8) below, which allows the real exchange rate to be interpreted as a marginal rate of substitution on the part of households between goods that are sold for different types of currency, and which makes 'purchasing power parity' a consequence of perfect substitutability between currencies. Finally, condition (5) rules out 'Ponzi schemes' on the part of households, which are otherwise allowed to borrow an unlimited amount (i.e. hold unboundedly negative quantities of the various types of bonds). The choice of currency 1 as the one in terms of which present discounted values are defined in (5) is arbitrary.

Now this is formally identical to a standard multi-country cash-in-advance model, if one identifies household types with countries and goods types with goods produced in different countries, except that our notation allows a given household to supply many different goods. Given that interpretation, it would appear that the model assumes a rigid cash-in-advance constraint (a given country's goods can be purchased only using that country's currency) that makes no allowance for currency substitution whatsoever. But the same formalism can be given an alternative interpretation. In the interpretation intended here, the different 'types' of goods do not differ except in the kind of means of payment used to purchase them, so that the fact that it is possible for both consumers and producers to shift from one 'type' of goods to another indicates the possibility of changing the degree to which one currency is used rather than another for transactions.[4] If one 'type' of good supplies a greater marginal utility to a given household than another, this indicates that it is more convenient for that household to use the first currency in transactions than the other, and, if different 'types' of goods are imperfectly substitutable, this indicates the costs involved in currency substitution. The limiting case of perfect substitutability among currencies corresponds to a utility function (1) of the form

$$V^h = \Sigma_{t=0}^{\infty} \beta_h^t U^h(\Sigma_i c_t^{hi}; \Sigma_i n_t^{hi}) \tag{1'}$$

Optimization by households with perfect foresight can be characterized by the following conditions. Since households are assumed to be able to sell the various types of bonds short, a solution to any household's optimization problems exists only if

$$\frac{R_t^i e_{t+1}^i}{e_t^i} = \frac{R_t^j e_{t+1}^j}{e_t^j} \tag{7}$$

for every two currencies i, j. This is the usual interest rate parity condition that follows from perfect capital mobility.[5] Optimization then requires the first-order conditions

$$\frac{\lambda_t^{hi}}{\lambda_t^{hj}} = \frac{p_t^i e_t^i}{p_t^j e_t^j} \tag{8}$$

$$\frac{\nu_t^{hi}}{\nu_t^{hj}} = \frac{p_t^i e_{t+1}^i [\alpha^j R_t^j + (1 - \alpha^j) I_t^j]}{p_t^j e_{t+1}^j [\alpha^i R_t^i + (1 - \alpha^i) I_t^i]} \tag{9}$$

$$\frac{\lambda_t^{hi}}{\nu_t^{hi}} = \frac{R_t^i}{\alpha^i R_t^i + (1 - \alpha^i) I_t^i} \tag{10}$$

$$p_t^i c_t^{hi} = M_t^{hi} + \alpha^i p_t^i n_t^{hi} \qquad \text{if} \quad R_t^i > I_t^i \tag{11}$$

$$p_t^i c_t^{hi} < M_t^{hi} + \alpha^i p_t^i n_t^{hi} \qquad \text{only if} \quad R_t^i = I_t^i \tag{11'}$$

$$\frac{\lambda_t^{hi}}{\beta_h \lambda_{t+1}^{hi}} = \frac{p_t^i R_t^i}{p_{t+1}^i} \tag{12}$$

Here λ_t^{hi} denotes the value (in utility units) to household type h in the securities trading subperiod of period t of an additional amount of currency i sufficient to allow purchase of one more unit of type i consumption goods, and v_t^{hi} denotes the value of the same quantity of currency i if received in the goods market subperiod of period t. Condition (10) is the relation that must exist between these quantities given the possibility of borrowing currency i during the securities trading period and repaying the loan out of revenues received in the goods market trading period. The shadow prices λ_t^{hi} and v_t^{hi} must furthermore be positive, and satisfy

$$U_c^{hi}(t) = \lambda_t^{hi} \qquad \text{if} \quad c_t^{hi} > 0$$

$$U_c^{hi}(t) < \lambda_t^{hi} \qquad \text{only if} \quad c_t^{hi} = 0$$

$$U_n^{hi}(t) = - v_t^{hi} \qquad \text{if} \quad n_t^{hi} > 0$$

$$U_n^{hi}(t) < - v_t^{hi} \qquad \text{only if} \quad n_t^{hi} = 0$$

where $U_c^{hi}(t)$ denotes $(\partial/\partial c^{hi}) U^h(c_t^{h1}, \ldots, c_t^{hn}; n_t^{h1}, \ldots, n_t^{hn})$, and so on. In the case of equations (11)–(11'), as in the similar pairs of complementary slackness conditions involving the marginal utilities, it is to be understood that the two cases listed exhaust the possibilities consistent with optimization, so that one or the other must apply. Finally, assuming nonsatiation, optimization requires that the household completely exhaust its budget, so that

$$\Sigma_i[M_t^{hi} + (B_{t+1}^{hi}/R_t^i)]e_t^i = \Sigma_i[W_t^{hi} - p_t^i \tau_t^{hi}]e_t^i \tag{13}$$

$$\lim_{T \to \infty} [e_T^1 \Pi_{s=0}^{T-1} R_s^1]^{-1} \Sigma_i W_T^{hi} e_T^i = 0 \tag{14}$$

A perfect foresight equilibrium is then a state of affairs in which each household optimizes in the manner just described, and in addition all markets for goods, currencies, and bonds clear, so that

$$\Sigma_h c_t^{hi} + g_t^i = \Sigma_h n_t^{hi} \tag{15}$$

$$\Sigma_h M_t^{hi} + p_t^i g_t^i = M_t^i \tag{16}$$

$$\Sigma_h B_{t+1}^{hi} = B_{t+1}^i \tag{17}$$

for $t = 0, 1, 2, \ldots$, and for $i = 1, \ldots, n$. Here g_t^i denotes goods purchased by government i in period t; it is assumed for the sake of simplicity that governments purchase goods only with their own currencies. M_t^i denotes the supply of currency i in period t (to be precise, at the end of the financial markets subperiod), which is equated in (16) to the sum of private demands and government i's demand for currency to be used in making its purchases. Finally, B_{t+1}^i denotes the supply of bonds by government i maturing at time $t + 1$; again, it is assumed for the sake of simplicity that governments only issue bonds denominated in their own currencies. The quantities of goods purchased by the governments and the evolution over time of the money supplies and stocks of government debt depend upon governments' monetary and fiscal policies. Various assumptions will be made below about these, but they must always satisfy the government budget constraints

$$(M_t^i - M_{t-1}^i I_{t-1}^i) + ((B_{t+1}^i / R_t^i) - B_t^i) = p_t^i(g_t^i - \Sigma_h \tau_t^{hi}) \tag{18}$$

$$\lim_{T \to \infty} [\Pi_{s=0}^{T-1} R_s^i]^{-1}(M_{T-1}^i I_{T-1}^i + B_T^i) = 0 \tag{19}$$

(Note that only $n-1$ of each of these sets of equations represent additional, independent, equilibrium conditions, since the last of each set is implied by the other $n-1$ and the household budget constraints (13) and (14).) An equilibrium is then a set of sequences for the endogenous variables satisfying (4) and (6)–(17), given some specification of the monetary and fiscal policy variables of the governments that is consistent with (18)–(19).

It will often be convenient to simplify the model by considering the case of a world representative household, by which I mean the case of a single household type that is taxed by all n governments and that both supplies and purchases all n types of goods. One might interpret such households as being made up of a large number of extended family members who are linked by altruistic transfers and as a result act jointly so as to maximize a single household utility function, with different members of the family living in different jurisdictions, and working in regions where different currencies are most conveniently used. Lest this seem an extravagant fantasy even at a conference concerned with post-1992 Europe, I might point out that the common use of representative households for individual countries is most plausibly defended, not on the ground that authors believe that most households in a single country have roughly similar economic circumstances, but rather on the ground that the effects of the distribution of wealth (as opposed to the aggregate wealth of the country) on aggregate consumption and labour supply are believed to be small and so need not be modelled. A similar hypothesis regarding the insignificance of the international wealth distribution for world aggregate consumption and labour supply ought equally well to justify consideration of a world representative consumer.

The assumption of a world representative consumer greatly simplifies all of the above equilibrium conditions, eliminating the need for separate state variables and separate first-order conditions and budget constraints for the separate households. (I will still, however, keep a superscript h on the household's demands for currencies, to distinguish these from the corresponding money supplies.) This furthermore immediately allows the variables c_t^i to be eliminated from all equilibrium conditions, using the substitution $c_t^i = n_t^i - g_t^i$, because of (15). Equations (10) are then a set of n

equations that can be solved for the n unknowns $\{n_t^i, i = 1, \ldots, n\}$; let us suppose that there is a unique solution[6] and let it be denoted

$$n_t^i = n^i(R_t^1/I_t^1, \ldots, R_t^n/I_t^n; g_t^1, \ldots, g_t^n) \tag{20}$$

Then using his and also (16), equations (11) and (11') become[7]

$$M_t^i/p_t^i = (1 - \alpha^i)n^i(R_t^1/I_t^1, \ldots, R_t^n/I_t^n; \\ g_t^1, \ldots, g_t^n) \\ \text{if} \quad R_t^i > I_t^i \tag{21}$$

$$M_t^i/p_t^i > (1 - \alpha^i)n^i(R_t^1/I_t^1, \ldots, R_t^n/I_t^n; \\ g_t^1, \ldots, g_t^n) \\ \text{only if} \quad R_t^i = I_t^i \tag{21'}$$

Substitution of (20) for the arguments of the representative household's utility function allows us to define

$$U_c^{hi}(t) = \lambda^i(R_t^1/I_t^1, \ldots, R_t^n/I_t^n; g_t^1, \ldots, g_t^n)$$

Substitution of this in turn into (8) and (12) then yields

$$\frac{\lambda^i(R_t^1/I_t^1, \ldots, R_t^n/I_t^n; g_t^1, \ldots, g_t^n)}{\lambda^j(R_t^1/I_t^1, \ldots, R_t^n/I_t^n; g_t^1, \ldots, g_t^n)} = \frac{p_t^i e_t^i}{p_t^j e_t^j} \quad \text{if} \quad (R_t, I_t, g_t) \in C \tag{22}$$

$$\frac{\lambda^i(R_t^1/I_t^1, \ldots, R_t^n/I_t^n; g_t^1, \ldots, g_t^n)}{\beta\lambda^i(R_{t+1}^1/I_{t+1}^1, \ldots, R_{t+1}^n/I_{t+1}^n; g_{t+1}^1, \ldots, g_{t+1}^n)} = \frac{p_t^i R_t^i}{p_{t+1}^i} \tag{23}$$

where R_t, I_t and g_t denote n-vectors giving the corresponding quantities for each currency, and where C is the set of values of (R_t, I_t, g_t) for which (20) implies that $c_t^i > 0$ for all i. Given a specification of monetary and fiscal policies consistent with (18)–(19), a perfect foresight equilibrium (in which all n currencies are used at all times to purchase private consumption goods) is then a set of sequences $\{p_t, R_t, e_t\}$ for $t = 0, 1, 2, \ldots$, that satisfy (6), (21)–(21'), (22) and (23) for $t = 0, 1, 2, \ldots$ The remaining equilibrium conditions are all implied by these, in the single-household case. Thus the assumption of a world representative household allows us to reduce the equilibrium conditions to a system of $3n - 1$ difference equations for $3n - 1$ state variables (eliminating one variable using (6)). The equations are only slightly more complex in the case of equilibria in which not all currencies are used by the representative household in some periods.

It will be observed that this system bears a certain resemblance to the sort of *ad hoc* equation systems postulated in previous studies of currency substitution. Equations (21)–(21') can be interpreted as a set of money demand functions, in which the demand for each currency is shown to depend upon the interest rate spreads between bonds and currency for all of the currencies.[8] (Equation (21′) indicates that money demand becomes infinitely elastic when the interest rate spread is set to zero, since currency and bonds then become perfect substitutes, in the deterministic environment assumed here.) Equations (22) equate real exchange rates to marginal rates of substitution between the goods purchased with the different currencies (which marginal rates of substitution the theory determines as a function of the other state variables), while equations (23) are Fisher equations for the various currencies (with the real interest rates identified with marginal rates of substitution that again the theory determines).

This derivation may shed some light upon the relation between the various formulations employed in previous analyses, contrasted in Thomas and Wickens (1989). Some, such as Girton and Roper (1981), have assumed that the demand for currency i should be an increasing function of the currency i interest rate and a decreasing function of other currency interest rates, because the interest rates being discussed are I^i versus I^j. Others, such as Miles (1978), have assumed that the demand for currency i should be a *decreasing* function of the level of interest rates in country i and an *increasing* function of the level of interest rates in other countries, because the interest rates in question are R^i versus R^j.[9] Both sorts of effects of foreign and domestic interest rates are consistent with the model presented here, where the demand for currency i depends upon the spreads R^i/I^i and R^j/I^j, and where, if substitution effects dominate, it will be a decreasing function of R^i/I^i and an increasing function for R^j/I^j, for all $j \neq i$.[10]

Of course this derivation is adequate only if one cares only about the determination of a world demand for each currency. Determination of separate national demands would require heterogeneous households, the simplest possible case being that of a representative household for each country. In this case one cannot derive money demand functions as simple as (21). However, equations (8), (10) and (15) represent in this case a system of $2n^2$ equations that can be solved for the $2n^2$ variables representing consumption and output of each 'type' of good in each country. Let us denote the solutions

$$c_t^{ij} = c^{ij}(R_t^1/I_t^1, \ldots, R_t^n/I_t^n;$$
$$p_t^2 e_t^2/p_t^1 e_t^1, \ldots, p_t^n e_t^n/p_t^1 e_t^1; g_t^1, \ldots, g_t^n)$$

$$n_t^{ij} = n^{ij}(R_t^1/I_t^1, \ldots, R_t^n/I_t^n;$$
$$p_t^2 e_t^2/p_t^1 e_t^1, \ldots, p_t^n e_t^n/p_t^1 e_t^1; g_t^1, \ldots, g_t^n)$$

Substitute these into (11) and (11′), we obtain equilibrium conditions of the form

$$M_t^{ij}/p_t^i = m^{ij}(R_t^1/I_t^1, \ldots, R_t^n/I_t^n;$$
$$p_t^2 e_t^2/p_t^1 e_t^1, \ldots, p_t^n e_t^n/p_t^1 e_t^1; g_t^1, \ldots, g_t^n) \qquad \text{if} \quad R_t^j > I_t^j$$

and a corresponding generalization of (21′). Note that in general the demand for each currency will depend not only upon the interest rates in all countries but also upon all countries' real exchange rates.

2 Effects of currency substitution on price level and exchange rate determinacy

In this section I wish to consider whether a particular set of monetary and fiscal policies on the part of the n governments result in a determinate perfect foresight equilibrium path for the various price levels, exchange rates, and interest rates, and in particular to consider how the degree of substitutability between different 'types' of goods in households' utility functions) affects the answer to this question. In order to simplify the analysis, it is useful to restrict our attention to the case of a two-currency world with a world representative household. I also consider only monetary policies that involve fixing an exogenous constant rate of growth, and an exogenous constant rate of interest payments on money holdings, for each of the currencies, and allowing exchange rates to float. There is also assumed to be no government debt outstanding, and government purchases are assumed to be constant. Finally, the number of parameters entering the equations below is reduced by restricting attention to the case of perfect symmetry between the two currencies. That is, I assume the same money supply growth rates and rates of interest on money in the case of both currencies, the same constant levels of goods purchases by the two governments, perfect symmetry of the utility functions between the two currencies, and equal values for α^i.

Let us consider only equilibria in which both currencies are used to purchase consumption goods by the representative household. (This does not rule out the possibility of equilibria in which one currency ceases to be used asymptotically.) Then combining (10) and (12) yields

$$- U_n^i(c_t; n_t) = \alpha U_c^i(c_t; n_t) + (1 - \alpha) \beta I U_c^i(c_{t+1}; n_{t+1}) \frac{p_t^i}{p_{t+1}^i} \qquad (24)$$

for $i = 1, 2$, where c_t denotes the vector (c_t^1, c_t^2), and likewise for n_t.

Let g denote the constant level of purchases by both governments, and define

$$\hat{n}_1(n_2) = \arg \max_{n_1} U(n_1 - g, n_2 - g; n_1, n_2)$$

$$\hat{n}_2(n_1) = \arg \max_{n_2} U(n_1 - g, n_2 - g; n_1, n_2)$$

$$\bar{n} = \arg \max_{n} U(n - g, n - g; n, n)$$

Note that $\hat{n}_1(\bar{n}) = \hat{n}_2(\bar{n}) = \bar{n}$. Also note that $n_1, n_2 \geq \bar{n}$ imply that at least one of the inequalities $n_1 \geq \hat{n}_1(n_2)$ or $n_2 \geq \hat{n}_2(n_1)$ must hold, and that $n_1, n_2 \leq \bar{n}$ imply that at least one of the inequalities $n_1 \leq \hat{n}_1(n_2)$ or $n_2 \leq \hat{n}_2(n_1)$ must hold. Then (11), (11'), and (15) imply

$$n_t^1 = m_t^1, \ n_t^2 = m_t^2 \qquad \text{if} \quad m_t^1 \leq \hat{n}_1(m_t^2), \ m_t^2 \leq \hat{n}_2(m_t^1) \tag{25a}$$

$$n_t^1 = m_t^1, \ n_t^2 = \hat{n}_2(m_t^1) \qquad \text{if} \quad m_t^1 \leq \bar{n}, \ m_t^2 \geq \hat{n}_2(m_t^1) \tag{25b}$$

$$n_t^1 = \hat{n}_1(m_t^2), \ n_t^2 = m_t^2 \qquad \text{if} \quad m_t^1 \geq \hat{n}_1(m_t^2), \ m_t^2 \leq \bar{n} \tag{25c}$$

$$n_t^1 = n_t^2 = \bar{n} \qquad \text{if} \quad m_t^1, m_t^2 \geq \bar{n} \tag{25d}$$

where $m_t^i = M_t^i/p_t^i$, $i = 1, 2$. Equations (25a)–(25d) show that the complete allocation of resources in a given period t (recalling that $c_t^i = n_t^i - g$) can be determined as a function of the levels of real money balances (m_t^1, m_t^2) alone. The four different cases correspond to whether one, the other, both, or neither of the cash-in-advance constraints are binding in the period in question. Let the pair of continuous functions defined in (25a)–(25d) be denoted $n_t^i = n(m_t^1, m_t^2)$, for $i = 1, 2$.

Then, substituting (25a)–(25d) into (24), we obtain a pair of difference equations for the perfect foresight equilibrium dynamics of the two price levels of the form[11]

$$F^i(m_t^1, m_t^2) = (\beta I/\mu) G^i(m_{t+1}^1, m_{t+1}^2) \tag{26}$$

for $i = 1, 2$, where

$$F^i(m) = m^i[- U_n(n^1(m) - g, n^2(m) - g; \\ n^1(m), n^2(m)) \\ - \alpha U_c(n^1(m) - g, n^2(m) - g; \\ n^1(m), n^2(m))]$$

$$G^i(m) = (1 - \alpha)m^i - U_c(n^1(m) - g, n^2(m) - g; n^1(m), n^2(m))$$

and where μ is the common growth rate of the two currencies (i.e. M_{t+1}^i/M_t^i). Conditions (26) describe the determination of the demand for both types of real balances (and hence of the price levels) in period t as a function of the expected price levels in the following period.

Finally, substitution of (12) allows (14) to be put in the form

$$\lim_{T \to \infty} \beta^T \Sigma_i G^i(m_T) = 0 \tag{27}$$

Any pair of sequences $\{m_t^1, m_t^2\}$ satisfying (26)–(27) represents a perfect foresight equilibrium; that is, given such sequences, one can find unique sequences of value for the price levels, interest rates, and so on, that satisfy all of the other equilibrium conditions. Hence it is the uniqueness of solutions to (26)–(27) with which we are concerned. Since there are no initial conditions for the difference equations (26), it is evident that there could be as large a set of equilibria as a two-dimensional continuum, corresponding to different possible initial levels of real balances (m_0^1, m_0^2).

I propose to interpret the effects of switching to a single, common currency for all transactions as corresponding to a utility function for the representative household of the form

$$U^*(c; n) = U(c, c; n, n)$$

where c and n represent consumption goods purchased and output sold using the common currency. In this case it is easily seen that perfect foresight equilibria of the economy with a common currency correspond exactly to those equilibria of the symmetric two-currency economy in which $m_t^1 = m_t^2$ for all t. As a result, *requiring the use of a common currency cannot increase the number of equilibria*. Furthermore, if there exists a continuum of equilibria even in the case of a common currency, there must be a continuum of equilibria in the case of multiple currencies, *regardless of the degree of substitutability of the different currencies*. Hence the only interesting case to analyse is the one in which perfect foresight equilibrium is unique in the case of a common currency; we can then consider whether equilibrium may nonetheless be indeterminate in the case of multiple currencies, and we can consider how currency substitution affects this.

In the case of a common currency, the model presented here reduces to the model of Lucas and Stokey (1987); the determinacy of equilibrium in this model is analysed in Woodford (1988). It is shown in the latter paper that a sufficient condition to rule out the existence of multiple equilibria in which the level of real balances goes neither to zero nor to infinity asymptotically is to assume that the functions $F(m) = F^1(m, m) = F^2(m, m)$ and $G(m) = G^1(m, m) = G^2(m, m)$ satisfy

$$F' > 0, \quad G' > 0, \quad F'/F > G'/G \tag{28}$$

for all m. The first and third inequalities hold in the case, for example, of additive separability of consumption and leisure within periods. The second holds in the case of sufficient intertemporal substitutability of consumption. This is also an assumption that implies that the demand for real balances will be a monotonically decreasing function of expected inflation, which is surely the most realistic case. It is also shown that a sufficient condition to rule out the existence of equilibria in which real balances asymptotically approach zero is for G to remain bounded above F as m approaches its lowest feasible value. If $g > 0$, the lowest feasible value is $m = g$ and the property must hold.[12] In the case that $g = 0$, it is necessary to assume that

$$\lim_{m \to \infty} G(m) > 0 \tag{29}$$

This means that the marginal utility of consumption rises sufficiently steeply as the level of consumption goes to zero, a not implausible stipulation. Finally, it is shown that equilibria in which the level of real balances asymptotically becomes infinite exist if and only if the rate of money growth μ satisfies $\beta I < \mu < I$; there exists a continuum of solutions of this kind to the difference equation (26) for any $\mu > \beta I$, but the solutions (in which real balances grow asymptotically at the rate $\mu / \beta I$, and so in which $G(m)$ grows asymptotically at that same rate) also satisfy the transversality constraint (27) only if $\mu < I$. Hence (28) and (29), or just (29) if $g > 0$, and $\mu \geq I$ suffice to ensure the existence of a unique rational expectations equilibrium, in which the price level grows at the same rate as the growth rate μ of the common currency.

I wish to maintain assumptions (28) and (29) in the case of two currencies, but consider whether there can exist additional equilibria in which $m_t^1 \neq m_t^2$. Again, these assumptions (together with $\mu > \beta I$) imply the existence of a unique symmetric stationary equilibrium in which $m_t^1 = m_t^2 = m^*$ for all t, and in which both cash-in-advance constraints always bind. Can there also exist asymmetric stationary equilibria in which both currencies are used for consumption purchases? A further reasonable assumption on preferences is that

$$-\frac{U_c^i}{U_n^i} > -\frac{U_c^j}{U_n^j} \qquad \text{if} \quad c^i < c^j, n^i < n^j \tag{30}$$

for $i, j = 1, 2$. This is also a property that necessarily holds, for example, if U is strictly concave and additively separable between consumption and output. It then follows that $m^i < m^j$ implies $F^i/G^i < F^j/G^j$, from which it follows that one cannot have $F^i/G^i = F^j/G^j = \beta I/\mu$. Hence assuming (30), there can be no stationary equilibria in which both currencies are used, other than the symmetric one (m^*, m^*).

A further simple question to address is whether there exist other perfect foresight equilibria in which both m_t^1 and m_t^2 remain near m^* forever (e.g. non-stationary equilibria that converge asymptotically to the stationary values). Linearizing (26) around the stationary equilibrium, we obtain a pair of equations of the form

$$\Delta m_t^i = \Sigma_j M_{ij} \Delta m_{t-1}^j$$

for $i = 1, 2$, where Δm_t^i denotes $(m_t^i - m^*)/m^*$. The two eigenvalues of the matrix M are

$$\xi^1 = \frac{\mu F_1^1 + F_2^1}{\beta I G_1^1 + G_2^1}$$

corresponding to an eigenvector whose components are equal, and

$$\xi^2 = \frac{\mu F_1^1 - F_2^1}{\beta I G_1^1 - G_2^1}$$

corresponding to an eigenvector whose components are of equal magnitude but opposite sign, where the derivatives of F^1 and G^1 are evaluated at (m^*, m^*). It follows from (28) that $\xi^1 > 1$. Furthermore, if we interpret a change in the degree of substitutability of currencies as a change in U that does not affect the reduced form utility U^*, then changes in the degree of substitutability of the two currencies will not affect the size of ξ^1.

Changes in the degree of substitutability will not affect the location of the stationary equilibrium (i.e. the value of m^*) either, but they will affect the size of ξ^2. In particular, it is easily seen that in the case of perfect substitutability (1'), $F_1^1 - F_2^1 = F^1/m^1$ and $G_1^1 - G_2^1 = G^1/m^1$, so that $\xi^2 = 1$, *whereas in the case where purchases and sales using one currency are not at all substitutable for those using the other, so that the marginal utility of purchases or sales of one kind is independent of the quantity of purchases and sales of the other type*, $F_2^1 = G_2^1 = 0$, so that $\xi^2 = \xi^1 > 1$. In general we are interested in cases intermediate between these two, so that we should expect $1 < \xi^2 < \xi^1$. In fact (30) implies

$$\frac{F_1^1 - F_2^1}{F^1} > \frac{G_1^1 - G_2^1}{G^1} \tag{31}$$

If we assume in addition (as just suggested) that we are interested in the case of partial substitutability, so that U_{cc}^{12}, $U_{nn}^{12} < 0$, then $F_2^1 > 0$, $G_2^1 < 0$, and (28) then implies that the right hand side of (31) is positive. Then (31) together with these latter inequalities implies that $1 < \xi^2 < \xi^1$.

It follows that regardless of the degree of substitutability of currencies, as long as it is less than perfect, both eigenvalues are greater than one, and there will exist no equilibrium other than the symmetric stationary equilibrium that does not eventually diverge from values of real balances near (m^*, m^*). In this regard the case of *perfect* substitutability is qualitatively different from that of even very great (but still imperfect) substitutability. For with perfect substitutability, every pair (m^1, m^2) satisfying $m^1 + m^2 = 2m^*$ is equally a stationary equilibrium, so that perfect foresight equilibrium is indeterminate even if only equilibria remaining forever near the symmetric stationary equilibrium are considered.[13] This may well correspond to a difference as respects global uniqueness of equilibrium as well, since, as explained below, solutions to (26) that involve diverging levels of real balances for the two currencies may after some number of periods reach extreme values that prevent solution of the difference equations for further periods. Hence analyses of exchange rate determinacy (such as Kareken and Wallace, 1981) that assume perfect substitutability may be misleading as guides to the consequences of increased substitutability.

On the other hand, there is a sense in which the analysis just given indicates that increased substitutability may increase the volatility of exchange rates and prices. For increased substitutability will move ξ^2 closer to one. And a value of ξ^2 only slightly above one implies that a change in expectations regarding fundamentals far in the future (future tastes, future transactions costs, future money growth rates) can have a significant effect upon the current equilibrium price levels and exchange rate. In the model analysed formally here, I have assumed perfect fore-knowledge of fundamentals into the indefinite future, and this may lead to a unique perfect foresight equilibrium. But in reality there will certainly be uncertainty and constant changes of opinion about the future, and, even if (presumably quite volatile) expectations regarding the very distant future have a large impact upon equilibrium, one must suppose that this will increase instability. With less substitutability of currencies, the smallest eigenvalue may be significantly above one, so that only expectations about fundamentals over a relatively short horizon have much effect upon equilibrium, in which case speculative instability should be less of a problem.

Another class of non-stationary equilibria that are easily analysed are those in which real balances of one currency decline to their minimum possible value, g (i.e. the private sector ceases eventually to use that currency for purchases), while real balances of the other currency approach a constant positive long-run level, m^{**}.[14] In the case of equilibria which may involve zero private sector purchases using one currency, equations (26) must be generalized to

$$F^i(m_t^1, m_t^2) \geq (\beta I/\mu) G^i(m_{t+1}^1, m_{t+1}^2) \tag{32}$$

with an equality if $m_t^i, m_{t+1}^i > g$, for $i = 1, 2$. (The derivation is the same as for (26), but now allowing for a possible discrepancy between the marginal utilities and the shadow values of real balances, and I assume here that $g > 0$, so that necessarily $n_t^i > 0$.) Let us suppose, without loss of generality, that currency 1 is the one that eventually ceases to be used for private consumption purchases. Then the asymptotic level of real balances of currency 2, m^{**}, must satisfy

$$F^1(g, m^{**}) \geq (\beta I/\mu) G^1(g, m^{**}) \tag{33a}$$

$$F^2(g, m^{**}) = (\beta I/\mu) G^2(g, m^{**}) \tag{33b}$$

However, if $0 < g < n^*$, then (33b) and (30) imply that (33a) cannot hold. Hence in this case no equilibria of this kind are possible, even in the case of preferences of a sort that would allow such equilibria when $g = 0$.[15]

When $g = 0$, (33a) can hold, in fact with equality, even though, because of (33b) and (30),

$$- U_n^1 < [\alpha + (1 - \alpha)\beta I/\mu] U_c^1$$

In this case, there necessarily exists an m^{**} satisfying (33b), and sufficient conditions for the existence of a continuum of perfect foresight equilibria in which $m_t^1 \to 0$, $m_t^2 \to m^{**}$ (and similarly, a continuum of equilibria in which $m_t^2 \to 0$, $m_t^1 \to m^{**}$) are

$$\lim_{m \to 0} F^1(m, m^{**}) = \lim_{m \to 0} G^1(m, m^{**}) = 0 \qquad (34)$$

together with the condition that $F^1(m, m^{**})$ be positive for all small enough $m > 0$. On the other hand, a sufficient condition to rule out such equilibria is that

$$\lim_{m \to 0} G^1(m, m^{**}) > 0 \qquad (35)$$

This rules out equilibria in which one currency asymptotically ceases to be used, for the same reason that (29) rules out equilibria in which both currencies asymptotically cease to be used. Condition (35) requires that the marginal utility from purchases of goods using a particular currency becomes very large fast enough as the quantity of goods purchased using that currency goes to zero. It is thus a condition expressing a sense in which the use of that currency, for at least some purchases, is essential.

Now an increase in the substitutability of currencies need not imply that (35) should cease to hold. In particular (35) might hold despite the existence of an arbitrarily high degree of substitutability between currencies, up until the point where one currency is used for only a very small number of purchases. Hence, again, analysis of the case of perfect substitutability is a poor guide to what must happen in the case of highly but not perfectly substitutable currencies. But, on the other hand, it should be pointed out that substitutability of currencies can result in (34) holding, despite the fact that (29) holds, as indeed must be the case if there is perfect substitutability; while in the case that U is additively separable between transactions involving the two different currencies, (29) implies (35).

Finally, we can consider the possibility of equilibria in which real balances of one currency become unboundedly large asymptotically. It is easily seen that in any solution of (26) of this form, real balances of the currency in question grow asymptotically at the rate $\mu/\beta I$, so that (27) is satisfied only if $\mu < I$. Hence, assuming that $\mu \geq I$, equilibria of this kind can be ruled out, regardless of the degree of substitutability of the two currencies. If $\beta I < \mu < I$, equilibria of this kind do exist, but again this is independent of the degree of substitutability of currencies.

However, it is arguable that the rate of money growth should not be independent of the degree of substitutability of currencies; indeed, this is the main argument of the proponents of 'competing currencies' for the desirability of increased substitutability. The usual argument (see, e.g. Girton and Roper, 1981) is some variant of the following.[16] Suppose that each government chooses a path $\{\mu_t^i\}$ for the rate of growth of its currency, and a path $\{I_t^i\}$ for the rate of interest on holdings of its currency, taking as given the rate of growth of and rate of interest on the other currency, so as to maximize its seigniorage income from money creation.[17] To simplify the analysis, let us restrict attention to strategies for each country in which money growth is held constant in all periods $t \geq 1$, and in which the interest rate on money is held constant in all periods $t \geq 0$, although μ_1^i may differ from μ_0^i owing to the existence of a special constraint on the period zero choice. The most important advantage of this restriction is that it allows us to make a natural choice regarding what equilibrium prices the countries expect to result from a given choice of money growth rates and interest payments. Specifically, we may assume that each country expects that from period one onward, the equilibrium that will exist will be the unique stationary equilibrium in which both currencies are used.[18] That is, each government assumes that given (μ^1, μ^2, I^1, I^2), the constant values expected to prevail for all $t \geq 1$, an equilibrium will result in which real balances of each currency are constants (m^1, m^2) for all $t \geq 0$, satisfying

$$F^i(m^1, m^2) = (\beta I^i / \mu^i) G^i(m^1, m^2) \tag{36}$$

in which nominal interest rates in each country are constants (R^1, R^2) for all $t \geq 0$, satisfying $R^i = \mu^i / \beta$, and in which inflation in each country is equal to μ^i for all $t \geq 1$, for $i = 1, 2$. This results in a well-defined non-cooperative game between the two countries.

Now the government budget constraints (18)–(19) may equivalently be written as a single infinite-horizon constraint for each government, which in the case of a stationary equilibrium of the kind just described reduces to

$$\sum_{t=0}^{\infty} \beta^t [g_t^i - \tau_t^i] = (1 - \beta)^{-1} m^i [1 - (\beta I^i / \mu^i)] - \sum_h W_0^{hi} / p_0^i \tag{37}$$

where $\sum_h W_0^{hi}$ is an initial condition. It is reasonable then to take the right-hand side of (37) to be the quantity that government i wishes to maximize. The second term on the right-hand side of (37) can also be expressed $(\sum_h W_0^{hi} / M_1^i)(m^i / \mu_0^i)$. Then, using (36) to define m^i, both governments' objectives are specified as functions of their joint strategies and the initial conditions $\Sigma_h W_0^{hi}/M_1^i$.

It is immediately obvious that, given any choice of I^i/μ^i by the two countries, country i can increase the right-hand side of (37) by increasing μ_0^i. Hence, in the absence of any further constraint, the optimization just described should lead to choice of an unboundedly large rate of money growth in the initial period. Apart from the fact that this makes equilibrium prices undefined, this result is undesirable because, as is well known, the optimizing behaviour described is not time-consistent. One solution to this problem is to suppose that each government must commit itself a period in advance to an inflation target for each period, and is in the subsequent period constrained to choose a policy that results in an equilibrium price level no higher than the pre-announced target level.[19] With such a constraint in addition to the initial condition $\Sigma_h W_0^{hi}$, country i's optimal policy will be to choose I^i/μ^i so as to maximize $(1 - \beta)^{-1}m^i$ $[1 - (\beta I^i/\mu^i)]$, given that the other country's choice (which affects the determination of m^i through the pair of equations (36)), and then to choose μ_0^i so as to make p_0^i equal to the pre-announced target. These policies not only lead to finite price levels, but are time-consistent.

The optimal choice of I^i/μ^i, taking as given the policy of the other country, will then satisfy a first-order condition[20]

$$[1 - (\beta I^i/\mu^i)] \, \partial m^i/\partial(I^i/\mu^i) - \beta m^i = 0 \tag{38}$$

where $m^i(I^1/\mu^1, I^2/\mu^2)$, for $i = 1, 2$, denote the solutions to the pair of equations (36).[21] Considering again the case of a symmetric two-country economy, the symmetric Nash equilibrium of the monetary policy game will involve a common choice for I/μ, and a common level of real balances m^*, that satisfy

$$F(m^*, m^*) = (\beta I/\mu) \, G(m^*, m^*) \tag{39}$$

$$[1 - (\beta I/\mu)] = (2m^*/G(m^*, m^*))[Z_+^{-1} + Z_-^{-1}]^{-1} \tag{40}$$

where

$$Z_+ = (F_1^1 + F_2^1) - (\beta I/\mu)(G_1^1 + G_2^1)$$

$$Z_- = (F_1^1 - F_2^1) - (\beta I/\mu)(G_1^1 - G_2^1)$$

with the derivatives evaluated at (m^*, m^*). For the reasons discussed above, an increase in currency substitutability will reduce Z, for any given m^*, with Z approaching zero (regardless of the value of m^*) as substitutability becomes perfect. As a result, the Nash equilibrium value of I/μ must approach the value β^{-1} from below. From this one may conclude that a sufficient degree of substitutability will imply a Nash equilibrium with $\mu < I$. On the other hand, in the case of a common currency (again interpreted as implying the utility function U^*), the optimizing policy choice by the single central bank will correspond to a stationary equilibrium in which

$$F(m^*, m^*) = (\beta I/\mu) G(m^*, m^*) \tag{39'}$$

$$[1 - (\beta I/\mu)] = (m^*/G(m^*, m^*)) Z_+ \tag{40'}$$

A change in the degree of currency substitutability has no effect upon the form of the function $Z_+(m, m)$ or of the function $G(m, m)$, and so has no effect upon the solution to (39')–(40'). It follows that the solution may well involve $\mu > I$ even in the case of a transactions technology that would imply extremely high substitutability of currencies.

This is, of course, exactly the sort of reasoning behind the usual arguments for 'competing currencies'; multiple currencies with a high degree of substitutability lead to a deflationary equilibrium while a single currency controlled by a single supra-national central bank may well lead to an inflationary equilibrium (as is warned of in the UK Treasury paper). But the result that one should expect $\mu < I$ in the case of sufficiently great substitutability of currencies has other implications besides the existence of a low-inflation steady state. Another consequence, as was shown above, is that equilibrium price levels and exchange rates will be indeterminate; not only will there exist a two-dimensional continuum of possible perfect foresight equilibria (in which one or the other or both kinds of real balances asymptotically grow without bound), but there will exist a large class of rational expectations equilibria in which both the price levels and the exchange rates vary stochastically in response to 'sunspot' events. In this sense, too high a degree of currency substitutability may lead to the adoption of monetary policies that actually increase the degree of instability of price levels and exchange rates, even under exactly the sort of assumptions about the nature of policy interaction between governments that are behind the arguments for 'competing currencies'.

3   Currency substitution and the stability of learning dynamics

Another question relevant to the likely stability of exchange rates in the case of increased currency substitution concerns not the uniqueness of rational expectations equilibrium, but instead how likely it is that the expectations of traders will in fact converge to those that characterize such an equilibrium. That is, if traders must learn what to expect about future exchange rate movements on the basis of their experience, can one be confident that even relatively crude adaptive learning rules would imply that a rational expectations equilibrium (and, in particular, the rational expectations equilibrium in which all currencies are used and their relative values change only at a rate dependent upon their relative growth rates) will eventually be reached? Or will disequilibium beliefs produce exchange rate movements that cause beliefs to diverge even farther from the rational expectations equilibrium beliefs, so that the latter are never reached even though they are theoretically determinate?

As in the previous section, I propose to address this question in the context of a world representative household and monetary policies that involve fixing an exogenous constant rate of growth, and an exogenous constant rate of interest payments on money holdings, for each of the currencies, and allowing exchange rates to float. Again, for simplicity, there is assumed to be no government debt outstanding, and government purchases are assumed to be constant, and again I specialize to the case of only two currencies with the same money supply growth rates and rates of interest on money, and the same constant levels of goods purchases by the two governments, and to the case of perfect symmetry of the utility functions between the two currencies and equal values for α^i. Finally, it will simplify the range of possible parameter variations that need to be considered if attention is also restricted to utility functions that are additively separable between consumption and work, i.e. that have the form $U(c^1, c^2; n^1, n^2) = u(c^1, c^2) + v(n^1, n^2)$.

First-order condition (10) can then be rewritten

$$U_c^i(c_t^1, c_t^2) = \beta R_t^i v_t^i \tag{41}$$

where

$$v_t^i = \left[\frac{p_t^i}{p_{t+1}^i} U_c^i(t+1) \right]^e$$

for $i = 1, 2$. Here the superscript indicates that what matters is the representative household's expectation at time t regarding the value of the quantity inside the brackets, which we will no longer assume must coincide with what actually happens in period $t + 1$. I assume in order to simplify the analysis of learning that these expectations are a simple point value for each of the quantities in question, rather than functions describing how the quantities in the brackets are expected to vary depending upon the household's decisions in period t. This is doubtless unrealistic, but I do not believe that the instability result below depends upon this aspect of the proposed learning rule.[22] Equations (41), together with (10) and (15), also for $i = 1, 2$, comprise a set of six equations[23] that can be solved for the six variables (c_t^i, n_t^i, R_t^i) as functions of the variables (v_t^i), given values for $g^1 = g^2 = g$, $I^1 = I^2 = I$, and $\alpha^1 = \alpha^2 = \alpha$. Let the solutions for the variables (n_t^i) be denoted

$$n_t^i = n^i(v_t^1, v_t^2) \tag{42}$$

Then equations (11) and (16) imply

$$\frac{M_t^i}{p_t^i} = (1 - \alpha) n^i(v_t^1, v_t^2) \tag{43}$$

These equations together with (8) allow us to determine the *temporary equilibrium* values for the complete set of state variables $(c_t^i, n_t^i, R_t^i, p_t^i, e_t^i)$ as functions of the money supplies at time t and the state of expectations (v_t^i).

We wish to analyse the evolution of a sequence of temporary equilibria of this sort, in response to exogenously growing money supplies and to changes in the state of expectations in response to observed rates of price change and marginal utilities. A simple but not entirely unrealistic rule for updating expectations is the *adaptive expectations* rule used by authors such as Cagan (1956). That is, expectations are adjusted in proportion to observed expectational errors:

$$v_t^i - v_{t-1}^i = \lambda \left[\frac{p_{t-1}^i}{p_t^i} U_c^i(n_t^1 - g, n_t^2 - g) - v_{t-1}^i \right] \tag{44}$$

Here $0 < \lambda \leq 1$ is a parameter indicating the speed of adjustment of expectations (the case of greatest interest being one where 'periods' are short but $\lambda \ll 1$). This sort of simple rule has at least the desirable property of consistency with the stationary rational expectations equilibrium. That is, suppose households happen to start out with exactly the expectations characteristic of that equilibrium, i.e. $v_0^1 = v_0^2 = v$, where v satisfies

$$v - \mu^{-1} U_c^i(n^1(v, v), n^2(v, v))$$

and where μ is the common growth rate of the two currencies. (This condition for v is the same regardless of the value of i, because of the assumed symmetry of the utility function.) Then, under the learning rule specified, the temporary equilibrium dynamics will generate constant (and hence rational expectations equilibrium) expectations $v_t^1 = v_t^2 = v$ for all t.

The temporary equilibrium dynamics are defined by the system of difference equations (42)–(44). We are interested in the stability under these dynamics of the stationary equilibrium. Substituting (43) into (44) we obtain

$$v_t^i - v_{t-1}^i = \lambda \left[\frac{n_t^i}{\mu n_{t-1}^i} U_c^i(n_t^1 - g, n_t^2 - g) - v_{t-1}^i \right] \tag{45}$$

Linearizing (42) and (45) around the stationary equilibrium values $v_t^i = v_{t-1}^i = v$, $n_t^i = n_{t-1}^i = n = n^i(v, v)$, we obtain

$$\Delta n_t^1 = \rho \Delta v_t^1 - \sigma \Delta v_t^2 \tag{46a}$$

$$\Delta n_t^2 = \rho \Delta v_t^2 - \sigma \Delta v_t^1 \tag{46b}$$

$$\Delta n_t^1 = (1 - \lambda) \Delta v_{t-1}^1 + \lambda[(1 - \gamma) \Delta n_t^1 - \eta \Delta n_t^2 - \Delta n_{t-1}^1] \tag{47a}$$

$$\Delta n_t^2 = (1 - \lambda) \Delta v_{t-1}^2 + \lambda[(1 - \gamma) \Delta n_t^2 - \eta \Delta n_t^1 - \Delta n_{t-1}^2] \tag{47b}$$

where Δn_t^i denotes $(n_t^i - n)/n$ and Δv_t^i denotes $(v_t^i - v)/v$, and using the notation

$$\gamma = - nU_{cc}^{11}/U_c^1 = - nU_{cc}^{22}/U_c^2$$

$$\delta = - nU_{nn}^{11}/U_c^1 = - nU_{nn}^{22}/U_c^2$$

$$\eta = - nU_{cc}^{12}/U_c^1$$

$$\phi = - nU_{nn}^{12}/U_c^1$$

$$\rho = \frac{\alpha\gamma + \delta}{(\alpha\gamma + \delta)^2 - (\alpha\eta + \phi)^2} \beta(1 - \alpha) \frac{I}{\mu}$$

$$\sigma = \frac{\alpha\eta + \phi}{(\alpha\gamma + \delta)^2 - (\alpha\eta + \phi)^2} \beta(1 - \alpha) \frac{I}{\mu}$$

where the derivatives of the utility function are evaluated at the stationary equilibrium allocation $(n - g, n - g; n, n)$. Substituting (46a–b) into (47a–b), we obtain a pair of coupled difference equations for the variables (Δv_t^i), of the form

$$\Delta v_t^i = \Sigma_j M_{ij} \Delta v_{t-1}^j$$

The stationary rational expectations equilibrium is then locally stable under the learning dynamics if and only if both eigenvalues of the matrix M are of modulus less than one.

One eigenvalue, corresponding to an eigenvector whose two components are equal, is

$$\xi^1 = \frac{1 - \lambda(1 + \rho - \sigma)}{1 - \lambda(1 - \gamma - \eta)(\rho - \sigma)}$$

The other eigenvalue, corresponding to an eigenvector whose two components are equal in magnitude but opposite in sign is

$$\xi^2 = \frac{1 - \lambda(1 + \rho + \sigma)}{1 - \lambda(1 - \gamma + \eta)(\rho + \sigma)}$$

We wish to consider the effects upon stability of varying the degree to which currencies are substitutable. Again, the natural experiment to consider is to fix the values of $\gamma + \eta$ and $\delta + \phi$, while varying the individual parameters; this means keeping constant the effect upon the marginal utility of one or another type of consumption or work of a proportional change in both types of consumption, or of a proportional change in both types of work, while varying the extent to which variation in one type of good by itself has the same effect as variation in the other type by itself. Concavity of the utility function requires that we fix values $\gamma + \eta$, $\delta + \phi > 0$. Imperfect substitutability exists as long as $\gamma > \eta$ or $\delta > \phi$. Currency substitutability is increased by increasing η (and correspondingly reducing γ) and by increasing ϕ (and correspondingly reducing δ); the limit of perfect substitutability is reached when $\eta = \gamma$ and $\phi = \delta$.

Under this experiment, if the value of λ is held fixed, the eigenvalue ξ^1 does not vary. Let us suppose that its modulus is less than one. (This is necessarily true for small enough positive λ, given any positive values for $\gamma + \eta$ and $\delta + \phi$.) Then stability depends upon the size of $|\xi^2|$. Noting that

$$\rho + \sigma = \frac{\beta(1 - \alpha)(I/\mu)}{\alpha(\gamma - \eta) + (\delta - \phi)}$$

we see that $|\xi^2| < 1$ if and only if

$$-1 < \frac{(2 - \gamma + \eta)\beta(1 - \alpha)(I/\mu)}{\alpha(\gamma - \eta) + (\delta - \phi)} < \frac{2 - \lambda}{\lambda} \tag{48}$$

It is then obvious that, if $\gamma - \eta$ and $\delta - \phi$ are both made small enough, the right-hand inequality in (48) is eventually violated. Hence, given a rate of adjustment of expectations λ, a great enough degree of substitutability between currencies implies instability of the stationary rational expectations equilibrium under the learning dynamics.[24] On the other hand, a low enough degree of substitutability can result in stability. For example, $\eta = \phi = 0$ (the case of preferences additively separable between the transactions involving different currencies) would imply $\xi^2 = \xi^1$, so that under the assumption made above both eigenvalues would then have a modulus less than one. Clearly it will in general not be necessary to reduce substitutability to this extent to ensure that $|\xi^2| < 1$. Hence this result provides an example of a case in which institutional barriers to currency substitution could improve exchange rate stability.[25]

It also provides an example of a case in which price level stability could be improved through adoption of a common currency. Let us assume, as in the previous section, that adoption of a common currency would result in preferences for the representative household of the form

$$U^*(c; n) = U(c, c; n, n)$$

as well as a value of α for the single currency equal to the previous common value. Then we can analyse, in the common currency world, the temporary equilibrium dynamics resulting from the representative household's adjusting its beliefs about the value of $U_c(t + 1)p_t/p_{t+1}$ according to a rule of the form (45). In this case, the matrix M has a single element, equal to the quantity ξ^1 defined above. Hence, under the assumptions made above, adoption of a common currency would result in local stability of the stationary rational expectations equilibrium under the learning dynamics. This would bring about a steady and fully anticipated rate of world inflation. Contrastingly, with multiple currencies and in the unstable case, the rates of inflation in terms of the two currencies would diverge from the stationary rational expectations equilibrium value, along with the exchange rate.

4 Feasibility of fixed exchange rates with currency substitution

Up to this point, I have analysed the consequences of increased substitutability of currencies in the case of a system of fully flexible exchange rates. There are some obvious reasons for analysis of the doctrine of 'competing currencies' within that context; in particular, the view that competition will result in pressure for lower rates of money growth presumes a world in which individual countries are free to choose their own rates of money growth, while a fixed exchange rate regime in the full sense of that term implies subordination of individual countries' monetary policies (in the case of all but one country, probably Germany for the EMS) to the need to maintain exchange rate parities. Nonetheless, Europe has made substantial progress towards fixed exchange rates within the EMS, and adoption of the proposal to stimulate increased competition between currencies would presumably be within a context of continued commitment to that goal; and the UK proposal explicitly reaffirms the UK's commitment to eventual participation in the current Exchange Rate Mechanism (HM Treasury, 1989, p. 2). Hence it is also of interest to ask what the consequences of increased substitutability of currencies would be within the context of an attempt to maintain fixed exchange rates.

Let us consider the character of a perfect foresight equilibrium in which exchange rates are fixed forever, and known in advance to be so fixed with certainty. Without loss of generality, we may suppose that the fixed exchange rates are $e_t^i = 1/n$ for all i and t. Condition (7) then implies the existence of a common world nominal interest rate on bonds each period, $R_t^i = R_t$ for all i. Let us now repeat the derivation of (32), again assuming a world representative consumer, but allowing for n currencies, not assuming symmetry, and not assuming a constant exogenous growth rate for the varius money supplies. We obtain

$$F'(m_t) = \frac{\beta M_t^i I_t^i}{M_{t+1}^i} \gamma_{t+1}^i \tag{49}$$

$$G^i(m_t) \le \gamma_t^i \tag{50}$$

with an equality in (50) if $m_t^i > g$. Here m_t denotes $(m_t^1, \ldots, m_t^n)$ and

$$\gamma_t^i = (1 - \alpha^i) m_t^i \lambda_t^i$$

I have also assumed that $g > 0$, for simplicity, so that $n_t^i > 0$ is assured. In terms of this notation, (12) becomes

$$\frac{\gamma_t^i}{\gamma_{t+1}^i} = \beta R_t \frac{M_t^i}{M_{t+1}^i} \tag{51}$$

The aspects of monetary policy that remain to be exogenously specified, given the fixed exchange rates, are a set of $n + 1$ variables per period, one (either M_t^i or I_t^i or some function of the two) for each country that is responsible for maintaining its exchange rate, and two (both M_t^i and I_t^i, or one of these and the world interest rate R_t) for the country that is not so constrained.[26] Given a full specification of world monetary policy in this sense, equations (49)–(51) are then a system of $3n$ equations per period to solve for the remaining $3n$ of the variables

$$\{M_t^1, \ldots, M_t^n, I_t^i, \ldots, I_t^n, \gamma_t^1, \ldots, \gamma_t^n, m_t^1, \ldots, m_t^n, R_t\}$$

Now (49)–(51) taken together imply

$$F'(m_t) \ge (I_t^i/R_t) G^i(m_t) \tag{52}$$

with an equality if $m_t^i > g$. These n equations taken together determine the demands for real balances of the n currencies as a function of the n spreads I_t^i/R_t.[27] These are again just the money demand functions derived in section 1. I have here written these relationships in the form (52) to make it clear what determines whether there is a positive private demand for all of the currencies. If

$$\lim_{m^i \to g} \frac{F'(m)}{G^i(m)} > 0 \tag{53}$$

where the m^j, $j \ne i$, are fixed at values greater than g, then, for given interest rate spreads for the currencies $j \ne i$, there will exist a maximum spread θ such that $I_t^i/R_t > \theta^{-1}$ is necessary in order for currency i to be used for consumption purchases. Condition (53) necessarily holds if $g > 0$, and even if $g = 0$ (or if government purchases do not require cash in advance, or governments do not insist on using their own currency), currency substitutability may result in such a condition holding, as discussed in connection with condition (34) above. Without fixed exchange rates, this would simply that there is a limit to the extent to which nominal interest rates on bonds can be raised in a given country if that country's currency is not to be driven out of circulation. With fixed exchange rates, a given country has no possibility of controlling nominal interest rates on bonds, so that now the condition can be ensured only by making the nominal interest payments on money high enough. Hence it may not be possible for a country to ensure that its currency continues to be used unless interest payments on money are available as an instrument of monetary policy.

This is especially a problem in the case of a high degree of substitutability between currencies. In the case of perfect substitutability (1′), one has for all currencies i

$$\frac{F^i(m)}{G^i(m)} = \frac{\rho(m) - \alpha^i}{1 - \alpha^i}$$

where $\rho(m)$ denotes the common marginal rate of substitution between output and consumption. It follows that (52) can hold with equality for each of two currencies (so that both can be used for consumption purchases in equilibrium) only if $\alpha^i + (1 - \alpha^i)(I_t^i/R_t)$ is identical for the two currencies. hence variations in α^i across payments systems must be compensated for by variations in I_t^i. If it is not possible pay interest on money balances, then *only the currency with the highest value of α^i can be used for consumption purchases in equilibrium, under a fixed exchange rate regime.* Since it is reasonable to suppose that payments systems must differ to some extent in the time lags associated with transactions,[28] this means that all but one currency should be driven out of use, through a sort of reverse Gresham's Law. Nor is such an outcome dependent upon exactly perfect substitutability. If substitutability is very great (although not perfect), the marginal rates of substitution between consumption purchases and output sales in the case of the different currencies will still be close to one another, even if the quantities transacted in terms of the various currencies are very different, and so it may not be possible to satisfy (52) with equality in the case of the low-α^i (i.e. high transaction cost) currencies, given that it holds with equality for the high-α^i currencies, without having differential interest payments upon cash balances of the different kinds.

Nor is this problem solved if it can be arranged that α^j be the same for all currencies, due to adoption of a common technology or even perhaps a common payments system. For there would remain the problem of speculation about future adjustments of the exchange rate parities, that would continue to be a possibility as long as one did not move to a common currency. Perfect capital mobility implies that expectations of the possibility of such an adjustment must be reflected in differentials across currencies of the nominal interest rate on bonds. Then even with a common value for α^j and a common (institutionally fixed) value for I^i, it will not in general be possible for $\alpha^j + (1 - \alpha^j)(I^j/R^i_t)$ to be identical for any two currencies, with the result, in the case of perfect substitutability, that only the lowest-R^i_t currency (i.e. the currency thought least likely to be devalued in the future) will be used for consumption purchases.

Again, the problem persists in the case of high but not perfect substitutability of currencies. In this case, *the greater the degree of substitutability of currencies, the smaller the change in expectations required to drive currencies out of use by the private sector.* Even an arbitrarily small positive probability of even an arbitrarily small realignment suffices to drive out all but one currency, in the event of great enough substitutability, although in the event of a given probability and of a given size of realignment, the degree of substitutability needed for such an outcome is less than perfect. Hence in the event of a great increase in currency substitutability, a fixed exchange rate regime will become extremely unstable (in terms of the volatility of the rates of growth of the various currencies that will be required to maintain the exchange rate parities), and quite possibly unmanageable as a practical matter, unless the nominal interest rate on money balances is available as a policy instrument in each country that is responsible for maintaining the exchange rates. And this instrument would have to be able to be adjusted very precisely and very rapidly in response to speculation regarding future exchange rate realignments. Since no such independent instrument of monetary policy is currently used in the European Community or elsewhere, pursuit of the UK's program of stimulating 'competition' between currencies, were it possible, would likely be incompatible with maintenance of the sort of Exchange Rate Mechanism currently in force.[29]

For this reason, as well as those summarized above, increased currency substitutability would likely be a source of greater instability. And insofar as it is regarded as either desirable (for reasons unrelated to the supposed stabilizing consequences of competition between currencies) or inevitable (as a consequence of the removal of barriers to trade in financial services), this would be a reason to regard it as desirable to move towards adoption of a common currency.

NOTES

I would like to thank John Flemming, Alberto Giovannini, Michael Mussa, Philippe Weil and the participants in the CEPR workshop on 'Currency Substitution', for helpful comments on earlier presentations of this material, and the (US) National Science Foundation for research support.

1 Giovannini (1989) also argues that the process of European integration will lead to increasing substitutability of currencies, quite apart from the Delors Report proposals.

2 Some especially influential prior analyses of competition between currencies, of the sort that presumably provide the reasoning behind the UK proposal, are collected in Salin (ed.) (1984).

3 It is also closely related to the models of Svensson (1985a, b). For an overview of uses of this general modeling strategy in international monetary economics, see Stockman (1989).

4 This suggestion is analogous to Lucas and Stokey's use of substitution between 'cash goods' (subject to a cash-in-advance constraint) and 'credit goods' (subject to no such constraint) by consumers and producers as a way to represent the possibility of substitution away from the use of money to carry out transactions.

5 I assume perfect capital mobility throughout the present exercise, on the ground not only that capital is already much more mobile within the European Community than are currencies substitutable, but that the UK proposal to promote currency substitutability as an alternative to a common currency is made within a context of a consensus regarding the Community's commitment to moving toward completely unrestricted capital mobility as part of Stage 1 of economic and monetary union.

6 It can be shown that concavity of the function U implies the existence of a unique solution, at least for all values of $(R_t^1/I_t^1, \ldots, R_t^n/I_t^n)$ in a neighbourhood of $(1, \ldots, 1)$, i.e. if the spread between the return on bonds and on money is small enough for all currencies, by a direct extension of the argument in the single currency case. If the various types of goods and leisure are all sufficiently substitutable, there will also exist a unique solution globally.

7 Note that it should be understood here, as in the case of (11) and (11'), that either the case described by (20) or that described by (20') must occur, for a lower interest rate on bonds than on money would imply that households would wish to hold an arbitrarily large quantity of the currency in question, financed by selling short a similarly large quantity of bonds.

8 Measures of the volume of private transactions do not appear as arguments of these money demand functions because in the present model, with no supply shocks allowed for, the complete allocation of resources is a determinate function of the interest rate spreads and governments purchases. In a stochastic model with shocks to the household's disutility for supply of goods, these preference parameters would also be arguments of the money demand functions. One could then substitute for them the vector of supplies or consumptions, in order to obtain a money demand function of a more standard form.

9 See the references in Thomas and Wickens (1989) for other examples of the two contrasting approaches.

10 On the other hand, this derivation does not necessarily provide support for the view that the appearance of foreign interest rates in a money demand equation

is in itself proof of the importance of currency substitution. For it must be recalled that the equations derived here are equally applicable to a model in which each country's products must be purchased with that country's currency, and the n 'types' of goods represent goods produced in different countries. In that case the effect of foreign interest rates spreads upon the demand for a particular currency results from substitution away from purchase of goods produced in countries whose currencies are particularly costly to hold due to a large interest rate spread, and not from any change in the currencies used for a particular type of transactions.

11 This form makes it clear to what extent the difference equations obtained are a natural generalization of the equation obtained in Woodford (1988) for the single-currency case.

12 Concavity of U implies that $G(m) > F(m)$ for all $0 < m < \bar{n}$.

13 In this case there will also exist among the possible rational expectations equilibria what are sometimes called 'sunspot equilibria', in which permanent exchange rate and price level shifts occur in response to random events that convey no information about any changes in the 'fundamental' determinants of price levels and exchange rates.

14 An even broader set of possibilities arises if we consider stochastic equilibria (i.e. 'sunspot equilibria') as well as deterministic ('perfect foresight') solutions. For example, stochastic equilibria can occur in which the ratio between real balances of one currency and those of the other follows a random walk, visiting arbitrarily small and arbitrarily large positive values infinitely often, while the total level of real balances of both kinds remains bounded both above and away from zero. See, e.g. Chiappori and Guesnerie (1989).

15 Hence the use of their own currencies by governments can play a crucial role in rendering determinate the equilibrium value of currencies, even if the share of government purchases is relatively small. See Giovannini (1989) for a related discussion.

16 It might seem odd that the only account here given of how 'competition' between currencies is supposed to work is presented in the context of a floating exchange rate system, when the UK Treasury paper explicitly envisions 'competing currencies' within a system of fixed rates. But the existing theoretical justifications of the supposed advantages of 'competing currencies' (e.g. Girton and Roper, or Salin (ed.), 1984) are in fact in the context of a floating exchange rate world. Indeed, there would seem to be no possibility for competitive monetary policies in the case of a fixed exchange rate system, if this is interpreted as an asymmetrical peg of the kind discussed in section 4 below. The case of a 'common currency' with independent central banks discussed by Casella and Feinstein (1989) cannot be interpreted as a fixed exchange rate system of the usual sort, in which only central banks are obligated to exchange the various currencies at par, but rather represents a world in which private sellers are required to exchange the various currencies at par (e.g. because they are physically indistinguishable). In any event, in the latter case, currency substitution has the consequence that non-cooperative, seigniorage-maximizing central banks would choose a higher rate of money growth, rather than a lower one, than would prevail in the case of less substitutability of currencies or in the case of cooperative behaviour; so that such a regime cannot be what the author of the UK Treasury view have in mind either.

17 This objective is not the only possible one, but provides a simple explanation for why governments might wish to avoid policies that involve inflations so great that the use of their currency is severely reduced.

18 Here we make an assumption with little obvious justification that avoid some very serious difficulties with the argument for 'competing currencies'. For without an arbitrary selection as to which equilibrium is expected to prevail in the case of any given pair of monetary policy choices, there is no well-defined game being played by the two countries. Furthermore, not all possible selection rules imply existence of the kind of 'competitive' pressures usually assumed to result from currency substitution. For example, in the case of very high substitutability between currencies, all perfect foresight equilibria in which at least one currency is used forever, except those in which the ratio of the level of real balances of country 2's currency to real balances of country 1's currency is initially and forever extremely low, involve real balances of country 1's currency that asymptotically approach zero (while those of country 2's currency approach a positive constant), if I^1/μ^1 is even slightly *larger* than I^2/μ^2. And if (34) holds, a continuum of such equilibria exist. (In the case of perfect substitutability, this is true of all equilibria in which positive levels of real balances exist for both currencies, as shown by Kareken and Wallace.) This might be taken to indicate that countries with higher rates of money growth (or lower rates of interest on their currencies) are rewarded with greater eventual use of their currencies, rather than the reverse. The argument is somewhat doubtful, because the initial levels of real balances are not given as an initial condition for the dynamics, but are instead determined by expectations about the future. And the fact that 'most' initial level of real balances correspond to one asymptotic behaviour rather than another does not imply that that long-run income is the one that should occur; for example, reasonable 'learning' dynamics may converge to exactly the equilibrium that all but one perfect foresight paths diverge from (Grandmont, 1985; Marcet and Sargent, 1989). But the grounds for a belief that a pressure toward lower rates of money growth should exist are also far from certain.

19 This is the essential point of Girton and Roper's assumption of a convertible currency.

20 This is an obvious analog for the two-country case of the kind of first-order condition obtained by authors such as Friedman (1971), Auernheimer (1974), and Calvo (1978).

21 Note that there is a determinate optimal value only for the ratio, not for I^i or μ^i separately: similarly, in the Nash equilibrium of the policy choice game, only the ratio is determined for each country. The additional restriction that I^1 is determined technologically to equal I will not affect the character of the game or the results obtained below.

22 The analysis given here can be rigorously justified if utility is linear in the various types of consumption, so that each household is simply forecasting the expected rate of change of prices in terms of the various currencies.

23 I assume that (10) holds at all times in the analysis of this section, for we are only interested in local stability of the learning dynamics near a stationary equilibrium in which both currencies are used, and so both currencies will be used along all paths sufficiently near that equilibrium.

24 It will be observed that for any given values of the other parameters, (48) is satisfied for small enough positive λ. Hence the instability could be avoided, in

the event of even a very great increase in the substitutability of currencies, if for some reason λ declined sufficiently at the same time, i.e. if expectations began to be adjusted sufficiently slowly. But it is hard to see why this should occur.

25 The asymptotic behaviour of the temporary equilibrium dynamics in the unstable case cannot be determined from a purely local analysis of the kind presented here. A plausible outcome would appear to be the eventual complete displacement of one of the currencies, but it is not clear that perpetual disequilibrium fluctuations in expectations can be ruled out.

26 Note that if the interest rate on money is fixed institutionally (e.g. if it is necessarily zero), then the only aspect of world monetary policy that remains to be exogenously specified is a single variable per period chosen by the unconstrained country.

27 Derivation of a determinate relationship of that sort would be possible here even without the assumption of a world representative consumer, because of the fixed exchange rates. Recall the derivation at the end of section 1.

28 See Giovannini (1989) for discussion of this.

29 On the desirability of a system of fixed exchange rates within the European Community, see Giavazzi and Giovannini (1989)

REFERENCES

Auernheimer, L. (1974) 'The honest government's guide to the revenue from inflation', *Journal of Political Economy* **82**, 598–606.

Cagan, P. (1956) 'The monetary dynamics of hyperinflation', in M. Friedman (ed.), *Studies in the Quantity Theory of Money*, Chicago: University of Chicago Press.

Calvo, G.A. (1978) 'Optimal seigniorage from money creation', *Journal of Monetary Economics* **4**, 503–18.

Casella, A. and J. Feinstein (1989) 'Management of a common currency', in M. de Cecco and A. Giovannini (eds.), *A European Central Bank: Perspectives on monetary unification after ten years of the EMS*. Cambridge University Press.

Chiappori, P-A. and R. Guesnerie (1989) 'Self fulfilling theories: the sunspot connection', London School of Economics discussion paper.

Friedman, M. (1971) 'Government revenue from inflation', *Journal of Political Economy* **79**, 846–56.

Giavazzi, F. and A. Giovannini (1989) *Limiting Exchange Rate Flexibility*, Cambridge, MA.: MIT Press.

Giovannini, A. (1989) 'Currency substitution and monetary policy', unpublished, Columbia University Presented at CEPR conference on 'Managing Change in the EMS', Madrid, May 1989.

Girton, L. and D. Roper (1981) 'Theory and implications of currency substitution', *Journal of Money, Credit, and Banking* **13**, 12–30.

Grandmont, J-M. (1985) 'On endogenous competitive business cycles', *Econometrica* **53**, 995–1046.

HM Treasury (1989) 'An evolutionary approach to economic and monetary union', discussion paper, released 2 November 1989.

Kareken, J.H. and N. Wallace (1981) 'On the indeterminacy of equilibrium exchange rates', *Quarterly Journal of Economics* **96**, 207–22.

Lucas, R.E. Jr. (1982) 'Interest rates and currency prices in a two-country world', *Journal of Monetary Economics* **10**, 335–59.

Lucas, R.E. and N.L. Stokey (1987) 'Money and interest in a cash-in-advance economy', *Econometrica* **55**, 491–514.

Marcet, A. and T.J. Sargent (1989) 'Least-squares learning and the dynamics of hyperinflation', in W.A. Barnett, J. Geweke and K. Shell (eds.), *Economic Complexity*, Cambridge University Press.

Miles, M.A. (1978) 'Currency substitution, flexible exchange rates, and monetary independence', *American Economic Review* **68**, 428–36.

Salin, P. (ed.) (1984) *Currency Competition and Monetary Union*, The Hague: Martinus Nijhoff.

Stockman, A.C. (1989) 'The cash-in-advance constraint in international economics', in M. Kohn (ed.), *Finance Constraints and the Theory of Money*, Boston: Academic Press.

Svensson, L.E.O. (1985a) 'Money and asset prices in a cash-in-advance economy', *Journal of Political Economy* **93**, 919–44.

(1985b) 'Currency prices, terms of trade, and interest rates: A general equilibrium asset-pricing cash-in-advance approach', *Journal of International Economics* **18**, 17–41.

Thomas, S.H. and M.R. Wickens (1989) 'Currency substitution and vehicle currencies: Tests of alternative hypotheses', unpublished, University of Southampton. Presented at CEPR workshop on 'Currency Substitution', London, October 1989.

Woodford, M. (1988) 'Monetary policy and price level determinacy in a cash-in-advance economy', unpublished, University of Chicago, December.

10 Currency competition and the transition to monetary union: currency competition and the evolution of multi-currency regions

PHILIPPE WEIL

What is, compared with the Delors Report objective of achieving European monetary integration by institutional reform, the theoretical case for the United Kingdom Treasury proposal (HM Treasury, 1989) that the determination of the eventual nominal anchor of a unified Europe be left to Darwinian market forces through the removal of obstacles to currency substitution?

This question – crucial from a policy perspective, and challenging from a theoretical standpoint[1] – has recently been addressed by Michael Woodford (1991) in a very skillful and thought-provoking paper. Woodford suggests, in essence, that we make two simplifying assumptions to study currency competition. First, he argues, we should think of currency substitutability as an attribute of preferences, and thus 'represent' institutional reforms that increase substitutability of currencies in transactions and portfolios as changes in the utility function, without having to worry about the formalization of institutions themselves. Second, Woodford submits that not much generality is lost by studying currency substitution within the context of an integrated world (or regional) equilibrium with a representative world (or European) consumer, as monetary issues themselves and not the pattern of intra-European trade flows are at the core of the debate on European financial integration.

The two theoretical shortcuts which these assumptions provide allow Woodford to construct a very powerful, but also very complex, model of currency substitution based on an n-good, n-currency cash-in-advance model with linear production. Each good should be thought of as a commodity which must be purchased with a specific currency; the substitutability in utility between the different goods, and the substitutability in utility between labour allocated to the production of each good, indirectly reflect the restrictiveness of institutional barriers to currency substitution.

290

My objective is to show that Woodford's two strategic theoretical simplifications can be incorporated into a money-in-the-utility function model[2] to provide, in section 1 of this paper, an extremely simple framework in which to study, in sections 2 and 3, the effect of the removal of obstacles to currency substitution on the evolution of multi-currency regions such as the EEC. In doing so, I hope to answer at least partially the question posed at the outset of this paper – what are the theoretical merits of the UK Treasury proposal? – and also to demonstrate, if need still be, the power and appeal of the theoretical approach to currency substitution suggested by Woodford's work.

1   A simple model of currency substitution

1.1   Governments

The world economy is administered, for simplicity,[3] by two separate entities (governments, regional reserve banks) which compete in the issuance of currencies and interest-bearing liabilities. Each government, indexed by j, must finance an exogenously given and constant path of per capita public consumption g_j $(j = 1, 2)$ by either seigniorage or debt creation.[4]

To concentrate on simple (and realistic) policies, I assume that monetary authorities follow constant-growth-of-the-money-supply rules, with $\sigma_j \geq 0$ being the instantaneous rate of growth of the nominal money supply in country j. I also assume, to focus on the monetary aspects of the model, that there is a single consumption good in the world economy.[5] Then, without ambiguity as to the unit in which real quantities are measured, let m_j denote per capita real money balances, and π_j the inflation rate in country j. By definition of real balances, and assuming population is constant, it follows that[6]

$$\dot{m}_j = (\sigma_j - \pi_j)m_j \tag{1}$$

Since each government must balance its budget, real *per capita* public debt b_j in country j evolves over time according to

$$\dot{b}_j = [g_j + rb_j] - \sigma_j m_j \tag{2}$$

where r denotes, assuming perfect international capital mobility, the world real interest rate. In other terms, the stock of public debt increases (decreases) to cover the shortfall (excess) of the sum of government consumption and interest payment on the debt over seigniorage.

1.2   Consumers

Following Woodford's first crucial simplifying assumption, I assume that the world economy consists of a large number of identical and infinitely lived consumers and only study, in the tradition of trade theory, the integrated world, or regional, equilibrium.

   Time is continuous, and every consumer receives, per unit of time, a constant non-produced endowment $y > 0$ of the non-storable consumption good. Consumers can hold four assets: currency and interest bearing liabilities of each country.[7]

   In line with Woodford's second insight, it is fruitful to think of currency substitutability as an attribute of consumers' preferences. Specifically, I assume that each currency provides to consumers a flow of utility services which is proportional to the stock of real balances they hold. Formally, a representative consumer's utility at time 0 is

$$\int_0^\infty e^{-\delta t}\{U[c(t)] + V[m_1(t), m_2(t)]\} dt \qquad (3)$$

where $\delta > 0$ denotes the instantaneous subjective discount rate, $U[.]$ is increasing and concave, and $V[.,.]$ is increasing and concave in both arguments. The separability of the utility function between goods on the one hand and real balances on the other is assumed to concentrate on the monetary aspects of the model, for – as is well-known and will be shown below – the money-in-the-utility-function (MIUF) model dichotomizes when utility is separable.

   As always in MIUF models, the function $V[.,.]$ should be viewed as an indirect utility function whose properties reflect not only tastes but also transactions technology and institutions. As a consequence, the effect of institutional reforms which increase competition and substitution between currencies – in particular the UK Treasury Proposal (HM Treasury, 1989) – can be represented by an increased elasticity of substitution between m_1 and m_2 in the function $V[.,.]$.

   Let

$$w = m_1 + m_2 + b_1 + b_2 \qquad (4)$$

denote financial wealth, and

$$i_j = r + \pi_j \qquad (5)$$

the nominal interest rate in country j. A representative consumer maximizes utility U, given in (3), subject to the instantaneous budget constraint

$$\dot{w} = rw + y - [c + i_1 m_1 + i_2 m_2] \tag{6}$$

with $w(0)$ given. The term in brackets is 'full consumption', i.e. the sum of consumption on goods and of the costs of holding wealth in non-interest bearing, but utility providing, monetary form when the nominal interest rate is positive.

To avoid trivialities, one must also subject consumers to the asymptotic solvency constraint

$$\lim_{t \to \infty} e^{\int_0^t r(s)ds} w(t) \geq 0 \tag{7}$$

The jointly necessary and sufficient conditions for a consumption optimum are, together with (6),

$$U'(c) = \lambda \tag{8}$$

$$\dot{\lambda}/\lambda = \delta - r \tag{9}$$

$$V_j(m_1, m_2) = \lambda i_j \qquad j = 1, 2 \tag{10}$$

$$\lim_{t \to \infty} e^{\int_0^t r(s)ds} w(t) = 0 \tag{11}$$

1.3   Equilibrium

In equilibrium, the goods market must clear. Since output is non-storable, this requires

$$c = y - g_1 - g_2 \tag{12}$$

The constancy over time of y, g_1 and g_2 immediately implies, from (9), that the real interest rate is constant and equal to the subjective discount rate:

$$r = \delta \tag{13}$$

Using the definition of the nominal interest rate in (5) together with (1), the portfolio condition (10) then immediately provides the equilibrium law of motion of real balances in each country:

$$\dot{m}_j = (\delta + \sigma_j)m_j - m_j V_j(m_1, m_2) \qquad j = 1, 2. \tag{14}$$

For the given nominal money supply rules, these two equations determine the equilibrium real price of each currency, thus completing the characterization of equilibria.

In the next two sections, I analyse in detail the equilibrium dynamics of real balances when currencies are (i) perfect substitutes and (ii) imperfect substitutes.

2   Perfect currency substitution

When the two currencies are perfectly substitutable,

$$V(m_1, m_2) = V(m_1 + m_2) \tag{15}$$

and $V_j(m_1 + m_2) = V'(m_1 + m_2)$ for $j = 1, 2.$[8] Equilibrium real balances then obey, together with (11) and the condition that they be non-negative, the following laws of motion:

$$\dot{m}_1 = (\delta + \sigma_1)m_1 - m_1 V'(m_1 + m_2) \tag{16}$$

$$\dot{m}_2 = (\delta + \sigma_2)m_2 - m_2 V'(m_1 + m_2) \tag{17}$$

If both m_1 and m_2 are strictly positive, equations (16) and (17) imply that:

$$\frac{\dot{m}_2}{m_2} - \frac{\dot{m}_1}{m_1} = \sigma_2 - \sigma_1 \tag{18}$$

whence the following:

Proposition 1   If both (perfectly substitutable) currencies are valued, then the share in real world balances of the faster[9] growing currency monotonically tends to 100% in the long run.

Proof: Suppose, without loss of generality, that $\sigma_1 > \sigma_2$. Equation (18) holds if both currencies are valued, so that

$$\frac{m_1(t)}{m_1(t) + m_2(t)} = [1 - e^{(\sigma_2 - \sigma_1)t}]^{-1}$$

which monotonically increases towards 1 as $t \to \infty$.

There is, therefore, a Gresham's law of currency substitution:[10] the currency of the country which under autarky would experience the highest inflation will, in real terms, eliminate in monetary portfolios that of the tight money country. Thus, contrary to the view which underlies the UK Treasury proposal, the removal of obstacles to currency substitution will result, according to this model in the Irish pound, rather than the Deutsche mark, being the principal component of real European money balances.

To understand why this happens, it suffices to notice that, when currencies are perfect substitutes in utilities/transactions, equation (10) requires that

$$i_1 = i_2 \tag{19}$$

i.e. that nominal interest rates, which measure the opportunity cost of holding wealth in monetary form,[11] be equalized across countries. Because we are studying an integrated world economy with free international capital mobility, the equilibrium real rate of return on bonds is, from (13), the same in both countries: $r = \delta$. But, then, (19) requires that the inflation rate be the same in both countries:

$$\pi_1 = \pi_2 \tag{20}$$

Since prices grow at the same rate in each country, it must be the case that real balances grow faster in the country in which the nominal money stock grows faster – which is the essence of proposition 1.

Note that the equalization of inflation rates, despite divergent money growth, implies that the eventual real elimination of the tightly managed currency is consistent with a fixed, but indeterminate, exchange rate e between the two currencies, as

$$\dot{e} = \pi_2 - \pi_1 = 0 \tag{21}$$

This result proceeds from the same basic principle which underlies the results of Kareken and Wallace (1981): the exchange rate between two monetary instruments which are perfect substitutes in utilities/transactions (like nickels and dimes) is conventional but constant in equilibrium. This principle applies whether the currencies under consideration are intrinsically useless as in Kareken and Wallace, or useful in transactions as in this model. The Gresham-like results of proposition 1 are therefore extremely general as they rest solely on an arbitrage foundation. Removing the obstacles to currency substitution while maintaining fixed parities must result in the eventual elimination of the slow growing currency.

To complete the characterization of the equilibrium dynamics of this economy, it is useful to draw a phase diagram in (m_1, m_2) space. Following Obstfeld and Rogoff (1983), it is necessary to distinguish between two cases, depending on whether positive real balances of both currencies are essential or not for utility/transactions, i.e. on whether $\lim_{m \to 0} mV'(m)$ is strictly positive or zero.

2.1 Essential real balances

When $\lim_{m \to 0} mV'(m) > 0$, Obstfeld and Rogoff establish, in a one-currency MIUF model, that no finite amount of consumption can compensate a consumer for the infinite disutility he incurs if real balances are zero, since it is then the case that $\lim_{m \to 0} V(m) = -\infty$. They show that, as

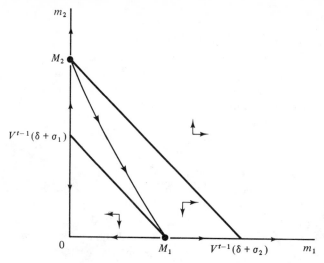

Figure 10.1   Perfect substitutes (money essential)

a consequence, hyperinflationary dynamic paths in which the real value of the one currency is eroded away are not admissible equilibria.

When there are *two* perfectly substitutable currencies, the essentiality of money implies that dynamic paths in which *both* currencies become worthless in real terms cannot be valid equilibria. Paths in which only *one* currency becomes worthless in real terms are however admissible.

These results are immediate from the phase diagram in figure 10.1, which shows that there are three possible types of equilibria. First, a steady-state equilibrium M_1 in which only currency 1 is valued. Second, a steady-state equilibrium M_2 in which only currency 2 is valued. Third, a continuum of non-stationary equilibria in which both currencies are valued, which lie on a saddlepath connecting M_2 to M_1. From proposition 1, these non-stationary paths all converge, assuming $\sigma_1 > \sigma_2$, to M_1. Hyperinflationary paths starting below the curve $M_1 M_2$ are ruled out by the condition $\lim_{m\to 0} m V'(m) > 0$, as it implies that they leave the positive quadrant in finite time – an infeasible event since prices cannot be negative under free disposal. Finally, one can show by adapting an argument in Obstfeld and Rogoff (1986) that, because $\sigma_j \geq 0$, hyperdeflationary paths starting above the curve $M_1 M_2$, along which both m_1 and m_2 become infinite, are ruled out by the transversality condition (11) if preferences satisfy the mild restriction $\lim V(m) < \infty$.

$$m \to \infty$$

To summarize, the equilibrium outcome of currency competition when money is essential for transactions is (i) either one currency being valued

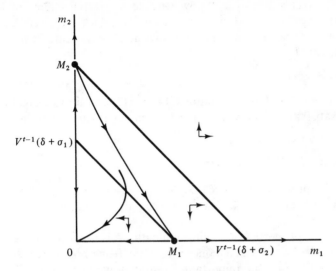

Figure 10.2   Perfect substitutes (money inessential)

or (ii) both currencies being valued, with the real value of the slow growing currency being driven to zero in the long run. Equilibria of the latter type may occur despite the fact that money is essential because no currency *alone* is ever essential for transactions or utility when financial liberalization has removed the obstacles to currency substitution.

2.2   Inessential real balances

When $\lim_{m \to 0} mV'(m) = 0$, it is possible to have, in addition to the equilibria described in the essential case, hyperinflationary equilibria in which *both* currencies become worthless in the long (or even short) run because money is not essential for utility.[12] Figure 10.2 draws the phase portrait of such an economy when $\sigma_1 > \sigma_2$.

3   Imperfect currency substitution

To contrast the case of imperfect substitutability between currencies with the one studied in the previous section, it is simplest[13] to consider a specific symmetric parameterization of the utility function for real balances:

$$V(m_1, m_2) = (m_1 m_2)^{1-\alpha}/(1 - \alpha) \quad \alpha \geq 0, \alpha \neq 1,$$
$$= \ln m_1 + \ln m_2 \qquad \alpha = 1. \tag{22}$$

While in the previous section I focussed the analysis on the implications of divergent money growth for the evolution of a multi-currency region when currencies are perfect substitutes, I now wish to study the effects of imperfect substitutability *per se* on equilibrium dynamics. I therefore henceforth assume[14] that nominal money grows at the same rate in the two 'regions', i.e. that

$$\sigma_1 = \sigma_2 = \sigma > 0 \tag{23}$$

Under this assumption, and using equations (14) and (22), equilibrium real balances must satisfy, together with (11) and a non-negativity constraint,

$$\dot{m}_1 = (\delta + \sigma)m_1 - (m_1 m_2)^{1-\alpha} \tag{24}$$

$$\dot{m}_2 = (\delta + \sigma)m_2 - (m_1 m_2)^{1-\alpha} \tag{25}$$

It is useful for later purposes to notice that these two equations imply that any path which starts along the 45 degree ray from the origin remains on its forever.[15]

To characterize the properties of equilibrium paths, it is necessary, once again, to distinguish cases in which money is essential from those in which it is not – with the obvious, but important *caveat* that, while no currency in isolation can ever be essential in the perfect substitutes case (both currencies taken together may be essential, but one can in principle always use the other currency for transactions), this is not the case under imperfect substitutability. Conveniently, the utility function specified in (22) – which features a *unit elasticity of substitution* between the two currencies – includes both the case in which each currency is essential ($\alpha \geq 1$) and the case in which each is inessential ($\alpha < 1$) since, for instance,

$$\lim_{\substack{m_1 \to 0 \\ m_2 > 0}} m_1 V_1 = \lim_{\substack{m_1 \to 0 \\ m_2 > 0}} (m_1 m_2)^{1-\alpha} = 0 \tag{26}$$

if and only if $\alpha < 1$. In what follows, I consider, for the sake of specificity, the qualitatively representative cases $\alpha = 1$ and $\alpha = 0$.

4   Essential currencies ($\alpha = 1$)

When $\alpha = 1$, each and every currency is essential, and equations (24) and (25) become

$$\dot{m}_1 = (\delta + \sigma)m_1 - 1 \tag{27}$$

$$\dot{m}_2 = (\delta + \sigma)m_2 - 1 \tag{28}$$

The phase portrait of this pair of difference equations, drawn in figure 10.3, reveals, together with the transversality condition (11), that the only admissible equilibrium is the steady-state equilibrium M in which real balances are constant over time. All other paths violate either the transversality condition or the non-negativity constraint on prices.

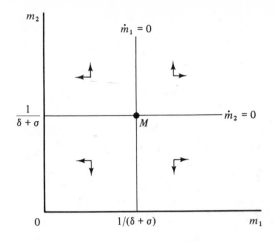

Figure 10.3 Imperfect substitutes (money essential)

The qualitative difference, when money is essential, between equilibrium dynamics under perfect and imperfect substitutability is striking.[16] In the former case, there are many equilibria, notably hyperinflationary in which one currency loses its real value while, in the latter, there is a unique equilibrium. This difference, which is at the source of the distinction between this model and the one-currency world studied by Obstfeld and Rogoff (1983), arises from the already noted fact that essentiality of money does not have the same implications under perfect and imperfect currency substitutability: it does not rule out that one (but not every) currency be worthless under perfect substitutability, whereas it does under imperfect substitutability.

5 Inesssential currencies ($\alpha = 0$)

When $\alpha = 0$, positive real balances are not essential for utility, and equilibrium dynamics must satisfy

$$\dot{m}_1 = (\delta + \sigma)m_1 - m_1 m_2 \tag{29}$$

$$\dot{m}_2 = (\delta + \sigma)m_2 - m_1 m_2 \tag{30}$$

a system of differential equations represented in figure 10.4.

Using the transversality condition (11) and non-negativity constraint on prices, it is easy to show that the only admissible paths lie on the 45 degree ray from the origin. Equilibrium paths are of three types. First, a steady-state equilibrium M in which both currencies are valued. Second, a steady-state equilibrium in which neither currency is valued. Third, a

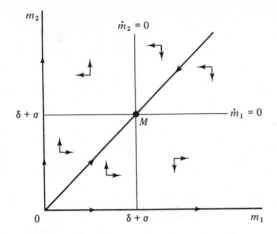

Figure 10.4   Imperfect substitutes (money inessential)

continuum of non-stationary equilibria which all converge to M in the long run.

Comparing these results with those of section 2.2, it is again clear that imperfect substitutability reduces the scope for hyperinflationary equilibria, as the non-monetary equilibrium (the origin) is locally unstable under imperfect substitutability but stable when currencies are perfect substitutes.

6   Concluding remarks

The main lesson to be drawn from the foregoing exercise is that increasing the substitutability of currencies in an integrated multicurrency region may well have perverse effects. First, there is a Gresham's law of currency substitution: under perfect capital mobility and perfect currency substitution, simple arbitrage considerations dictate that the real value of the slow growing currency must, if both currencies are valued, collapse to zero over time. Second, removing the obstacles to currency substitution increases the scope for hyperinflationary equilibria, since no currency alone is ever essential for transactions when currencies are perfectly substitutable.

Therefore, making currencies more easily substitutable provides no guarantee whatsoever that the currency of the monetarily 'virtuous' country will eventually emerge as the nominal anchor of a multicurrency region: the theoretical presumption is indeed the opposite. Further, perfect substitutability makes a multicurrency region more vulnerable to hyperinflations.

These results provide a strong argument against the UK Treasury proposal: currency competition will not promote 'the use of low inflation currencies at the expense of high inflation ones in both transactions and deposits',[17] and perfect substitutability will make speculative hyper-inflations more likely. As economists, however, we should be careful of not adjudicating issues solely on the basis of the qualitative nature of equilibria, as welfare considerations are paramount. It is here, unfortunately, that the simplifying modelling strategy suggested by Woodford and pursued in this paper – namely that currency substitutability should be thought of as an attribute of the utility function – fails us: it is simply impossible to make any welfare statement in this model, or in Woodford's, as to the relative merits of the UK plan versus the Delors proposal, as each is 'represented' by a different utility function. Bearing this *caveat* in mind, the conclusion of this paper should not be that the UK proposal is not desirable, but that it may be conducive to perverse, and expectationally driven, phenomena probably not envisaged by its authors.

NOTES

The ideas developed in this article originate from my discussion, at the January 1990 CEPR/IMI conference on European financial integration, of Michael Woodford's paper (in this volume). I thank Alberto Giovannini and Maurice Obstfeld for their comments.

1 Except for recent work by Kiyotaki and Wright (1989), there is a dearth of rigorous models which explain the endogenous emergence of some assets as monetary instruments as a function of tastes, technology and institutions.
2 Models with money in the utility function are as black a box, and as *ad hoc*, as cash-in-advance models which rely on arbitrary assumptions on the timing of market openings and the nature of payment systems. I therefore do not feel that the latter are at all more general, or more satisfactory theoretically, than the former.
3 Introducing more countries only increases the dimensionality of the problem without providing additional insights.
4 Since I consider below a world in which Ricardian equivalence holds, there is no loss of generality in assuming that lump-sum taxes, while in principle available, are not used to finance public consumption.
5 Equivalently, all consumption goods are perfect substitutes.
6 Dots denote derivative with respect to time. Time arguments are omitted when no confusion results.
7 I do not introduce a market for inside credit, as it must be inactive in equilibrium in a world with identical consumers.
8 Symmetry is inessential; it depends on the choice of monetary units.
9 I omit for the sake of brevity the analysis of the uninteresting case in which $\sigma_1 = \sigma_2$, as it is essentially identical to a one-currency economy in which an arbitrary but constant fraction of the money stock receives a new name.

10 Its theoretical foundations, explored below, are of course distinct from the bimetallic base of the traditional Gresham's law.
11 The nominal interest rate in currency j is $i_j = r - (- \pi_j)$: it is the difference between the real rate of return on bonds and the real rate of return on currency j.
12 Note that the non-stationary equilibria which converge to the origin do satisfy proposition 1.
13 It is easy to extend the results of this section to a more general utility function. This is not done here for the sake of brevity.
14 It is straightforward to relax this assumption.
15 This is of course a reflection of the symmetry intentionally built into the equilibrium dynamics, and not a general result.
16 This point can be made more precisely by specializing the analysis of section 2.1 to the case in which $V(m_1, m_2) = \ln(m_1 + m_2)$.
17 HM Treasury (1989), p. 3.

REFERENCES

Kareken, J. and N. Wallace (1981) 'On the Determinacy of Equilibrium Exchange Rates', *Quarterly Journal of Economics* **96**, 207–22.
Kiyotaki, N. and R. Wright (1989) 'On Money as a Medium of Exchange', *Journal of Political Economy* **97**, 927–54.
Obstfeld, M. and K. Rogoff (1983) 'Speculative Hyperinflations in Maximizing Models: Can We Rule Them Out?' *Journal of Political Economy* **91**, 675–87.
    (1986) 'Ruling out Divergent Speculative Bubbles', *Journal of Monetary Economics* **17**, 349–62.
HM Treasury (1989) 'An Evolutionary Approach to Economic and Monetary Union', Discussion paper, November 2.
Woodford, M. (1991) 'Currency competition and the transition to monetary union: Does competition between currencies lead to price level and exchange rate stability?' (this volume).

Discussion of chapters 9 and 10

JOHN S. FLEMMING

The origin of Philippe Weil's paper in his discussion of Michael Woodford's ensures a high degree of consistency between them. Weil building, as he says, on Woodford's insights, spends less time on the foundations and offers the more intuitively accessible account. From this common story several points emerge both as conclusions and as limitations of the analysis.

The first point is that, since it is not disputed that in these models the utility function that includes money(s) is an indirect utility function, it is relatively difficult – and no attempt is made – to obtain welfare conclusions.

The second point is that under perfect substitutability (and zero real growth) the 'virtuous', more slowly growing, currency asymptotically accounts for a negligible proportion of the whole and aproaches (in the aggregate) zero purchasing power. Although Weil suggests that this is an example of Gresham's law, I do not see it as such. What we have here is two printing presses generating virtually identical notes at different rates. As a user, I have no interest in hoarding those from one press while passing-on the others – they have a single relative value of unity to all holders. The proposition in fact has no behavioural content beyond what is implied by the assumption of perfect substitutability and indefinite compounding.

Woodford's foundation for the analysis are ingenious and powerful but the assumption required for his aggregation to a representative global individual are very similar to those which have been shown to imply that 'everything is neutral' (Bernheim and Bagwell, 1988) – which does not give one confidence that essential features of reality have not got lost in the process.

In fact my greatest doubts about the relevance of this analysis relate to the abstraction from uncertainty. This has implications at two levels; at the consumer level uncertainty would add another (portfolio) margin of (limited) substitutability between currencies. More important, however, is its role in relation to the monetary authorities.

Although in his section 3 Woodford considers learning dynamics as opposed to full information rational equilibria his authorities always either fix the growth rate of (and interest on) their money or fix exchange rates – in both cases immutably.

This specification immediately makes clear that *no competitive process* is involved. Monetary authorities' policies do not interact, they do not attempt to steal a march on each other, or need to look over their shoulders, or redouble their efforts to stay in the pack of contenders on the race track. In this respect, though Woodford's analysis is presented as being of the UK Treasury's proposals, something very important is clearly missing.

The UK proposal is explicitly set in the context of the ERM which is characterized by both a band of permitted fluctuation about central parities and the possibility of occasional adjustment of these parities. It is not a proposal either for the competitive supply of perfect substitutes or for the passive working out of pre-ordained growth of possibly imperfectly, but perhaps increasingly, substitutable moneys. It is quite possible that as substitutability increased towards some finite limit it might be possible to narrow the band or lower the expected frequency of realignments. I say finite limit because HM Treasury's proposal is not for monetary union, as usually understood, but for a competitive process which is claimed to have an anti-inflationary bias relative to one offering less scope for competition. Nonetheless it is recognized that equilibrium is not unique; that, while a single currency could be imposed by fiat, the multi-currency equilibrium is not easily broken – as Woodford acknowledges on his second page. There he says that 'experience suggests (that) the cost advantages of using a (the?) local currency for payments within local markets are such as to deter (complete?) currency substitution except in cases of extremely large inflation differentials (so that) it is not clear how much discipline can be expected from this channel'.

This seems to concede that *some* discipline is involved. How is this notion of discipline captured in models in which monetary authorities only ever make one decision? The competition concerned, like the exercise of discipline, involves reputational considerations which play little or not part here. They do elsewhere, in the literature of repeated policy games, and some marrying of those approaches with that of these papers might be more revealing as to the validity, if any, of the UK Treasury's arguments.

REFERENCES

Bernheim, B.D. and K. Bagnell (1988) 'Is Everything Neutral?', *Journal of Political Economy* **96**, 308–38.

11 Problems of European monetary integration

RUDIGER DORNBUSCH

The debate on European Monetary Integration of the past year has been driven by the French amibition to transform economic realities by institutional arrangements and the German fear that they might succeed. Following the strong impetus of the Delors Committee, and reinforced by a strategic exploitation of the developments in Eastern Europe, against German and UK resistance, European monetary integration is now in the mail.

A poll of 1,036 European business leaders conducted in 1988 showed that 86% (ranging from 60% in Germany to 98% in Italy and France) favoured a common currency. A majority of those questioned (from 52% in Germany to 87% in France) favoured a currency unit that represented an average of the EC currencies such as the ECU rather than a single currency.[1] The Delors Report (pp. 14–15) has pushed the discussion much further, defining the issues and the agenda:

> A monetary union constitutes a currency area in which policies are managed jointly with a view to attaining common macroeconomic objectives. As already stated in the 1970 Werner Report, there are three necessary conditions for a monetary union:
> – the assurance of total and irreversible convertibility of currencies.
> – the complete liberalization of capital transactions and full integration of banking and other financial markets, and
> – the elimination of margins of fluctuations and the irrevocable locking of exchange rate parities.
> The first two of these requirements have already been met, or will be met with the completion of the internal market programme. The single most important condition for monetary union would, however, be fulfilled only when the decisive step was taken to lock exchange rates irrevocably.

But what does monetary integration mean in practice?[2] More conservative monetary policy in Italy, Germany surrender to European inflation complacence, fiscal austerity for Greece, common funds that support exchange rates that are out of line with fundamentals? We argue here that monetary integration means fixed exchange rates and that implies that a burden is shifted onto countries' fiscal institutions and onto the wage–price process to conform. The issue is not to bring about monetary discipline, but rather that countries need to take on their unions and tax payers. In fact, monetary policy today is tight in soft currency countries and one must therefore ask what are the steps that are actually required to implement a credible fixed exchange-rate program.

A strong further move on the monetary front in Europe is now essential; the EMS was a useful instrument in bringing about disinflation, but that process is running out of steam. A sharper and more differentiated tool is now needed to cut through the current state of limbo. Spain, France, Italy and Germany share an exchange-rate regime that is neither here nor there; it does not assure basically zero inflation for Germany and it implies high interest rates for Italy or France; it involves unsustainable real appreciation for Spain and it makes no sense whatsoever for Greece or Portugal. This is a useful point in time for some EMS members to join into a fully fixed-rate regime and others to split off into a crawling peg arrangement.

Some of the questions about monetary union concerns the institutional arrangements, in particular the design of a common central bank, the independence of that institution and the distribution of the seigniorage. But even more important is the question of the transition: assuming a move to permanently fixed rates, how can inflation rates be brought fully into line, fast? We will argue that this transition has more to do with unions than with central banking and the growth rate of money.

1   The EMS as a convergence mechanism: 1978–90[3]

In the period of the EMS, since 1978, inflation rates of member countries have declined substantially and the differences in inflation have narrowed. There are now basically three groups of countries in Europe: Germany, the Netherlands, Austria and Switzerland form a block of hard currency countries. The second tier is made up of Belgium, Ireland, the UK and possibly Italy. In this group inflation is moderate, though decidedly higher than in the first tier. And then there are the high inflation countries which only recently joined the Common Market: Greece, Portugal and Spain (see Table 11.1).

How much of this phenomenon can be attributed to the EMS, and through what channels or mechanisms did the operation of the EMS bring about these results?

The hypothesis in support of a special disinflation mechanism emphasizes either the direct operation of a fixed exchange rate or else credibility effects:[4]

Table 11.1. *Inflation rates in the EMS, 1974–90* (%)

	1974–81	1982–88	1989*	1990*
EMS	12.2	6.5	4.9	4.6
Belgium	7.1	4.4	3.1	3.6
Denmark	10.0	6.2	3.8	2.8
Germany	4.7	2.6	2.4	2.7
Greece	16.3	18.7	15.0	15.2
Spain	17.0	9.6	7.3	6.6
France	11.0	6.6	3.3	2.7
Ireland	14.8	7.0	4.4	4.1
Italy	17.7	9.8	6.3	6.6
Luxembourg	6.7	4.2	3.2	3.5
Netherlands	6.9	1.9	1.4	2.3
Portugal	19.6	19.2	12.4	12.0
UK	15.9	5.4	6.7	5.3

Note:
*Forecast, October 1989.

Source: Commission of the European Communities.

Inflation has a significant inertia component due to explicit or implicit backward-look indexation. The change over to a fixed exchange rate changes the inflation process. Once and for all changes in indexation or incomes policy are required to achieve the transition.

'Imported Credibility' effects: Germany enjoys a substantial reputation for a low tolerance for inflation. Other countries do not have quite the same reputation, but they can piggyback on the German reputation by entering into exchange-rate commitments which then translate into increased credibility of announced policy, lower cost of disinflation and therefore more vigorous disinflation.[5]

The EMS has changed the institutional arrangements for inflation policy. It has created the responsibility for maintaining, until further notice, a pegged rate and it has made realignments subject to multilateral negotiation. Two effects emerged from this process. First, inflation problems of any one country became internationalized because they had an incidence on their joint performance and the cohesion of the exchange-rate regime. Second, central banks became relatively more independent in the soft-currency EMS countries. In this fashion the EMS has mustered more forces on the side of disinflation.

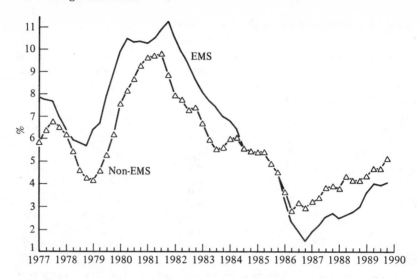

Figure 11.1   Disinflation in the EMS and outside, 1977–90

A substantial body of research has failed to demonstrate conclusively a shift in expectations or in credibility.[6] Moreover, the operation of the EMS, at least at the outset, did not imply fixed rates, nor was the intent to adhere to more nearly fixed rates tantamount to an ability and willingness actually to do so. In fact, a number of arguments can be brought to suggest that the disinflation may have little to do with the EMS *per se*, but rather reflects common factors in European inflation performance.

(a) Countries who did join the EMS were predisposed to bring about disinflation. Accordingly the EMS performance reflects a selection bias, not a performance effect.

(b) Following the inflation bulge of the late 1970s, most industrialized countries felt that disinflation was a priority. As a result, there is basically no difference in the disinflation experience of countries who have and have not joined the EMS. The hypothesis of special EMS disinflation effects should not be accepted too readily. Disinflation has been pervasive in the 1980s and success in this dimension is not limited to EMS partners.
 In fact, figure 11.1 shows the disinflation of EMS members and a group made up of Austria, Finland, Sweden, Norway and Switzerland. Inflation rates of the EMS and the outsiders respectively are made up of the GDP-weighted rates of the members of each group. The figure shows the striking coincidence and extent of disinflation, casting serious doubt on an EMS effect.[7] This evidence suggests strongly a common inflation

experience, independent of EMS membership. In fact the correlation of inflation rates of the EMS and the Non-EMS groups rose from 0.60 in quarterly data in the period 1970–88: 4 to 0.83 in the 1978–89 period.

(c) It is possible, of course that the improving inflation performance of the EMS group provided, through whatever mechanism, disinflation. This raised the costs to outsiders of not sharing the experience. As a result, they, too, disinflated by adopting an informal EMS policy in the form of DM exchange-rate targets. With exchange-rate targets the operative mechanism, the performance of the outside group was indistinguishable from the insiders.

In sum, there is no satisfactory way of deciding to what extent the disinflation and convergence can be attributed to the operation of the EMS. Countries outside, for example Austria, have experienced disinflation just as much as insiders. In fact the same applies to the US in the 1980s. Methodologically, it is a mistake to focus exclusively on the EMS experience, trying to document credibility effects when much the same experience characterizes most other countries without their having in place special mechanisms. The only satisfactory procedure is to construct the counterfactual experiment of a particular country (small enough not to affect the experience of the remaining ones) and ask whether EMS partnership brought to bear special constraints or opportunities which favourably influenced the scope for disinflation.

Specifically, would an EMS membership of Portugal make it more likely that inflation could come down over the next few years? If Portugal did join the EMS now and disinflation succeeded, no doubt membership would be credited with the result. Clearly, Portugal can achieve disinflation on her own; the interesting question is not whether a country can disinflate but whether membership makes that process easier and hence more acceptable. There is certainly no evidence that it makes it harder, hence countries proposing to disinflate might do well to join. But these countries must not believe that there is any evidence to suggest that it eases the task.

The argument mustered for EMS membership as a disinflation device, as was seen in Spain in the year or so before the 1989 membership decision or in Portugal today revolves around a strengthening of the Central Bank and a determined effort to extricate monetary policy from a responsibility for economic performance other than on the inflation front.[8] The cause is good, but it is still fair and appropriate to cast doubt on the assertions because the costs of disinflation are not demonstrably reduced by the EMS. If ending inflation at any price is the objective, then EMS membership provides a good vehicle; if cost effective inflation fighting is the objective than incomes policy remains perhaps a better or indispensable instrument.[9] Of course, it might be argued that EMS membership represents a superior, though implicit, form of incomes policy, better than time-worn wage-price controls.

2   Inconsistencies

The current system, after the narrowing of inflation differentials, suffers from three problems. In Germany inflation is too high, in Denmark (or Italy and Ireland) interest rates are too high and in several countries, notably Britain and Spain, the external deficits may be unsustainably large. Each of these features shows a problem of the current state of monetary limbo.

2.1   The German problem

The actual narrowing of differentials reflects a potentially unsustainable averaging of inflation rates. German inflation, in the absence of fixed rates with a narrow band would be lower and French inflation, for example, would be higher. This is the perennial curse of Germany, imported inflation, which emerged under the Bretton Woods system and has become an almost institutional feature of the EMS.

Hamada (1985) was the first to formulate this problem in a suggestive game-theoretic approach. The subsequent literature has emphasized that the EMS can work as an instrument of disinflation by enhancing the credibility of soft-currency members.[10] But in the current experience the aspect of free riding in the disinflation effort may deserve equal emphasis. If, as is surely the case, success is measured by how close one can come to the German inflation rate, then raising Germany's inflation rate is just as successful a strategy as is lowering one's own. And since the former is less painful it must be the common ambition of most EMS members.

These pressures cannot be effectively resisted: Germany can try and restrain domestic spending, but the resulting gain in cost competitiveness increases the external surplus and thus rapidly becomes in that fashion a source of demand and inflation. Since German restraint does not automatically force restraint in the partner countries, as was the case in the mid-1980s, the game has changed and Germany is forced into imported inflation. Once the presumption of depreciation that offsets inflation differentials cannot be taken fully for granted and as long as partner countries are willing to have high interest rates relative to Germany they can readily finance their imbalances, until further notice.

In principle the imbalances that evolve from differential cost performance

Table 11.2. *Increases in unit labour costs, 1988–90*
(% per annum)

	1988	1989	1990
Germany	0.0	0.7	1.3
France	1.1	2.1	2.0
Italy	6.1	6.5	5.4

Source: Commission of the European Communities.

provide a check, but this mechanism is quite imperfect. There are two reasons. One is that they are easily financed and the other is that Germany's surpluses can be presented as a German problem, to be eliminated by expansion in Germany rather than contraction abroad. Once the mechanism works in a way that places at least part of the adjustment on Germany much of the disinflation dynamics is lost. We then face one of two possibilities: either German restraint is entirely frustrated because it leads to offsetting expansion abroad so that total demand for German goods and services is virtually unchanged. Or else restraint works temporarily and helps contain costs, but the gain in cost competitiveness translates into an improved external balance which restores the initial level of demand.

One way or the other there is no effective instrument to check demand for German goods and services and hence inflation.[11] As long as imbalances are easily financed there is no discipline. In the mid-1980s countries had to work down their own inflation rate or else suffer depreciation. With the narrowing of inflation rates far more of the burden falls almost inescapably on Germany, (see table 11.2).

2.2 The interest rate problem

The EMS was invented to shield Europe by the creation of a zone of monetary stability in Europe from financial instability exported by the US. It then became a project of disinflation.[12] But, even though the experience of the 1980s has established a progressive hardening of *nominal* exchange rates, there remain doubts about just how fixed exchange rates are and how permanently inflation differentials have vanished.

Assets markets clearly have not taken the view that exchange rates are now fixed. The last realignment, prior to the Italian shift of margins in January 1989, had occurred in January 1987 preceded by general

Table 11.3. *Interest rates and inflation in the EMS, 1989: II*
(% per annum)

	Money market[a]	Gov't bond[a]	Inflation[b]
Belgium	6.6	8.4	3.1
Denmark	8.7	10.6	3.8
France	8.6	8.8	3.3
Germany	6.2	7.0	2.4
Ireland	9.2	9.1	4.4
Italy	12.5	10.6	6.3
Netherlands	6.6	7.2	1.4
Spain	14.1	13.9	7.4
UK	12.9	9.6	6.7

Notes:
[a]1989: II. [b]Inflation of the GDP deflator in 1989.

Source: EC, IMF and Morgan Guaranty.

realignments in 1986 and 1983. In fall of 1989 the possibility of another realignment was widely discussed, but it then did not occur. The fact that inflation differentials have narrowed sharply and no realignment occurred in two and a half years has not translated into an equalization of long-term interest rates. Yield differentials remain very substantial as table 11.3 shows.

Although the disinflation effort has been quite successful, the step to a system of fully fixed exchange rates has not been taken formally. That opens a precarious possibility: interest rates reflect the possibility of further exchange-rate realignments even though governments are almost or entirely committed to no further exchange-rate changes. For countries with high debt ratios this represents the worst possible situation because realized real interest rates are high and debts are growing rapidly.

The convergence of inflation rates is not systematically reflected in either short or long-term interest rates. The implication is that if exchange rate actually remain fixed between Germany and Ireland, for example, Irish *realized* real interest rates will be exceptionally high.[13] Given the high debt ratio in countries like Ireland or Italy, this is a major source of fiscal instability.[14]

The countries who have the weakest fiscal position are also the ones who are most committed to fixed rates and who have the highest interest rates. As a result their budget deficits are large and their debt ratios are growing. The problem is worse the more a government is actually committed to

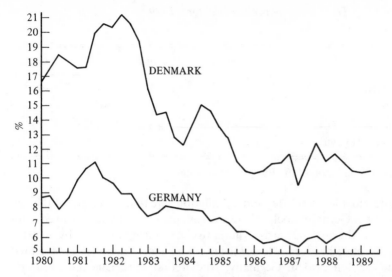

Figure 11.2 Long-term interest rates in Denmark and Germany, 1980–9

maintaining exchange rates and the less it is believed: in that case large realized real interest rates add year after year to the debt burdens.

Consider for example the case of Denmark, shown in figure 11.2. Since 1987 the EMS has not had any realignments and the Danish inflation rate has not been very far above that of Germany. Even so, long-term interest rates in Denmark substantially exceed those in Germany; the differential is presumably a reflection of the anticipation of depreciation some time in the future.

Interestingly, the term structure of interest rates is quite flat.[15] One cannot therefore take the view that there is either a near-term high probability realignment (the case of a negative term structure) or a distant one, reflected in a 'peso problem' term premium. In fact, it is not clear what the yield differential relative to Germany is trying to suggest other than that fixed rates for ever is not the presumption.[16] And this lack of certainty about exchange rates translates into a fiscal problem in countries with high debt as we shall now discuss.

For Greece and Portugal there is simply no question; their inflation rates exceed by so far the community average, and even more so the German rate. They cannot expect to maintain their exchange rates; they might succeed for a year or even two, but that attempt would be certain to condemn them to a typical Latin American experience.

The issue of exchange-rate expectations becomes more interesting in the case of Denmark, Italy, Ireland and the UK. Here are countries that have

Table 11.4. *The European problem debtors, 1989*
(% of GNP)

	Belgium	Ireland	Italy	Greece
Debt/GNP	127.9	117.5	97.8	76.5
Deficit				
Total	5.9	5.1	9.9	12.8
Primary	− 4.5	− 4.3	1.0	3.2
Real interest payments	7.1	5.7	3.8	− 0.7

Source: Commission of the European Communities.

high nominal interest rates and an inflation rate that is in sight of the low rates of the German block. There is a genuine issue of whether fixed rates help make the last 100 yards. Alternatively, reducing inflation by an extra point becomes harder the lower the rate – an experience well-documented in the US but also in Germany. And if that were true the fixed-rate strategy could well imply a losing battle where the fiscal implications of high *realized* real interest rates built up an important debt problem.

In 1985–7, for example, realized short-term interest rates averaged 2.1% in Germany. By contrast, they averaged 4.3% in Italy, 9.4% in Denmark and 6.4% in Ireland.[17] Because of these high realized real interest rates debts kept growing relative to GDP (see table 11.4).

A related difficulty, also the by-product of the low inflation policy, was the shift in deficit finance. Prior to the disinflation and fixed exchange-rate commitment, Italy, for example, had financed a significant share of the deficit by money creation. But with fixed exchange rates and low inflation the scope for inflationary finance was gone and debt creation was the rule.[18] The growing debt ratios of course imply increased tax burdens in the future. Although the form and incidence of these taxes is uncertain, the presence of these future tax burdens makes high-debt countries poor locations for production.

The debt issue points to the need for major reform in two directions. One is to reduce the exchange-risk premia that there are now in real interest rates, the other is to reduce the budget deficits. The two policies are strictly complementary. Increasing ratios of debt to GDP are clearly not possible for a long time once the 100% threshold has been passed. Unless there is a prospect of significantly higher growth or much lower future real interest rates there is a need for reduced deficits. Without a prospect of deficit reduction and lower real interest rates asset holders must ultimately expect debt repudiation in some form. That expectation would lead to yet larger risk premia and even more rapid growth in debt.

Of course, high real interest rates also affect real aggregate demand and may create an unsustainable slump. But this effect is quite differentiated: high realized real interest rates translate into high real incomes for debt holders and to that extent may well be expansionary, not contractionary. High real interest rates are also a poor measure of the extent of fiscal restraint: major corporations, and increasingly medium-sized firms, can finance themselves in foreign exchange and across borders. If their gamble pays off their real cost of capital is actually even lower than that in Germany. The exchange rate rate limbo thus introduces potentially undesirable distortions in the capital market and uncertainty that may distort investment patterns.

2.3   Sustainability of current accounts

The EC studies of the Europe 92 project (see Emerson *et al.*, 1988) envisage that cross-border competition in financial services will have a major impact on financial service prices, spreads and the cost of capital. Compared with the average of the four lowest-price countries, Germany for example has at present a very high cost of consumer credit, for example, while Belgium has a low cost. Price divergences at the retail level would shrink substantially for banking services, insurance and security transactions. In Spain the decline in financial service prices might be as large as 21%, in Germany 10% and in the Netherlands only 4%.[19]

Trade in financial services, and financial deregulation which will be an important part of Europe 92, are likely to have an impact on credit rationing. Restrictions on capital mobility for asset holders and inability to compete in services across borders at present leaves the national saving pools (and even the regional pools) substantially unconnected. In the wholesale Euro-dollar there is already substantial mobility as Giavazzi and Giovannini (1989a, b) have documented. But that does not preclude a retail market in which many forms of credit remain segmented and non-traded. There is local lending of local deposits and small and medium-sized firms are typically unable to obtain credit except locally. Credit rationing then is pervasive and financial integration, drawing on the US experience with securitization, may be a very radical experiment.[20]

The likely effect of financial integration is twofold. One is that, while spreads narrow, interest rates which are now repressed may actually rise throughout Europe and especially in high saving countries like Spain. At the same time firms and households will find it easier to finance them-selves in a more competitive market so that credit rationing is less pervasive.

In the past, in the presence of budget deficits credit rationing crowded

Table 11.5. *External balances, 1978–90*
(% of GNP)

	1978–87	1988–90
Italy	− 0.3	− 1.1
Spain	− 0.3	− 2.7
UK	− 0.2	− 3.5

Source: Commission of the European Communities.

out business investment and consumer spending. With the internationalization of markets this tendency can lessen significantly as firms can tap the European capital market, crossing national borders. The possibility therefore emerges that those countries where credit rationing has kept investment low will now borrow in the European capital market both to finance public sector deficits and increased investment rates as well. Table 11.5 shows this effect for Spain and Italy where external balances already reflect the increase in national investment rates.

In judging the sustainability of these deficits we encounter the problem of knowing their primary cause: misaligned exchange rates, normal development finance or budget deficits. The distinction is important because deficits that are the result of exchange-rate misalignment cannot last: they are financed by high interest rates and ultimately fall of their own weight. A more transparent exchange rate regime can help avoid the ambiguity about deficits that is present now. Once exchange rates are either fixed-fixed or crawling the financing of deficits is driven less by interest rates and more by fundamentals.

In the case of Spain, more so than for other countries, there is a genuine question about the sustainability of the external deficit. The deficit seemed appropriate while Spain could claim to be a preferred manufacturing location in the context of Europe 92. The real appreciation of the past two years (see table 11.6) would be a reflection of a new real equilibrium associated with the development phase where investment inflows easily finance the external imbalance. But if the developments in Eastern Europe imply the arrival of 100 million low wage workers in the European Space then Greece, Ireland, Portugal and Spain must be among the principal losers; a substantial readjustment of their real exchange rate would seem likely in that event.

3   Moving ahead

When capital movements are fully liberalized and margins shrink, monetary policy will have to carry even more of a burden, at even an higher

Table 11.6. *Real exchange rates and the current account, 1989: II*

	Real exchange rate[a]		Current Acct. (% of GDP)
	Morgan	IMF	
Belgium	95.3	92.8	0.8
Denmark	97.7	100.4	− 2.0
France	94	96.5	− 0.5
Germany	94.3	96.4	5.3
Ireland	n.a.	96.0[b]	2.0
Italy	105.4	101.4	− 1.3
Netherlands	90.5	92.7	2.1
Spain	109.7	106.2	− 2.9
UK	104.1	107.3	− 4.1

Notes:
[a]Value in 1989: II, index 1987 = 100, based on manufacturing prices.
[b]Based on consumer prices.

Source: Morgan Guaranty, IMF and Commission of the European Communities.

price to public finance. This is a good time to move far ahead and be done with all and any exchange margins.

Monetary integration is often interpreted in terms of the loss of independence of monetary policy and the creation of joint monetary institutions. But realism requires one to recognize that there is no longer significant independent monetary policy in Europe. The only question is whether exchange rates are or are not fixed for the foreseeable future. And that has little to do with monetary policy but is rather a question of wage behaviour and fiscal policy.

In most European countries monetary policy has become almost powerless. Exchange-rate expectations are governed by accumulated imbalances and loss of competitiveness, and by political squabbles about who 'makes' inflation and who 'suffers' from it, not by short-run monetary policy. Monetary policy only serves to postpone exchange rate crises, but it does so at an important cost to the budget. For most EMS members monetary policy has basically become an instrument for managing the balance of payments and only in the nth country, Germany, is it devoted to setting the EMS inflation trend. Even in economies where there is no crisis in sight there is invariably a concern for realignments in the system, and hence the possibilities of any particular country staying with the average rather than with Germany. That in turn requires a level of interest rates that includes a 'peso problem' premium.

Once the ability to conduct any kind of independent monetary policy is so far gone one can ask why countries should not go ahead and abandon the pretence altogether. There are several answers:

> The current arrangement allows the soft-currency countries as a group to put pressure on Germany. Until these countries have demonstrated their willingness and ability to sustain low inflation, and have developed the implied fiscal conditions, Germany will not allow monetary policy to be made at the Community level.
>
> Several countries have been unable to get better control of their wage–price dynamics. As a result they fear that on a fixed exchange rate they will be driven into a situation of overvaluation and stagflation. They therefore might prefer to work on disinflation further before moving to a fixed rate.
>
> Some countries are running large budget deficits. They plan to correct these and recognize that to assure full employment a gain in competitiveness is required once budget cutting is achieved. They prefer to keep the exchange rate option rather than having to rely on deflation.
>
> In some countries unions control the wage dynamics and governments are unwilling to fight the unions on this issue. They leave to much later the question of the equilibrium real exchange rate. This is presumably the UK position.

In most cases these obstacles merely postpone, and without much justification, the necessary adjustments and the move to fixed rates. But that answer does not apply with equal strength to all EC countries. Some, like Greece, Portugal or Spain are far out of line with the rest, and should therefore receive separate and differentiated treatment that may stretch over a number of years.

4   Transitional adjustment: zero margins

The momentum now pushes towards institutionalizing monetary integration. One direction, favoured by Germany, is to increase rapidly and on a broad scale the scope for capital mobility. This is seen as a means of testing just how seriously the partner countries are willing to go even further in the direction of German monetary policy. With sharply increased capital mobility nothing short of German performance can be consistent with the free flow of capital and fixed rates.

The same direction is favoured by Central Banks in Italy especially, but also in Spain or France where they traditionally have been appendices (or cash windows) of the national Treasuries. The disinflation experience of the 1980s in which exchange-rate stability was central to establishing lower inflation and possibly, in addition, a reputation for anti-inflation commitment had an extraordinary side effect: it made central banks independent. The bureaucratic response, especially in Italy, has been a fervent commitment to more of the same – deepening of monetary integration.

A more rapid implementation of a firmly committed exchange-rate policy must now be put in place for the core countries. To avoid the fiscal costs associated with exchange-rate uncertainty governments in soft-currency countries like Italy can press for increasing exchange-rate fixity. They can immediately discard exchange-rate margins altogether. This would signal a much stronger commitment to fixed rates. The strategy is attractive because it is already widely believed in Europe that monetary policy is no longer effective, except to provide financing for the external balance. European monetary policy is made in Frankfurt and any independence is not only an illusion, but is also expensive in terms of domestic debt service.

There is no need at this stage for any joint institutions to manage European money. Central bank consultation as it has occurred in the past 2 or 3 years can assure continuing efforts at disinflation. But exchange rate fixity must become more believed and for that purpose governments must take on bigger *actual* commitments. The more governments put at stake the more credible their policy. The chief issue how to manage the transition. That problem will be just as difficult 2, 3 or 5 years from now. It will always be inconvenient to give up an option, and because government retain the option capital markets retain the risk premium. For all intents and purposes the policy of retaining the option of changing nominal exchange rates, but not exercising it, is extremely expensive in terms of public finance. Recognition of this fact should lead governments to take the radical steps required to move within a short time span – less than a year – to a fully fixed rate.

In this spirit the Netherlands, Denmark, Italy and France should fix their exchange rates *without any margin* to the DM. In the case of Italy the occasion should be used for redenomination to eliminate the almost tropical excess of zeros and achieve a simple 1:1 relation.

4.1   The payments mechanism with zero margins

How is such a system implemented? Three institutional arrangements of the payments mechanism help impose the fixed rate.

First, economic agents in the core group that has adopted zero margins should be allowed to write cheques in any of the core-group currencies. Second, banks in the core-group countries must clear all cheques at par, independent of origin or denomination.[21] Third, central banks organize a core-group clearing system. These arrangements assure that rates are in fact fixed at par.[22] The only departure would stem from confidence crises.

The zero margin proposal highlights the need to rethink the role of exchange-rate margins. These might serve two entirely different purposes. One is to create a sufficient room for realignments to occur only at discrete intervals even though the trend of fundamentals leads to a drift in the equilibrium real exchange rate over time. In this perspective a 6% margin, for example, might lead to an interval of a year or two before a resetting of the margin is required to accommodate a trend depreciation. The alternative role is as a deterrent to one-way speculation. Here the purpose is to create increased uncertainty for speculators and thus lessen the need for the authorities to undertake corrective action to ward off one-way speculation. It is assumed in the profession that with a single money there is no reason to have margins, but that with different monies, even if the intent is to practice fixed rates, that there should be margins. The absence of any literature on the appropriate band highlights that this is an area that deserves further study.

Further monetary integration requires as a first step that countries abandon the ambiguity about trend depreciation that continues, notably for countries with a wide band. Thus Italy's adoption of a narrower band should not translate into more frequent realignments but rather into a reinforced vigour in eliminating the sources of trend depreciation. Incomes policy, as noted below, must be brought into play for that purpose.

Consider then the role of margins that are maintained as a device to contain speculation. If the government is unambiguously committed to maintaining the margins then they serve no purpose but create volatility of both exchange rates and interest rates. The within-margins flexible rate stops accommodating banking flows and as a result stops the interest rate-smoothing function of capital flows. And to the extent that interest differentials emerge, these will force offsetting exchange-rate adjusted yield differentials.

Consider a simple model with risk-neutral speculators. Let there be white noise disturbances in interest differentials and let e be the expected future exchange rate. The interest differential is thus given by the disturbance term u_t. The condition for exchange-adjusted yields to be equalized becomes:

$$e/e_t - 1 = u_t \tag{1}$$

or

$$e_t = e/(1 + u_t) \tag{1a}$$

$$e_{min} < e_t < e_{max}$$

Within the exchange margins disturbances to interest rates are reflected in offsetting exchange-rate fluctuations. At the margins monetary policy becomes endogeneous and this limits interest differentials. Interest-rate disturbances thus translate into exchange-rate fluctuations. If margins were eliminated capital flows would provide the endogeneous smoothing of differentials as is the case across regions in a payments zone.

Moreover, in the presence of risk-aversion the potential volatility of exchange rates makes debt denominated in the two currencies imperfect substitutes. As a result disturbances in the capital markets translate into exchange-rate and interest-rate fluctuations because the capital markets have been arbitrarily segmented by the introduction of a noise zone. With zero margins capital flows would smooth interest fluctuations across countries without the noise and transactions costs associated with exchange-rate fluctuations.

Accommodating capital flows would emerge spontaneously once exchange-rate fluctuations (by contrived margins) were eliminated. An increase in interest rates in Italy, say because of a money demand disturbance, would lead to a capital inflow and expansion of reserves in the banking system in Italy. Rather than have the lira appreciate, thereby interfering with trade flows, banking flows would fully accommodate financial disturbances. Par clearing assures that the transactions costs in providing this arbitrage function are radically reduced.

The argument establishes that the case for margins (given the alternative of zero margin with par clearing) must hang either on the authorities' wanting to retain the option of realignments or on the objective of consciously creating uncertainty. The former is understandable but may well involve a 'bad' equilibrium as a result of a lack of commitment on the part of the authorities. The latter – contrived uncertainty – has no microeconomic foundation.

Within countries par clearing is routine. Exchange margins are a legacy of the gold standard and were adopted, almost by mistake one would think, as part of the Bretton Woods system. It pays to reexamine whether they serve any useful function whatsoever. And if they do, surely one would have to demonstrate whether a 1, 2 or 6% margin represents the optimum.

4.2 Transitional arrangements

Two issues emerge immediately with the decision to have zero margins:

adjustment in capital markets – interest rates on assets denominated in different currencies will converge strongly, though perhaps not fully

inflation performance up to this point has been inconsistent with a fully fixed rate and pressure on Germany to inflate has been effective.

The capital market problem emerges in two ways. First, countries like Italy or France will experience incipient capital inflows. Rather than allowing reserve accumulation, and hence strain on the low-inflation countries and the system, the central banks of high-inflation countries should expand domestic credit by retiring public debt. But the expansionary demand effects should be offset by a sharp tightening in fiscal positions. Therefore a country like Italy would use the move to a fixed rate as the occasion to clean up its public finances. There will be no better time to do what needs to be done anyway.

To the extent that debt contracts are medium-term and carry an inflation premium, there is also a need to make a readjustment here. Both for the outstanding medium-term public debt and for time deposits, rates should be scaled down. At the same time it would be convenient to consolidate the debt into long-term instruments. We discuss below fiscal prerequisites, but we immediately note that in Italy monetary reform should be accompanied by eliminating the excessive number of zeros on its currency.

The transition period must also be used to break the inertia of inflation which today puts in question continued fixed exchange rates. A shift to a fixed rate will influence expectations, but if wage adjustments are backward-looking care must be taken to avoid an overvaluation in the initial phase. It is therefore appropriate in some countries, for example Italy, to accompany the shift to a fixed rate by a temporary wage freeze coupled with *ex post* indexation.[23] This is an extraordinary step to take and that is the purpose: it makes it clear (at great cost to the government) that the regime has changed. At the same time the intervention in the wage process can be used to bring about desirable changes in wage arrangements: specifically they could provide for *ex post* indexation and real-wage flexibility on a regional basis. Once the exchange rate ceases to be an instrument of change in competitiveness the wage has to do far more of the work. The advantage of such a system over exchange-rate adjustment is the scope for regional relative wage adjustment. Of course, that presupposes departing from national wage setting.

It would be a grave mistake to fix rates, free capital movements and then use supertight money to defend the system against overvaluation. This is where incomes policy can and should play a role, not to cut real wages, but to avoid the new system going astray at the very beginning. Without incomes policy, and supporting fiscal restraint, the step to fully fixed rates is not plausible.

4.3   Fiscal prerequisites

Substantial fiscal convergence is commonly recognized as the *sine qua non* for full monetary integration.[24] Those countries who have set for themselves a record of monetary responsibility cannot accept that their performance be threatened by the fiscal problems of countries with a poorer record. Thus the transition to a zero-margin policy requires fiscal action, but it also provides the opportunity for such action.

Fiscal problems such as Italy conspicuously experiences can affect monetary policy decisions in several ways.[25] First, a government may simply have recourse to the printing press to finance a portion of the deficit. Second, a government may be tempted to inflate away an excessively burdensome debt. Finally, when debts and hence debt service are large, it is tempting to run a low interest-rate policy so as to reduce the cost of debt service. In one way or another, fiscal problems taint the ability to conduct a serious monetary policy. The issue is all the more serious because a country like Italy does have a debt problem and would clearly stand to benefit from a *joint* monetary easing.

Even when there is no outright inflationary pressure exerted by the fiscal stance, there is another possibility to be concerned about: in a repressed financial system deficits are financed at relatively low interest cost because private investment is crowded out. Once the capital market is liberalized, as will be the case after July 1990, interest costs may increase and that in turn might then translate into pressures on the monetary authorities. Of course, it is also possible that the liberalization of capital markets leads to external financing at lower interest cost. In this case partner countries might be concerned that one country's budget deficits are financed by a joint intervention fund at the cost of a monetary expansion in the entire area.

The move to zero margins should therefore introduce a transition period of 2 years during which the fiscal and wage–price preconditions for joint monetary poicy are established and demonstrated. In this transition period soft-currency countries would adapt to and follow German monetary policy. After that period the move to common monetary institutions will be appropriate.

5   The UK case

In the UK the transition to fixed exchange rates would be a far larger problem than elsewhere. The pound is certainly overvalued at normal levels of demand. It would therefore be necessary to have an initial real depreciation. But unions would be most unlikely to accept a real depreciation and therefore wage pressure and inflation would be the result.

The plain fact is that the UK will not fit into a European monetary arrangement until the union problem has been solved. High real interest rates and a slump can check union pressure for real wages, but that comes at the cost of unemployment. Even abstracting from the need for an initial real devaluation, wage-setting is driven by unions without regard for inflation and exchange-rate targets. British wage–price–exchange rate relations continue to be an issue of political rift rather than co-responsibility.

Because the process differs so radically from what is now basically accepted on the continent monetary union is implausible at this stage or under this government.

6   Concluding remarks

It is not obvious that a fixed nominal exchange rate offers a solution for every one of the EC members at this time. Spain has an inflation rate of 7%, in Portugal it is 13% and in Greece 15%. Clearly these countries are far away from German inflation and any use of fixed nominal exchange rates to control inflation is misguided. It will only produce overvaluation and a devaluation crisis in short order. A fixed exchange rate, as we know from endless Latin American experiments, is not a lasting measure against homemade inflation. Governments must come to grip with the forces of inflation, specifically unions or inertial pressure on inflation and fiscal imbalances.

But for countries whose performances has narrowed down to the level where trend depreciation, if any, is more of a nuisance than an advantage and where exchange-rate uncertainty is predominantly an impediment to trade rather than a defence against speculation further hesitation is no longer warranted. There is never a situation where all uncertainties melt away. Countries must take a leap of faith and commitment at some stage and the preconditions are now right for that jump.

NOTES

I am indebted to Alberto Giovannini and Michael Emerson for helpful discussions.

  1 These date are reported in 'European Business and the ECU' published by the Association for the Monetary Union of Europe, Paris, 25 October 1988.
  2 For extensive discussion of the EMS and further detailed references see

European Economic Commission (1989c), Giavazzi and Giovannini (1989a, b), Giavazzi and Spaventa (1989), Padoa-Schioppa *et al.* (1987), Folkerts-Landau and Mathieson (1989), Ungerer (1989), Cobham (1989), de Grauwe and Peeters (1989), Thygesen (1988) and McDonald and Zis (1989).

3 The extent of convergence is elaborated in detail in European Communities (1989a).

4 See Giavazzi and Pagano (1988), Giavazzi and Giovannini (1989a, b) and Collins (1988).

5 Exchange rate-based stabilization was very common in Latin America in the 1970s. Both the Argentinian and Chilean experiments ended in disaster, not because the announced policies were not followed, but because the expected results failed to be achieved.

6 The statement does not intend to belittle the important research effort in defining and carrying out tests. It simply is a reflection of the great difficulty in constructing a convincing counterfactual experiment.

7 See de Grauwe (1989a) for a similar figure.

8 See Viñals (1990) and Torres (1990).

9 See Collins (1988) and de Grauwe (1989a, b) on the costs of disinflation.

10 See Giavazzi and Pagano (1988), Giavazzi (1988) and Giovannini (1990).

11 See the 1989–90 *Annual Report* of the European Economic Commission which raises concerns along these lines.

12 See Giavazzi and Pagano (1988), Giavazzi and Giovannini (1989a, b), Giavazzi, Micossi and Miller (1988), de Cecco and Giovannini (1989), Ungerer (1989), Cobham (1989) and Schinasi (1989).

13 As inflation rates narrow down to only a few points it becomes increasingly difficult to judge which particular price index is appropriate. It becomes likewise to decide whether inflation differentials translate into a loss of competitiveness. The reason is the Balassa effect – countries with high productivity growth will experience relatively higher inflation even though they are gaining in international manufacturing competitiveness.

14 For an earlier discussion of this issue in the context of Ireland see Dornbusch (1988) and Kremers (1990).

15 See Anderson and Risager (1988) on the relation between credibility, exchange rates and the term structure of interest.

16 For a further discussion see Dornbusch (1989) and Giavazzi and Giovannini (1989).

17 See OECD *Economic Outlook. Historical Statistics*, July 1989.

18 On this point see Dornbusch (1988) and Giavazzi (1989).

19 See Emerson *et al.* (1989), p. 105.

20 The analogy with the US mortgage market is useful. In the 1960s local S&Ls collected local deposits and made local loans. Today US mortgages are securitized and traded internationally.

21 The provision of par clearing was an essential innovation associated with the Federal Reserve system. The fact of a currency area, already prior to the creation of the Federal Reserve, was not enough to create fixed rates between various cities. The evidence has been analysed by Garbade and Silber (1987).

22 An inconsequential exception can be made for currency. Because of the cost of carrying inventories, there is no reason to impose zero margins here.

23 Of course, the indexation clause would exclude oil shocks and the like.

24 For discussion of the fiscal policy issue see van der Ploeg (1989), Masson and Melitz (1990) and European Commission (1989b).

25 In the US, until the 'Accord' in the 1950s, the Fed maintained low interest rates to accommodate debt management. This helped reduce the debt income ratio from more than 100% in the 1940s to less than 60% in the early 1950s. Since the pegging of interest was suspended there is no evidence of a link between deficits and the stance of monetary policy.

REFERENCES

Andersen, T. and O. Risager (1988) 'The Role of Credibility for the Effects of a Change in the Exchange Rate Policy', *European Economic Review* **32**, 669–79.

Canzoneri, M. and C. Rogers (1989) 'Is the European Community an Optimal Currency Area: Optimal Taxation versus the Cost of Multiple Currencies?' Mimeo, Georgetown University.

Cobham, D. (1989) 'Strategies for Monetary Integration Revisited', *Journal of Common Market Studies* **27**, 203–18.

Collins, S. (1988) 'Inflation and the European Monetary System', in F. Giavazzi, S. Micossi and M. Miller (eds.), *The European Monetary System*, Cambridge University Press.

Commission of the European Communities (1988) *Annual Economic Report 1988–89, European Economy* No. 38, November.

(1989a) 'Facing the challenges of the early 1990s', *European Economy* No. 42, November.

(1989b) *Report on Economic and Monetary Union in the European Community*, Luxembourg.

(1989c) *Collection of Papers Submitted to the Committee for the Study of Economic and Monetary Union*, Luxembourg.

de Cecco, M. and A. Giovannini (eds.) (1989) *A European Central Bank? Perspectives on monetary unification after ten years of the EMS*, Cambridge University Press.

de Grauwe, P. (1989a) 'The Cost of Disinflation and the European Monetary System', CEPR Discussion Paper No. 326.

(1989b) 'Disinflation in the EMS and in the Non-EMS Countries: What Have We Learned?' Discussion Paper, Center for Economic Studies, Catholic University of Leuven.

de Grauwe, P. and T. Peeters (eds.) (1989) *The ECU and European Monetary Integration*. London: Macmillan.

Dornbusch, R. (1988) 'Money and Finance in European Integration', in *Money and Finance in European Integration*, Geneva: EFTA.

(1989) 'Credibility, Debt and Unemployment: Ireland's Failed Stabilization', *Economic Policy* **4**(8), 174–209.

Emerson, M., M. Aujean, M. Catinat, P. Goybet and A. Jacquemin (1989) *The Economics of 1992*. Oxford: Oxford University Press.

Folkerts-Landau, D. and D. Mathieson (1989) *The European Monetary System in the Context of the Integration of European Financial Markets*, IMF Occasional Papers No. 66.

Garbade, K. and W. Silber (1979) 'The Payment System and Domestic Exchange Rates: Technological versus Institutional Change', *Journal of Monetary Economics* **5**(1), (January), 1–22.

Giavazzi, F. (1989) 'The Exchange Rate Question in Europe', CEPR Discussion Paper No. 298, January.

Giavazzi, F. and A. Giovannini (1989a) *Limiting Exchange Rate Flexibility*. Cambridge, MA.: MIT Press.

(1989b) 'Can the EMS Be Exported? Lessons From 10 Years of Monetary Policy Coordination in Europe', CEPR Discussion Paper No. 285.

Giavazzi, F., S. Micossi and M. Miller (eds.) (1988) *The European Monetary System*. Cambridge University Press.

Giavazzi, F. and M. Pagano (1988) 'The Advantage of Tying One's Hands: EMS Discipline and Central Bank Credibility', *European Economic Review* **32**, 1055–74.

Giavazzi, F. and L. Spaventa (1989) 'The New EMS', CEPR Discussion Paper No. 369.

Giovannini, A. (1990) 'The Transition Towards Monetary Union', mimeo (presented at the Institut d'Etudes Européennes, Bruxelles), Columbia University, March.

Hamada, K. (1985) *The Political Economy of International Monetary Interdependence*, Cambridge, MA.: MIT Press.

Kremers, J. (1990) 'Gaining Credibility for a Disinflation: Ireland's Experience in the EMS', *IMF Staff Papers* **37**, 116–45.

Masson, P. and J. Melitz (1990) 'Fiscal Policy Independence in a European Monetary Union', EMF Working Paper WP 90/24, March.

McDonald, F. and G. Zis 'The European Monetary System: Towards 1992 and Beyond', *Journal of Common Market Studies* **27**, 183–202.

Padoa-Schioppa, T. *et al.* (1987) *Efficiency, Stability, and Equity*. Oxford: Oxford University Press.

Schinasi, G. (1989) 'European Integration, Exchange Rate Management, and Monetary Reform: A Review of the Major Issues', Board of Governors of the Federal Reserve, International Finance Discussion Paper No. 364.

Thygesen, N. (1988) 'The European Monetary System: Introduction', in F. Giavazzi, S. Micossi and M. Miller (eds.), *The European Monetary System*, Cambridge University Press.

Torres, F. (1990) 'Portugal's Monetary Integration into a Changing Europe: A Proposal', Mimeo, European University Institute and CEPS.

Ungerer, H. (1989) 'The European Monetary System and the International Monetary System', *Journal of Common Market Studies* **27**, 231–48.

van der Ploeg, F. (1989) 'Fiscal Aspects of Monetary Integration in Europe', CEPR Discussion Paper No. 340. August.

Viñals, J. (1990) 'The EMS, Spain and Macroeconomic Policy', CEPR Discussion Paper No. 388, March.

Discussion

FRANCESCO GIAVAZZI

The Delors Report, and the decisions taken by the EC Council of Ministers in June and December 1989, lay out a clear, but very slow process towards monetary unification in Europe. Until the start of Stage II – that is not before 1993 – realignments of EMS central parities will remain possible, and exchange-rate bands will not be reduced below the current 2.25% margins. The transition to irrevocably fixed parities is not foreseen before the start of Stage III – that is, not before 1996. A single currency shines high above the horizon, but its distance is indeed astronomical – not before the end of the decade.

Dornbuch challenges the EC blueprint, arguing that Europe can only lose from holding up the process of monetary unification: 'In most European countries monetary policy has become almost powerless. [. . .] Once the ability to conduct any kind of independent monetary policy is far gone, one can ask why countries would not go ahead and abandon the pretence altogether.' The cost of not doing so is an unnecessary high tax burden. This is because, as long as currencies are allowed to fluctuate in bands, the bands are not irrevocably fixed, interest rates in 'weak-currency' countries – e.g. Ireland and Italy – are higher than they would be if their exchange rates were irrevocably linked to the Deutsche mark without any margin. Since these countries are also those suffering from large budget deficits and exceptionally high public debt levels, a prolonged transition will have long-lasting consequences: it will keep the cost of debt service unnecessarily high, and will thus require an even higher tax burden in the future.

I share the view that a lengthy transition is a potential source of instability, but for quite different reasons. The interest rate differentials that we presently observe among EMS members are a temporary phenomenon, largely unrelated to the size of the band, or to the fact that officials have not declared the current bands irrevocably fixed. Their source lies primarily in the yet incomplete integration of European financial markets, which allows central banks to retain some monetary independence, and thus the ability to prevent a fall in domestic interest rates by sterilizing capital inflows.

In the EMS, the recent abolition of exchange controls has been accompanied by a shift towards greater exchange-rate fixity: policy-makers seem to have realized that, once exchange controls are gone, realignments become virtually impossible, since the mere possibility of a realignment could stir up an unsustainable speculative attack. After the failure of repeated attempts to prove to the contrary, the authorities' commitment to stick to the existing parities has become credible. The abolition of exchange controls, however, has not yet translated into a full integration of European financial markets. In many countries, for example, households are still prevented from borrowing in foreign currency: 'local lending of local deposits' is still the rule, rather than the exception. However, the ability of central banks to sever the link between domestic financial markets and the international market – the main source, in my opinion, of the interest-rate differentials that we currently observe – is rapidly disappearing, and so will the interest-rate differentials. When these have converged to the lower bound consistent with the operation of the band, their magnitude will become negligible relative to the effects of factors such as market liquidity and default-risk premia.

The potential source of instability, in the transition to a single currency, is the failure of inflation differentials to decrease along with the disappearance of nominal interest rate differentials. Exchange-rate stability and financial integration reduce the real cost of borrowing in the countries where inflation is relatively high, and put upward pressure on domestic demand. The expansionary effect of the fall in real rates may more than offset the loss of competitiveness that results from fixing the nominal exchange rate while inflation is still higher at home than abroad. The result is an expansion of domestic demand which, if left unchecked, would work against the convergence of inflation.[1] This explains why central banks in countries such as Spain and Italy use what is left of their monetary sovereignty to prevent a fall in nominal and real interest rates. However, financial integration and the firm commitment to fixed exchange rates make such attempts increasingly powerless.

Therefore I share the view that the transition to fixed exchange rates should be accompanied, in the high-inflation countries, by 'a sharp tightening in fiscal positions', and by government intervention in the wage-setting process. As noted by Dornbusch, 'governments must take on bigger *actual* commitments'. However, fixing the exchange rate to the Deutsche mark with zero margins may not be sufficient: it may in fact amplify the expansionary impulse to domestic demand.

1   Interest-rate convergence in the EMS

Dornbusch points to an important and long neglected aspect of the EMS experience – the relation between interest-rate differentials and the size of the band. This may indeed become an important issue in European

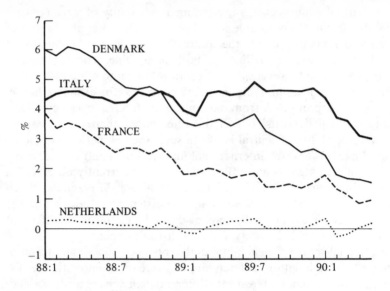

GERMANY   weighted average of all government bonds with average maturity of more than three years. Source: IFS;
FRANCE   average yield to maturity of national equipment bonds. Source: IFS;
DENMARK   yield of the 3 1/2 percent perpetual bond. Source: IFS;
NETHERLANDS   average yield to maturity of the more recent issues with original life of at least 10.5 years. Source: IFS;
ITALY   average net yield to maturity of Buoni Poliennali del Tesoro (BTP). Source: Bank of Italy

**Figure 11A.1   Long-term   yield   differentials   relative   to   DM-bonds,   1988–90
(government bonds, %)**

financial markets, if central parities are fixed, but the size of the band fails
to be reduced.[2] However, the interest-rate differentials that we currently
observe across EMS currencies are orders of magnitude larger than what
could be explained by the presence of finite bands.

Figures 11A.1 and 2 show the yield differential between long-term bonds
denominated in four EMS currencies (lire, French francs, Dutch guilders
and Danish krone), and bonds denominated in Deutsche marks. I have
chosen long-term bonds since these incorporate long-term expectations
on the relative value of currencies. The data are monthly, and the sample
starts in January 1988, just after the speculative attacks on the lira and the
French franc, that took place in the late summer and fall of 1987, were
successfully resisted, marking an important turning point in the EMS: for
the first time in the history of the system the West German central bank
lowered interest rates in order to avoid a realignment. (As is well known,
there have been no realignments of central parities since January 1987.)

Two facts emerge from figures 11A.1 and 2. First, for all currencies
except the lira, the differential *vis-à-vis* the Deutsche mark declines

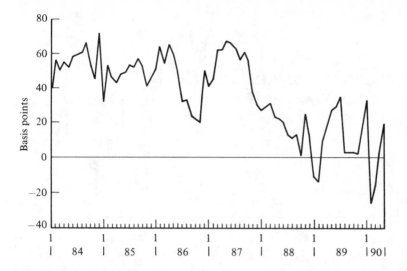

Figure 11A.2   Yield differentials between guilder and DM-bonds, 1984–90 (basis points).
Source: See figure 11A.1

throughout the period. In the case of the guilder (reported on a different scale in figure 11A.3) the differential has been equal to zero, on average, since mid-1988.[3] Second, interest rates on lira-denominated bonds remained four percentage points above German rates until the beginning of 1990: since then the differential has steadily declined. The turnaround in the differential between Italian and German bond yields coincides with the reduction of the fluctuation band of the lira from 6 to 2.25% on each side of the central parity – an observation that would seem to support Dornbusch's view that the smaller the band, the lower the interest-rate differential. It also coincides, however, with the removal of the last remaining barriers to capital mobility. The effect of these measures has been to make capital flows more responsive to interest-rate differentials (Table 11A.1 documents the acceleration of net capital inflows in the first months of 1990.) Financial liberalization has made sterilization virtually impossible, and has forced the Italian central bank to accept an interest-rate differential consistent with the credibiity of its exchange-rate target.

NOTES

1 The convergence of inflation, or lack of it, in a regime of fixed exchange rates and free capital mobility is analysed in Giavazzi and Spaventa (1990).

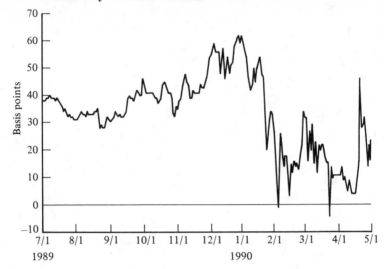

DEUTSCHE MARK BOND   *Bundesrepublik*, 6¾%, 21st June, 1999.
GUILDER BOND   *Dutch Government*, 7¼%, 15th July, 1999.

Figure 11A.3   Yield differential between a DM and a guilder government bond, 1989–90.
Source: Bloomberg, L.P.

Table 11A.1. *Italy: the current account and private capital flows, 1988–90* (billion US dollars)

	1988 (March–Dec.)	1989 (Jan.–Dec.)	1990 (Jan.–April)
Current account	− 9.4	− 16.1	− 11.5
Private capital inflows	27.1	39.9	30.5
Private capital outflows	− 9.3	− 12.1	− 12.4
Net capital inflows	17.8	27.8	18.1
Change in central bank reserves	8.4	11.7	6.6

Source: Bank of Italy.

2 The role of EMS bands is analysed in Bertola and Caballero (1990). Some preliminary empirical results relating the interest-rate differential to the size of the band and to the location of the exchange rate in the band are presented in CER (1990).
3 Figures 11A.1 and 2 compare weighted averages of the yields on long-term government bonds. To investigate to what extent the current 2.25% band can

account for the divergence between long-term nominal interest rates, I report in figure 11A.3 the yield differential between two government bonds, one in Deutsche marks, the other in guilders, of almost identical maturity. Yields to maturity are computed from the bid prices at which a transaction could actually take place. The differential is almost always positive, and can be as large as 60 basis points.

REFERENCES

Bertola, G. and R.J. Caballero (1990) 'Target Zones and Realignments', CEPR Discussion Paper No. 398, March.
Centro Europa Ricerche (CER) (1990) *Rapporto*, 1990: 1, Rome, February.
Giavazzi, F. and L. Spaventa (1990) 'The New EMS', CEPR Discussion Paper No. 369, January.

NIELS THYGESEN

Rudiger Dornbusch has perceptively and with customary brutality identified at least four problems of European monetary integration:

(1) the transition to Economic and Monetary Union (EMU) is the most difficult issue, rather than the design of a final stage of EMU and its institutional underpinnings;
(2) in that transition the roles of budgetary and of incomes policies are more crucial than that of monetary policies;
(3) different groupings of countries are visible within the European Communities (EC) and potential additional members: a hard core group, a second tier the members of which might aspire to participate in the first after a short transition, and a third tier for which monetary integration is a more distant prospect; and
(4) for the hard core group, and possibly some countries in the second tier, the paper proposes to move rapidly – in 'less than a year' – to a fully fixed exchange rate, without any fluctuation margin, with the DM.

On all of these four points the paper is refreshingly more blunt than most official documents, including the Delors Report and efforts to follow up on it. Yet it reflects quite realistically in several respects more radical thinking among many officials and academics in Europe, and particularly in the Federal Republic of Germany, about a more direct approach to European monetary integration than the gradualist and institutional – 'bureaucratic' in Dornbusch's terminology – approach which appears to dominate among policy-makers and in EC bodies.

These virtues make it a pleasure to discuss the paper. But they also make it possible to pinpoint what in my view is the main weakness of the paper: the neglect of – almost the disdain for – institutional mechanisms which could help to assure the success of the radical central proposal in the paper, listed here as (4). Let me take up the four points in succession.

1   Transitional problems are central

Here it is hard to disagree with Dornbusch. Although the Delors Report was asked to study and propose concrete stages leading to EMU, the Report concentrated more on the nature of the final stage and did not reflect any sense of urgency about getting there. If anything, it suggested that the process would necessarily be long and gradual. The absence of any proposed time frame is the most evident illustration. It was at its most specific in discussing how a final stage of so-called irrevocably fixed exchange rates could be run by a European System of Central Banks and coordinated with other economic policies. Particular attention was paid to the mandate for the ESCB to pursue a monetary policy oriented towards price stability, to the independence of the bank from political instructions and to its account-ability for its performance. These issues are discussed in an ahistorical way with little linkage to the initial conditions from which the process towards EMU starts, both in terms of the nature of the present EMS and the differences in national economic performance of the participants: inherited inflation, public and external deficits and unemployment. The reasons for the emphasis on the longer-run systemic issues and on monetary policy are easily understood: prescribing policy adjustments for the transition of particular countries towards EMU was too delicate a task for a committee consisting of central bankers. Furthermore, criticism of the starting point of the present EMS for being 'neither here nor there', as Dornbusch says, could not easily have been voiced by the managers of that system.

However, we are in 1990 trying to prepare for 1993 or 1995, not in year t and planning for year $t + s$. Much of the policy debate is now turning to performance criteria which should be met or approached by participants before entering the final stage of EMU. The desirable degree of convergence of price and wage trends and the sustainability of government debt accumulation are, as in the Dornbusch paper, the central topics.

Despite the sense of urgency which the focus on the transition, rather than on the systemic issues in the final stage, brings to the debate, it may be politically easier to accept a rapid and forceful adjustment programme to become ready for permanently fixed exchange rates than to accept the more permanent infringements of sovereignty implied, in particular, by the mandatory rules for national budgetary policies suggested by the Delors Report for the final stage of EMU. Both transitional and permanent understandings among the participants would in my own view be warranted, the permanent 'rules' helping to assure that national governments perceive their long-term budget constraints as clearly as the latter appear in economic analysis. Yet there is a limited tradeoff between the short and the long run; without demonstrable progress on inflation convergence and budgetary stance in the transitional stage, the insistence on proof of readiness to submit to permanently constraining rules could become crushing. Hence, both in a real and in a tactical sense, the emphasis on the transition in the paper is helpful for advancing European monetary integration.

2   Taking on tax payers and unions

In the transition the essential step is, in Dornbusch's view, less to conduct an essentially unified monetary policy – because that has already largely been forced into existence and could be completed by rigid exchange rates with no fluctuation margins – than to take on tax payers and labour unions. In the final section I come back to my reasons for believing that Dornbusch is too casual about the feasibility of fixed rates without an institutional framework for monetary policy. But let us accept the argument that budgetary and incomes policies have to play major roles in the transitory adjustment of those economies that do not obviously belong in the hard core of the EMS.

It is justified to take on tax payers – and, one could add, the users of public services and recipients of transfer payments – both because of intitial budgetary imbalances in some countries and because the transition to EMU will imply a major easing of monetary policy. As Dornbusch explains, an important motive for undertaking that transition is to squeeze out the risk premia on otherwise very similar financial instruments in different currencies (see his table 11.3). The convergence of nominal, and in the longer run also real, interest rates and the further weakening of any residual rationing elements as capital controls are fully removed and financial integration is deepened through very stable exchange rates, will provide a strong stimulus to debt-financed demand. As most EC economies are already set on relatively rapid growth rates for the next few years with signs of strains on productive capacity, not least in those countries in southern Europe which would be the prime beneficiaries of lower interest rates, there is a strong case for tightening of budgetary policies in these countries.

It is particularly important to remind policy-makers of these arguments, because three short-term political considerations could easily push them in the direction of more, rather than less, budgetary laxity: (1) measured budget deficits will decline in countries with large public debt, as the effects of lower interest rates on the outstanding debt work their way through, leaving more apparent scope for a deterioration in the non-interest balance; (2) less concern over any external deficit may seem justified, as external finance will be more readily available with advancing monetary integration and as the instrument of devaluation recedes more definitively into the background; and (3) pressures to lower taxes on capital income and corporate earnings and to reduce indirect taxes increase as a result of deeper integration of financial and goods markets, hence eroding some sources of public revenue.

In these circumstances it will be no easy task for governments in, say, Italy, Belgium, Denmark and Spain to explain to their tax payers (and users of public services) that an extra effort has to be made to assure that the budgetary position does not, during the transition, become difficult to reconcile with long-run participation in an EMU. The temptation will be to relax, rather than to tighten, and the danger signals may not flash early since monetary and exchange-rate policies are becoming more credible. But the latter development provides also, as Dornbusch says, the opportunity for better budgetary convergence.

Taking on the unions is, as the paper argues, a particularly important task in the transition for the authorities in the United Kingdom. In the Benelux countries and France, and more recently in Ireland and Denmark, there is evidence of a significant degree of convergence of unit labour cost trends towards German rates; the process is much less advanced in Italy and Spain and, not surprisingly, unobservable in the three EC countries that have not been subject to the exchange-rate discipline of the EMS. There is a tendency in policy-making circles to assume that the credibility effects of the EMS commitments have played a major role in this convergence, since, to quote Dornbusch, 'it might be argued that EMS membership represents a superior, though implicit, form of incomes policy, better than time-worn wage–price controls'. (p. 310) One might add that most of the governments that have had some success with this mechanism have tried to make it more explicit to domestic unions and employers.

This is the crucial issue in evaluating the feasibility of UK participation in EMU and in the transition. The UK authorities have a double problem. On the one hand they have put great emphasis over the past decade on allowing the exchange rate to move quite widely, first by the massive sterling appreciation of 1979–81 which broke inflation more radically than elsewhere in Europe, and more recently by allowing, in 1986 and in 1988–90, two large downward adjustments of the currency. The latter experiences have brought home the point that there is an escape route from excess inflation through the exchange market. Real wages have continued to rise, and the political investment that would have to be made to commit to what most domestic actors would see as an arbitrary exchange-rate target, now seems very large. On the other hand the UK government has been anxious to move as far as possible from the notion of an incomes policy, which on the Continent can be invoked to underpin a fixed exchange rate, because the framework for such a policy was thought to have been undermined by the failures of policies in the 1970s and, in any case, to be undesirably corporatist.

What does it mean then to 'take on the unions'? There is little evidence in the UK wage experience that reforms in the labour market have performed as a substitute for the restraining influence of an ambitious exchange-rate policy cum incomes policy that has worked elsewhere. It is difficult in these circumstances to disagree with Dornbusch that a monetary union comprising the United Kingdom 'is implausible at this stage or under this government'. (p. 324).

3   Three groups of countries in the EC?

An important contribution of the paper is that it tackles head on the hypocrisy that all EC countries should ideally progress together towards EMU. The initial conditions are too different for that. A differentiated approach is required.

The paper distinguishes three group of countries, and although I have quarrels with the precise groupings suggested, the basic framework is helpful. The first, or hard core group, consists of Germany and those other countries for which 'trend depreciation (*vis à vis* the DM), if any, is more of a nuisance than an advantage'. (p. 324). That necessarily loose criterion would, certainly according to policy-makers in the countries concerned, comprise the Netherlands, Belgium–Luxembourg (for some purposes put into a second tier by Dornbusch) and France. A second tier consists of countries where one or more indicator of macroeconomic imbalance is visible: Denmark and Ireland, where stabilization has left unemployment relatively high and inflationary convergence is less complete than in the first group, and Italy where both budgetary and incomes policies have to be adjusted. Dornbusch also includes the United Kingdom in this tier – in section 1 – but his subsequent comments in section 5 on the UK economy suggest that she rather belongs in the third group. The latter consists otherwise of the three most recent EC members (Spain, Portugal and Greece), the 'high-inflation countries'. It is not clearly justified why Spain is in this third group, since inflation is similar to that in Italy and budgetary imbalance much smaller, but Dornbusch advances two arguments: as a recent participant in the real and financial integration of Europe, Spain must necessarily feel more uncertain about the proper level for her exchange rate. And that uncertainty is enlarged by the economic reform process in Eastern Europe which could have particularly strong effects on Spain's ability to grow fast, led by exports to Europe and substantial capital inflows to build up productive capacity.

My main point is not to quibble with Dornbusch's precise classification of countries, important as it is. Basically it makes good sense to distinguish first between those countries that are in the EMS narrow arrangements or could join it (Spain?) and the three others (UK, Greece and Portugal) for whom such a step would appear more than hazardous; and then to distinguish with the first eight or nine countries between those that could establish permanently fixed DM-rates within a year without further policy adjustments and those for whom a transitory period of budgetary and/or incomes policy adjustment would be required. For that second tier Dornbusch recommends a two-year transition period 'during which fiscal and wage–price preconditions for joint monetary policy are established and demonstrated' (p. 323). In the Italian case, which is the only one explicitly discussed in section 4, the transition would comprise a temporary wage freeze coupled with *ex post* indexation.

The proposals in the paper are radical when compared to the effort of the EC countries to negotiate a Treaty revision on EMU acceptable to and accessible for all member states. They are less at variance with a more pragmatic view in several of the hard core countries that, while it is of great importance to arrive at a commonly accepted long-run framework, participation by some in advanced stages of monetary integration, or even union, should not be precluded by the inability or unwillingness of some to bypass a long period of transition. This eventuality was also foreseen in the Delors Report, which recommended (para. 44) 'allowing a degree of flexibility concerning the date and conditions on which some member countries would join certain arrangements'.

4   Fixed exchange rates within the hard core in 1990?

The most specific and the most provocative proposal in the paper is for the hard core countries, and those from the second tier who undertake whatever transitional adjustments are seen to be required and mutually agreed, to move rapidly to fixed exchange rates with zero margins.

To take the last point first, the paper contains a persuasive subsection (4.1) as to why zero margins are superior to the present EMS extended into a system with permanently fixed central rates, but some arbitrary margins – 2.25% or narrower – around them. Only a system in which both the central banks and private banks undertake par clearing, i.e. stand ready to convert from one participating currency to another without any transctions cost, would eliminate exchange rate uncertainty and enforce strong convergence of national interest rates. In fact par clearing would take us far towards a single currency; national monies would indeed become very close subsitutes. The Delors Report did say that margins of fluctuations should disappear in the final stage of EMU in preparation of the single currency (and be narrowed in the second stage), but it was not specific on whether the bid-ask spreads for currencies in private banks should be eliminated. The Dornbusch proposal telescopes much of stages one, two and three of the Delors Report into the near future – 'within a year' – for the, possibly enlarged, hard core group.

I have sympathy also for his other, and main, proposal that a rapid move to fully fixed central rates – the irrevocable nature of the commitment being underlined by the elimination of margins, though less efficiently than by a single currency. If the non-German members of the EMS are not prepared to use realignments anyway, they might as well make that intention more visible. But I fail to see how the fixing of DM-rates in itself without any institutional underpinnings – Dornbusch states explicitly: 'there is no need at this stage for any joint institutions to manage European money' (p. 319) – could be adequate, particularly to Germany. This is all the more puzzling, since the author clearly has German concerns about imported inflation in the present EMS very much in mind.

Somehow he seems to assume that 'European monetary policy is made in Frankfurt'(p. 319) and that this would become even more visible as capital controls disappear – and that residual divergences in economic performance would be taken care of by the suggestions he has sketched for budgetary and incomes policies in those countries in the enlarged hard core group that would need such adjustments in the transition period. This view of natural gravitation towards German monetary policy does not square with the experience in the EMS since 1987 when the system appears to have become more symmetric and less amenable to German dominance. The paper even gives a persuasive account (pp. 310–11) of why Germany has found it increasingly difficult to check the demand for German goods and services and hence German (and European) inflation in the recent period.

It can be argued, of course, that, with the transitional arrangements envisaged, these German concerns would fade, because a more direct influence on the evolution on nominal demand outside Germany would substitute for the indirect disinflation dynamics which worked more visibly in the EMS prior to the last few years. Present concerns will fade gradually to the extent that the transitional adjustment is successful and no major tendencies to free riding in monetary policy appear. But the proposed step would not in my view look assuring either to a Germany policy-maker or to his colleague in, say, France, Italy and Spain – assuming they all take part. The nominal anchor function would not be well defined from the perspective of the former without some jointly formulated monetary policy, and the latter group of non-German policy-makers would not readily accept the absence of an institutional framework within which a joint policy could be designed. In this sense, the efforts to set nationally coordinated monetary targets among the EMS-countries in stage one and to move to a European System of Central Banks as soon as possible may appear to both groups of monetary officials more reassuring than Dornbusch's proposals.

In summary, the paper is refreshing by aiming to redress the imbalance that may have developed in the European debate between monetary and non-monetary approaches to EMU. Monetary integration cannot advance durably without some progress in budgetary and wage–price performance, yet the time is ripe for more radical ideas on the European exchange-rate system than the gradualist approach which dominates official thinking. Dornbusch has revised his own earlier ideas about the dangers of European monetary integration, see notably Dornbusch (1988), and now finds early move to fixed exchange rates feasible for a larger group of countries, given some transitional efforts. With some additional attention to institutional implications the basic proposals could attract wide support.

REFERENCES

Dornbusch, R. (1988) 'The EMS, the dollar and the yen', in F. Giavazzi, S. Micossi and M. Miller (eds.), *The European Monetary Syustem*, Cambridge University Press.

Index